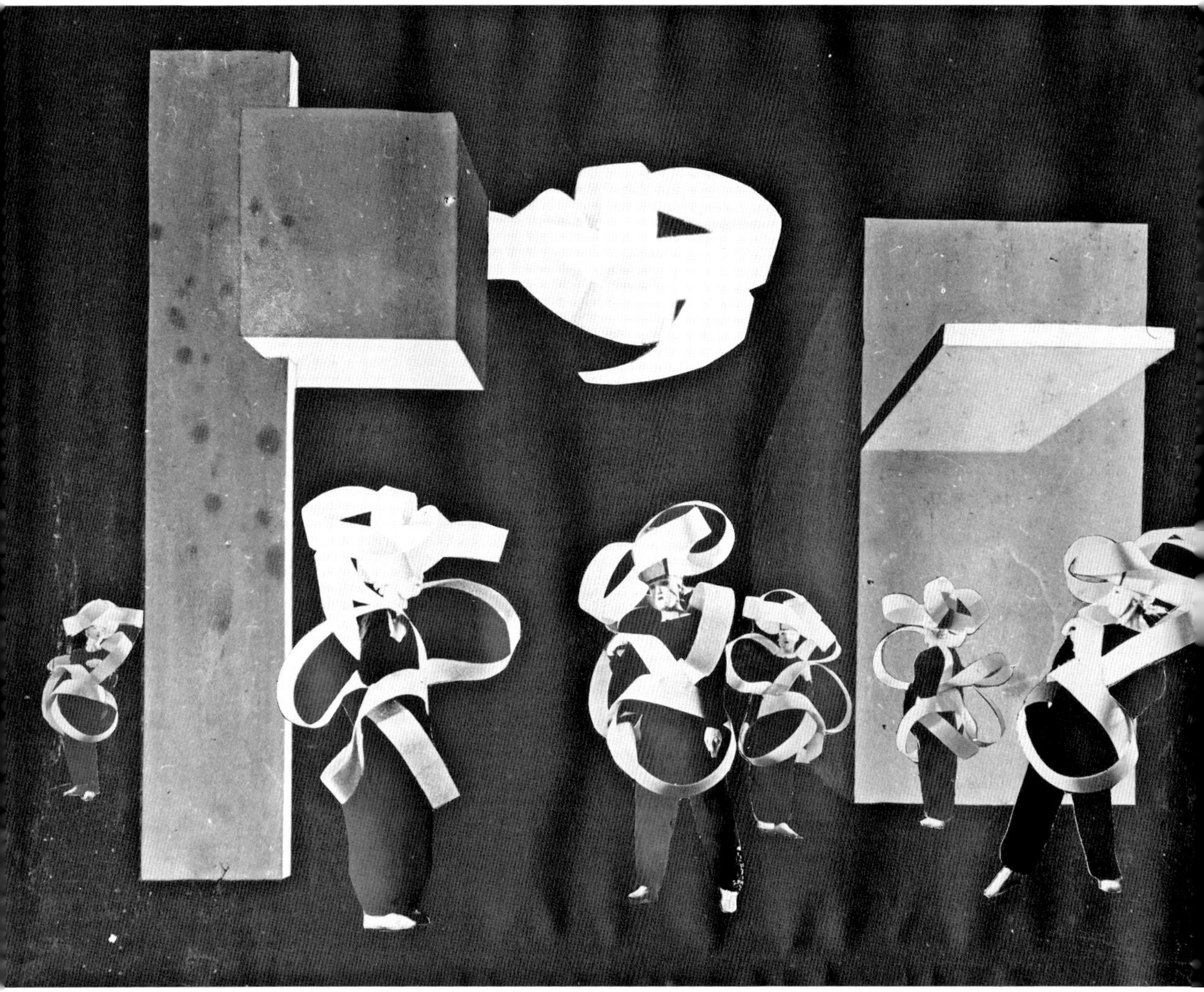

the experimenters

chance and design at black mountain college

eva díaz

THE UNIVERSITY OF CHICAGO PRESS
CHICAGO AND LONDON

Eva Díaz is assistant professor of art history at the Pratt Institute.

The University of Chicago Press, Chicago 60637
The University of Chicago Press, Ltd., London

Printed in the United States of America

24 23 22 21 20 19 18 17 16 15 2 3 4 5

ISBN-13: 978-0-226-06798-8 (cloth)
ISBN-13: 978-0-226-06803-9 (e-book)
DOI: 10.7208/chicago/9780226068039.001.0001

Library of Congress Cataloging-in-Publication Data

Díaz, Eva, 1977- author.
The experimenters : chance and design at Black Mountain College / Eva Díaz.
pages cm
Includes bibliographical references and index.
ISBN 978-0-226-06798-8 (hardcover : alkaline paper) — ISBN 978-0-226-06803-9 (e-book) 1. Black Mountain College (Black Mountain, N.C.)—History. 2. Arts—Experimental methods—History. I. Title.
NX405.B55B553 2014
707.1′175688—dc23
2013037749

Frontispiece
Xanti Schawinsky, *Spectodrama 8: Building (Tensional)*, 1936–37. Photocollage on paper, 16 × 21.1″. The Xanti Schawinsky Estate.

Publication of this book has been aided by a grant from the Neil Harris Endowment Fund, which honors the innovative scholarship of Neil Harris, the Preston and Sterling Morton Professor Emeritus of History at the University of Chicago. The Fund is supported by contributions from the students, colleagues, and friends of Neil Harris.

∞ This paper meets the requirements of ANSI/NISO Z39.48-1992 (Permanence of Paper).

contents

acknowledgments

It is no understatement to say that many more talented people besides Josef Albers, John Cage, and R. Buckminster Fuller—the figures upon whom this book focuses—were drawn into the orbit of Black Mountain College. I have greatly benefited from these individuals' innovative teaching methods, the challenge and originality of their work, and the generous spirit of intellectual exchange that characterizes so much of the College's history and legacy. I am enormously thankful that Lore Kadden Lindenfeld, Merce Cunningham, and Kenneth Snelson allowed me to interview them in depth. Clemens Kalischer extended himself in discussing the project with me over the years; his ebullience is remarkable and always cheering. The legacy of the College's creative energy continues to pull fascinating people into the gravitational field of Black Mountain College studies. Many of these individuals have helped guide me in producing this book, and many have provided invaluable support in making materials available for the project.

While at Princeton University, I was lucky to receive invaluable support from the faculty there. Hal Foster, one of my mentors, patiently read drafts, gave insightful comments throughout the process, and provided invaluable advice—advice that made a writer of me. Rachael DeLue, Brigid Doherty, and Branden Joseph generously offered considered and constructive suggestions regarding the manuscript. Carol Armstrong supported the project at its early moments, and her direction in framing its parameters early on encouraged me to undertake it. The Graduate School and the Department of Art and Archaeology at

Princeton University enabled me to conduct research on this topic, and the Jacob K. Javits Fellowship and the Andrew Mellon Fellowship in Humanistic Studies generously aided me throughout all stages of the research process. The Wyeth Foundation for American Art's College Art Association Professional Development Fellowship assisted greatly in the completion of the final portions of the book.

The Experimenters was revised and expanded during my years teaching at Pratt Institute in Brooklyn. My colleagues in the History of Art and Design Department have bolstered the difficult work of revision with their enthusiasm for the project, and I thank Pratt's Faculty Development Grant Fund for supporting me.

I am deeply grateful to Martin Duberman and Mary Emma Harris for their inspiring work on Black Mountain College. Almost two decades have passed since I first read Duberman's *Black Mountain: An Exploration in Community*, which stimulated this project by providing an entirely different history of the rather sleepy Appalachian town where I used to spend my summers as a child. Mary Emma in particular has kept the memory of the College alive by founding the Black Mountain College Project, which has kindly provided me with materials over the years. My thanks also to Vincent Katz for his support, and for his book on Black Mountain College. Bill Wilson, James Jaffé, and Shoji Sadao generously shared their encyclopedic knowledge of the period and its players with me at the early stages of my research, making me feel that my book would be a positive contribution to these excellent precursors.

I would like to acknowledge the support of several archives that opened their doors to me. The Josef and Anni Albers Foundation made Josef Albers's work and archives available, and allowed me to stay at the foundation while conducting research; curator Brenda Danilowitz provided important advice and assistance, and her work on Albers has helped to bring him into contemporary consciousness. The North Carolina State Archives were a model of helpfulness; many thanks to their tireless staff. I am grateful to the Cunningham Dance Foundation for allowing me to research the Merce Cunningham Archives; scholar David Vaughan extended every courtesy to me in his capacity as archivist. Laura Kuhn of the John Cage Trust was always supportive, and many thanks are due to librarians Jeanette Casey and Jim Hobbs and their staff at Northwestern University Music Library for their generous assistance in making the John Cage Collection available to me. The Sterling Memorial Library at the Yale University Library allowed me to conduct research with the Josef Albers Papers; I extend my thanks to their staff for making materials available to me. The staff at the Department of Special Collections at the Stanford University

Libraries allowed me to access the R. Buckminster Fuller Collection; thanks to Hsiao-Yun Chu in particular for her assistance.

Along the way to seeing this book published, numerous conversations, writing projects, curatorial endeavors, and public events shaped my thinking about it, and I am profoundly grateful for all these opportunities. Caroline Collier, at that time director of the Arnolfini Gallery in Bristol, and Michael Harrison, director of Kettle's Yard at Cambridge University, gave me my first opportunity to publish on Black Mountain College in the book accompanying their retrospective on the College, *Starting from Zero: Black Mountain College, 1933–1957*. Thanks also to Beth Venn for putting Pam Myers, director of the Asheville Art Museum, in touch with me; curating a series of shows there on the College permitted me a hands-on involvement with artwork crucial to my project, and Pam's invitations to me to return for talks continue to offer opportunities to connect with many Black Mountain College friends and alumni. Richard Powell and Marianne Wardle at the *Art Bulletin* trenchantly guided the publication of an earlier version of my chapter on Albers; Lory Frankel's editorial comments on that project were superb. Sina Najafi and Jeffrey Kastner at *Cabinet* magazine published a portion of my work on Albers's influence beyond Black Mountain College, an essay that greatly facilitated the writing of the epilogue to this book. On the several occasions I spoke on Bucky Fuller at Sina's invitation, my work was treated to the inestimably compelling discussions that only *Cabinet* audiences can create. Howard Singerman's invitation to write on the Bauhaus for *Art Journal* gave me an opportunity to work through some of my newly developing ideas about Black Mountain College's influences and progenitors. More recently, Helen Molesworth invited me to return to topics related to Black Mountain College in her forthcoming catalog about the College at the ICA Boston. Thanks to all the individuals who have invited me to speak and teach on this material: at Yale, Harvard, Princeton, the Graduate Center of the City of New York, and the College Art Association, among many others. To all the people and organizations that helped with obtaining images for the book, I am extraordinarily grateful.

Jennifer King, Margaret Liu Clinton, Kaira Cabañas, Suzanne Hudson, and Ben Young generously gave suggestions on earlier drafts of this book. Ron Clark, Director of the Whitney Museum Independent Study Program, provided especially helpful comments. He has always been tremendously supportive of me in general and this project in particular; my deepest gratitude to him. My grandmother Sally Pack Thomas is to be thanked heartily: for acting as my native informant in Black Mountain, and for opening her home to me whenever I needed to go back to Buncombe County.

At the University of Chicago Press, I am deeply grateful to my editor, Susan Bielstein, for her commitment, and to Sandra Hazel and Anthony Burton for shepherding the book into print.

This book is dedicated to my family: my mother, Lynne Díaz-Rico, who has always been there for me when I needed her; to my husband, Michael Connor, who has supported me with immeasurable love through the long process of seeing this book to print; and to my daughter, Arizona, who constantly delights me.

introduction black mountain college between chance and design

In the years immediately following World War II, an unaccredited college in rural Appalachia became a vital hub of cultural innovation. Black Mountain College was an unlikely place for a *naissance*: usually it could offer little more than train fare and a bed for its faculty, and it never had more than a few dozen students enrolled at a time. Yet it was the site of a crucial transatlantic dialogue between European modernist aesthetics and pedagogy and their US counterparts, a conversation whose roster of participants—the faculty and students of the College—now reads like a *Who's Who* of postwar American art.

Artistic experimentation was one of the key themes of this conversation. Seemingly everyone who attended Black Mountain College shared a desire to experiment, though they did not necessarily agree on what this meant. In particular, competing and even incompatible approaches to experimentation were advanced by three of the College's most notable faculty members in its heyday of the mid-1940s to early 1950s: artist Josef Albers, composer John Cage, and architect-designer R. Buckminster Fuller.

The language of experimentation continues to play an important role in contemporary artistic practice, and the ideas and terms advanced by Albers, Cage, and Fuller serve as important reference points. And yet the conflicts that arose among their competing ideas of the "experiment" have not been clarified. This book asks, among other things, what do we mean when we talk about experimentation in art? And why is it important? It moves toward answering these questions by returning to that far-flung corner of North Carolina where decisive arguments about experimentation took place.

Black Mountain College was founded in western North Carolina on the grounds of a YMCA summer camp on the outskirts of a small mountain town by the same name, about twenty miles from Asheville (fig. I.1). In the aftermath of a faculty governance dispute at Rollins College, Florida, nine fired faculty members, including Black Mountain's first rector, John Andrew Rice, had gone before an American Association of University Professors mediation panel that vindicated them but ultimately could not reinstate them. Soon after, the discharged professors and a contingent of sympathetic staff decided to establish an educational institution that would avoid the pitfalls of autocratic chancellors and trustees and allow for a more flexible curriculum, thereby resolving the key issues in their clash with the Rollins administration. Black Mountain College was established immediately afterward in 1933, with the holistic aim "to educate a student as a person and as a citizen."[1] Inspired by the work of

Figure I.1
Claude Stoller, *Studies Building across Lake Eden, Black Mountain College*, 1941. Gelatin silver photograph. Courtesy of the State Archives of North Carolina.

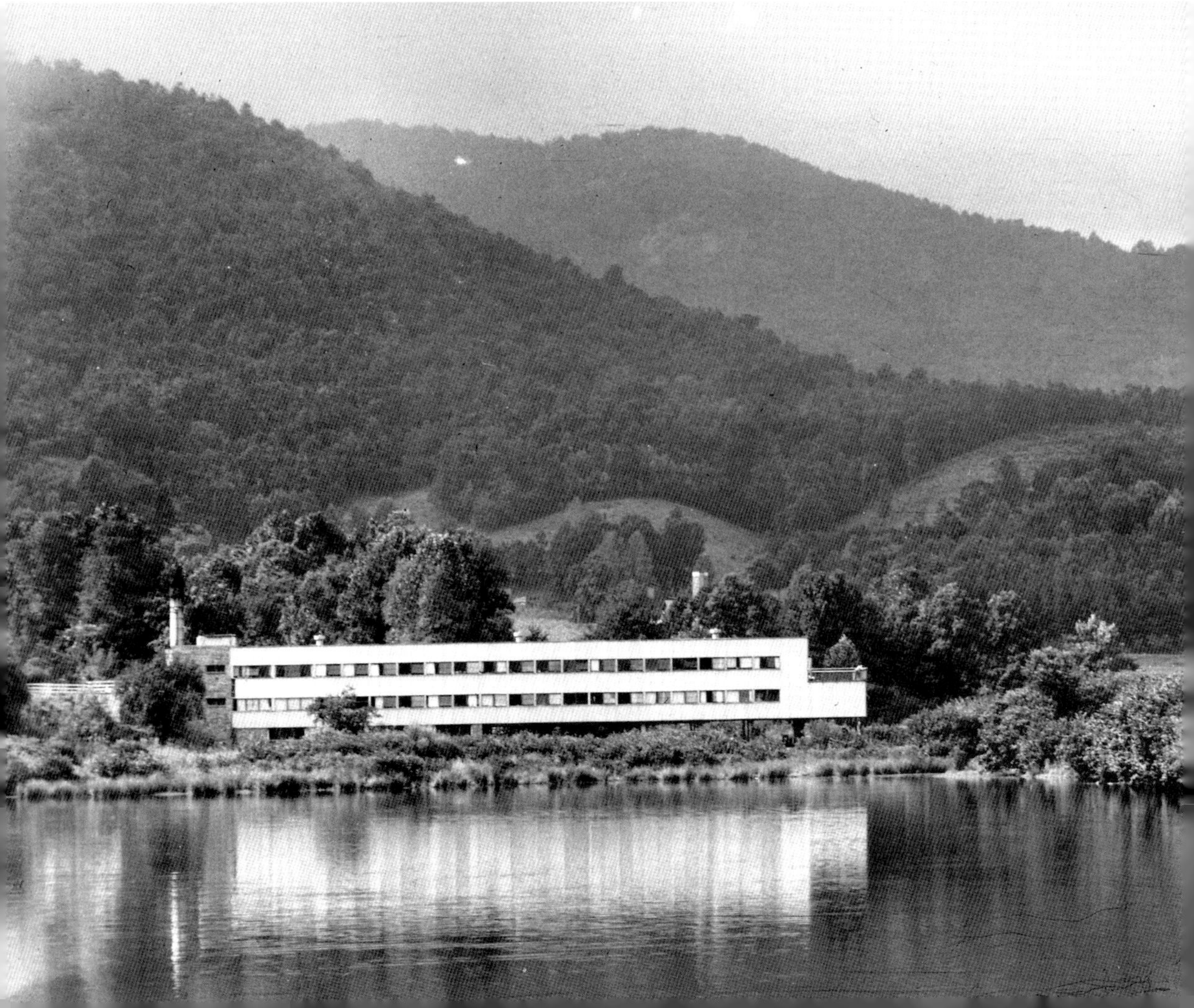

philosopher John Dewey (who soon joined the College's advisory board), its pedagogy emphasized arts training, and its founders hoped to loosen or altogether abolish the types of separations between student and faculty, and faculty and administration, that usually served to specialize roles and bolster hierarchical distinctions.[2] With minimal structure, born of both ideological inclination and economic necessity, Black Mountain's experiment in education was groundbreaking, though relatively brief. In 1957, when the College closed its doors, it had dwindled to less than a half a dozen paying students, with a little over a thousand students having attended since its inception.

Despite its short life and modest size, Black Mountain assumes a prominent place in the genealogies of widely disparate fields of thought. It has been heralded as one of the influential points of contact for European exiles emigrating from Nazi Germany; as a standard-bearer of the legacy of intentional (or planned) communities such as Brook Farm in Massachusetts; as the bellwether campus of Southern racial integration; as an important testing ground for proponents of progressive education; and, as this book takes up, as a seminal site of postwar art practices in the United States.[3] Adding to the College's legend, the number of famous participants—in addition to Albers, Cage, and Fuller, faculty included Albers's wife Anni, Merce Cunningham, Clement Greenberg, Franz Kline, Willem de Kooning, Robert Motherwell, and Ben Shahn; among the students were Ray Johnson, Kenneth Noland, Robert Rauschenberg, Dorothea Rockburne, Kenneth Snelson, and Cy Twombly—and the breadth of their artistic diversity have garnered it an impressive reputation, if an uneven historical treatment.

Among the many stories that could be told of Black Mountain College, this book follows the thread of a single concept: experimentation. It can be traced in the spirit of radical innovation at the core of the College's educational philosophy; for example, in a 1938 campus bulletin, weaving professor Anni Albers implored her students and other artists to employ "free experimentation . . . and leave the safe ground of accepted conventions."[4] She wasn't alone in espousing the rhetoric of experimentation; it is one of the terms most frequently applied to the College.[5] As with other repeatedly used concepts at Black Mountain such as "community," "experience," "innovation," or "freedom," "experiment" was and continues to be treated as a generically positive attribute, at once a broad endorsement of the College's progressive history as well as an encapsulation of its specific history and merits.[6] Whether in the context of education, community, or visual art and music, many aspirations became attached to experimental practices: collaboration and interdisciplinarity, countercultural ambitions, artistic avant-gardism, cultural improvement, and political progressiveness.[7] Experimentation was in fact a complicated and contested concept defined by projects as varied as geometric abstraction, serialized and mass production, dome architecture, chance-based musical composition, and explorations of monochromatic painting.

Yet a broad notion of experimentation in effect became a kind of glue binding the often-fragmented interdisciplinary discussions about the College. At the time the idea was used to rethink underlying assumptions that separated various disciplines into realms of discrete specialization. Prior interdisciplinary modernist explorations such as those practiced at the Bauhaus were revisited and expanded at Black Mountain: art merged with concerns of visual perception and environmental design; music composition flirted with arbitrary sounds and background noise; architecture and shelter design were pushed to redefine the conditions under which individuals, increasingly understood as members of wider communities, experienced space. Experimentation thus provided a shared terminology for College members to view their specific endeavors in relation to different though allied efforts in other disciplines. At Black Mountain, experimentation was professed to be a practice that could be shared by *all* creative producers.

The frequent invocation of "the experiment" by key Black Mountain figures cannot disguise the fact that the concept to which they appealed was, and remains, deeply contradictory. In large part, the contradiction reflects the compound meanings of the word experiment, and the historically shifting relation between concepts such as innovation and tradition, or originality and routine. Experiment shares with empirical and experience a common root in the Latin *experiri*, "to try or to put to the test." Until the eighteenth century, experience and experiment were interchangeable in English usage, though subsequently experience came to indicate that which has been previously tested, a past accumulation of knowledge or skill—"lessons as against innovation or experiments," in the words of Raymond Williams.[8] Yet experience continued to carry a second nuance, that of a full and active consciousness or awareness that may allow the experimenting with, testing, or trying of something. The complexity in the definition of experience as either the past (tradition) or that which is freshly carried out (innovation) had the effect of splitting the meaning of experiment into two definitions: "testing under controlled circumstances," as distinct from "innovative acts or procedures" more generally. Although experimentation is sometimes associated with systematic procedures such as the scientific method, which imply previously formulated hypotheses under test, the term is also invoked (both in art and in science) in trials of new or different experience in which results are not forecast beforehand. At Black Mountain, debates about the degree of freedom or control inherent or permitted in practices considered experimental, and not merely chaotic or improvisational, turned on this ambiguity.

Focusing on the rival methodologies of experimental forms as elaborated and practiced by key teachers Albers, Cage, and Fuller is not to say they were the only Black Mountain faculty that appealed to experimentation, but study of their work will help excavate three of the most clearly articulated positions of the period. For Albers, an experiment "embrace[d] all means opposing disorder and accident."[9] It represented a careful procedure of testing socially and historically constructed perceptual understandings in art against deceptive optical stimuli. To Cage, experimentation exceeded patterns of reasoning so as to unleash greater indeterminacy. As he stated, "The word 'experimental' is apt, providing it is understood not as descriptive of an act to be later judged in terms of success or failure, but simply as an act the outcome of which is unknown."[10] To Fuller, experimentation was the nearly opposite procedure of aligning specific failures of a method with the regularities of his holistically conceived system of "total thinking," a teleological process of discovering empirical truths.[11] Experimental procedures were those by which the "valid data" of "what is really going on in nature" could be formulated conceptually and tested by artists or other "comprehensive designers," thereby exposing the conventionalized knowledge claims or "myths" of an overspecialized society that inefficiently managed its resources.[12] Each of these men laid claim to a practice of experimental production stressing innovation without personal expression, and their rigorous procedures of testing—through both methods of chance and investigations of order and design—resulted in thorough redefinitions of what art could be.

If one considers the College in terms of its geographical locale, two of the most unlikely Black Mountaineers were Josef and Anni Albers. Exiles from Nazi Germany, both had been on the faculty at the Bauhaus, a school whose radical pedagogy encouraged new considerations of the function of art with respect to industrial production and modern society.[13] As it turned out, the Bauhaus—closed in 1933—and Black Mountain—opened that same year—shared many characteristics as progressive educational institutions and as zones of experimental art practice. Upon his arrival in Black Mountain, Albers famously declared, "I want to open eyes."[14] His pronouncement indicated a desire to create an audience—for his art, and for practices of abstraction more generally—that would be educated by the new perceptual strategies he was advancing. In the drawing, color, and design courses he taught at the College (from 1933 until his departure in 1949), Albers proposed an ordered and disciplined testing of the various qualities and appearances of readily available materials such as construction paper and household paint samples. His approach emphasized the correlation between formal arrangement and underlying structure, and placed a high value on economy of labor and resources. But understanding the material and appearance of form was part of a broader project; to him, art was the experimental arm of culture, an investigation of the better forms that precondition advanced cultural production and progress. He encouraged a reflexive relation between art production and a better society; as he stated, "For me studying art is to be on an ethical basis."[15] Albers's ethics of perception maintained that the arrangement of a work of art could mirror the way one organizes events outside what is traditionally called art, but only by testing received conventions with carefully controlled sets of visual and material experiments.

Chapter 1 takes up how Albers stressed the experience, rather than any definite outcomes, of a laboratory-like educational environment, and promoted forms of experimentation and learning in action that could dynamically change routine habits of seeing.[16] As he insisted, "Art is not an object but an experience"—an experience in and of perception that facilitates complex understandings of the visual world.[17] With his systematic exploration of subtle variations of form, he attempted to construct new techniques of pushing visual perception beyond habit. In this process of experimentation, he tried to influence patterns of transmission—transmissions of artistic tradition and of social pattern—by introducing the model of the perceptual test. The final section of chapter 1 traces Albers's work on tests of the contingency of form by charting the epistemology of the concept of experiment he drew from, positioning it within College sympathizer John Dewey's discussions about using experimentation as a test of the mutability of experience.[18]

The celebrated summer programs and institutes at the College supplemented regular faculty such as the Alberses with guests of tremendous energy and talent, often at very early stages of their careers.[19] One of the most significant of these sessions occurred during the summer of 1948, attracting John Cage, Merce Cunningham, Elaine and Willem de Kooning, and Buckminster Fuller, among others. Frequently these summer sessions produced unexpected and enduring collaborations, though just as often participants shared a language of experiment to effect vastly different projects. In particular, the Albersian definition of experimentation as a test of tradition—as a training of the eye and mind to recognize illusions by meticulously testing socially and historically constructed perceptual understandings—was being redefined by Cage as simply an act with unexpected results, without need for discursive or other interpretations.

Cage arrived at the College in 1948 as dance choreographer Cunningham's accompanist. His interest in French musico-aesthetic models of disorder and disruption antagonized many of the College's German émigrés, deeply invested as they were in the twelve-tone music of Arnold Schoenberg and the ordered architectonics of Bauhaus theater. Very schematically, the shift at Black Mountain from a model of experimentation as attention, order, and observation to dispersal, chance, and fragmentation can be understood as Cage's introduction to the College of his varied sources: his growing interest in Zen Buddhism, Dada, and surrealism, and in particular his often-expressed attraction to the writings and works of Erik Satie, Marcel Duchamp, and Antonin Artaud. Incorporating ideas and actions that had previously been explored by these figures, Cage increasingly viewed experimentation as a terrain of chance procedures and indeterminate outcomes. In his time at the College, he devised techniques to test the relationship of natural forces to human intention, privileging the former over the latter in a way that, some argued, forestalled art's potential to influence broader social practices.

Cage's 1948 theatrical production at Black Mountain of Satie's *The Ruse of Medusa*, characterized by absurd monologues and unrelated musical interludes, alerted him to the possibility of arbitrary relationships between actions within a performance. On his next extended visit to the College, in 1952, in a radical departure from existing traditions of performance at the College and elsewhere, he introduced overlapping activities and narrative fragmentation in the production of *Theater Piece No. 1*, also known as the first "happening."[20] In this later work, Cage recruited faculty and students to perform short, timed scripts, resulting in many unrelated events scattered throughout the performance space that could not be apprehended simultaneously. To Cage, the event represented "the centricity within each event and its non-dependence on other events," though he had in fact established strict time brackets and organized the event with particular temporal and locational guidelines.[21] Cage's employment of what I discuss as a "chance protocol" in *Theater Piece No. 1*, which involved particular parameters (duration, assignment of specific tasks to performers, or an agreed-upon use of certain tools or instruments) governing the execution of the work, represented an attempt to sever experimentalism from determining factors such as artistic intention or interpretive argumentation.

Chapter 2 addresses how Cage's version of the experimental test—the formulation of the chance protocol—was, as he termed it, a "purpose to remove purposes."[22] This directly contradicted Albers's project of experimentation as a rigorous and rational testing of carefully controlled and evaluated outcomes. To Cage, experimentation ruptured patterns of reasoning in which testable conditions were hypothesized; procedures of close attention and observation such as those proposed by Albers were impediments that served to control results and impose a restrictive order of calculated effects. The history of the changing nature of experimentation at Black Mountain therefore hinges on a comparison of Cage's efforts in exploring chance-derived scoring and events of indeterminate performance with the work at the College of European émigrés, who tended to share Albers's approach to experimentation. A principal one of these émigrés was Xanti Schawinsky, previously a student and collaborator of Bauhaus theater master Oskar Schlemmer in the 1920s. The Schlemmer-Schawinsky tradition of experimentation brought to Black Mountain at Albers's invitation emphasized ordered vision as a way to defamiliarize viewers in their habitual relation to space and its larger social context. Yet like Cage's 1948–52 events at the College, it, too, represented a larger shift in which experimental theater commingled with what came to be known as performance art, in that both models probed nonnarrative performance situations, employed experimental music, broke with strict theater in their use of spontaneous or unscripted events, and disrupted traditional spatial relationships of audience to stage.[23]

Buckminster Fuller, in contrast, was only obliquely interested in the conditional or accidental. His method of experimentation was oriented toward the acceptance of unforeseen tactical failures in the interest of long-term strategic goals.[24] Experimentation was the process of aligning specific faults of a tested form with the regularity of a holistically conceived system, a system he termed "comprehensive" or "total" design. The goal of design, to Fuller, was to convert traditionally compensatory political thinking into what he termed "anticipating and laboratory experimenting."[25] These experiments toward comprehensive knowledge—proposed and tested by Fuller and other nonspecialists—were ostensibly set forth for the greater good of society.[26]

This model of experimentation played out in the late 1940s through his research on the structural properties and social benefits of geodesics, defined as the arcs of great circles. Because they mirror the form of the earth itself, spheres were a main component in Fuller's argument that he was discovering the universal laws of nature on "Spaceship Earth."[27] His initial, unsuccessful attempt to assemble a geodesic dome took place during his first summer at Black Mountain in 1948. Then he became energized by College sculpture student Kenneth Snelson's innovations in what Fuller termed "tensegrity"—an engineering principle of discontinuous compression and continuous tension that reoriented Fuller from what he called "energetic geometry," physical models of energy and tension seen in closely packed spheres, for example. The geodesic dome, eventually prototyped to employ tensegrity, became a touchstone for Fuller's notion of holistic planning, an efficient *ur*-structure central to his reconsideration of postwar housing, transport, and communications as networked systems.

Yet the articulation of "total thinking," culminating in the successful erection of a geodesic dome on campus in 1949, was perhaps not the lasting consequence of Fuller's time at Black Mountain. It was his paradoxical stance of self-declared success in the face of apparent setback—his proposal of a model of experimentation that accommodated failure in the name of the larger holistic program—that proved Fuller's greatest contribution to the College, particularly in its selective adoption by Cage. In Cage's case, the acceptance of failure was enthusiastically embraced, and the programmatic element abandoned.

Chapter 3 addresses the implications of Fuller's "total thinking" as a model of experimentation. Though the comprehensive designer was charged with thinking expansively about social problems, the wider, more inclusive breadth of society was not necessarily invited to participate in the design process. Fuller's heady proposition of artist-scientists seeking truths beyond organized politics was a self-described "design revolution," the parameters of which could be understood only years into the future.[28] His utilitarian version of experiment as a test and proof of total systems found company with many postwar iterations of pattern and network theory emerging from the New Bauhaus in Chicago (later renamed the Institute of Design), where Fuller taught before Black Mountain. The middle part of this chapter, then, takes up Fuller's relation to his Institute of Design colleagues László Moholy-Nagy and Gyorgy Kepes. Design for these men was not a product but a social process (a distant echo, to very different effects, of Albers's "art is not an object but an experience"); experiment proved that "structures are not *things*" but patterns.[29] Design processes should reveal underlying, universal truths hidden in patterns and networks. The final portion of chapter 3 addresses how Fuller's still-controversial version of experimentation presented a picture of total design—contingency, alternative platforms, and even human agency itself eliminated—in a world of self-sacrificing nonspecialists risking failure to improve unproductive habits in society. Whereas Cage and Albers argued over degrees of contingency, Fuller regarded experimentation as a process moving knowledge toward a comprehensive, technocratic global order.

These three models of experiment initiated at Black Mountain College—the methodical testing of the appearance and construction of form in the interest of designing new, though ever-contingent, visual experiences (Albers); the organization of aleatory (chance-generated) processes and the anarchical acceptance of indeterminacy (Cage); and "comprehensive, anticipatory design science" that tests traditional artistic and architectural forms, and embraces temporary failures, in order to teleologically progress toward a utopia of efficiently managed resources (Fuller)—represent incipient directions of postwar art practice and social praxis, elements of which would be sampled, if not wholly adopted, by Black Mountain students and subsequent practitioners.[30]

Despite their different proposals for experimental art practice—from explorations of contingency to schemes of total design—the cases presented here all attempted to establish experimentation in opposition to self-expression or immediacy. To explore this difference, consider the case of Charles Olson,

Black Mountain's final rector and its guiding influence in the 1950s. Expressionism at the College, embodied in visual art practices such as those of teachers de Kooning, Franz Kline, and Robert Motherwell, and paralleled in expressive literary modes such as those of poets Olson and Robert Creeley, counterposed (in ways that came to define the postwar artistic scene in the United States) the experimental models represented by Albers, Cage, and Fuller.

Olson advocated a quixotic form of rapid collaboration in the interest of immediacy, spontaneous production, and personal expression. His student at Black Mountain, poet Jonathan Williams, quotes him as saying—and one could imagine similar words spoken by de Kooning, Jackson Pollock, or any number of postwar expressionists—"You've got to take hunches, you've got to jump and then see what [happens]—you've got to operate as though you knew it."[31] Discussions at Black Mountain about the complicated nature and effects of experiment must be seen as themselves in dialogue with such countertendencies toward direct action and expression. Expressionists' condensation of self with presence and immediacy was anathema to experimentalists' methods. For Olson, the velocity of a creative process reflected the hope that the individual could become the prime agent for exploration of what he termed the "kinetics of experience . . . the kinetics of themselves as persons as well as of the stuff they have to work on, and by."[32] In his 1950 essay "Projective Verse," he praised composition born of spontaneity. Believing that impulsive invention presented an unmediated path to unconscious thought, he was reluctant to either premeditate or revise his work, and claimed that speed effected the direct transcription of the purer material of the unconscious. As he proclaimed: "It is spontaneous, this way . . . at all points (even, I should say, our management of daily reality as of the daily work) get on with it, keep moving, keep in speed, the nerves, their speed, the perceptions, theirs, the acts, the split second acts, the whole business, keep it moving as fast as you can, citizen."[33] In proto-Beat fashion, spontaneity was a process of unveiling the essential expression of subjectivity; Olson was verifying the fidelity of the textual form to the "truth" of the unconscious. He and his cohort of expressionists at Black Mountain weren't alone in trying to find a form of uncorrupted immediacy in the postwar moment. It is a testament to Albers, Cage, and Fuller that they attempted to generate models of experimental process through their work and pedagogy which, however conflicting, sidestepped the growing tendency to define the project of art as untrammeled, self-revelatory immediacy.

The chapters that follow are each aligned along axes of methodology and place. The discussion of place maps a trajectory of spatial and discursive moves from

Europe to America—though sometimes from America to Europe—in particular, a cross-circulation of Bauhaus ideas and their stateside reception, as well as a consideration of the German audience for John Dewey's theories.[34] As the phrase "chance and design" in the book's subtitle indicates, the line of methodological inquiry in this book charts a continuum of experimental practices from the chance-derived to the highly ordered, designed, and, in the case of Fuller, technophilic. Plotting the routes these different men traveled toward their respective visions of experimentation in postwar America results in a particular organizational logic to this project. Such an exploration is suited to a case-study basis for the chapters' mostly monographic treatments of their subjects. In turn, the chapters relate to one another directly and interweave certain threads, though they are largely focused examinations of three disparate methodologies that characterized experimental practice at the College. Albers, Cage, and Fuller, though they returned to the concept repeatedly, were addressing radically different procedures when they invoked the matter of experimentation. For example, Cage can be seen as a wedge against Albers, moving his (Cage's) explorations of indeterminacy as a process beyond human agency toward Fuller's total design as a process beyond political means.

The coincidence that concepts and practices employing a notion of the experimental test took root at Black Mountain College, at the same early 1930s moment during which many European models of experimental social and aesthetic practice were being foreclosed upon by political persecution and the ensuing "call to order" of a return to artistic tradition, is also an implicit theme of this book. The Bauhaus project in particular—a utopian vision of aesthetic form integrated with society (art, architecture, design, and performance seen contextually and as part of modernist industry, transport, infrastructure, communication and media, housing, and education)—in its US reception fractured at times into a depoliticized notion of experimentation as mere interdisciplinary conversations. In recent years, art and architectural historians have been rethinking how form is taught to students and meaning is communicated in artworks, regrouping after years of cultural relativism in which criteria for evaluating projects of modernist innovation were deeply shaken. Above all, the Bauhaus was a program, or at least a series of competing programs, that offered students training in the observation of form and its creative rearticulation. It presented students with a persuasive sense of order and design as a means to think about the social stakes of form in a collaborative, interdisciplinary fashion and to rework outmoded, routinized production that led to repetition and stagnation. The minimization of explicit links between aesthetics and social praxis at Black Mountain, in contrast, left the College open to criticisms of its being a communitarian venture of artistic practitioners living a kind of enlightened social experiment of interdisciplinary affinities *as* social progress, divorced from earlier avant-gardes' aspirations to link developments in aesthetic form to wider, socially transformative ramifications.[35]

The specific post-wartime context of Black Mountain College's most propitious, creative years also has manifold implications for the rhetoric and practices of experimentation nurtured there. Not only did the College benefit from a bevy of talented veterans who brought generous GI Bill funding—students Kenneth Noland, Robert Rauschenberg, and Kenneth Snelson among many others took advantage of the US government's few-strings-attached cash payments for tuition and living expenses to attend the unaccredited, art-focused Black Mountain—but the widespread association in postwar society between experimentation and cultural value, following the immense technological advances of the war-driven economy, no doubt influenced the frequency of the term's invocations on the campus. In this light it is easy to see the invitation to Buckminster Fuller to head the College upon the Alberses' departure as endorsing his sense of the horizon of experimentation as opening onto questions of scientific truth and advancement.

If we can think of the experimental test in its postwar context through a range of meanings, from planned hypothesis to trials of experience more generally, it is indeed a productive term. While this expanded definition of experiment was being rethought at the College as a model of artistic practice that connected activities occurring in various disciplines, testing was simultaneously invoked as a technique to link practices to one another historically. Distinct methods of experimental practice along the continuum of chance and design must also be understood as not simply a triangulated configuration (Albers and Cage, Cage and Fuller, Albers and Fuller). Instead, the work of each figure must be positioned, as they are in this book, in relation to prior and contemporaneous explorations of experimentation they connected to their respective disciplinary practices. Cage's attraction to chance is appreciated only when his seemingly eclectic interests in Zen, Dada, and Antonin Artaud are linked to his developing notion of "void" spaces and experiences in performance; Fuller's technocratic design can be best elaborated by probing network and pattern theories developed at the New Bauhaus in Chicago by Moholy-Nagy and Kepes; and Albers's version of contingent design can be clarified when seen as a part of a broad conversation of geometric abstraction with Bauhaus concerns of visual apperception, Viennese logical positivism, and Theodor Adorno's contemporaneous theorization of experimentation. Each figure at Black Mountain defined, in his own practice, a particular, historically grounded method of experiment, and then attempted to chart its effects on his audience. Experiment as a single, unified practice never existed at Black Mountain, but Albers, Cage, and Fuller shared aspirations about testing new visual, theatrical, and structural forms and measuring their effects, however different the specific means that characterized their practices.

The analysis that follows thus posits a close interrelationship of experimentation and politics, suggesting that working "experimentally" in a cultural practice (in these cases, art, architecture, and music) casts a shadow venture, a project of posing models of how to test and organize new forms of political agency and social life, though sometimes in microcosmic fashion. For Albers, the "ethics" of a careful, trained visual attention to the world of form often substituted pedagogy and personal growth for forms of collective politics or social transformation. For Cage, indeterminacy in musical composition mirrored his idea of a fundamentally uncontrollable and anarchic world, though he created meticulous chance-protocol structures to eliminate personal bias and the crust of habit. And finally, for Fuller, total design in architectural form extended toward types of efficient technocratic social and political organization that, at times, shaded into forms of libertarian utilitarianism. Yet the attribution of a common experimental basis to their works and inventions, and their reinterpretations of tradition, bring to the fore a common impulse to change present and control future conditions. Experiment as a testing of the past or as a moving toward unforeseen experiences was nevertheless a quest for new, more adequate, and politically progressive and inclusive understandings of the world. One would not experiment if the current state of affairs—the status quo—was perceived as satisfactory. This extension of the project of artistic experiment to a redefinition of life conditions was of course as fraught as those preceding it in earlier moments of twentieth-century modernism.

The works of these three major teachers at Black Mountain College exemplify methods of experimentation that cannot, nor could they ever, harmonize, given their imperative to define, determine, and delimit quite differentiated life conditions beyond cultural practice. Each chapter of this book accounts for how these practitioners articulated distinct and nuanced procedures of experimentation; yet sometimes so great were the dissimilarities that they united merely in their mutual hostility toward expressionism and the subjectivization of creativity in its productive process as well as in its reception. In the case of figures such as Cage and Fuller, who were at Black Mountain intensely and briefly in the late 1940s and early 1950s, their elaborations of experimentation should be seen contextually in the traditions they displaced at the College (Bauhaus theater, in the case of Cage), or in practices that represented alternative genealogies of the Bauhaus theory so central to the College's educational mission (the Institute of Design, in the example of Fuller).

Ultimately, this book analyzes perhaps *the* crucial midcentury modernist practice—experimentation—that has not been studied in depth elsewhere, though the concept was explored to a nearly unparalleled degree at Black Mountain during these years. The legacy of Black Mountain College is precisely bound up with these figures' contradictory visions of modernism as inextricably interwoven with the logic of experimentation—the interest in testing as an exploration of a paradoxical "fact of contingency," to use Louis Althusser's phrase.[36] This book investigates what chance, design, and the unforeseen mean when a fertile and disputed term like experimentation is the site of discursive struggles as well as historic collaborations.

It should be clear that the Black Mountain idea of experimentation, when treated critically and differentially rather than descriptively, elucidates a crucial conflict surrounding American artistic purpose in the late 1940s. In proposing experiment as a model for understanding art practices at Black Mountain College, a clearer understanding can emerge of the College's role in generating new methods and objects of artistic production, and also innovative critiques about the constitution and uses of form in its time, to develop working means to effect those critiques. Black Mountain participants' ambitions to transform habits of perception, systems of intention, and patterns of tradition have essential implications for understanding not only modernist but subsequent art practices.

chapter one

josef albers and the ethics of perception

Experimentation means learning by experience.

Josef Albers, 1941[1]

A most poignant document of Black Mountain College's early years is the snapshot of Josef and Anni Albers's arrival, published in North Carolina's *Asheville Citizen* on December 5, 1933 (fig. 1.1). "Germans to Teach Art Near Here," the caption reads, though "Fresh Off the Boat" would do just as well; the grainy newsprint depicts the couple posed tensely in formal attire—he in tie and jacket, she in fur, cloche, and veil. Tightly angled in a corner, they look very much the anxious, recent immigrants. While Anni's mild gaze seeks out the viewer, Josef averts his eyes, his stiff bearing and tightly clasped hands registering trepidation, even strain. Fleeing the Nazi regime, the couple left Berlin for the site of a newly founded experimental school in rural Appalachia, a quite improbable relocation under other circumstances. Though they came from the Bauhaus, one of the most radical art institutions of the era, to what was vociferously announced as its successor in the United States, this evidence of a nervous arrival is testimony to their unexpectedly providential exile from Europe.

Josef knew but a few words in English, though Anni was fluent. In their first years, she would serve double duty as both faculty member at the recently founded college and as his patient translator. The newspaper article does not mention this, nor does it quote his famous response to their welcoming ceremony. Rallying his scant English when asked what he hoped to accomplish in the United States, Josef declared simply, "I want to open eyes."[2] Typical of his plain and frank manner, Albers's pronouncement nonetheless encapsulates two concerns that characterize his years in the United States. Most obviously,

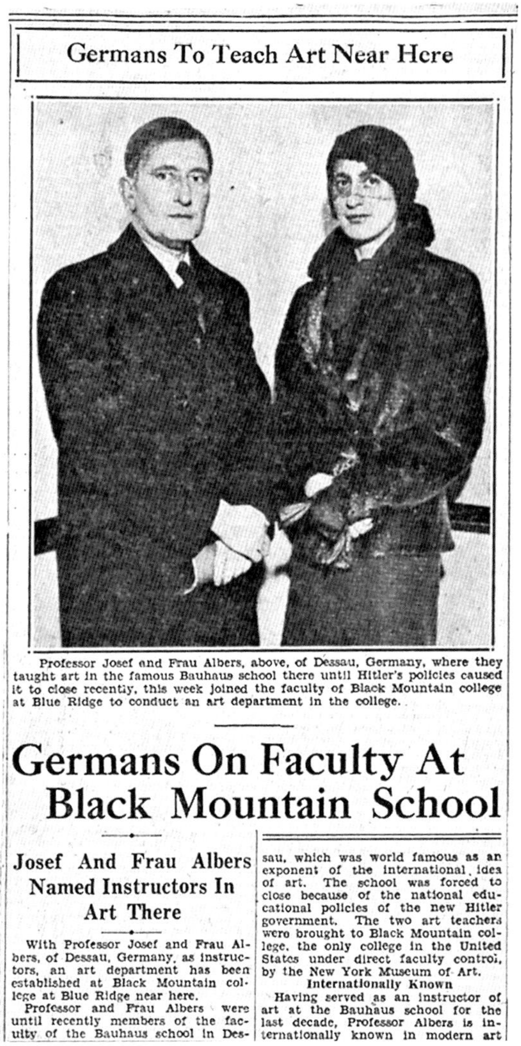

Germans To Teach Art Near Here

Professor Josef and Frau Albers, above, of Dessau, Germany, where they taught art in the famous Bauhaus school there until Hitler's policies caused it to close recently, this week joined the faculty of Black Mountain college at Blue Ridge to conduct an art department in the college.

Germans On Faculty At Black Mountain School

Josef And Frau Albers Named Instructors In Art There

With Professor Josef and Frau Albers, of Dessau, Germany, as instructors, an art department has been established at Black Mountain college at Blue Ridge near here.

Professor and Frau Albers were until recently members of the faculty of the Bauhaus school in Dessau, which was world famous as an exponent of the international idea of art. The school was forced to close because of the national educational policies of the new Hitler government. The two art teachers were brought to Black Mountain college, the only college in the United States under direct faculty control, by the New York Museum of Art.

Internationally Known

Having served as an instructor of art at the Bauhaus school for the last decade, Professor Albers is internationally known in modern art

Figure 1.1
"Germans on Faculty At Black Mountain School," *Asheville (NC) Citizen*, December 5, 1933. Photograph by Tim Nighswander. Courtesy of The Josef and Anni Albers Foundation / *The Asheville Citizen-Times*.

it indicates the centrality of his pedagogical commitment (the same newspaper article proclaimed Albers as "internationally known . . . for his unusual method of art instruction"). His statement also foregrounds the preeminence of a study of *vision* in his pedagogy and in Bauhaus teaching more generally—it is eyes he wants to open, after all.[3] Pedagogy and vision: together, his words represent a desire to craft an audience for abstraction and, more particularly, for his art, an audience that would be tutored in the perceptual strategies he was developing in his teaching.

The key elements of these perceptual strategies were set out in Albers's three-pronged Preliminary Course, or *Vorkurs*, brought from the Bauhaus to Black Mountain and later to Yale University. In these drawing, color, and design

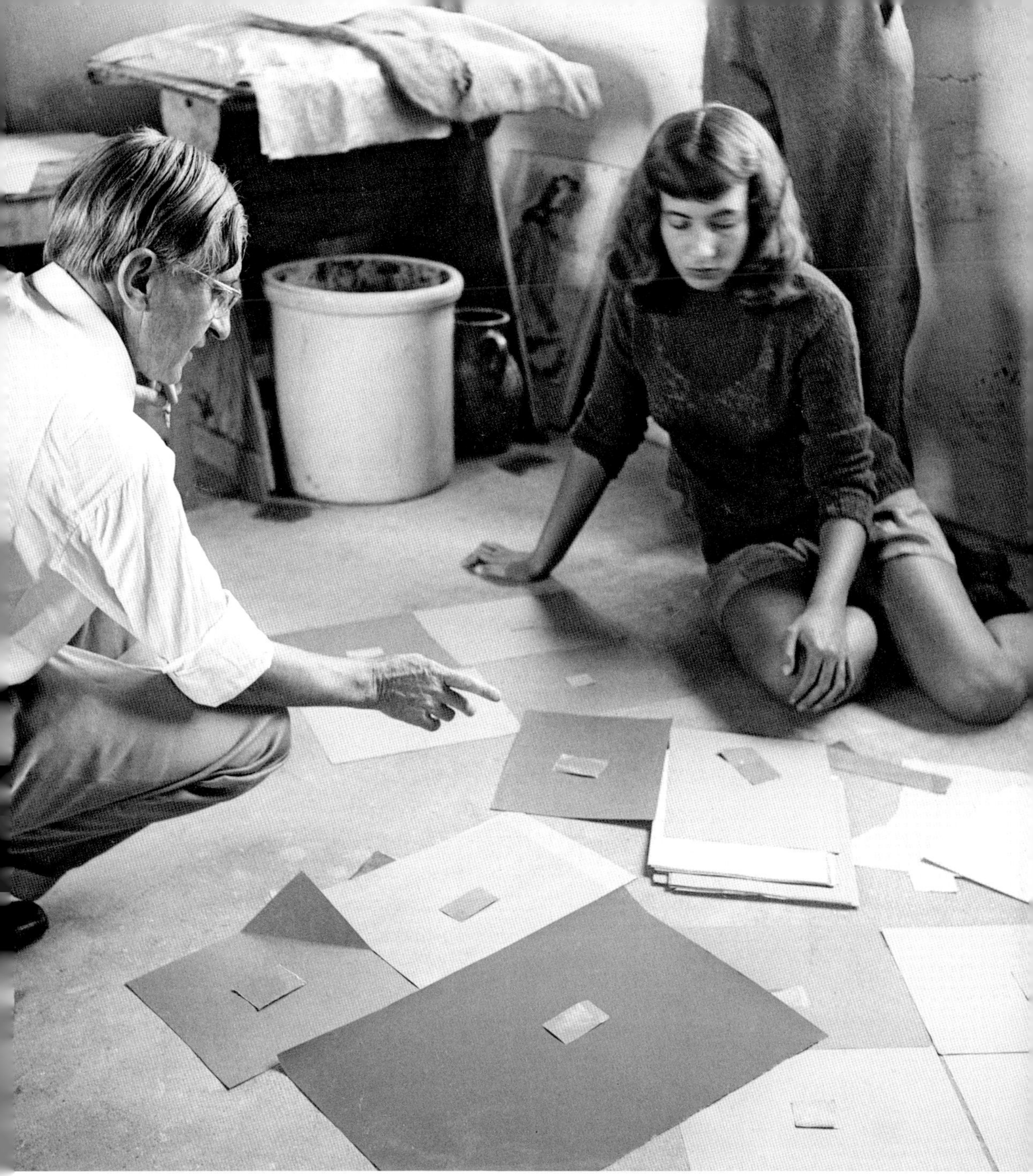

Figure 1.2
Josef Breitenbach, *Josef Albers' Color Class, Summer 1944*. Gelatin silver photograph © The Josef and Yaye Breitenbach Charitable Foundation, New York. Courtesy The Josef Breitenbach Archive, Center For Creative Photography, University of Arizona, Tucson.

classes, he proposed an ordered and disciplined testing of the various qualities and appearances of readily available materials such as construction paper and household paint samples. His approach brought out the correlation between formal arrangement and underlying structure, and placed a high value on economy of labor and resources. He stressed the *experience*, rather than any definite outcomes, of a laboratory educational environment and promoted forms of experimentation and learning in action that could dynamically change routine habits of seeing.[4] He began his drawing and design courses with mirror writing, a simple exercise in defamiliarization. He invited students to draw their names, for example, backward and in cursive, as if reflected in a mirror, and then asked them to render this script using their nondominant hand. Drawing by automatic motor sense invariably becomes a crutch, overwriting any direct consciousness of how the actual forms of a signature are produced. Mirror exercises provided students with a sure way to begin challenging sterile habits of observation, "to develop awareness of what we do out of habit as opposed to choice."[5]

To grasp Albers's proposal of what he came to term a "new visual expression" through acts of experimentation, it is crucial to understand the discursive field he produced around geometric abstraction, that is, how he explained the importance of a continuous study of the constitutive elements of form.[6] The first section of this chapter will undertake a close reading and analysis of Albers's large body of unpublished texts written in his budding English, which can shed light on the process of testing variations in form that his pedagogical strategies elaborated. (One could argue that given its minimal denotation of form and its refusal of naturalistic representation, geometric abstraction always relied heavily on discursive interpretations, offered both in the artists' own writings and by critics.) He redesigned the experience of looking at art as one of "direct seeing," whereby attention to perceptual habits marks routine cognitive associations as social constructions and allows these associations to be influenced and possibly transformed.[7] In that vein, the second section of this chapter will connect Albers's pedagogy with his own work. With careful study of his sketches, studies, and paintings undertaken at Black Mountain (and a few from his subsequent decades in the United States), it will be possible to address how Albers developed methods of articulating form that highlighted its contingency and endless mutability.

The final section of this chapter will explore how Albers went further to find in form an ethics of perception, which he developed in theories of progressive pedagogy concerning experimentation and social change. Drawing on the work of John Dewey, Albers presented the methodology of the experimental test as a forceful corrective against stagnant perceptual habits in the culture at large, bringing attention to the tremendous stake of progressive education in combating forces of social reproduction, that is, the tendency of dominant cultural values to be reproduced as the privileged traditions of a society. He maintained that learning to observe and design form made an essential contribution toward cultural transformation and growth. In brief, in Albers's ethics of perception, careless habits—habits that inhibit self-actualization and social progress—can be overcome with the disciplined study of the constitution of forms, forms that themselves compose the ubiquitous, though often overlooked, material and appearance of our surroundings.

PERCEPTION BETWEEN SCIENCE AND INTUITION

Elements of Josef Albers's teachings have become so familiar and ingrained in current art curricula that it is difficult to recall how radically art education was altered by the widespread adoption of his methods. Developed at the Bauhaus in the early 1920s through 1933 and continued at Black Mountain College from 1933 to 1949 and at Yale from 1950 to 1958, Albers's Preliminary Course consistently challenged conventional art teaching. Indeed, it is important to remember the great influence of Black Mountain's teaching methods generally—especially during Albers's nearly two decades at the College—in positioning invention and experiment as central elements of educational practice in the United States, and to bear in mind that in the years preceding its implementation elsewhere, "it was heresy," according to Albers, "to consider art a central part of a college curriculum or a means of general education."[8]

Visual arts training in the early twentieth century, in Europe as in the United States, took place in specialized art academies modeled on classical Beaux-Arts instructional models or in technical institutes featuring drawing for industrial design, rather than in liberal arts colleges such as Black Mountain. In academies, distinctions among various media were reinforced, and the rendering from life, above all the study of the nude, was central. The emphasis was on repetition (in life studies) and duplication (in copying past works). Advancement was secured by a review process that paradoxically assessed a pupil's fidelity to precursors and his (rarely *her*) departure from precedent in an "original" work—the academy study of the male nude. In its technical application, drawing accentuated the repeatability of objective nature by creating a strict geometry of form (and in this sense, to use M. Norton Wise's phrase, "drawing is the language of engineering").[9] This language of reproduced form, as Molly Nesbit contends, was routinized by drills in elementary and higher education toward "blueprints of production" in industrial product design.[10] Even attempts to devise hybrid guild-workshop models of art education spawned by the Arts and Crafts movement, as Howard Singerman has noted, tended to attach more importance to craft traditions than to creative work in art and design.[11] Whatever the model—academy, technical college, or workshop—visual art training beyond high school was not closely integrated with liberal arts concerns or with experimental or progressive approaches.

Albers bemoaned the persistence of such models in the United States:

> I believe dominating education methods in this country are not at all typically American with their stereotyped requirements, standardized curricula and mechanized evaluation of achievements. Why do we still have the belief in academic standards while our living reveals variety, youth and freshness . . . ? Why must exploration and inventiveness, two American virtues, too, play such a minor part in our schools?[12]

He found particularly grating the assumption in standardized art education that talent and an aptitude for art were inherent gifts and prerequisites to creativity. Instead, he fostered a general training in the fundaments of art as "more democratic [and] . . . giving a chance to many more people," not just to the exceptional or advanced student.[13] In this sense, Albers was a good fit for Black Mountain; the centrality of art education was emphasized in the College's 1933 inaugural publication shortly before his arrival: "Fine Arts, which often exist precariously on the fringes of the curriculum, are regarded as an integral part of the life of the College and of importance equal to that of the subjects that usually occupy the center of the curriculum."[14] The goal was not to produce professional artists but to consider all individuals as possible creators and to offer training for what Albers termed a "flexible and productive mind that wants to do something with the world . . . we are on the way to the researcher, discoverer, to the inventor, in short to the worker who produces or understands revelations."[15]

Art practice offered the ideal site in culture from which to encourage broad-minded thinking, as training in experimentation steered a course toward "coordination, interpenetration . . . conclusions, new viewpoints . . . for developing a feeling or understanding for atmosphere and culture."[16] The as yet unrealized prospect of education thus could consist of a richer understanding of "action or life," not a stockpiling of mere information or knowledge.[17] Developing an attuned visual sensibility involved testing, dynamism, and action, not the passivity and stasis of education based on study of precedent alone.[18] Albers's series of foundational courses promoted independent thinking and a close study of the mutable nature of form. On a visit to Black Mountain in 1944, Walter Gropius praised Albers's innovation: "He has discarded the old procedure to hand over to the student a ready-made formulated system. He gives

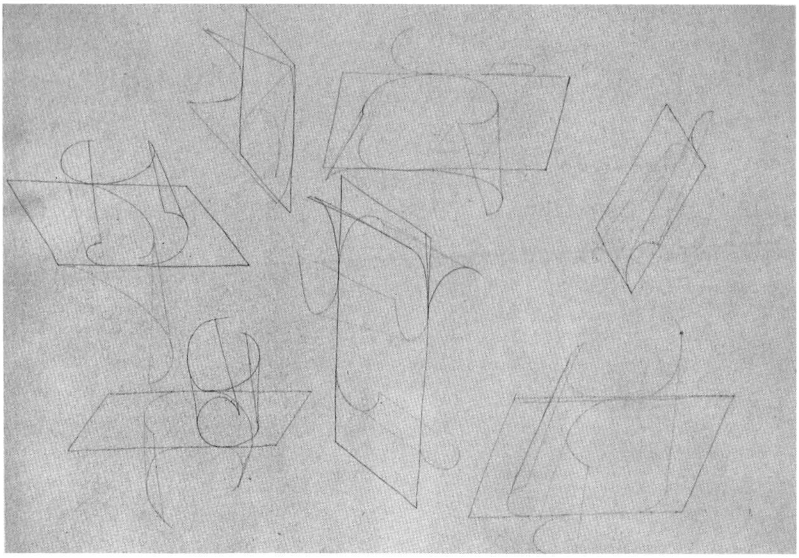

Figure 1.3
Unknown artist, *Drawing Study*, n.d. Reproduced in J. Albers, *Search Versus Re-Search* (Hartford, CT: Trinity College Press, 1969), 51. © Trinity College Trustees. Courtesy of the Watkinson Library, Trinity College, Hartford, Connecticut.

them instead objective tools that enable them to dig into the very stuff of life. . . . This ever-changing approach seems to me pregnant of life, present and future."[19]

Albers's battery of courses constituted a broad foundation in the "stuff of life": a general education in the fundamental elements of visual perception, broken down into a sequence of three classes covering the "main provinces of form"—drawing, color, and design.[20] Yet "fundamental" and "foundational" should not be understood as merely elementary. Rather, through the observation of form's shape, material (in its structure, surface, and appearance), and coloristic qualities, Albers offered a basic training in articulating form, and possibly in rearticulating it creatively. As Peter Galison has observed, this program of "building up from simple elements to all higher forms" was perhaps the central feature of Bauhaus pedagogy.[21]

Albers's first course—Basic Drawing—concentrated on shape through the exact observation and transcription of form in space. Drawing was conceived as a "test of seeing" that graphically reported visual data honed by exercises in foreshortening, overlapping, distance, and nearness.[22] Albers encouraged students to observe the disposition of line in various contexts; in one study (fig. 1.3), the depiction of repeated bent and scrolled planes tested the precise spatial translation of two dimensions into three. Such trained observation excluded what Albers termed "expressive drawing" as a beginning, that is, the depiction of conditions that could not be assessed with some objectivity; the length of each mark in figure 1.3 maps the real behavior of a line in space with respect to qualities of depth and movement.[23] His teaching exercises employed

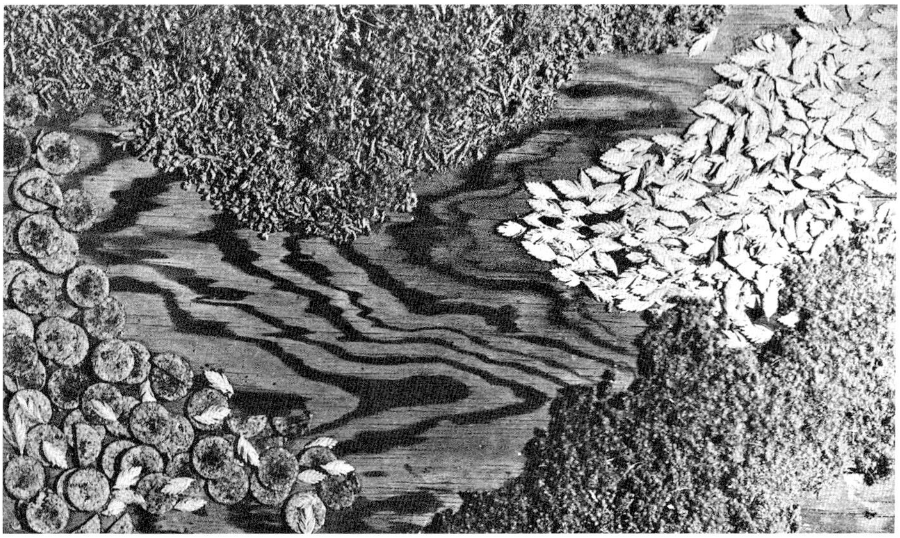

Figure 1.4
Unknown artist, *Matiere Study*, n.d. Reproduced in J. Albers, *Search Versus Re-Search* (Hartford, CT: Trinity College Press, 1969), 77. © Trinity College Trustees. Courtesy of the Watkinson Library, Trinity College, Hartford, Connecticut.

uncomplicated geometric forms such as squares, triangles, and ellipses, as well as simple figures such as letters and numbers, to perform changes in perspective and to create anamorphic effects that demonstrated a mastery of spatial representation. He avoided studies of the nude or classical model, "because that's the hardest thing to do and you come maybe only for the nudes and not for the drawing."[24]

Basic Design (the key *Werklehre*—handicraft, or literally, the study of how to work—portion of the Preliminary Course) involved explorations of the material constitution of form. Albers divided the subject into two components, which he termed *matière* and *material*, and focused on exploration using commonly found materials and the fewest possible tools. *Matière* studies concerned the *appearances* of materials, distinguishing among structure, facture, and texture, and sought to characterize materials by their tactile or optical perception.[25] For example, a trompe l'oeil representation of wood grain on paper gave the optical appearance of wood but the tactile experience of paper (fig. 1.4). Essentially, the practice of combining and confusing the superficial qualities of materials tested (mis)perceptions of the appearances of surfaces.[26]

Material studies concerned the immanent *capacities* of materials, evaluated structurally and analyzed according to features such as compression, elasticity, and firmness, tested through folding and bending. Here, Albers concentrated on the internal organization of forms and their relation to one another, encouraging dynamic relations rather than strictly symmetrical or mathematically predictable ones. An understanding of the dimensional, spatial, and volumetric qualities of form was accomplished through construction exercises, whose parameters were defined through formal economy, that is, the "ratio of effort to effect."[27]

Albers believed the disciplined study of the material organization of form to be a necessary condition of art production. As he reasoned, "Every art work is based on a thinking out of the material."[28] And in pre-Columbian sculpture he found the signal example of a sophisticated understanding of the technical potentials and limitations of medium. Once Albers relocated to the United States, he amassed an extensive collection of Mexican pre-Columbian pottery and figurines; he felt such work amplified the characteristic tendencies of its material, establishing a reflexive relation between an object's structure and appearance. In contrast to many uses of clay in Western art, in which it is applied over a hidden armature, pre-Columbian art keeps "clay clay-like," building "cake-like flat elements or little globular or sausage-like forms"[29] (fig. 1.5). Stonework commonly uses compact forms lacking delicate protrusions that

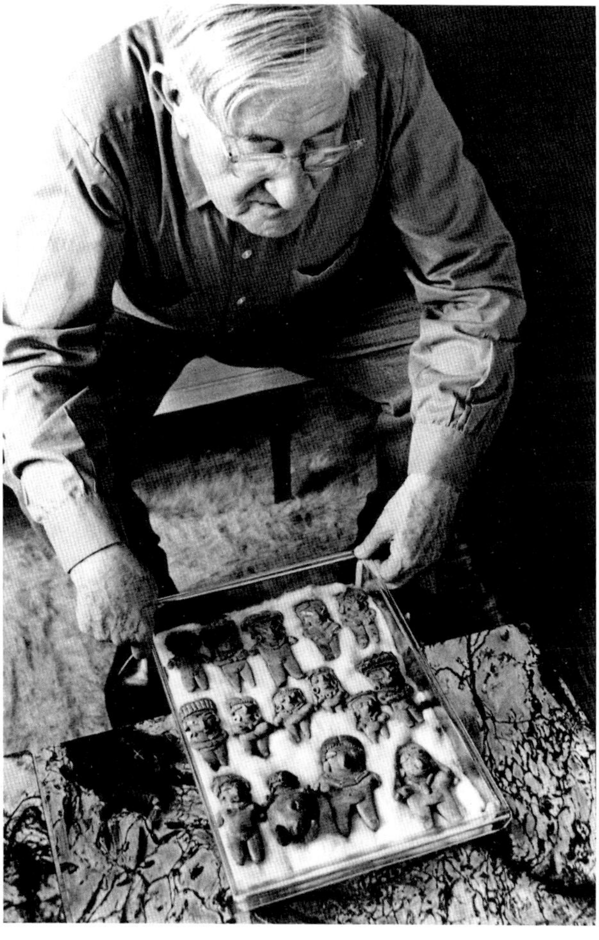

Figure 1.5
Henri Cartier-Bresson, *Josef Albers with Pre-Columbian Figurines*, 1968. Gelatin silver photograph. Courtesy Magnum Photos.

can break. This construction is "proof that the artist has not overaimed and that the material has not been over-charged."[30] Rather than simulating something else, the materiality of pre-Columbian art evokes the constructivist credo: it "teaches us [to] be truthful with materials."[31] Though the appearance of any material can mimic another, its underlying structure and technical capacity can never be successfully imitated. The trompe l'oeil woodgrain drawing on paper, however naturalistic, cannot be mistaken for actual wood in its strength or durability (fig. 1.4).

Color study was conceived as the foundational technique of painting, each brushstroke or application of the palette knife the bearer of a dab of colored paint. Albers's color course encouraged students to tackle the process of painting with clear intentions and proper execution—"to prepare for a disciplined use of color and to prevent accident, brush, or paint-box from taking authorship."[32] Again, as in his other courses, Albers emphasized active "laboratory study" over the theoretical study of color systems, since "the ability to see color and color relationship is more important than 'to know about' color."[33]

Despite the renown Albers later won through his influential 1963 manual *Interaction of Color*, the study of color was relatively undeveloped in his repertoire upon his arrival in the United States. At the Bauhaus, he had radically shifted the Preliminary Course away from explorations of expression and gestural improvisation to rigorous material studies. The increasingly unpopular fixation with the subjective and emotional potential of color demonstrated by Johannes Itten, his predecessor, hastened his departure (triggering perhaps the most productive schism in Bauhaus ideology, one concerning the role of expression as opposed to design in art).[34] Though diverging from Itten's methods, Albers well understood the subjective dimension of color perception. When presented with irrefutable physical evidence—for example, the demonstration of a particular red shade—"all group members will have the same visual perception. But still the individual associations and emotional reactions will differ vastly."[35] Color is always relational; its perception is influenced not only by neighboring colors but by the surrounding light and atmospheric conditions. In addition, "visual memory is amazingly poor" as compared with, say, auditory memory, and suggests that "color is deceiving us all the time"; these influences on vision have the effect of converting "the optical (physio-physiological) susception ['stimuli'] into a psychological effect (perception)."[36] Because optical impressions and reactions are highly susceptible to manipulation or error, our understanding of and reflection on visual data—that is, the way we "image" or represent the world in the process of perception—must be carefully trained. This education in vision works to prevent the ease and apparent lack of mediation of optical vision to stand in for a more robust process of challenging meanings commonly assigned to forms. The fallibility of perception, its reliance on deceptive optical registrations, indicates the mutability of cognitive (that is, abstract/conceptual) comprehension, built as it is on those self-same illusions. "Color is the most relative medium in art," Albers asserted, and this relativity puts into question how cognitive understandings of the world are founded, maintained, and possibly altered.[37]

Deliberate evaluation of the data of perception marks habits of cognition as such, denaturalizing them and making them receptive to change. In the long history of aesthetic discourse, theorizing perception as indebted to habit was early proposed by British empiricists. John Locke was forcefully skeptical about the "naturalness" of perception; he contended that reactions to the testimony of the senses organize knowledge and experience in ways that become ingrained. Casual relations to such sensory stimuli generate "habitual customs" that reformulate new visual appearances into familiar cognitive patterns: "We are further to consider concerning perception, that the ideas we receive by sensation are often, in grown people, altered by the judgment, without our taking notice of it." Previous experiences of events—traditions and precedents—model subsequent experiences in their image; therefore, it is important "to consider how much [one] may be beholden to experience, improvement, and acquired notions."[38]

Locke's recognition that perception is "beholden to experience" and susceptible to routinization became a touchstone of late nineteenth-century philosophical debates about the nature of attention under conditions of growing industrialization and mechanization. Positivists such as Hermann von Helmholtz problematized the "apparentness" and immediacy of visual comprehension with tests of the enervation of visual attention in situations of optical fatigue, citing Johann Wolfgang von Goethe's experiments with the vulnerability of visual evidence in the phenomenon of afterimages. Nonetheless, von Helmholtz was prey to the conceit, according to Jonathan Crary, that "habitual repetition was part of what maintained an orderly social world and affirmed the validity and durability of existing relations."[39] For Crary, Henri Bergson's arguments about the close connection between habit, repetition, and automation in modernity (as against forms of personal memory) best corrected von Helmholtz's tendency toward functionalism. Crary detected in Bergson's work that "the more 'determined,' that is, the more habitual and repetitive one's perceptual response to one's environment is, the less autonomy and freedom characterize that individual existence."[40]

Citing Bergson's work, Russian formalists developed theories of vision that focused on remaking perceptual experience.[41] Significantly, Viktor Shklovsky's exploration of "habituation" as a process of rendering perception automatic and unconscious brought to the fore the key role of art in catalyzing new forms of awareness:

> The purpose of art is to impart the sensation of things as they are perceived and not as they are known. The technique of art is to make objects "unfamiliar," to make forms difficult, to increase the difficulty and length of perception because the process of perception is an aesthetic end in itself and must be prolonged.[42]

To Shklovsky, the "purpose [of an image] is not to make us perceive meaning, but to create a special perception of the object—it creates a 'vision' of the object instead of serving as a means of knowing it."[43]

It can be argued that Shklovsky's type of formalism, by privileging the "special perception" of art over knowledge, elevated art to a category of direct experience surpassing epistemology, and even attempted to negate the "ends" of meaning production in favor of an "ends" of "means": the process of sensation. In contrast, Albers's troubling of habituation was undertaken not merely as "an aesthetic end." Rather, he contended that the entire structure of perception was related to the growth and transformation of cognitively assigned meanings in art and in the world at large. Albers saw art as an epistemological project, as a *form* of knowledge; to him, the better "vision" that attentive perception provokes can in fact increase awareness about routinely assigned meanings, and thus can encourage people to transform their customary patterns of comprehension. To Albers, "Every perceivable thing has form . . . and every form has meaning."[44] But through routine the richness of the visual and material world is frequently overlooked. The diverse forms of modernity are themselves always changing, yet habit-driven behaviors reinforce accustomed understandings of forms and their existing, known relations to one another.[45] Maintaining an alert attention to the appearance and constitution of form short-circuits assumptions that corroborate preexisting categories.

In short, Albers wanted to connect visual to social habits. If, for example, one can recognize how a work of art maintains a dynamic construction through careful imbalances of color and form—if a particular color to which one might automatically assign the name "black" is brought out of its familiarity and shown to be perhaps a little purple in one light and a little gray in another—the routine cognitive associations of "blackness" (dirt, gloom, death, and so on) can be made similarly unstable. The potential of color study to uncouple sterile associations he dubbed its "psychological effect."[46] In his color exercises (note the comparative study from *Interaction of Color*, adapted from his Black Mountain–era exercises of making the same color appear different depending on its background [plate 1]), Albers tested the mutability of perception, demonstrating how the reception of color shifts dramatically and is deeply situational. Though the two central forms in each study are identical in shape and color, the gray rectangle on a warm yellow field appears brown and static as compared with its more dynamic, though lower-contrast counterpart on a cool blue ground. The illusion, even in close proximity, is persuasive; as the eye compares, it remains difficult to reconcile the fundamental semblance of the two forms. The ambiguity of the gray shade—lively in one instance, dull in another, and therefore utterly dependent on its immediate context for definition—reveals the extraordinary attention and subtlety every visual experience demands of viewers. Careful study of the discrepancy between optical trickery (they *appear* as two different colors) and material reality (they actually *are* the same) can activate a fresh awareness of the constructedness of all habits of meaning in the world, as well as trigger an ambition to redesign them conscientiously.

Albers saw experimentation as the preeminent method by which the new and changing experiences of modernity could be expressed and its "modern problems" addressed (first and foremost, how to develop a student's "independence, critical ability, and discipline"), and he envisioned its practice as a disciplined testing process encouraging innovative visual articulations.[47] Art itself was the experimental arm of culture, investigating the "better forms" that are the prerequisite of cultural production and progress.[48] As he wrote:

> To understand the meaning of form is the indispensable preliminary condition for culture. Culture is the ability to select or to distinguish the better, that is, the more meaningful form, the better appearance, the better behavior. Therefore culture is a concern with quality. Culture can be manifested in two ways: through recognition of better form and through producing of better form. The latter direction is the way of art. Art as the acting part of culture and therefore its proof and measurement.[49]

Art was more broadly both an "intuitive search for and discovery of form" and "the knowledge and application of the fundamental laws of form."[50] Experimental processes constellate these interreliant features of artistic production: intuition and intellect. To Albers, this dialectic had profound social effects. In one respect, practices of teaching and learning were mutually informing and interdependent; in an egalitarian educational climate it was possible to "break through the boundary between those teaching and those being taught, because then everybody will be teacher and student at the same time."[51] The problems posed in the classroom setting and as homework assignments should be stimulating to all—novice and expert, instructor and pupil.[52] In breaking down hierarchies of expertise, Albers by no means advocated the dissolution of all categories of pedagogical distinction. Rather, he required of himself consummate skill; students would then "estimate as more competent . . . the one with more experience and insight."[53] The goal was discovery, not demonstration: to shift from "giving information to giving experience."[54] Experimentation, the testing operation that characterizes creative processes, builds skills of evaluation and assessment: "This one is better than that one and this shows more your expectations and your aims and all your efforts, then you are on the way to build up yourself."[55] The procedure of the test joins *comparison* and what Albers termed *competition*; it is both self-driven and motivated externally by variations in performance among members of a group:

> Because this comparing includes of course competition—nothing is big, or nothing is small, when we do not see it in [the] neighborhood of something bigger or smaller. . . . That's the relativity of all evaluation, and if I want to evaluate myself by comparing my work with other work . . . that is comparison and is also competition.[56]

Competition—not antagonism—impelled personal growth and progress within a group by encouraging careful evaluations of subtle changes in performance.[57]

In this explicit focus on competition, Albers differed from other geometric abstractionists at the College, notably Ilya Bolotowsky, Albers's replacement when he went on sabbatical in 1946–47. In Bolotowsky's classes, students were urged to produce "mature" work regardless of whether it emulated the styles of other artists, resulting in some conflict at the College as he effectively repealed Albers's group exercise techniques. Bolotowsky's courses at Black Mountain propounded a "universal plastic language with sufficient room for individual difference" in which "originality is encouraged."[58] He was Albers's junior by twenty years, and he and other abstract painters based in New York City such as Fritz Glarner had been highly receptive to Piet Mondrian and neoplasticism in the 1930s. Bolotowsky took it on faith that abstraction, not "nature," was the preeminent modern practice because it captured the essence, not the appearance, of form. Though he and Albers were founding members of the American Abstract Artists (AAA) group in 1936, Bolotowsky's emphasis on universal characteristics of representation precluded any comparative or experimental testing framework. As he explained in language indebted to Mondrian's more Neoplatonic moments, "The majority [in AAA] felt that all worthwhile art has to begin somewhere in nature and then become the essence of it, but a few of us would simply start abstractly and reject nature. . . . Abstract art is striving to depict an essence of harmony."[59] Bolotowsky's emphasis on the immanence of abstraction and the rejection of nature stood in direct opposition to Albers's methodology, especially as the latter's model of the test demanded careful observation of the order of existing appearances of "nature," in the interest of rearticulating them.

Albers's investigations of form, in contrast to Bolotowsky's, were not undertaken in the interest of generating immediately viable, mature art practices. The goal of the courses was not necessarily to produce anything useful but rather to train observation. As Albers stated, "In designing there are besides technical and economical problems also problems of form which are independent of a purely functional approach."[60] To help students avoid succumbing to tendencies of habit or to pressure them to supersede work of the past, Albers advocated "experiment without aiming to make a product."[61] He identified intuitive elements in art production available to those with trained vision, recognizing that there are "many unknown and incalculable X's which makes it impossible to find every solution by figuring, reckoning and calculating."[62] He counseled students to devise exceptional situations in which his "worst enemies"—symmetry and predictability—were most effectively supplanted by dynamism and discovery.[63] The unlabored exercise frequently succeeded; one student recounted how Albers's first assignment in Basic Design supplied only a few newspapers with the task to "try to make something out of them that is more than you have now." Dismissing the resulting cut and pasted boats, animals, airplanes, little figurines, and masks as "kindergarten studies which could have been made better in other materials," Albers alighted on a study of great simplicity in which a young architect folded the newspaper lengthwise and stood it up to resemble a standing screen. "Albers explained to us how well the material was understood and utilized—how the folding process was natural to paper . . . now that the paper was standing up, both sides had become visually active. The paper had lost its tired look—its lazy appearance. After a while we caught on to his way of seeing and thinking."[64]

An expanded notion of art as mediating between material and culture led Albers to maintain, "Art is a province in which one finds all the problems of life reflected—not only the problems of form (e.g. proportion and balance)" but also what he termed "spiritual problems," problems of "philosophy, of religion, of sociology, of economy."[65] In broadening the definition of art to include visual and material explorations of all sorts, Albers's pedagogy posited the role of creativity in society as a consciousness to the breadth of aesthetic experience, beyond those observed in the "laboratory" of the classroom. Attentiveness to details of form meant, to Albers, an alertness to the ways in which the individual was sited in the larger field of social relations. Everything in the world has form; training the eye in the composition of form was a precondition for understanding and possibly transforming the material appearance and immaterial relations in the world. Albers believed that above all, "our art instruction attempts first to teach the student to see in the widest sense: to open his eyes to the phenomena about him and, most important of all, to open to his own living, being, and doing."[66]

THERE ARE NO MASTERPIECES: SERIALITY AND VARIATION

The practice of the experiment, seen in the light of Albers's body of writings on the test in art and in art education, helps unpack his own body of work in various media undertaken during his years in the United States. His production at Black Mountain in particular was tremendously catholic; though he had begun his career at the Bauhaus as a glass artist, there and at the College he produced photographs, photomontages, furniture, lithographs, wood- and linoleum cuts, pen-and-ink drawings, and oil paintings. In spite of this diversity, Albers's work from Black Mountain can be divided into roughly two long-term projects: the black-and-white *Graphic Tectonics* lithographs (1942–48) and the oil-on-Masonite *Variants* (1947–53), which were inspired by adobe architecture he'd seen in Mexico. Leaving Black Mountain to teach at Yale, he continued to develop the concerns about color perception, initiated in the *Variants* series, in the later *Homage to the Square* series (1950 until his death in 1976), as well as those of dimensional perception from the *Graphic Tectonics* in his subsequent *Structural Constellations* (1949–58).

Albers's work reflected a deliberate experimentation with the constitutive elements of form, centering on the coloristic and geometric relations organizing the appearance of forms on a two-dimensional surface. The scheme of each construction produces internal frictions and instabilities and must be provisionally extricated from multiple and contradictory dimensional readings. For instance, in Albers's linoleum cut *Fenced* (1944), interlocking irregular trapezoidal and triangular forms are demarcated in a regular pattern of vertical lines in two contrasting widths (fig. 1.6). As one follows the diagonals to find the outline of a half-perceived three-dimensional object, the impossibility of extracting such an illogical dimensional form from the matrix of surrounding verticals summons once again an overall flatness to the image. The contingent structure of the jigsawed composition in *Fenced*—is it more two dimensional than three dimensional? is it a unified shape or several intersecting or even disparate, overlapping forms?—generates optical challenges (though Albers

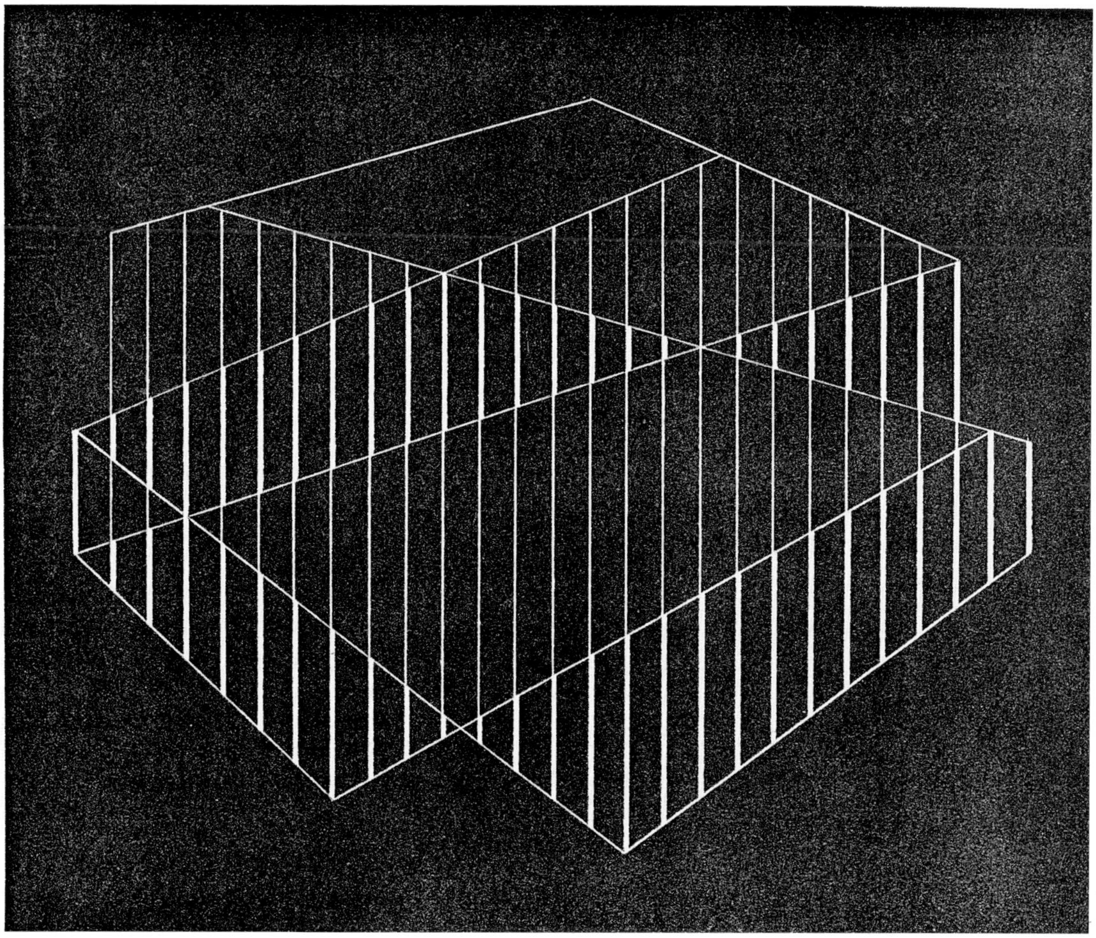

Figure 1.6
Josef Albers, *Fenced*, 1944. Linoleum cut, Biltmore Press, Asheville, 10 × 12". Photograph by Tim Nighswander © The Josef and Anni Albers Foundation / Artists Rights Society, New York.

disdained association with the later op art moniker) and exposes the rudimentary representational conditions necessary to construct spatially ambiguous images. As Albers observed of a similar work, "No matter where you start to read, you will never find a logical conclusion. And this, despite the fact that there is no arbitrary point or line, every part is mathematically derived from the underlying square."[67]

The distinction between the optical and the conditions under which opticality is understood cognitively was vital in Albers's work. To him, "In all visual perception, the initial reaction is optical"—that is, there is a physical fact of seeing that results in what he termed a "retinal projection."[68] Yet the effects of optical stimuli elicit varied perceptual responses that go beyond mere opticality; they are "post-retinal" and occur as the mind synthesizes the visual data

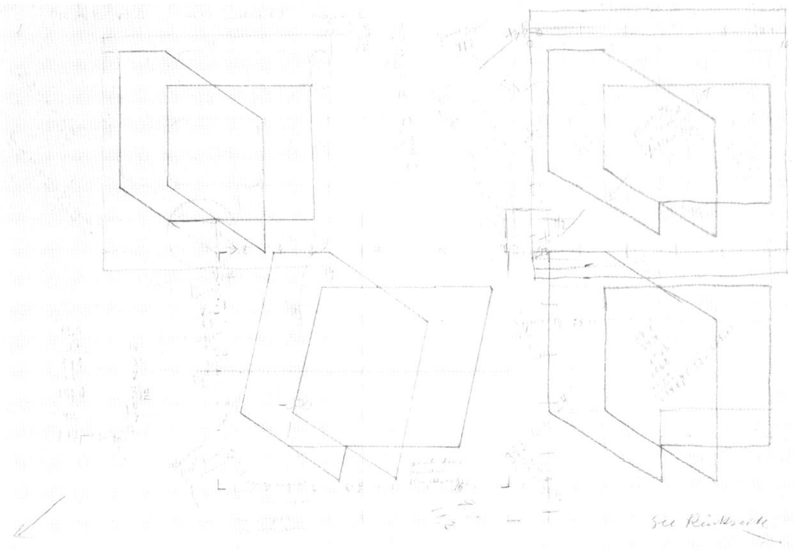

Figure 1.7
Josef Albers, *Studies for Abstract Paintings*, ca. 1937. Pencil and red pencil on wove paper, ruled in pencil, 9¼ × 13¾". Photograph by Tim Nighswander © The Josef and Anni Albers Foundation / Artists Rights Society, New York.

of a retinal projection. As Albers was fond of repeating, "Only there [in the mind] occur such important changes (reactions, results) as, for instance, that gentlemen prefer blondes."[69]

Perceptual responses in turn condition cognitive understandings of the world and one's ability to formulate and change the comprehension of objects and events. (Here, Yve-Alain Bois's paraphrase of the Russian formalist conception of representation—"form is always ideological"—is worth bearing in mind when considering Albers's circuit of testing perception against cognitive meanings.)[70] Perception mediates the physical fact of seeing and the socially and psychologically determined effects of vision. This zone of perception, as opposed to optics, is where Albers couched his artistic practice, tagging it "perceptual art."[71] And in this zone, he emphasized above all "perceptual ambiguity" as opposed to mere "optical deceptions," which occur in all representation but fail to educate the viewer in more attentive observation.[72] Revealing the mechanisms of perception could be accomplished with very limited visual data, hence his predilection toward abstraction. As Albers asserted, "The *how* is more important than the *what*."[73]

Albers's sketches and studies reveal the systematic trial-and-error process that each work underwent before completion, showing how "finished" works are composed of systematic variations and are produced in series. In a pencil study from about 1937, for example, careful calculations of surface area determine alterations in the size and placement of each form, and a series of measurements analyzes the spacing of the central forms as separated from the edges

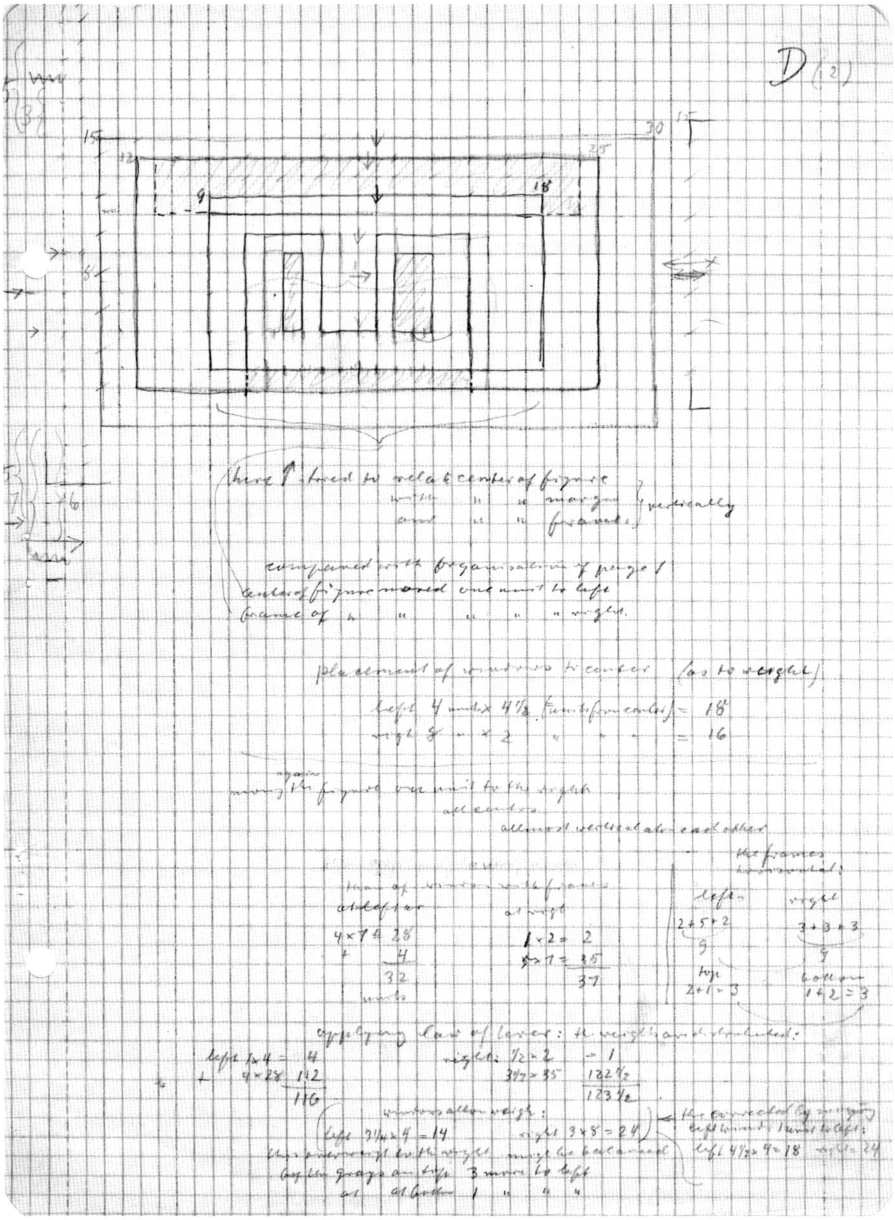

Figure 1.8
Josef Albers, sketch for *Variant D(2)*, n.d. 8½ × 11". © The Josef and Anni Albers Foundation / Artists Rights Society, New York.

of the future work (fig. 1.7). Minute adjustments and transpositions of certain elements of the repeated forms are worked out in subsequent iterations of the innermost form. For the late 1940s *Variants,* Albers filled dozens of graph-paper sheets with precisely drawn sketches surrounded by detailed calculations of distances, area, and proportions (fig. 1.8). The "windows," as he termed the central squares of the *Variants,* are indicated in different positions in relation to

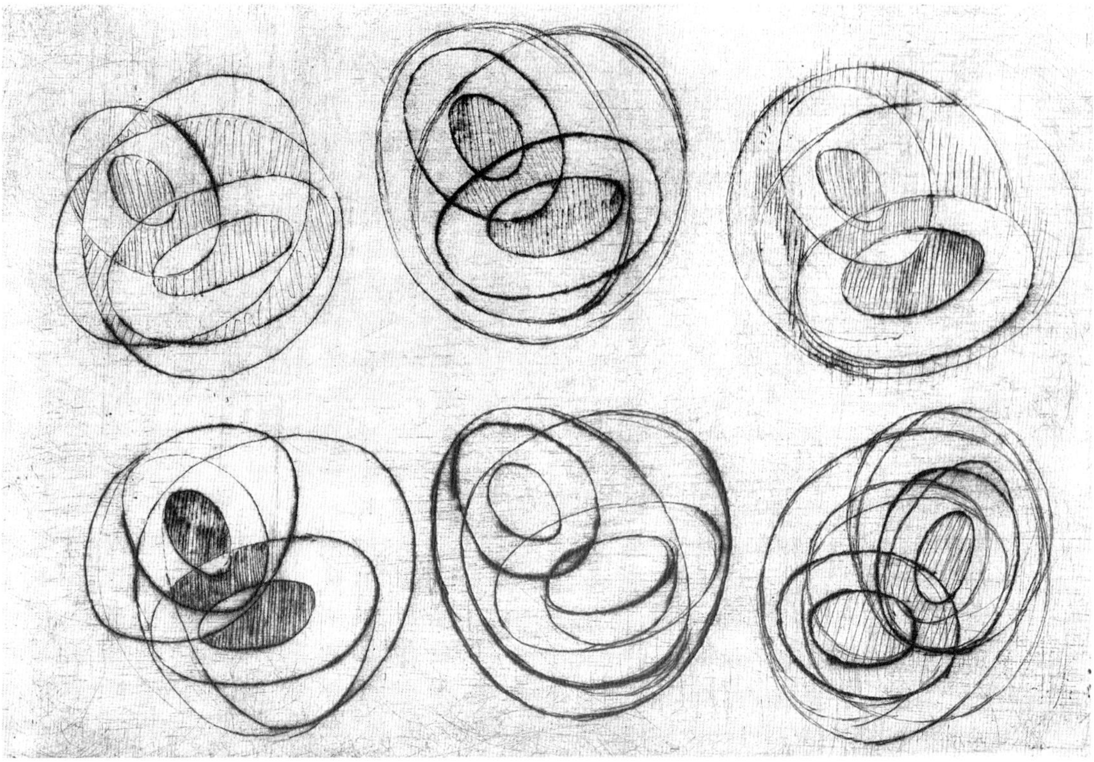

Figure 1.9
Josef Albers, *Variants*, 1942. Drypoint, edition 20, printed at Swan Press, Chicago, 6 × 8⅞". Photograph by Tim Nighswander © The Josef and Anni Albers Foundation / Artists Rights Society, New York.

the surrounding "frames." Various figures drawn in colored pencil are carefully marked off by the number of graphed squares they occupy. In Albers's close script, meticulous reactions to the tested schemas are noted. One page contains the following registration of different placements of a single window:

> Have tried to relate center of figure (vertically) with center of margin (vertically) and with the center of frame (vertically) . . . compared with organization of page 1 center of figure moved one unit to left, frame of figure moved one unit to right . . . moving again the figure one unit to the right, all centers almost vertical with each other . . . this movement to the right must be balanced by the grays on top, 3 more to the left, and at bottom 1 more to the left.

This systematic testing and factoring of each altered variable governed the subsequent iterations of the work's structure.

Similarly, his drypoint engraving *Variants* (1942) represents a series of virtually identical forms subjected to a methodical procedure of modification and recombination on the basis of a test figure's orientation (figs. 1.9, 1.10). Alternating segments of each individual form-group are shaded in different

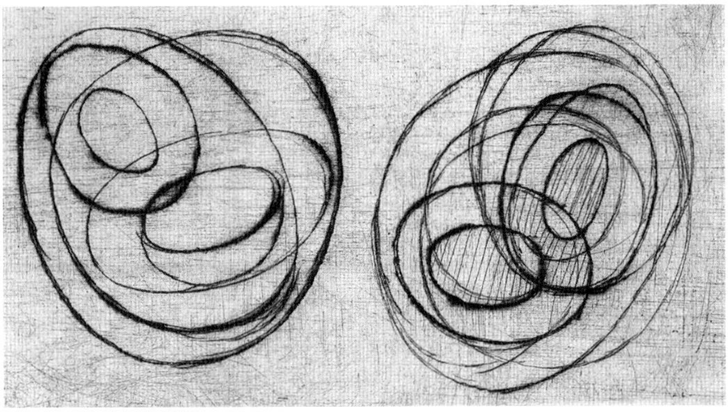

Figure 1.10
Josef Albers, *Variants*, 1942, detail. Photograph by Eva Díaz

arrangements; in the lower-right shape, the orientation is transposed. In his sketchbooks, Albers would carefully draw figures and then invert them, using heavily marked areas as reference points in the reversals in order to test the changing perception of dimensionality in each. Under a shaded version of one sequence is written in pencil: "The right angles—the square—around the figure do not remain—frontal!" Albers's attempts to adapt the figure test the visual effect of the interlocking forms in various orientations, charting variation among the forms subject to doubling and reversals. This can be seen in a sketch of nine related figures where Albers maintained as a constant a double series of *X*s in each figure, varying the angles slightly as he embedded cubes within their armature. As the figure is rotated in space, the *X*s are seen torqued, transposed, and eventually resolved, as with the upper-right figure, when a new set of angles has in turn become the control factor.

Describing these controls, Albers distinguished between the casual approach he termed "variety" and the experimental rigor of "variance":

> The word variety, although recently a favored design term, has become discredited because of increased abuse. It has become a pretentious recommendation for designs of questionable merit. It is applied to protect hurried changes, to excuse poor alterations, or to defend any accidental and meaningless whim. . . . Thus the excuse "for variety's sake" remains a warning signal.
>
> To replace this negative criterion, we are in favor of a related word of better reputation, the design term "variant." As variety usually concerns changes of details, variant means a more thorough re-doing of a whole or of a part within a given scheme. Although variant may remind us slightly of imitative plagiarism, normally it results from a thorough study. Because of a more comprehensive comparison forth and back, it usually aims at a new presentation. On the

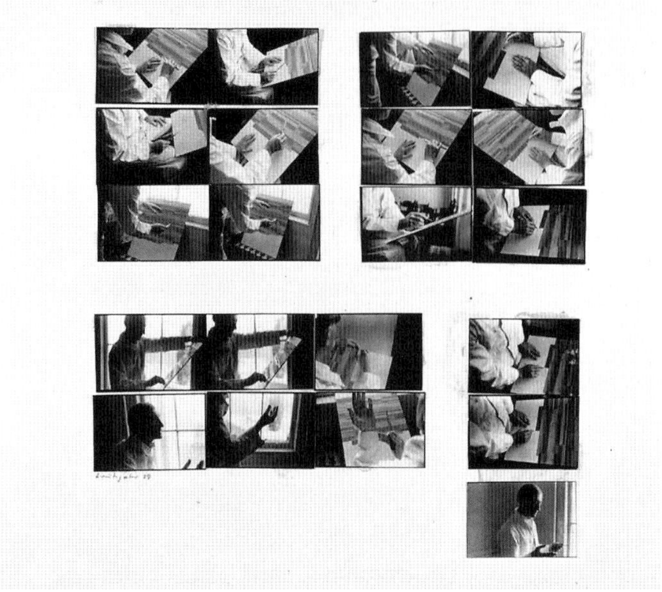

Figure 1.11
Josef Albers, *Spring 39 (Josef Albers Painting at Black Mountain College)*, 1939. Photocollage of 21 images, 8 × 9". Photograph by Tim Nighswander © The Josef and Anni Albers Foundation / Artists Rights Society, New York.

> whole, variants demonstrate, besides a sincere attitude, a healthy belief that there is no final solution in form; thus form demands unending performance and invites constant consideration—visually as well as verbally.[74]

As he later reformulated this idea, "The final ending, the end quality of all form will not be—cannot be—decided upon."[75] What Albers advocated was not simply following a set of rules, but rather *reworking* continually, being a perpetual student of the complex organization of forms in the world. The notion of competition as elaborated in his teaching method undergirded this interest in testing—each iteration a test of the qualities of the material and of the ability of the artist to discern growth and change. He explained, "In my own work I am content to compete with myself . . . so I dare further variants."[76]

In his many studies for the *Variants* paintings, Albers devised tools and techniques to facilitate his tests of possible color arrangements and orientations in the series. Detailed preparation studies functioned as "experimental tryouts" for paintings that were themselves intelligible only within a schema of experiments in formal possibilities, rather than discrete and final entities.[77] In a sequence of templates (for example in figure 1.12 and plate 2), Albers painted concentric borders in alternating colors on several different cardboard mats. He then overlaid these "frames" around different central arrangements, testing the possibilities of color and scale organization of the work by changing the different panels. Varying the interrelated borders by alternating the order of the panels, Albers used the visual "data" to assess more appropriate contrasts and to create the most dynamic compositions. In other studies for the *Variants*, he often tried out several color combinations, painstakingly labeling the constitutive elements by application technique and manufacturer. As the orientation of the embedded elements was altered, he would calculate the relations of the various surface areas, weighing the components by their color and volumetric intensity. Each of the penciled recipes noted the precise constitution of the study and permitted Albers to adjust specific factors until a desirable result was obtained; his paintings include these protoconceptualist instructions on their reverse sides as well (plate 4, fig. 1.13). Because of the serial quality of the *Variants*, however, Albers believed that "new and different cases [would] be discovered time and time again."[78]

The criteria that substantiated the successful completion of a particular work were intelligible only within a context of continual variation. Using the principle of dynamism—palpable when a composition refused simple harmony and remained asymmetrical, imbalanced, and syncopated—Albers attempted to maximize the contrast between elements in a given composition. With the potential for countless renditions, each work completes an intricate process of testing, and also demands evaluation and comparison between completed works. There are no "masterpieces" in Albers's

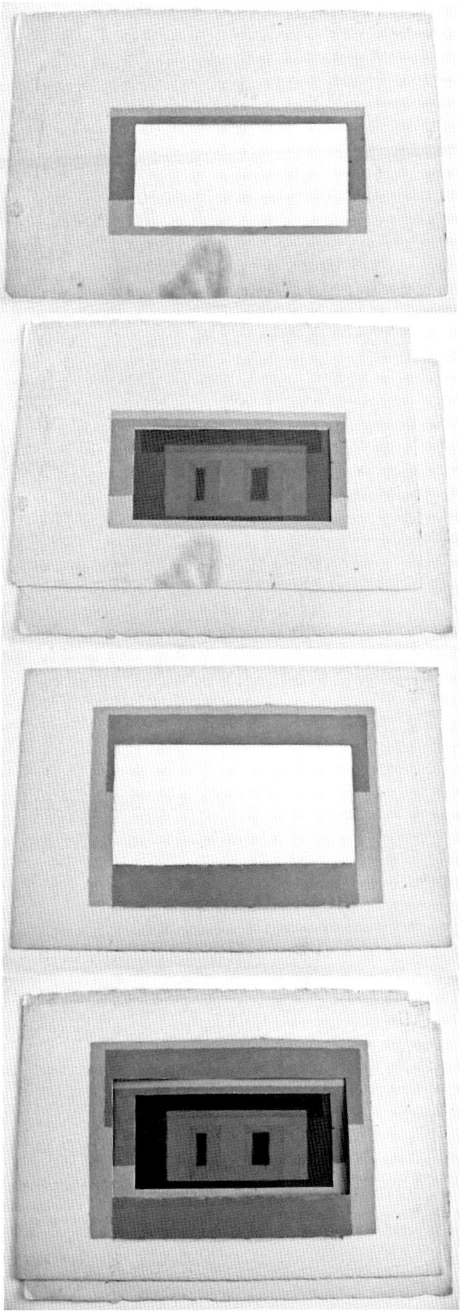

Fig. 1.12
Josef Albers, templates for a *Variant* study, n.d. 12 × 19". Photographs by Eva Díaz © The Josef and Anni Albers Foundation / Artists Rights Society, New York.

Figure 1.13
Josef Albers, *Variant: Southern Climate,* 1948–53. Oil on Masonite, 12¼ × 22½", reverse side. Photograph by Tim Nighswander © The Josef and Anni Albers Foundation / Artists Rights Society, New York.

career; each work emerges from the success of its forerunner and initiates the explorations of its successor.

He maintained other "control" factors that made possible a judicious analysis of the element under inspection, be it orientation, surface area, color, or dimensional ambiguity. When painting the *Variants,* Albers used the same basic "checkerboard-like structure . . . which provides a definite relationship of all the parts" to one another.[79] This allowed modulations in color and orientation to remain measurable when compared with one another. Unmixed colors were spread with a palette knife straight from the tube onto Masonite panels (rose and pink were exceptions, as they are unavailable without mixing), and were applied in one coat without underpainting; striking textural differences often resulted from the distinct consistencies of different paint brands (see the purple section of *Variant* [plate 3], for example). The always unshaded surfaces of the various sections create flat expanses of color that are tightly abutted by their neighboring hues. Yet for all the precision of the sketches, marked as they are on graph paper in scrupulous ruled lines, in the painted *Variant* Albers relished a rapid application of color with the knife. The resulting edges, seemingly flawless from afar, are in fact loose and sometimes inexact, with visible facture and the pilled texture of the Masonite evident in certain sections, as in the detail of *Variant: Southern Climate* (1948–53) (plate 4). The performance was so stringently rehearsed in preparatory studies that the paintings themselves profited from Albers's facility with the knife; he painted the hard edges with penciled-in guidelines but with no masked-off tracing edges.

In his yellow, green, white, and gray *Variant* from the late 1940s, the appearance of depth is illusionistically suggested in certain areas but refused in others[80] (plate 6). Here, Albers was interested in the perception of proximate or adjacent areas of darker or lighter color as either transparent overlays or areas of opacity. Through a meticulous and methodical process of color and compositional studies, as in *Study for a Variant (III), C* (1947), Albers applied bands of color to contiguous sections of the concentric rectangles, confusing the optical impression that the various forms are either embedded in or superimposed on one another (plate 7). Areas of translucency and overlap and, hence, impressions of spatial recession—for example, the appearance of the gray horizontal band in *Variant*—are contradicted by colored zones that project over and around the ostensibly covered-over section, such as the bright elevation of the area of white (plate 6).

Each of Albers's techniques of illusion implicates viewers, inviting them to become students of the processes of visual perception at play in his work, just as he was in the work's creation. What Svetlana Alpers has termed "pictorial equivocation" is very much in operation for Albers: "The possibility of the painter representing the perception of a thing, and representing it for viewers, in such a way as to encourage the mind to dwell on perceiving it as a process: the painter's experience of an object as coming into its own, distinguishing itself from others, taking shape."[81] The sense of perception as a process—the "how" and not the "what"—is derived from Albers's conception of "gestalt," or form, as an active procedure: "If I had to determine the task of a designer, an artist, or of any kind of creative worker I would use the German verb 'gestalten.'"[82] (As Albers was aware, *gestalten* constitutes a vast subject in German thought; in his writings he connected it to Gestalt psychology's evaluation of a form element in relation to a whole.) *Gestalten* can be defined a variety of ways: to arrange, to create, to design, to frame, to fashion, to organize, or to form; form in Albers's rhetoric was therefore positioned as a practice and procedure, not as the artifact of a process, as demonstrated in *Variant: Southern Climate*.[83] Here, two sand-colored central windows appear to project over the surrounding bright and muted orange frames, yet are simultaneously pulled back toward the top sand-toned horizontal plane that deceptively appears to be the overall ground. The oscillation between foreground and background emphasizes the inherent temporality of the process of perception, and brings home the fundamental ambiguity of seeking any final, stable resolution to the pictorial problems Albers explores. The viewer vacillates between two roles that Albers himself occupies as creator: acting as subject of the experiment in vision, and as organizer of the mutable effects transpiring in the visual field as the image's components are scanned. Experiencing the basic acts of perception, his audience is invited to work through sections of the picture plane, to weigh imbalances and test dynamic relations. Donald Judd, commenting on an Albers work he owned (plate 8), observed of this process, "The painting is one single whole and is as complex as a metope. The scheme of squares and the corresponding change of color provides changes in proportion . . . as in a Mobius strip."[84] The appearance of squares as either embedded or superimposed in the *Variants* is contradicted by the visible adjacency of the paint application seen in the thin strips where they meet and the narrow windows revealing stripes of background. In the seemingly elementary demonstration of concentric squares and rectangles, the complicated language of vision is built up so that illusions of representation are confronted by the materiality and inherent flatness of paint.

Concentrating on the elements of perception, Albers participated in a shared German-Austrian modernist project of the 1920s and early 1930s in which, according to Peter Galison, "all knowledge . . . would be built up from logical strings of basic experiential propositions."[85] Not coincidentally, there existed a close association of Bauhaus ideology with Vienna Circle logical positivist philosophy, which grew out of the work of Ludwig Wittgenstein and was expounded in the lectures of Otto Neurath and Rudolf Carnap at the Dessau Bauhaus in the late 1920s. According to Carnap, the organization of knowledge from a repertoire of fundamental perceptual experiences unified all modernist endeavors, whether visual or linguistic. In explaining his "constructional program," he noted, "It attempts a step-by-step derivation or 'construction' of all concepts from certain fundamental concepts . . . all concepts can in this way be derived from a few fundamental concepts."[86] Concerned with how basic units of perception organize knowledge, Neurath postulated that one could backtrack, too, from gestalt to basic compositional units. That is, if forms in combination could be seen as gestalt wholes, what was to stop their constituent parts from being reduced to gestalts themselves in an endless recursion toward an immanent and universal *ur*-structure of communication? However, Neurath's quest for common codes of perception—namely his attempt to invent a visually transparent international pictographic language (fig. 1.14)—departed from Albers's interest in applying the knowledge of fundamental forms toward further complexity, contingency, variation, and visual ambiguity. Albers's own attempt at representing language was a font (a version of which is used throughout this book) composed of variations on modular forms, in which a series of ten basic components could be recombined to form sans-serif lowercase letters and numbers[87] (plate 9). (Though one could argue that both attempts suffer from a surfeit of visual information; each of Albers's letters needs to be

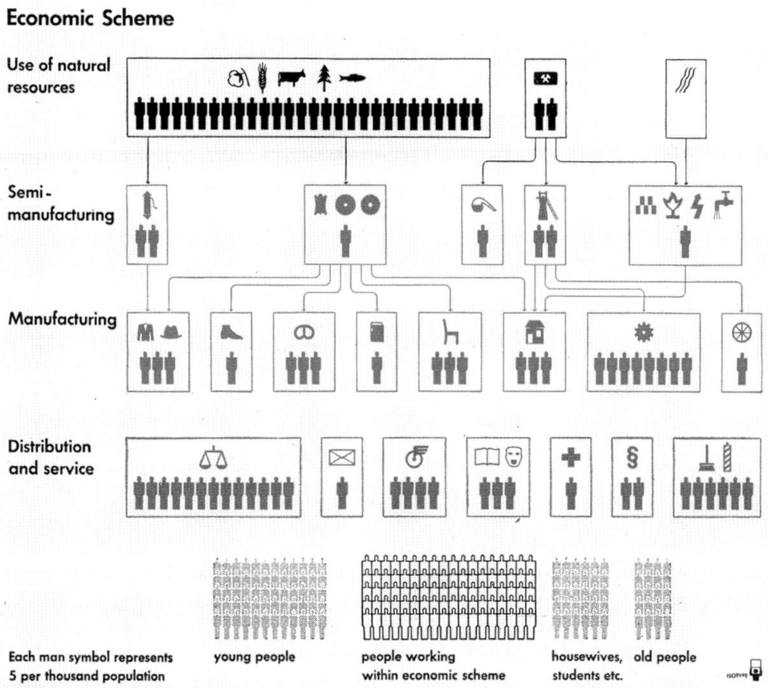

Figure 1.14
Otto Neurath, *Economic Scheme*; Isotype (International System of Typographic Picture Education) designed by Gerd Arntz. From *Modern Man in the Making*, 1939. © 2012 Artists Rights Society, New York/Beeldrecht, Amsterdam.

painstakingly assembled from many constituent parts, and Neurath's ostensibly universally recognizable isotype icons are both culturally particular and excessively descriptive—note how many symbols are necessary to convey that a coal worker uses mechanized mining in Neurath's schema, or how many components are necessary to make a single *x* in Albers's typeset.)

Indeed, Albers's audience is invited to extend this concern with destabilizing vision to other aspects of how the world is perceived, represented, and understood. Albers's mode of geometric abstraction is far from the detachment of art from social conditions advocated by contemporary American formalist critics such as Clement Greenberg.[88] Rather, Albers's goal was to impel us to discover "which of certain art problems are related to our own life."[89] (One could make similar claims for the work of Kasimir Malevich, Mondrian, and others who viewed geometric abstraction as an exploration of perception in which art was part of a larger project telescoping outward to environmental design and possibly to social transformation.) The task was to test the relevance of certain rules that result from inherited experience *and* to devise parallels between problems common to life and art, recognizing that in "the problems of balance or proportion—that they are tasks of our daily life too."[90] Or, to put it another way, the objective was to demonstrate "that a fundamental art problem is a fundamental problem of life and therefore also of education."[91]

Nonetheless, the reflexive relation between better art production and a better performance in life could never reach a point of conclusion. As in his courses, the goal of repeatable exercises was to enforce that "every evaluation is relative and changing," that even in the same exercise different solutions emerge.[92] Rather than impulsive self-expression, conscientious experimentation set forth criteria that could be used to compare different artists and individual works and encouraged "discovery of the varied perceptions of others."[93] Realizing the contingency of all evaluation therefore underscored the profoundly social relation of art. In developing a common set of explorations, art was intelligible only within a community of understanding—"recognizing oneself and developing oneself in relationship to others."[94]

Self-expression was to be avoided for another reason that carried tremendously high stakes. For Albers, the stress on personal expression had come to justify all forms of trivial explorations, novel effects, and differences for the sake of difference. As he argued, "To produce something better [would] be more convincing than to do something merely different."[95] He found the importance of art in personal and social growth immense, but growth was always qualitatively assessed, not measured by specious indicators of artistic originality. Albers thought of originality as nothing more than "forced individualism." An artist's "expression, style and/or contemporaneousness is an unavoidable by-product of personality" understood by the virtues of "honesty and modesty," not as the "result of stylization" that most often corroborates originality.[96] The ambition was to design something better—not necessarily more useful, individuated, or newer, but better in the sense of altering habits of perception and therefore improving the sensitivity of individuals to the construction and organization of the world. Only after detailed study and observation, and with a clear knowledge of how to articulate the appearance and behavior of forms, could one articulate form creatively.[97]

In erecting a foundation in visual analysis and active construction, Albers provided tools for self-improvement through creative production. This, however, was in no way a normative standard for art making more generally. As he claimed, "There is no objective interpretation of what is art. I do not believe that there are any definite rules or systems by which to evaluate art, or, to distinguish between art and non-art."[98] In fact, fulfilling the goal of "more initiative and more imagination . . . means encouragement of experiments," regardless of the likelihood of failure. Summoning courage to try was the main thing: "To me it is uneducational to be afraid of minor results. Everyone has to start as a beginner. And mistakes are not the worst media for progress if we develop at the same time articulation and judgment."[99]

But mistakes must be recognized as such and not be exploited as an excuse for carelessness or acceptance of accident. As Albers firmly held, "Every art work is built (i.e. composed), [it] has order, consciously or unconsciously."[100] Intellect must be applied, order demonstrated. Though a trained intuition was essential, art was not the realm of unmitigated passions, the negative example being "those painters in New York who can paint only when they get mad and drunk."[101] Albers demanded order not in the sense of symmetry or harmony but rather as a dynamic consideration of a work's components and their organization with respect to the whole, to the gestalt form.[102] "You tell the brush and pencil where to go. Not you follow the brush."[103] Spontaneity and improvisation were to be discouraged as ends in and of themselves: "In my paintings I adhere to what in other arts is considered a matter of course. Namely, that performance is prepared by rehearsal, that exercises precede recital, or plans, execution."[104]

As Albers lamented, "Without comparison and choice there is no value. And why are we afraid that thinking and planning—necessary in all human activities—will spoil the painting of a picture?"[105] To take such a question seriously requires probing which methods of art production are sanctioned, and assessing how these methods relate to conceptions of social order. Albers's ethics of perception maintains that the arrangement of a picture is a mirror to the way one organizes life: "There is order . . . and in this sense this is [the order] of life. In art we have to present an example in which we might live together, and not shoot each other . . . that's our collective little baby. . . . For me studying art is to be on an ethical basis."[106] Better design alters habits of perception and can improve society—a nervy claim, perhaps, and yet a thoughtful argument for artistic responsibility.

This "ethical basis" was possible only through commitment demonstrated by competence. In progressing beyond mere observation to begin rearticulating the forms of the world in a creative way, one could then incorporate elements that came intuitively and somewhat spontaneously. This was only achievable, though, when the mastery of techniques of formal articulation became so ingrained—the mind controlling the hand and not the other way around—that the artist could trust in his or her own innovation. In his 1969 book *Search Versus Re-Search,* Albers quoted scientist Louis Pasteur on the topic: "In research, chance only helps those whose minds are well prepared for it," inserting his own comment: "Is that different from art?"[107] The radical repositioning of art practice as subject to unconscious desires advocated by surrealism, for example, was anathema to Albers; it mistook what he argued as the incommunicability of the unconscious as an object of interest. Pinpointing what he considered the fallacy of surrealist-derived automatic drawing, in which an ostensibly unmediated relationship of the hand to the unconscious could be tapped, he explained, "Automatism is a good point of departure but rarely an end of lasting interest. Let us be clear that there is no hand nor tool nor medium quick enough to follow adequately the speed of the 'stream of the unconscious.'" Continuing in this vein, he contended, "The saying that the freshness of the first sketch cannot be repeated is admitting impotence."[108] To Albers, surrealists' attempt to mediate art and the unconscious muddled the prospect of art, which was not to mimic the structuring principles, however disordered, of involuntary functions of the mind. Rather than search for the repressed material of the unconscious, Albers sought to convey the principles underlying the apperception of everyday life. Understanding and changing routines of visual perception was the goal of art. He maintained, "There is no extraordinary without the ordinary, and the root of both is order."[109] Given Albers's interest in expressing the contingency of forms through repeated trials, this insistence on order may seem paradoxical, but to him art, at its root, possessed a crucial strategy—*design*.

In 1949 Albers claimed, "Progress does not depend on accidents only. Without order and control we will drown or suffocate in chaos and decay."[110] Design was the force that held chaos at bay: "To design is to plan and organize, to order, to relate and to control. In short it embraces all means opposing disorder and accident."[111] The role of art was to articulate forms out of the flux of "mess, chance, and confusion" that was too often symptomatic of poor execution and lax thinking.[112] The practice of being economical with materials demonstrated the deliberation that went into production: "Nothing *unused* is permitted in any form, otherwise the calculations will not work out. Because chance has played a role. Chance has not been accounted for, and therefore it is *thoughtless*, because it derives from habit."[113] The imperative to design, in Albers's schema, epitomized the valued sign of cultural progress and change, not the chaotic acceptance of circumstance.

Albers's stance on restraint and aesthetic intention found company with Theodor Adorno, who likewise understood the dialectical relation of control to expression as a defining element of experimentation: "The need to take risks is actualized in the idea of the experimental, which—in opposition to the image of the artist's unconscious organic labor—simultaneously transfers from science to art the conscious control over materials."[114] Order, control, and design, or what Adorno together termed "construction," pose the greatest and most sustained challenge to the culture industry's processes of recuperating artistic practices as novelty or entertainment. Art, activated with more objective processes of control and design, is thus able to conceive outcomes that could never be possible in tactics of fun and play, which, though they seem to result in the unexpected, are after all predictable features of entertainment culture. "The concept of construction . . . always implied the primacy of constructive methods over subjective imagination. Construction necessitates solutions that the imaging ear or eye does not immediately encompass or know in full detail."[115]

Improvisation for its own sake, for Adorno as well as for Albers, was generally rebellious posturing or, worse, merely the appearance of spontaneity. As Adorno noted, most musical improvisation, for instance, is actually rehearsed or habit-driven: "Improvisations conform largely to norms and recur constantly."[116] When control is forfeited, process (or means) is separated from socially effective or intelligible ends. Experimentation, when it partakes in practices of construction and design, results in "efforts filtered through critical consciousness in opposition to the continuation of unreflected aesthetic practices."[117] When artistic experimentation refuses control and reflection, when it stresses chancy "contents that are not foreseeable in the process of production" and that are arrived at by subjective criteria, what results is not greater contingency (the unforeseen as an effect) but more likely a "subject [that] ratifies its self-abdication."[118]

The clear evidence of the artist's control in a process of creation constituted, to Albers and Adorno, a profound ethics of truth and integrity. For Albers, "truth" was a reflexive test of the individual's intention for the resulting articulation of that intent. "Integrity" arose from a vision developed through observation:

> I have very carefully watched not to be a bandwagon guy. That's my greatest warning to all my students, "Please keep away from the bandwagon, from what is fashion and seems now successful or profitable. Stick to your own bones, speak with your own voice, and sit on your own behind." That's—and how can we say that in ethical terms? Or in moral terms? [To] be honest, and modest, are the greatest virtues of an artist.[119]

PEDAGOGY AND THE POLITICS OF EXPERIMENTATION

Albers was renowned for his teaching strategies and, of course, for his long and prolific artistic production. Yet his contribution to highlighting how traditional pedagogy serves to maintain the status quo, though frequently sidelined, was equally important.[120] The "honesty and modesty" of his ethics derived from a project of community education that has been rarely matched since. In a speech from the early 1940s he declared, "Education is the most decisive factor in people's lives."[121] He saw education as an often underestimated but determining factor in social reproduction. In his view, the effects of traditional education tended to limit creative potential with rote exercises that in turn produced rote individuals.

Albers was aware of the limitations of tradition as generally defined in educational processes. Entering the Bauhaus in 1920 as an undergraduate in his early thirties, he had previously taught primary school and later art, coming into contact with the flourishing education reform movement in Germany.[122] He followed John Dewey (whose *Democracy and Education* appeared in German translation soon after its publication in 1916, and in an interesting transatlantic cross-pollination, its call for "learning by doing" rallied progressive educators throughout Europe) in describing traditional education as an operation of both selective cultural transmission and social control. For Dewey, in transmitting the "legacy" of the past, blind adherence to tradition obscured the reality that "a great deal [of that] which passed for knowledge was merely the accumulated opinions of the past, much of it absurd and its correct portions not understood when accepted on authority."[123] In a scathing critique of traditional hierarchies in education, Albers, drawing on Dewey, complained that the professor "passes on so-called 'established' facts: knowledge, methods, rules, to enable historical thinking. . . . The old school seeks, in addition to its main goal of popular education, to pass on abilities but only a few essential ones."[124]

During his early years at the Bauhaus, Albers attempted to repeal traditional models of art education by devaluing the role of tradition itself. At times, this represented a wholesale abandonment of the concept of history as a reference point for artistic production. With typically modernist zeal, he commented that "today's youth notes the wrong direction: that . . . historical knowledge hinders production. . . . A lot of history leaves little room for work. The reverse—little history and much work—is our task."[125] Prior hierarchies of knowledge could be sidestepped by substituting testing operations for the historical or scholarly study of art: "Experimenting takes priority over studying."[126]

In these Bauhaus-era writings, Albers tended to conflate tradition with retrograde, authoritarian models of education. After moving to the United States, his vituperative language softened and was supplanted by a voice more attuned to the merits of alternative traditions. He came to view tradition and history as residual formations that, though demanding vigilant testing, must be frequently resuscitated and never dispensed with entirely. The urgency of thinking historically in the present prevents the debasement of real struggles and gains in the past. Like Albers, Walter Benjamin argued that a faithful articulation of history must always contest the adulterations of contemporary novelty-based capitalist culture. He believed it was necessary to

> retain that image of the past which unexpectedly appears to man singled out by history at a moment of danger. The danger affects both the content of the tradition and its receivers. The same threat hangs over both: that of becoming a tool of the ruling class. In every era the attempt must be made anew to wrest tradition away from a conformism that is about to overpower it.[127]

For Benjamin, revitalizing perceptions of traditions under threat of ever-encroaching revisionism could awaken alternatives obscured by the dominant culture. Rather than annulling previous models, Albers, like Benjamin, lobbied instead for their augmentation with experimental techniques. Since, for Albers, tradition and experiment were dialectically related, "there is no art which is only traditional or only experimental."[128] The skewed preference in education toward tradition had made it an end, yet tradition and experiment "are only a means, namely towards art, or if you prefer, towards culture."[129] With all the attention given to the artifacts of the past, the *process* of creation had become neglected.

To Albers, *change* was a privileged term, but only because most art pedagogy either neglected it entirely or blindly encouraged it wholeheartedly. Teaching approaches that instead concentrated on design and experimentation enhanced the understanding of the now, of modernity; too often, art practice was initiated from a position of art historical survey. Albers saw this reliance on history as promoting an attitude of retrospection that treated precursors as hallowed and predetermining, stunting innovation and divorcing art from both present conditions and future possibilities.[130] The *work* of art was not historical study; rather, "its traditional task [was] to find again and again new visual expression of our mentality which changes from generation to generation."[131]

Dewey believed that processes of experimentation such as those proposed by Albers, and performed at Black Mountain more generally, provided techniques toward progressive pedagogy, and he publicly lauded their ambitions and successes.[132] For Dewey, education enhanced an individual's ability to appreciate self-crafted experiences rather than legacies rationalized as truth. Education thus becomes "an attack upon so-called purely rational concepts on the ground that they either needed to be ballasted by the results of concrete experiences, or else were mere expressions of prejudice and institutionalized class interest."[133] This reproduction of circumscribed possibilities has been termed the "selective tradition" by Raymond Williams: "the way in which from a whole possible arena of past and present, certain meanings and practices are chosen for emphasis, certain other meanings and practices are neglected and excluded."[134] The process of refining the objects of historical interest and cultural transmission to a rehearsed and often static canon or tradition regulates and diminishes the capacity for social and cultural change.

For sociologist Pierre Bourdieu, however, Dewey's stress on individual experiences and their curtailment by "mere" prejudice or institutional interest gave too much importance to the role of the individual subject. To Bourdieu, education functions as a central node in the transmission of dominant cultural values *in the name of* individual experience or success; educational institutions are possibly the most rearguard elements in the self-legitimating processes of social reproduction. He believed that the central "contribution made by the educational system to the reproduction of the structure of power relationships and symbolic relations between classes, [is] by contributing to the reproduction of the structure of the distribution of cultural capital among these classes."[135] Specifically, this system operates by enforcing hierarchies of preexisting knowledge based on cultural "inheritance"—the almost unconscious fluency of those reared in dominant class backgrounds with the dominant class culture that is privileged in traditional education. "By doing away with giving explicitly to everyone, the educational system demands of everyone alike that they have what it does not give."[136] Educational structures implement dominant cultural mores in subtle (and not-so-subtle) hierarchical methods such as testing, tracking, and early specialization (generally legitimated in ideologies such as equality of opportunity—as opposed to equality of outcomes—and the justification of meritocratic selection).[137] This makes education a political battleground, disenfranchising alternative viewpoints that challenge the class power of the privileged.

In order to avoid types of social reproduction that favor traditional values (and here Bourdieu helps us see "traditional" as often no more than "dominant-cultural"), alternative pedagogical practices mount a two-pronged attack: downplaying preexisting knowledge bases (high culture masquerading as tradition) and dedifferentiating specialized sectors (between disciplines or between expert and layperson, for example).[138] The task of experimentation in pedagogy is doubly difficult: managing to revoke certain historical processes that have contributed to the reproduction of existing structures of society while transmitting conceptions of history that can be marshaled toward a more forceful remediation of present problems. Dewey, too, recognized this seeming paradox of education: "We have the problem of ascertaining how acquaintance with the past may be translated into a potent instrumentality for dealing effectively with the future. We may reject knowledge of the past as the *end* of education and thereby only emphasize its importance as a *means*."[139]

The means Albers envisioned were of individuals' creative possibilities unleashed by their trained perception of the complex and ever-changing world. Disciplined work freed subjects from unrecognized habits of behavior that inhibited their autonomy and will. In a speech Albers gave in 1940 peppered with references to the ongoing war against Fascism in Europe, he asserted, "Freedom, if understood as being free from something, has no positive sense at all. Only being free *for* something has [an] active and productive meaning."[140] Though predating Isaiah Berlin's influential 1958 essay "Two Concepts of Liberty," Albers's weighing of "freedom for" above "freedom from" directly opposes Berlin's conservative critique of "positive freedom" ("freedom for") as the corrupting tendency of self-determining and collectively controlled social processes to lapse into authoritarian structures. Albers saw "freedom for" exploration and experimentation as antithetical to the "negative freedom" (freedom from) of "someone who is the passive recipient of specific rights," a distinction political theorist Chantal Mouffe has articulated.[141] The role of the test in developing self-mastery and expressing positive freedoms demonstrated how knowledge of form could release individuals from habit. What Albers supplied, therefore, was a "training in [the] ability to *choose*."[142] To return to his 1944 print *Fenced* (fig. 1.6), readings of the possible dimensional orientations of the work can be substantiated only by close consideration. Each path of inspection leads to manifold possibilities—forms project, recede, overlap, torque, and flatten. The image allows for various choices about how it is received and shrugs off a definitive reading. Albers offered a forum in which to both teach and perform observation of forms that brought emancipation from simplistic visual assumptions. To be able to see as many complicated structures in the world, and to see them particularly in conditions of deceptive simplicity, was a form of liberated vision. This "freedom [was] competence"—a seemingly paradoxical condition in which lack of restriction was earned in the restraint of discipline.[143]

Empowering individuals with attentive perception laid the foundation for an educated citizenry challenging regressive, outdated customs and sowing greater freedom in the world, or so Dewey and Albers hoped. While affording a means toward keen observation, any *specific* program with which to marshal such knowledge or achieve concrete change remained ambiguous. It might involve a more equitable distribution of resources, greater social or economic equality, or collective self-determination; Albers's calls for freedom and reform did not detail the particular social ends of alert perceptual strategies, other than broadly stated "betterment" or "improvement." For him, providing tools for the conscientious rearticulation of form sufficed; the outcomes of such explorations were not elaborated. This was perhaps a liberating proposition for students. The ethical dimension—the language of realization, responsibility, and improvement—was stressed above an active political program or explicit goals.

Given the tenuous position the Alberses found themselves in as exiles—without citizenship they were constantly vulnerable to residency restrictions and possible deportation—Josef's caution with respect to the political effects of his methods is somewhat understandable. Whether an educational program can coexist with a political program was always a contentious issue in insular environments such as the Bauhaus and Black Mountain. The politicization of the Bauhaus program by Marxist Hannes Meyer (successor to Gropius as director of the Bauhaus in 1928) was tendentious and short-lived, as conflicts between radicalized students and local government sponsors quickly developed. Likewise, Black Mountain was always fraught with the question of whether it was a community, with attendant political responsibilities, or an educational institution (which is not to say that the latter does not have a politics, that is, concerns about representation, fairness, and justice).

Albers consciously defined his role as that of an educator *within* institutions and avoided explicitly politicized or revolutionary rhetoric. Instead, he trained students in the basic understanding of how the world looks and the high stakes in re-presenting it innovatively. He railed against previous models of education, but in his own project he used a language of careful change, reform, and improvement. As a teacher he *belonged* to institutions, with their attendant concerns of sustaining state or private funding; he was not anti-institutional, though he lambasted the inattentive habits reproduced in institutions and in culture. Albers provided tools for educating artists and did not dictate the topics or approaches they might take when their formal education ended. Whether his avoidance of direct sociopolitical application of his method merely demonstrated an émigré's conformism would be difficult to say. Indeed, the central argument of his method did not concern outcomes so much as sharpening perceptions that different practices could wield to various ends. In his art and pedagogy, the study of abstract elements of form was paramount, though Albers remained open to many different kinds of practice. Much to his credit, he was personally responsible for inviting diverse (and divergent) practitioners to join him as faculty at Black Mountain, including neoplasticist Ilya Bolotowsky, realists Jean Charlot and Jacob and Gwendolyn Lawrence, and expressionists Willem and Elaine de Kooning and Robert Motherwell, as well as various other fields' future luminaries, such as John Cage, Buckminster Fuller, and Charles Olson, nurturing a community of practices that privileged no single teaching or artistic methodology.

"Art is visual documentation of human mentality through (visual) form," Albers claimed.[144] He looked not for "solutions," political or otherwise, but instead posed questions about the nature and understanding of form. His technique of testing subtle distinctions in vision used basic forms as containers for variation, though this work of comparison was sometimes deemed *too* subtle and restrained. Greenberg in particular singled out Albers as a "sensuous, even original colorist," while bestowing the faint commendation that his "strictly rectilinear art . . . adheres to the dogma of the straight line."[145] This was not the first time Albers's artistic method had been characterized as rigid and repetitive—or, for that matter, his teaching dismissed as doctrinaire. The testimony of his students often strikingly refuted such claims, however, for they recognized that as a pedagogue he trained them not to produce work that looked like his own but, with the help of his methodology of experiment, to represent the world liberated of sterile habit. Years after his studies at Black Mountain, Robert Rauschenberg praised Albers's method:

> I'm still learning what he taught me, because what he taught had to do with the entire visual world. He didn't teach you how to "do art." The focus was always on your personal sense of looking. When he taught water color, for example, he taught the specific properties of water color—not how to make a good water-color picture. When he taught drawing, he taught the efficient functioning of line. Color was about the flexibilities and the complex relationships that colors have with one another. I consider Albers the most important teacher I've ever had, and I'm sure he considered me one of his poorest students.[146]

When asked about Rauschenberg's comments in an interview, Albers responded:

> We were not on great admiring terms. With each other. Rauschenberg. He was a little stubborn and doing his own [thing]—but what he is doing now is much more a part of my classes he participated in than he will ever recognize. We have done quite a bit with, at Black Mountain—we have had the tendency—dada was in the air, to do dada, you see? Surface correspondences, you know? Dada—not as Itten did it, as just emphasizing that as different from that, you see? No, we played a lot with combination of materials, "combination" was a great word in our [vocabulary]—and changing surface qualities, . . . changing of articulation, that was a very exciting study at Black Mountain. And I think that is what lives on in his work now.[147]

That an artist changes the articulation of forms in the world and influences their perception: *that* was high praise coming from Albers.

For him, a determined process of experimentation produced results whereby contingency—the carefully tested permutations of a form's appearance that can continually be subjected to new variations—could be most clearly maintained. The understanding of contingency as "trial and error experimentation" with the endless possibilities of methodically tested differences was both a pedagogical practice and a methodology guiding his own work.[148] This type of experimentation—Albers's ethics of perception—served as an important impetus to perceptual and possibly cognitive change; indeed, he believed it "[could] lead to illusions, to new relationships, to different measurements, to other systems." His is perhaps the most concise description of the importance of explorations of form in transforming understandings of the world.

Albers insisted that "art is not an object but an experience"—an experience in and of perception that facilitates complex understandings of the visual world.[149] With his rational exploration of subtle mutations and variations of form, he attempted to construct new modes of visual perception. With his process of experiment, he endeavored to influence patterns of transmission—transmissions of tradition and of social pattern—by introducing the model of the test. It is interesting to note that Black Mountain also fostered the "next generation" of Americans concerned with experiment, notably Cage and Rauschenberg, who sought to sever it from its empirical, deterministic connotations.[150] As Cage argued in a 1955 essay, "The word 'experimental' is apt, providing it is understood not as descriptive of an act to be later judged in terms of success and failure, but simply as of an act the outcome of which is unknown."[151] Here we come full circle, with Cage embracing the indeterminacy that Albers wanted to excise. Whether Cage's invocation of experiment was similarly concerned with history and tradition is an interesting question, one that likely treads closer to experiment as the "new" and "innovative" than experiment as elaborated in careful variation.

chapter two

john cage's chance protocols

Where do we go from here? Towards theatre. That art more than music resembles nature.

John Cage, 1957[1]

Defining exactly what constituted an "experimental" artistic practice was a consistent feature of intellectual life at Black Mountain College, and these debates moved into an intense new phase after World War II. As the previous chapter set forward, one consequence of the close connection between John Dewey and the College's Bauhaus-derived ("Albersian," as we could describe the Bauhaus influence at Black Mountain) model of art pedagogy was that experimentation came to be understood as a creative process, nonetheless one characterized by degrees of preparation, considered intention, and technical competence. Similarly, the art practices and pedagogy of Black Mountain's early Albersian-Deweyan period—from the year of its founding in 1933 to approximately the end of the Second World War—sought to align the dehabituating, ethical, and personal-growth aspects of artistic practice with other forms of production in culture, particularly by associating the experimental test with scientific practice, advanced technological design, and sociocultural progress. In offering parameters for such a conception of artistic work, by the mid-1940s the neo-Bauhaus model at the College held experimentation to be a practice of changing ingrained habits of perception by testing the contingency of form in controlled situations.

By 1948, however, several factors—including logistical ones such as the departure or retirement of founding or early-era faculty members; the influx of a pool of less malleable (or sometimes merely anti-Germanic) older students and veterans on GI Bill funding who were attracted by the College's growing reputation for its summer art and music programs; and, most pressingly, the arrival of first-generation abstract expressionists such as Franz Kline, Willem de Kooning, and Robert Motherwell—had the effect of reorienting the College from a broader liberal arts basis to a more focused concentration on visual, musical, and literary practices and polemics. Though Josef Albers was keen to invite guest faculty for the summer sessions whose work represented a wide spectrum of contemporary visual and cultural production, in 1948 his faculty picks proved to be advocates of persuasive alternative arguments for what artistic experimentation could and should mean in the postwar period. These alternatives would challenge the predominance of Albers's model of art production, and throw into question the primacy of his pedagogical style at the College. Indeed, whether they acted intentionally or not, proponents of these other visions for (and sometimes against) experimentation undermined the framework (and I use the word *framework* pointedly: it was a *work* of framing aesthetic experience) of the Bauhaus model of attention and careful serial variation erected at the College, forevermore eroding its dominance and, by the 1950s, jeopardizing its legitimacy as one of the reigning projects of modernist art production in the United States.

The Black Mountain College summer session of 1948 surpassed in popularity and scope the vaunted 1946 incarnation that had elicited an influential cover profile about the College in *Design* magazine.[2] Among a rotating group of about twenty faculty in session from July through August 1948 were dancer-choreographer Merce Cunningham and composer John Cage, visitors to the College earlier that year who were asked back for the summer; artists Willem de Kooning and Richard Lippold, both recommended by Cage; architect R. Buckminster Fuller (whose version of experimentation is the topic of chapter 3 of this book), and Beaumont Newhall, previously in residence during the summer of 1946, who returned to teach the history of photography. They were joined by about seventy-five painting, sculpture, and theater students, including Ruth Asawa, Joseph Fiore, Betty and Peter Jennerhahn, Ray Johnson, Hazel Larsen Archer, Kenneth Noland, Arthur Penn, Kenneth Snelson, and Paul and Vera Williams. The Williamses later provided key financial support to Cage and Cunningham at Black Mountain—Cage's 1952–53 chance-based audiotape collage work *Williams Mix* was named for them—and they helped support the Merce Cunningham Dance Company, founded during the troupe's 1953 summer-in-residence at the College.

The first assault on the dominant Bauhaus model was blunt. Soon after de Kooning arrived to teach painting, he sowed seeds of resistance to the notion that studying art was necessary at all. According to his wife, Elaine, who was also on campus that summer, by the end of his time at Black Mountain

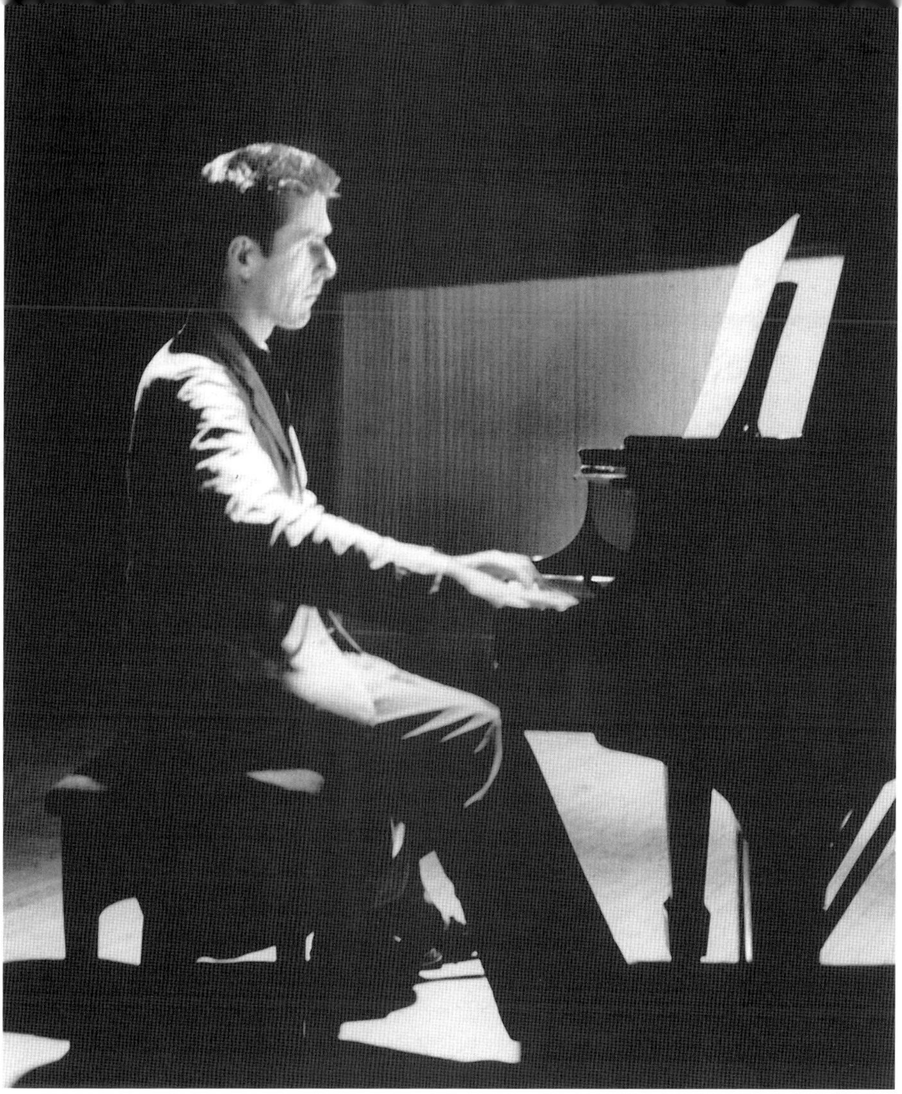

Figure 2.1
Clemens Kalischer, *John Cage at Black Mountain College*, 1948. Gelatin silver print. © Clemens Kalischer. Courtesy the artist.

> Bill had also become deeply involved with his students. Too involved, Albers thought. He said to Bill at the end of the summer, "You had ten students. Six of them are leaving the College to go to New York City this September. Do you know anything about it?" "Sure," said Bill. "I told them if they wanted to be artists, they should quit school and come to New York and get a studio and start painting." Albers seemed not to take this amiss. When he was appointed chairman of the Art Department at Yale two years later, Bill was the first artist to be hired to teach there.[3]

It could be expected that the example of the progressive, modernist art *school*, embodied most famously and perhaps most effectively by the Bauhaus and by

Black Mountain College, would be challenged by de Kooning and other New York school artists (despite their name). The centrality of *pedagogy* at both institutions—the transmission of ideas through teaching in formalized situations, of visual testing exercises loosely overseen by a master teacher in design-based artistic experiments—would no doubt grate against the libertarian, individualist streak of US-based abstract expressionism.[4] (Their allied critics, too, would challenge Black Mountain's pedagogy. Clement Greenberg, recommended to the College faculty by de Kooning, taught there in 1950. Though he credited the students with impressive intensity, he ultimately "felt that not much art came out of Black Mountain [only some famous names]."[5]) The claim that students at the College did not produce "mature" art, or the accusation that education suffocated creative practice by emphasizing technical skills acquired through trial, test, and peirastic dialogue, were historically quite frequent criticisms of higher education and art institutions leveled by expressionist artists.[6]

Albers, however, was prepared for assaults on the Bauhaus-derived Black Mountain curriculum by expressionists such as de Kooning; after all, he'd spent most of his life and work advocating creative explorations of form beyond the habituated constraints of artists' subjective or self-revelatory responses. Yet it was the wolf in sheep's clothing—John Cage's model of experimentation—for which Albers was ill-equipped. De Kooning, like his fellow expressionists, did not employ the language of experimentation in a rigorously defined manner; as was discussed in this book's introduction, in several ways expressionism is antithetical to the practice of the test or to the rhetoric of experimentation as a disciplined, systematic process of examining variables subject to thorough controls. Cage, unlike expressionists, arrived at Black Mountain in 1948 with a version of experimentation—a "marriage of order and freedom," as he phrased it—that he considered very much in line with Albers's.[7] Yet within a few years, the normally collegial Albers would end his friendship with Cage over the issue of the primacy of chance events in explorations considered experimental.

Cage's methodology of chance-based experimentation first emerged in the scores and events he composed when he taught at Black Mountain from 1948 through 1953; in many ways the seismic shifts in his practice during this period are tied to his close engagement with the College. In these scores and events, Cage initiated a series of practices that were highly structured, yet paradoxically attempted to sever the performance of a work from intention, argumentation, or "authorial" control. For Cage, the coupling of organized processes with aleatory (chance-generated) results made it possible to transcend predictable habits of composition and recital. How can one understand Cage's quixotic formulation of experimentation as a "purpose to remove purposes," so counter-intuitive to how an experiment was typically envisioned at Black Mountain?[8] To investigate this apparent contradiction in the careful organization of situations of greater contingency, of his use of order to obtain indeterminate outcomes, I propose a seemingly oxymoronic phrase: "chance protocol."

To Cage, the test was an exploration of uncertainty, not a careful examination of variables (à la Albers). Two watershed events staged at Black Mountain played a decisive role in Cage's formulation of experimentation in such a manner: first, his 1948 production of composer and poet Erik Satie's 1913 play *The Ruse of Medusa* (*Le piège de Méduse*) and second, his 1952 *Theater Piece No. 1* (sometimes referred to as *Untitled Event*), which was subsequently proclaimed the first "happening." In *Theater Piece No. 1*, despite a seemingly chaotic or random form, particular parameters governed the execution of the work: fixed durational segments, the assignment of specific tasks to performers, and an agreed-upon use of certain tools or instruments. This structure served as a chance protocol, allowing ever-greater unpredictability to emerge within predefined limitations. In the years that Cage was locked in a tight orbit with the College, his chance-protocol version of experimentation increasingly focused on chance-derived, durationally notated instructions as a means to create and organize contingent events. Initially he used chance processes to compose discrete and determinate scores; eventually he developed strategies that allowed a performance to retain as much indeterminacy as possible, usually by producing scores that were subject to alteration before and during recital, and that employed notation systems open to interpretation by the performers.

Cage's pioneering of new forms of composition and performance developed in a climate receptive to seeing experimentation as not merely a feature of visual art practices but also of time-based events and interdisciplinary collaborations. In fact, Black Mountain was one of the rare outposts in the United States during this period for in-depth work in experimental performance—that is to say, productions coming out of a background in the visual arts that emphasized improvisational workshopping or unrehearsed performances, nonnarrative methods (in other words, unscripted events lacking developed characterization or dramatic arc), and a close consideration of how to demarcate or collapse the spaces of performance and audience. Specifically, during the 1930s the College was the key US site invested in a "Bauhaus idea" of theater and live performance. This was due to the popularity of Bauhaus-influenced theater at the campus: throughout the mid-1930s, Bauhaus theater master Oskar Schlemmer's pupil and collaborator Xanti Schawinsky had staged several original productions of nonnarrative, participatory theater at the College, including *Spectodrama: Play, Life, Illusion* in 1936 and *Danse Macabre: A Sociological Study* in 1938. In his project of experimentation through careful observation, it is no coincidence that Schawinsky subsequently spent several years at "Albersian" Black Mountain further developing interdisciplinary theatrical models initially explored in Weimar and Dessau.[9]

The first section of this chapter will explore the existing tradition of Bauhaus experimental theater at Black Mountain, which would be challenged by Cage. Though ten years separated Schawinsky's departure from Cage's first extended visit, the models these men investigated and developed at the College represent two of the most radical explorations of US-based experimental performance taking place between the wars and after. (A third, I would argue, was Bertolt Brecht's notion of *Verfremdungseffekts* ["distancing effects"] and *Lehrstück* ["learning through participation"] in his "Epic Theater," which also found fertile ground at Black Mountain: Brecht's English translator Eric Bentley taught there for several years in the mid-1940s and staged productions of Brecht, including a 1944 reading with sound effects and music of *The Private Life of the Master Race*.[10]) Stage events at Black Mountain had also adventurously sampled other European precursors beyond Bauhaus performance—for example, poet M. C. Richards's productions of works by Jean Cocteau, including *Knights of the Round Table* in 1949 and a theater-in-the-round version of *Marriage on the Eiffel Tower* in 1950 (fig. 2.2). It is in Schawinsky's work, though, that we see a model of nonnarrative performance most clearly related though opposed to that which Cage came to embrace. By staging a comparison between these two models, the stakes of experiments in theater and other time-based media and events in the postwar period can begin to be elucidated. As we will see, the approaches to experimental performance Cage developed at the College soon rose to prominence (and a great deal of notoriety), overshadowing the Bauhaus model, which remains largely obscured to this day.[11]

The second part of this chapter will address how the "French" influences Cage introduced were, in actuality, a series of hybrid sources he was working through in the five years he taught at Black Mountain.[12] In this period, he joined several seemingly incompatible threads—French modernist theater from before and after World War I; Zen Buddhism (his fascination with the mystic Huang Po's strain of Zen arose during his time at the College); and Dada-surrealist employments of chance composition, most centrally those of Antonin Artaud and Marcel Duchamp.[13] His explorations of dispersion, disorder, and void-like mindlessness came to spurn purposeful communication between performer and audience, estranged the traditional, "scored" relationship between a composition and its performance, and began to draw on aleatory systems that paradoxically structured and controlled unexpected results beyond human prediction. The importance of Cage's practical and discursive move to the chance protocol is key to understanding the epistemic shift involved in repositioning

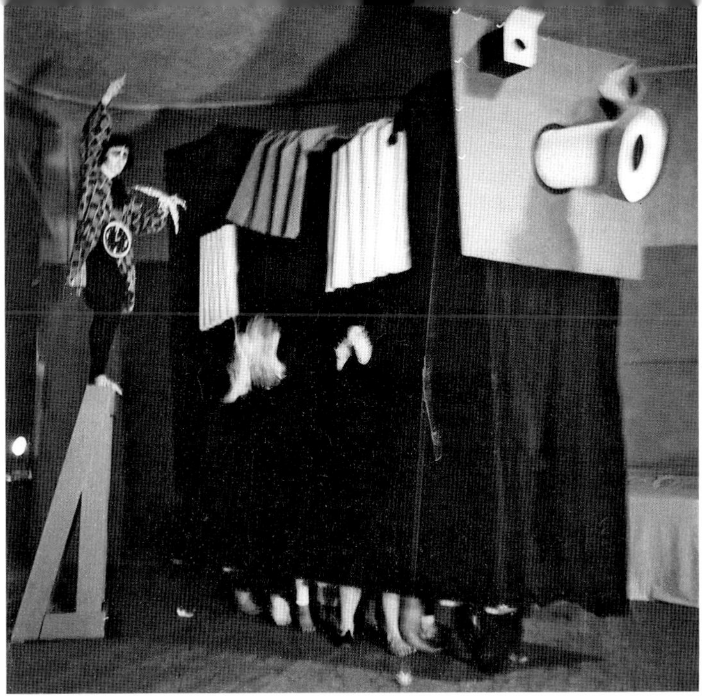

Figure 2.2
Hazel Larsen Archer, *June Rice Christensen as the Photographer in Jean Cocteau's "Marriage on the Eiffel Tower,"* Black Mountain College, 1950. Courtesy of the Estate of Hazel Larsen Archer and the Black Mountain College Museum + Arts Center.

experimentation as the production of events that were indeterminate as to their performance. In this, Cage's Black Mountain events radically altered the spectrum of possibility for art and performance: in his explorations of French-derived avant-garde theater, first of Satie's work and subsequently of Artaud's and Duchamp's, he inaugurated a new experimental model that came to define not only Black Mountain's future but the trajectories of Fluxus performance, Allan Kaprow–esque Happenings, Judson Dance Theater, and numerous other 1950s and 1960s events.

The third and final section of this chapter will take up how in *Theater Piece No. 1* Cage pushed experimental performance even further than his sources. Coupled with his analyses of Po's, Artaud's, and Duchamp's projects, Cage's admiration for Robert Rauschenberg's Black Mountain College–era works, particularly his 1951 *White Paintings*, helped Cage explore experimentation as a tool to "unfocus attention"[14] (fig. 2.3). The apparent emptiness of Rauschenberg's paintings encouraged him to "check my habits of seeing, to counter them for the sake of greater freshness . . . to be unfamiliar with what I'm doing."[15] Ultimately, Cage felt that Rauschenberg's work revealed that "art is the imitation of nature in her manner of operation," operations that Cage believed could be unburdened of human desire and interference. He believed his model of staging inattention and dispersion exposed art's pretentions to ordering life, better reflecting nature's own complexity, chancy-ness, and lack of single purpose.[16]

Figure 2.3
Robert Rauschenberg, *White Painting*, 1951. House paint on canvas, 72 × 72", four panels. © Robert Rauschenberg Foundation/Licensed by VAGA, New York, NY.

His perspective on chance operations as a mirror to the (dis)order of nature has proved a contentious point for artists and scholars, from Josef Albers to many in the present. As this last section considers, Cage's sense of the experimental chance protocol as handmaiden to anarchical freedom from sociopolitical determinants remains controversial.

In advocating notions of multisensory presentness and the diffusion of attention, Cage understood his work as exceeding the Bauhaus tradition at Black Mountain, replacing it instead with studies in Dadaist chance and simultaneity, as well as events inspired by Po's and Artaud's conceptions of void-like experiences. In his proposal of a chance protocol, Cage argued that a new dimension of perception could be revealed outside human faculties of organization and intention, a form of dispassionate quiescence he paradoxically spent most of his life actively scripting. In order to understand the stakes of the chance protocol's contravention of the Albersian model of experimentation as tests of controlled variables, we must therefore return to the origin of that tradition in performance—Bauhaus theater—and the genesis of the break—Erik Satie's *The Ruse of Medusa.*

ÉPATER LE BAUHAUS

Cage first arrived at Black Mountain College in April 1948 without a teaching commision: he was Cunningham's piano accompanist. But that was still a position of some visibility. In addition to theater and art, Black Mountain throughout the 1930s and 1940s was a notable outpost of experimental music; in 1944, for instance, it hosted a well-publicized and internationally renowned conference celebrating Arnold Schoenberg's seventy-fifth birthday.[17] As early as the late 1930s, when Cage was on the West Coast, he had heard rumors of Black Mountain as "an advanced place," and had written the school asking for a job; in 1942 he propositioned that the College found an on-site Center for Experimental Music.[18] Neither proposal panned out. By the late 1940s, Cage was facing resistance to his work as a composer, though not as a rather showy performer of his prepared piano compositions, performances in which he inserted objects between piano strings and played the instrument largely for its percussive qualities. He was therefore "delighted" when Albers offered him a teaching post at the College—his first for music composition—during the upcoming summer session of 1948.[19]

When Cage assumed his teaching responsibilities at the College, he further shifted his compositional strategy from the systemic explorations of atonality, seriality, and other recent developments in musical composition that Black Mountain's Schoenberg-oriented tradition was associated with. That summer, he brought with him nearly all eighteen extant musical scores by Erik Satie and a copy of Satie's only play, *The Ruse of Medusa*, proposing the College host an "amateur festival" of Satie's music. He proceeded to antagonize many of the College's German émigrés by performing Satie's oeuvre exclusively throughout his summer-long stay, rather than surveying, as he remembered it, "modern music in general"; particularly infuriating was one of Cage's introductory speeches that denounced Beethoven's harmonic tradition in favor of Satie's emphasis on rhythm and duration.[20] In contrast to the rancor his lecture stirred, Cage's production of Satie's long-neglected *The Ruse of Medusa*, translated that summer by Richards, was universally admired (fig. 2.4). Student Arthur Penn (later known for his films *The Miracle Worker* and *Bonnie and Clyde*) directed Buckminster Fuller as the Baron Medusa, Elaine de Kooning as his daughter Frisette, and

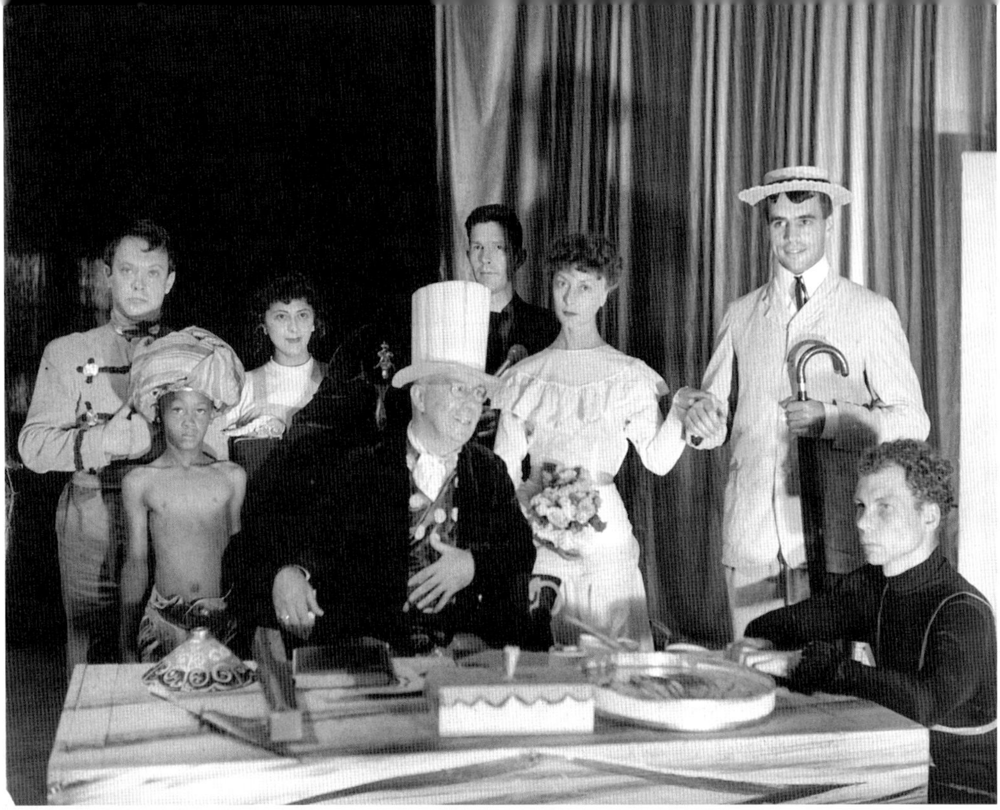

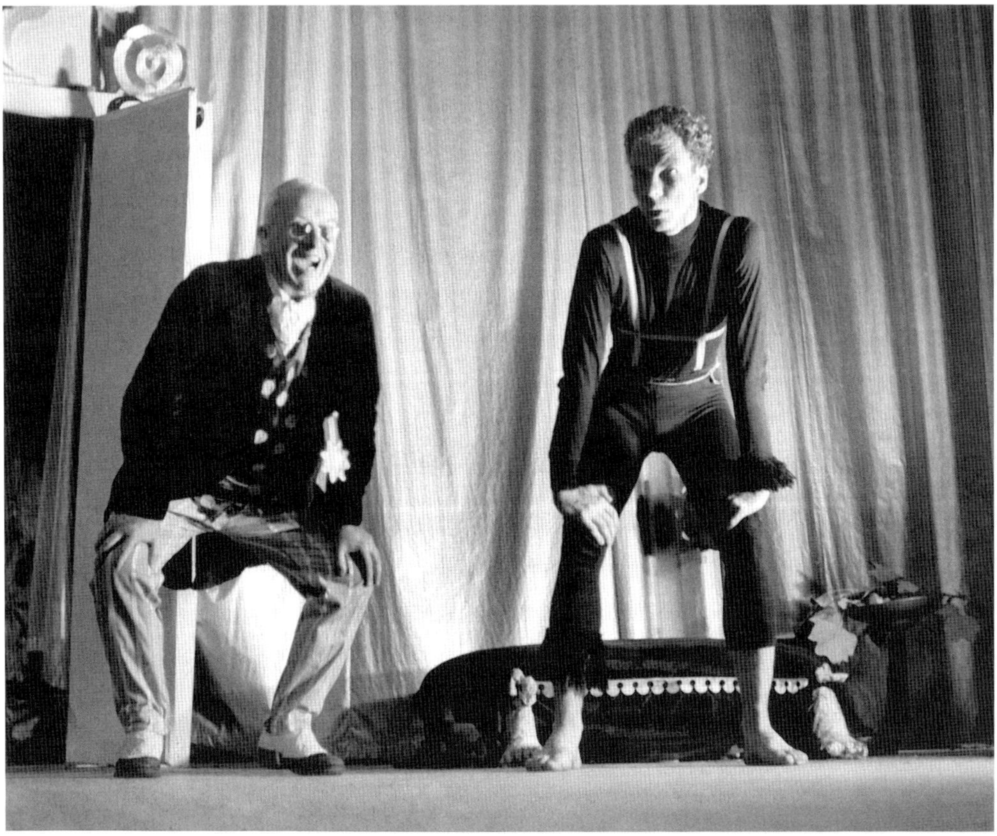

Figure 2.4 (above)
Clemens Kalischer, *Cast Portrait of "The Ruse of Medusa," including John Cage, Elaine de Kooning, Buckminster Fuller, and Merce Cunningham*, 1948. Gelatin silver print. © Clemens Kalischer. Courtesy the artist.

Figure 2.5 (below)
Clemens Kalischer, *Buckminster Fuller and Merce Cunningham in "The Ruse of Medusa,"* 1948. Gelatin silver print. © Clemens Kalischer. Courtesy the artist.

Cunningham as Jonas the "costly mechanical monkey," with sets and props by Fuller, Willem and Elaine de Kooning, and students Ruth Asawa, Ray Johnson, and others. The props included a velvet footstool with giant human feet, a monumental thermometer capped by an oversized paper bow, and a "baron's desk" painted in a "guild secret" trompe l'oeil technique de Kooning said he had learned as teenager in Holland; this was outfitted with enormous four-sided triangles around its legs (a tweak on the importance of tetrahedrons in Fuller's work)[21] (fig. 2.5).

The production set the groundwork for a renewed exploration of the College's experimental theater tradition that had remained mostly dormant since Schawinsky's departure in 1938. Satie's play features an eccentric, doddering aristocrat, his insolent and ever-defiant manservant, an obedient daughter, and her terrified straight-man fiancé. Consisting largely of rapid-fire puns and absurd nonsequiturs, the loosely sketched plot follows the Baron's attempts to wire one General Posthumous, a storyline designed as an excuse to frame the Baron's nonsensical pronouncements regarding the impending betrothal of his daughter. Scene changes are marked by short musical interludes danced by the mechanical monkey, written in a musical notation full of wisecracks and ironic comments (fig. 2.6). In one section, for example, the score's text reads at bottom, "Instructions in Roman text are for the choreographer, in italic for the pianist"; these begin with the following comments: "The Monkey's Dance, no. 1; **Quadrille** The monkey dances, sweetly, the following figure; *put yourself in the shade*; He goes crazy, or it looks as if he has; *Do not come out of your shadow / Behave yourself, please: a monkey is watching you*; The dance can end here."[22]

Satie's "lyrical comedy in one act" was rarely performed, though it was considered an important successor to Alfred Jarry's play *Ubu Roi* (1896) in a tradition of absurdist theater. Satie's emphasis on burlesque gestures and his creation of characters that sputtered childlike nonsense—"five plus three makes eleven . . . take four leaves six . . . two plus seven makes eighteen," or, a few lines later, "I am going to a billiards match. What a great match! Napoleon will be there. The billiards Napoleon, I mean of course! . . . THE REAL ONE"—made the entire production seem a farcical romp.[23] In an article Cage later penned on Satie, he pointed to the apparent freewheeling, illogical unpredictability of Satie's work and its disregard of musical seriousness as being its most compelling qualities. In the essay, set up as an imaginary conversation between the two men sourced from Satie's published statements, Cage quoted the composer:

> They will tell you I am not a musician. That's right. . . . Take the *Fils des Etoiles* or the *Morceaux en forme de poire*, *En habit de cheval* or the *Sarabandes*, it is clear that no musical idea presided at the creation of these works.[24]

*The Monkey's Dance (no. 1)**

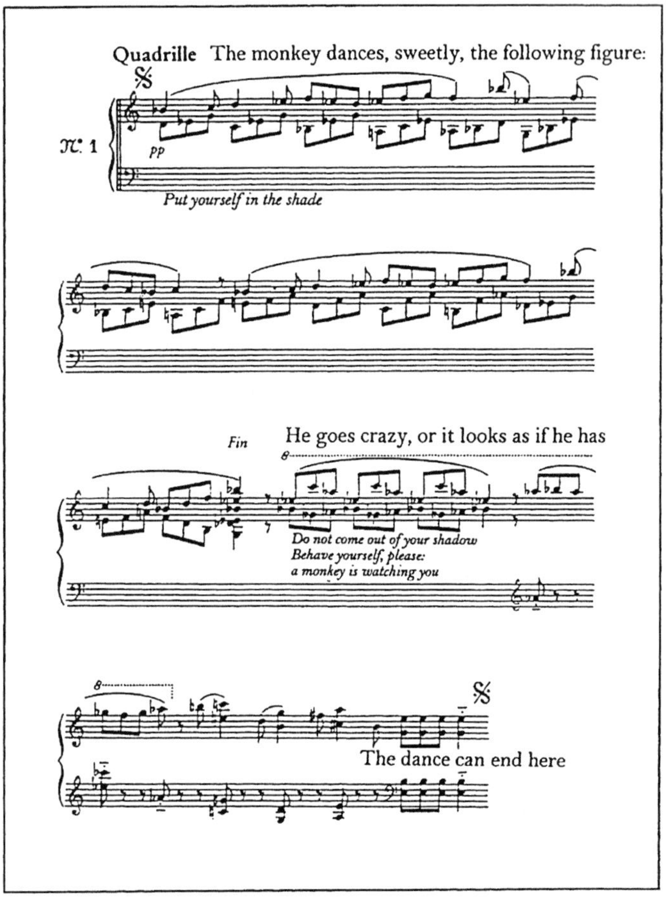

*Instructions in Roman text are for the choreographer, in italic for the pianist.

Figure 2.6
Erik Satie, "The Monkey's Dance (no. 1)." From *The Ruse of Medusa*, 1913.

The flippancy with which Satie dismissed musical intention delighted Cage. He concluded his "conversation" with the kōan that "to be interested in Satie one must be disinterested to begin with," a paradox of non-intentioned intention Cage often returned to in defining his chance protocol.[25]

Yet earlier in the essay, Cage claimed that Satie's *investment* (far from disinterestedness) in antagonizing or shocking his audience—the "power to irritate" expressed in Satie's call to "despise art"—inspired Cage's staging of the play at Black Mountain.[26] In particular, he was compelled by Satie's attempt to make "unpredictable" music that, in Satie's words, "will be part of the noises of the environment."[27] Satie's works demonstrated that music composition could reflect everyday events—not "musical ideas"—by representing ambient noises such as the sounds of eating or the pauses between conversations. To Satie, the radical neutrality of a sound not imposing itself on its audience as "music" fundamentally leveled hierarchies of distinction and quality; to Cage, such a move let "sounds be just sounds . . . just folk tunes, unresolved ninths, or knives and forks."[28] In studying Satie's other scores—particularly *Vexations* (1893), a cycle that can extend to nearly 24 hours in performance, based on 840 repetitions of a simple, fifty-two-beat theme whose four arrangements are alternately heard unaccompanied and then played with two variations of a short chord sequence—Cage was enthusiastic about Satie's concern with the durational aspects of sound.[29] In contrast to more complex qualities of aural information (pitch, frequency, amplitude, and so on), duration was the only feature that was unspecific: it could incorporate measures of both silence and the audible. The grand length of a performance of *Vexations*—a length that exceeded nearly any individual's ability to listen attentively—satisfied Satie's desire that his work be "furniture music" intended as background for other events. By stressing the durational aspect of sound over musical tone, in opposition to prior harmonic traditions, Cage argued that Satie accepted when "a sound is a sound . . . [one can] give up illusions about ideas of order, expressions of sentiment, and all the rest of our inherited aesthetic claptrap."[30] Important, too, was *The Ruse of Medusa*'s occasional use of instructions to the performer in durational—not musically notated—segments of simple time structures designated in cardinal numbers and plain language (this feature reemerged in Cage's own work during his next visit to Black Mountain in 1952).

Like several College productions before it, Cage's staging of *The Ruse of Medusa* encouraged intentionally unnaturalistic and stylized acting as well as innovative set and costume design. Yet there were important differences. Cage's sourcing of Satie as a precedent for a theater of cacophonous simultaneity and jest departed considerably from existing Bauhaus-oriented theater and performance that found its way to the College, though these were as dedicated to changing audience's perceptions through trained visual attention and concentration as Satie's was to doing so with fragmentary, incommunicable meanings and ambiguous gestures.

By the mid-1920s, an entire pedagogical and practice methodology dedicated to workshopping time- and motion-based compositions had been perfected at the Bauhaus in its second home in Dessau. This had not always been the case: early theater productions, under the direction of artist Lothar Schreyer, had been expressionistic and melodramatic, with highly charged emotional con-

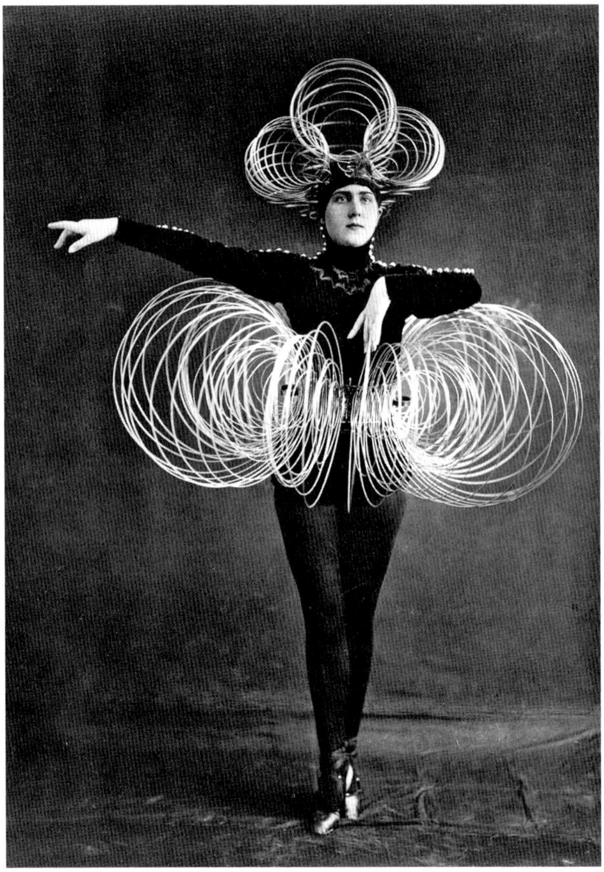

Figure 2.7
Oskar Schlemmer, *Triadic Ballet*, 1922, photograph 1925. Courtesy Oskar Schlemmer Theatre Estate and Collection. Photograph © Estate of Karl Grill. Reproduced by permission of The J. Paul Getty Museum, Los Angeles.

tent underscored by dramatic lighting and costumes. In contrast, when Oskar Schlemmer arrived at the Bauhaus in 1921 and subsequently assumed directorship of the stage workshop in 1923, he explicitly linked theatrical performance with the periodic festivals and costume parties hosted by the school. The emphasis, for Schlemmer, was not on festivity per se, but rather on the manner in which the masquerade of such events disguised and transformed the human body. He began staging masque-like shows in which performers' features were camouflaged by heavily padded costumes, elaborate papier-mâché masks, and helmetlike headdresses. In doing so, performers' bodies were extracted from "natural" or everyday experiences in order to be turned into archetypes of geometry and movement[31] (fig. 2.7).

Actors in Schlemmer's productions employed broad, pantomimic gestures and generally did not speak. For example, in *Gesture Dance* (1926), three performers wearing bulbous metallic masks outfitted with identical mustaches and spectacles execute flamboyant renditions of "everyday actions" including sneezing, laughing, and listening.[32] The characters' gesticulations are exaggerated to the point of being stilted, and the figures return to certain tropes of communication: hand cupped to ear indicates listening, palm shading mouth signs whispering, and boisterous rocking back and forth suggests laughter. The stylized gestures, combined with the use of masks and cumbersome costumes, disengaged the performing body from its habitual movements.

The emphasis on costume in Bauhaus theater also transfigured the human body and its everyday appearance by removing distinguishing characteristics and imposing an order of simple shapes and primary colors. According to Schlemmer, this abstracted the body and generalized its features in order to "reduce the differentiated parts . . . to simple, unifying forms."[33] These unified forms thereby permitted viewers to see "new totality" beyond previous habit-driven and subjective understandings of form.[34] In most theatrical performance, and indeed in most everyday social behavior, subtle work of visual discrimination routinely helps to organize, categorize, and ultimately hierarchize relatively minor differences in human appearances; for example, assessments of the size of a nose or the contour of a foot become paramount indicators of beauty or grace. In stressing general forms, Schlemmer rejected the meticulous morphologies of fashion, the superficial interpretations of physiognomic variation, or the cultural conditioning that patterned gesture and exploited arbitrary differences to create regimes of infinitesimal judgment and distinction. As these

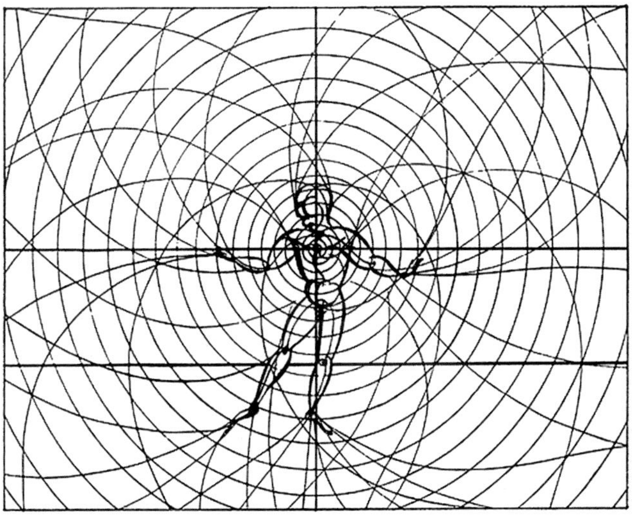

Figure 2.8
Oskar Schlemmer, drawing of Man as Dancer from *Man and Art Figure*, ca. 1921. Courtesy Oskar Schlemmer Theatre Estate and Collection.

historically specific, though relatively arbitrary, characteristics became naturalized, Schlemmer contended, they promoted fetishistic judgments regarding minute differences of form as compared with other fundamentally similar forms. In contrast, Bauhaus theater attempted to overturn this tradition of tiny visual distinctions made according to socially determined, often conflicting habits. It did so by heightening the artifice onstage so that rationally discerned details would throw habitual patterns into sharp relief. In Schlemmer's system, this perspicuous work of visual judgment focused on the close observation of the relationship of bodies—not as compared to themselves, but rather seen as embedded in larger perspectival contexts and environments. Reducing theater to such basic design elements as form and color represented "an undertaking whose purpose, contrary to nature, is order."[35] Denaturalizing the actors' movements and costumes encouraged spectators to remain self-conscious about the spatial relations surrounding the bodies onstage, estranging from habit their perceptions of, and judgments about, human form and gesture.

In contrast to Cage's emphasis on arbitrariness, distraction, and disconnection, the keywords of Bauhaus theater were unity, totality, and order. For Schlemmer, "unity" was an escape from the maddening simplification of life into trivial and fragmentary subcategories that effaced the larger interconnectedness of bodies, spatial contexts, and habits of social behavior. With concentration and attention, broader concerns could be assessed and judged, including the fundamental features of form (light, color, movement, and so on) that constituted the foundation of all perception. In the stripped-down environment of the new, "total" stage, spectators would be able to notice how the framing of a theatrical space marked conventions in everyday life to which they had become oblivious and conditioned.

In 1936, Albers invited the Swiss émigré Xanti Schawinsky, who had studied with Schlemmer from 1924 to 1928, to Black Mountain to teach painting and theater.[36] After fleeing persecution in Nazi Germany, Schawinsky had immigrated to Italy and had spent several years working in advertising for companies such as Illy Caffè, Cinzano vermouth, and Olivetti typewriters. He was best known for producing a widely circulated photomontage poster of Mussolini as the head of the masses to celebrate the twelfth anniversary of the Fascist revolution. (Schawinsky was an equal-opportunity designer, one could say: after leaving Black Mountain, he taught at the New Bauhaus in Chicago and with László Moholy-Nagy created patterns for a US Army project of equipment camouflage.)[37]

When he landed at the College, Schawinsky became the United States' sole proponent and performer of Bauhaus theater, and his ideas and productions remained very much part of the institutional memory and lore of the campus after

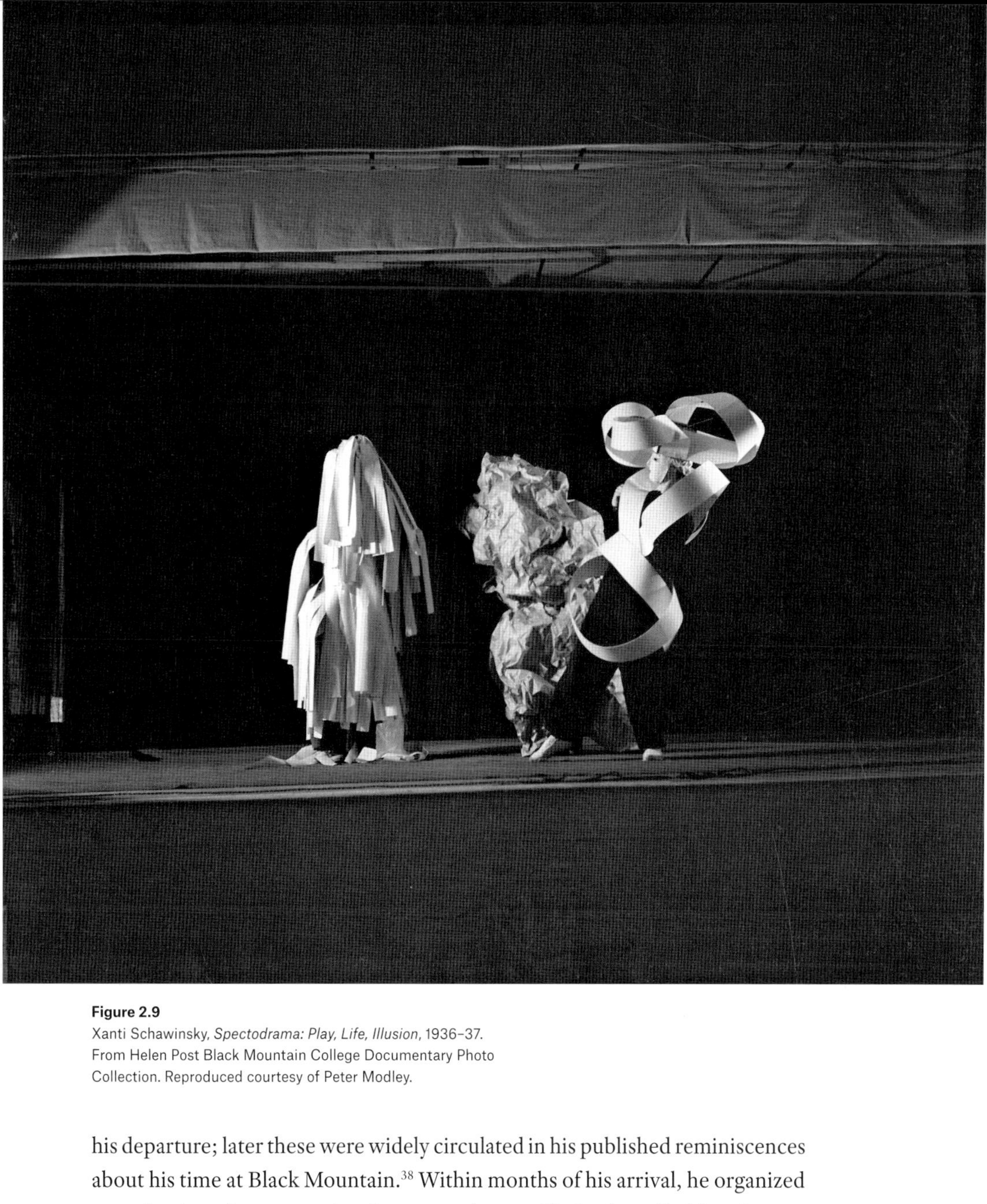

Figure 2.9
Xanti Schawinsky, *Spectodrama: Play, Life, Illusion*, 1936–37. From Helen Post Black Mountain College Documentary Photo Collection. Reproduced courtesy of Peter Modley.

his departure; later these were widely circulated in his published reminiscences about his time at Black Mountain.[38] Within months of his arrival, he organized a production of nonnarrative theater—a theater of what he called "total experience"—titled *Spectodrama: Play, Life, Illusion*, with music by Kurt Schwitters (his *Ursonate* [1922–32]) (see plates 10–12). In a series of episodes that had been previously "storyboarded" and rehearsed through improvisational techniques, *Spectodrama* staged short scenes of selected elementary concepts of theater, each falling into a specific category: "optics, form and color, acoustics, sound, language, music, time, space, architecture, technology, and illusion."[39]

In each vignette of *Spectodrama*, the performer's body, if evident at all (camouflage and illusion, and their constitutive elements of high-contrast geometric forms, were key features of the Bauhaus style), figures in a tableau of what Schawinsky termed "archetypal" geometric, spatial, or social situations: "play," "communication," "form," or "space." Each portion of the play contains elaborate sets and costumes designed so as to either conceal or set off the performer's placement and orientation with respect to the stage space and props. For example, one performer, trussed in a costume of stiff, intertwined white paper rolls, might emerge chameleonlike from a tangle of similarly twisted paper props and move toward the stark relief of a blank background. The figure's poses and the patterns of the props repeat throughout the space to create a "laboratory for demonstration" of the conditions of perceiving difference and similarity.[40]

Moholy-Nagy, also a key figure in Bauhaus theater, termed this research-like element of rational attention the "theater of totality," in which a body's movement transpired in a structured, architectonic space.[41] Rigorously ordering bodies in the theater demonstrated a kind of technical competence that, in orchestrating complex spatial relations onstage, extended the project of spatial organization into nontheatrical everyday life (the theater being a microcosmic exploration of the larger Bauhaus project of synthesizing the "living and working conditions of the environment").[42] Though spectators were seated and their attention carefully organized, "dynamism" in performance was nonetheless a frequently invoked term: kinetic sculptures and moving bodies were deployed in order to show that, to Moholy-Nagy, "material is employed only as the carrier of forces."[43] These forces charged the performance space with a temporal component that expressed the true "unity of life."[44] In contrast to architecture, static sculpture, or painting, theater was the arena for an examination of transient, time-based events and movements intersecting environmental conditions, and the body's temporal engagement with those sociospatial circumstances.

The search for universal gestures "common to mankind" took precedence over what Moholy-Nagy termed the "causal ties" of previous theater.[45] Stage design was emphasized, forcing "one to learn from the way an artist perceives" by estranging viewers' traditional emphasis on character and narrative in order to instead fabricate complicated illusions of spatial perception.[46] This model of integration—the performing body and space joined in an "indissoluble unity"—radically simplified performance to its "fundamental" components: "light, space, plane, movement, sound, and human being."[47]

Walter Gropius, too, was involved in theorizing performance strategies at the Bauhaus, and he underscored how spectatorial conditions of illusion and attention were influenced by the architecture of the theater itself. In the mid-1920s, he proposed a "Total Theater" in which "new interpretations of theatrical space" were to be explored.[48] In Gropius's model, an elliptical

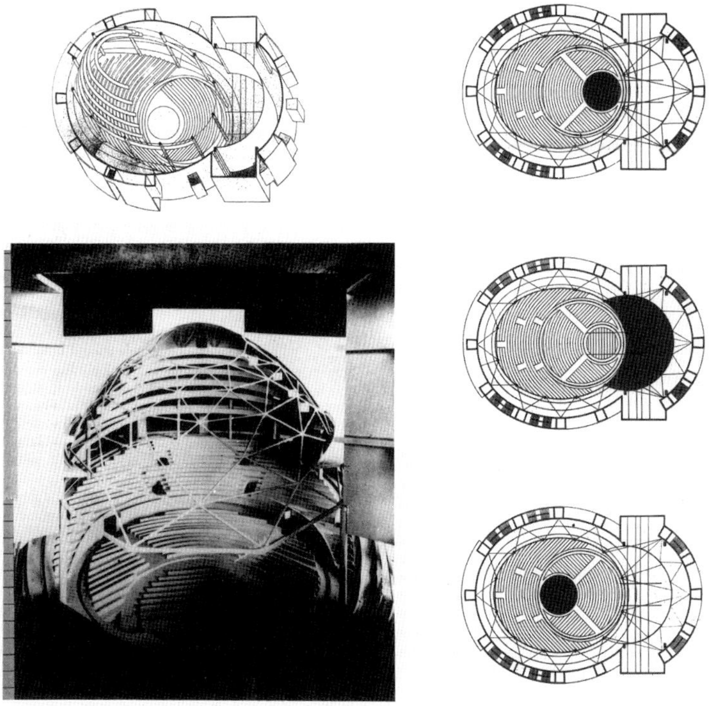

Figure 2.10
Walter Gropius, Photoboard with model, isometric with three diagrams showing uses of the stage in the "Total Theater," 1927. Courtesy Bauhaus-Archiv, Berlin. © Artists Rights Society, New York / VG Bild-Kunst, Bonn. Reproduced by permission of Bauhaus-Archiv, Berlin.

arrangement of ascending seats was clustered around an embedded, central circular stage flanking a second cylindrical back stage[49] (fig. 2.10). The inner circular stage was designed to rotate, accommodating various seating arrangements that represented the major performance traditions—the proscenium stage with a shallow performance space and fixed backdrop, the deep stage in which curtains and backdrops are arranged to reveal greater or lesser portions of the action and to accommodate more or fewer performers, and finally a theater-in-the-round setup. In the latter scenario, according to Gropius, "the play unfolds itself three-dimensionally while the spectators crowd around concentrically."[50] He connected this spectatorial arrangement, as Schawinsky did, to precedents in other public, collective events such as the circus, the bullring, and the sports arena.

Gropius's three staging possibilities in the "Total Theater" engendered various spatial effects; more important, his flexible architecture (the rotating core of the structure) could transform the space during performance, surprising the audience and impelling it to "shake off its inertia."[51] The dynamic possibility of moving the stage structure itself intensified the audience's awareness of the conditions of staging, and when the theater was arranged with a central platform surrounded by seating, the "spectator participate[s] in the drama."[52] In Bauhaus theories of spectatorship, in other words, the implied salutary social effects of heightening consciousness of the environment were part of the larger interest in concentration, focus, and order as transformative elements of vision. The actor, according to Schlemmer, was "space-bewitched"—"altered, transformed, or entranced" by the use of masks, props, and costumes so that "his habitual behavior and his physical and psychic structure are either upset or put into a new and altogether different balance."[53] This change in the actor's ingrained relation to gesture and its social intelligibility would impel an "inner transformation of the spectator" by his or her "receptivity" to the visual ordering of the theatrical field in performance.[54] Only a self-reflexive spectator could, "on the basis of the rational," understand the embeddedness of the actor in his or her surrounding space, a space that is itself "part of the larger total complex, building (Bau)."[55] As the performer acted out order in such a space, the spectator could rationally perceive the larger field of spatial and architectural illusions in which bodies are rooted contextually in their environments.

That this work of unification was enacted in the realm of time-based events was important to Schawinsky as he brought these ideas to Black Mountain; to him, theater explored the fundamental conditions of perception underlying *all* specific disciplinary explorations. As he wrote of theater's interdisciplinary nature, "Our theater can, I believe, get its impulse from studies that go through all phases of knowledge."[56] In Schawinsky's next major performance at the College, he attempted to push notions of spatial totality further. In the 1938 production *Danse Macabre: A Sociological Study*, adapted from a Latin hymn about the Last Judgment called *Dies Irae*, Schawinsky's theatrical staging—while still emphasizing elaborate masks and costumes modeled on abstract shapes, and employing dramatic spotlights and shadows—also included repetitive movements associated with funeral rites as well as highly mannered costuming (figs. 2.11 and 2.12). In staging a medieval morality tale, he chose the Middle Ages' "single absolute concept: death" in an attempt to "find the 'absolute' of our own time."[57] He sought the limiting experience that transcended performance/animation and background/stasis dichotomies—mortality—though he later distanced himself from the direct reenactment of the macabre source material blamed for the suicide of one of its student actors. The theater-in-the-round aspect of the performance, in which spectators were outfitted with robes and masks and given unconventional seating assignments in concentric circles around the central stage area, to him mimicked the "original plays [of the Middle Ages] which were

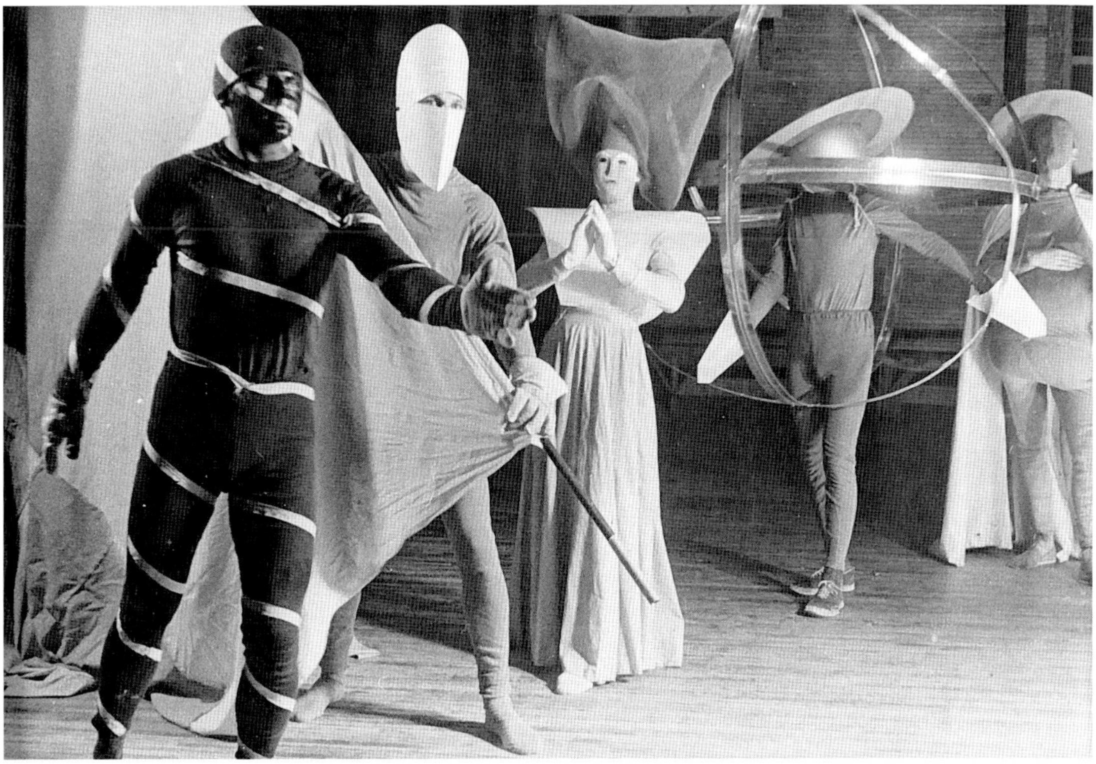

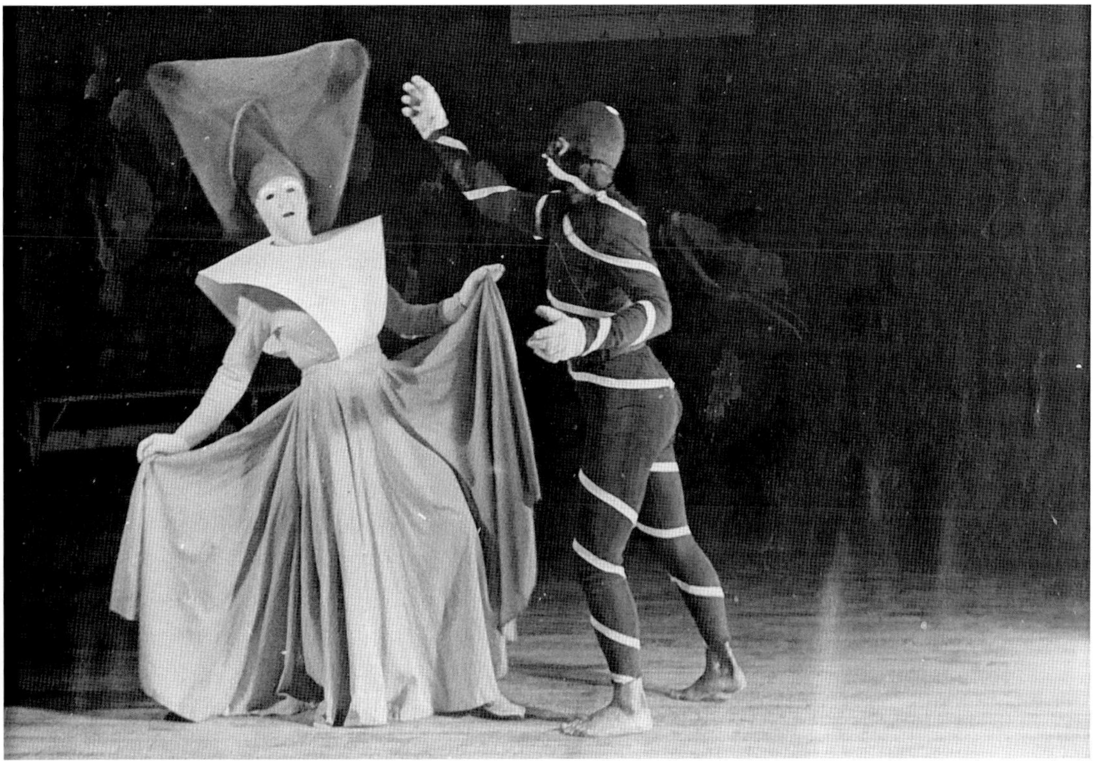

Figures 2.11 (above) and **2.12** (below)
Xanti Schawinsky, *Danse Macabre: A Sociological Study*, Black Mountain College, 1938. Courtesy of The Xanti Schawinsky Estate. Reproduced by permission of Bauhaus-Archiv, Berlin.

usually performed on the market place in front of the cathedral."[58] To Schawinsky, this focus on people and spaces outside traditional theater—for example, individuals in public space—updated Bauhaus precedents that focused on the circus and moved theater into the territory of history by studying constructions of social subjectivity. As he recalled, "While work at the Bauhaus theatre aimed at the modernization of theatrical means and concepts, and had a definite professional and artistic scope, at Black Mountain College an educational crack at the whole man seemed in order."[59]

What Schawinsky meant by such a "total experience" incorporating the "whole man" can be understood in relation to Schlemmer's explication of Bauhaus theater as a totality: to both men, the stage was a site of spatial unity that provided, according to Schawinsky, "a general study of fundamental phenomena."[60] He added that theater was the most appropriate location to explore concepts of basic perception, because "space on the stage was a very particular place . . . it is by nature a place of illusion."[61] Indeed, to Schlemmer, too, movements of bodies on the stage represented, by simplification and abstraction, the wider geometries of relationships in space perceived through *visual* illusion, and its inverse, penetrating observation. Bauhaus theater's work with perspective, with embedding the body in its space through complicated geometric formations, was often presented as a visual tableau in which the audience *perceives* space, but does not have any direct relation to the performer's *experience* of space. This results in the somewhat disembodied eye that the performances effect—why, for example, reproductions of Bauhaus performances look remarkably like friezes and pictures, or why Schawinsky envisioned the preparatory diagrams of *Spectodrama* as static tableaus (plates 10–12). The abstraction of Bauhaus theater and its exploration of visual illusions were "unified," to use Schlemmer's language, only by the audience's visually tracking the position(s) of the performer(s); Bauhaus and Bauhaus-derived theater expressly did not create cohesive spaces of unity between performers and spectators, and consistently maintained the illusion of the "fourth wall," even when seating arrangements were less frontally oriented.

These theatrical scenarios required spectators' orientation to the staged events to be fixed and their attention carefully focused in order to perceive the precise and subtly changing visual effects on the stage. An immobilized audience permitted Schlemmer and Schawinsky to apply the framing techniques of cinema to live performances. With such focused looking, a montage of visual effects could unfold, in order for each spectator to observe phenomena with close attention to the order and sequencing of events that he or she would not normally notice if watching as a casual bystander. Though a "play instinct" was encouraged of actors in workshopping, the final productions

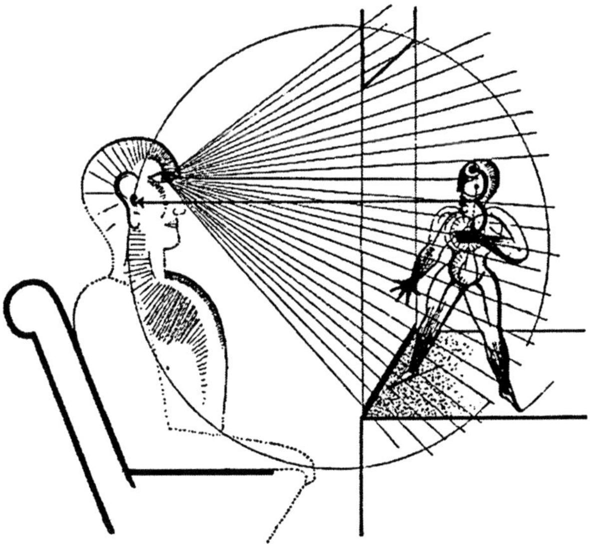

Figure 2.13
Oskar Schlemmer, drawing from *Man and Art Figure*, ca. 1921.
Courtesy Oskar Schlemmer Theatre Estate and Collection.

were predicated on passive spectatorship; Schlemmer wrote that the elaborate visual fabulations encouraged a concentration that rivaled the intensity of a "peep show"[62] (fig. 2.13).

In important ways, Schawinsky's work can be seen as a proxy, in time-based work, for what Albers's sensibilities hoped to accomplish in two dimensions. Much like Albers, Schawinsky promoted a model of experimentation that stressed order, concentration, and serial repetition, and employed careful variations of formal elements—color, gesture, costume, set design, and lighting—that could be measured, compared, and repeated. These tests of perception were undertaken to dynamically reappraise the seemingly self-evident nature of vision, and to question the habit-driven tendency of physical gestures to be reproduced unwittingly. The experimental practices of both Schawinsky and Albers can be seen as but a corner of a larger Bauhaus project demanding that the experimental act of perceptual testing produce dynamic outcomes in a serial practice of repeatable trials. Schawinsky's performances were part of a collective project at the Bauhaus in which *all* forms of perception were being reconsidered, those of time, space, and theatricality, too; for these reasons, the Bauhaus was the first art school to formally incorporate a performance department, then called a "stage workshop," into its curriculum. Just as Oskar Schlemmer envisioned his project as a "laboratory" exploration of space—isolating constitutive elements of light, color, and movement to attend to how underlying patterns and arrangements of forms outside the theater might function,

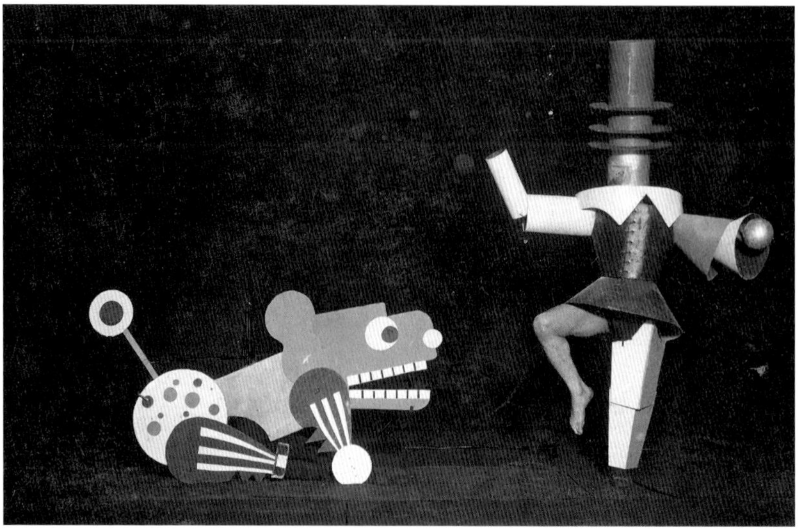

Figure 2.14
Xanti Schawinsky, scene from *The Circus*, first performance at the Bauhaus, 1924. Courtesy of The Xanti Schawinsky Estate.

Schawinsky pushed Albers's ideas of laboratory production toward concerns of duration, sound, and motion; toward the incorporation of bodies, theatrical audience, and three-dimensional space—concerns that have always been more pressing in theater than in visual art.[63]

Cage's production of *The Ruse of Medusa* was also a hybrid site of theater in a visual arts context, yet Erik Satie's script, in contrast to the Bauhaus precedents at the College, was dialogue-heavy and intentionally humorous, with quips addressed to the audience explicitly breaking down the fourth wall and engaging the spectator at a supravisual level. In Bauhaus productions from the 1920s, Schawinsky in particular often included comedic scenarios, particularly around the figure of the clown in circus theatrics, but they were largely explorations of pantomime: gesture in relation to the forms of props and the space of the stage (fig. 2.14). The emphasis in the Satie play on a script to be verbalized by actors characterizing fictionalized yet archly comedic roles also departed from Black Mountain precedents. Satie's 1913 script was, distinct from Bauhaus circus antics and pantomime, a proto-Marx Brothers slapstick full of ribald verbal repartee interspersed with burlesque-like visual gags—scene 2 ends with Baron Medusa, sounding very much like Groucho twenty years later, telling Frisette's fiancé Astolfo: "Get out now! . . . Off like a gun! . . . Come back in ten minutes . . . I shan't be here."[64]

The provocations of *The Ruse of Medusa*—its silly jesting and the disruption of narrative continuity in the play's sarcastic commentary (as Satie himself stated, "This is a play of pure fantasy . . . a joke")—were only part of its allure for Cage.[65] More important, the work was part of a Dadaist repertoire characterized by a particular *style* of writing and scoring. According to historian

Sandra Skurvida, Cage's fascination with the play stemmed from how "Satie introduced incongruence between language (musical, visual, notational, etc.) and meaning."[66] Satie's score and script become a fused and highly interpretable object pointing to a fundamental hybridity between aural and written information—*The Ruse of Medusa*'s musical score contains nearly as much textual as sound notation, and its script includes musical interludes interrupting the narrative (such as it is) with a nonverbal "Monkey's Dance" that is never clearly connected to the other events of the play. Performers must translate both forms of information, which, due to Satie's nonsensical asides, exceed the normal prescriptions of notation, and in this gap indeterminate interpretations are introduced that explore authorial misdirection or even unintended results (how, for example, as a pianist, would you "put yourself in the shade," as the score instructs?). As historian Liz Kotz has argued, such a hybridity in a work points to a "conceptual ambiguity" of text-based scoring that "derives from the use of the text as score [as] inseparably both writing/printed object and performance/'realization.'"[67] Cage's recovery of Satie was motivated in part by the latter's intentionally ambiguous scoring; the confusion between scripting and dialogue in the play resulted in a contingent performance full of unpredictable or unintended effects.

The Ruse of Medusa's ambiguities—its absurd monologues and unrelated musical interludes, combined with dance and physical slapstick—alerted Cage to the possibility of seemingly arbitrary relationships between actions in a performance. In the apparent randomness of its plotting, Satie's work departed from previous, more methodical theatrical events at Black Mountain. Even so, the production still drew from a script and rehearsals, in addition to functioning quite successfully as a comedic piece that lent levity to the provocation posed by Cage's lectures and his single-minded advocacy of Satie. (The play's sense of lightheartedness was especially pronounced as several Black Mountain faculty members performed self-deprecating, jokey roles in the production.)[68] An examination of the ordered unity of a visual field at the College was thus replaced, by the late 1940s, with diametrically opposed practices: dispersion, ambiguity, and inattention. Cage couched this shift in a return to Dada, by revisiting Satie's snappy and illogical explorations of the ludic and the disruptive effects of word, dance, and sound play.

Upon his next visit, Cage extended his methods into something one could more properly term experimental (in his case, the chance protocol)—his happening *Theater Piece No. 1*. For Cage, "Happenings . . . have this thing we've spoken of as carelessness in them. Carelessness comes about through . . . 'non-matrixed' activity."[69] Just how he composed and performed nonmatrixed or nonarranged activity is the crux of his chance protocol, and it pushes beyond Dada's attempt to trouble if not end "art" by exacerbating cultural illogic. It comes by way of a most quixotic pairing: Zen and early twentieth-century French art.

CIRCA 1952: SOMETHING IS HAPPENING HERE

In his first summer at Black Mountain, Cage was just beginning to make inroads in the new post-"German aesthetician" version of experimentation of which the Satie play and lectures were key mileposts.[70] As he recalled, in 1948 he still "saw eye-to-eye with Albers at the time, and our conversations were ones characterized by agreement."[71] Though separated by a generation, both men were equally zealous about defining and propagating their respective visions of modernist experimentation, and once Cage introduced chance into his practice, they would forever disagree about its role in art production.

The eventual split between the two emerged from a fundamental and intractable conflict between their visions for the role of the test in fostering unforeseen experiences in art. For Albers, because experimentation was the subtle and penetrating work of training the eye and mind to recognize illusion, art practice was therefore situated within a spectrum of design that began with technical proficiency and then produced subtle and carefully organized contingency through serial variation. For Cage, in contrast, contingency was a means of unleashing unpredictable aleatory processes that were nonetheless generated by systematic controls. By 1952, his procedures had the effect of drastically devaluing (in anarchic fashion) the role of authorial control in artistic production, encouraging new types of indeterminate performances in which events unforeseen by artist, performer, or audience could transpire.[72] Where Albers argued that "rehearsal precedes performance," such a notion of rehearsal was precisely what Cage attempted to remove, *without* substituting expressionistic improvisations on the part of the performer.[73]

Occluding the Albersian conception of experimentation he characterized as a "marriage of form and content," Cage's subsequent performance events at the College attempted to leave both the composition and the effects of performance actions intentionally open-ended, as much as possible.[74] Albers abhorred Cage's incitement of artworks left open to accident: as Cage explained, "When, in 1952, I took the path of chance, and later indeterminacy, our friendship was broken . . . he couldn't bear the real implications which I then carried out. And he felt that I was renouncing my responsibility as an artist."[75]

It was upon this visit, in 1952, that Cage radically disrupted previous models of performance at the College, including his own, by introducing overlapping activities and inaugurating both a dispersal of attention and a radical narrative fragmentation. With *Theater Piece No. 1*, Cage worked in the wake of Black Mountain legacies such as the theater-in-the-round, circus-like events previously organized at the College by the Light-Sound-Movement Workshop led by Betty and Peter Jennerjahn in the late 1940s, which were revived in the summer of 1951 by M. C. Richards and choreographer Katherine Litz. The Jennerjahns, for example, in collaboration with about a dozen College students and faculty, had improvised short theater pieces, sometimes "limited to a minute, or so," incorporating projected slides, improvised music, and dance elements.[76] Like these precursors at the College, Cage's *Theater Piece No. 1* eschewed extensive rehearsals and previously arranged scripting, costuming, music, and characterization; it emphasized simultaneously occurring events and immediacy, and closely considered how to organize the performance space with respect to the audience, who was often understood as a community of possible participants.

Drawing on these precedents, by 1952 Cage was developing chance-derived compositional methods obtained from parameters provided by the *I Ching*, or the *Book of Changes*, an ancient Chinese text of divination. In particular, his score for *Music of Changes* (1951) had been a turning point; during its composition he would "ask" specific "questions" about features of the score, and then make coin tosses or casts of the traditional yarrow sticks to assemble the hexagrams the *I Ching* requires; he then used the "answers" to select the duration, tempo, and other dynamics of the composition.[77] Cage expressly employed only the structure of the *I Ching*'s complex randomization features, not its divinatory aspects. As he contended of the innovation of chance composition, "My work became an exploration of non-intention. To carry it out faithfully I have developed a complicated composing means using *I Ching* chance operations, making my responsibility that of asking questions instead of making choices."[78]

Let's keep that phrase, "asking questions instead of making choices," in mind while considering *Theater Piece No. 1* and the works composed around it. In early August of 1952, Cage and his frequent collaborator, pianist David Tudor (also at Black Mountain that summer, though he had first arrived at the College in 1951 as piano accompanist to Litz), formulated ideas for a performance with multiple participants who would perform discrete activities during various overlapping time segments totaling forty-five minutes (see fig. 2.17). Cage proposed that College Rector Charles Olson and faculty member Richards read their poetry, student Robert Rauschenberg display his paintings and play records or project slides, and Cunningham dance. Tudor was to perform on the piano, and Cage would read from a previously prepared lecture on Zen and the medieval mystic Meister Eckhart. To Cage, the piece represented the possibility of events taking place without being causally related to one another; as he claimed, *Theater Piece No. 1* expressed "the centricity within each event and its non-dependence on other events."[79]

Cage had in fact established strict time brackets and organized the performance with particular time, content, and location parameters. His chance protocol, however, structured the piece's score around instructions that had many possible effects, which organized a set of open-ended possibilities. The most radical break of such a scoring in *Theater Piece No. 1* was the intentionally disorienting effect of the performance, what Richards called its "sensory bombardment"; it decentered attention away from the visual apperception of a theatrical event to the many intermittent, intermedia experiences Cage orchestrated in and around the body of the spectator.[80]

When it was performed at Black Mountain in mid-August, *Theater Piece No. 1* incorporated the last-minute addition of upside-down slides, likely projected onto the tilted surfaces of a canopy of Rauschenberg's monochromatic *White Paintings* (fig. 2.3; works I will discuss later); the canopy was arranged above and to one side of the central arrangement of chairs, which were organized as "a square composed on four triangles merging towards the center, but not meeting"[81] (fig. 2.15). The seating arrangement allowed performers mobility throughout the audience area, and directly followed, as will be discussed further, Antonin Artaud's pronouncement that "the spectator, placed in the middle of the action, is engulfed and physically affected by it . . . immerse[d] . . . in

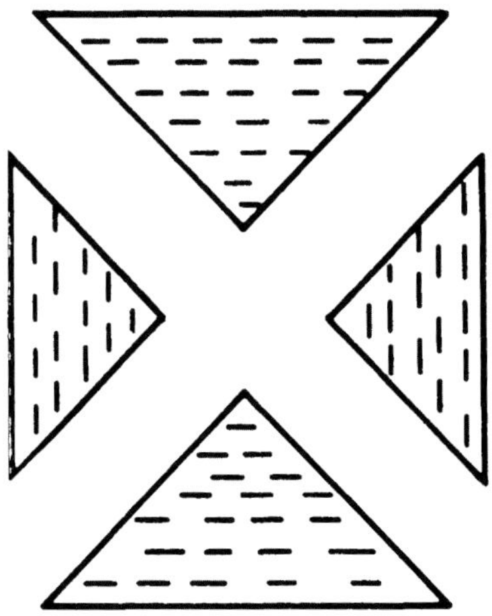

Figure 2.15
Performance seats and stage space for John Cage's *Theater Piece No. 1*, 1952. Published in Michael Kirby and Richard Schechner, "An Interview with John Cage," *Tulane Drama Review* 10, no. 2 (Winter 1965).

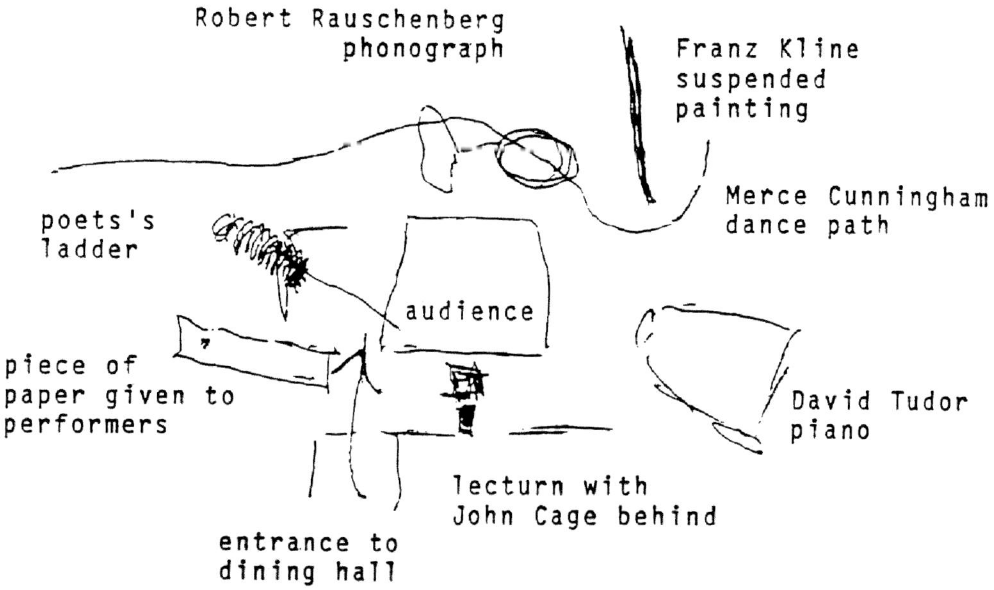

Figure 2.16
M. C. Richards's diagram of John Cage's *Theater Piece No. 1*, 1952. Reconstructed in 1989 for publication in James Fetterman, *John Cage's Theater Pieces* (New York: Routledge, 1996), 74. Courtesy of the Estate of M. C. Richards.

a constant bath of light, images, movements and noises."[82] Olson and Richards ascended a ladder at various points to read for their segments; some claim that Tudor played Cage's 1952 composition *Water Music*, and films were likely projected by student Nicholas Cernovich.[83] A dog or dogs barked at Cunningham throughout the piece, and hot coffee was served (as part of the performance) in cups that had been set at each seat, regardless of whether they had been previously used as ashtrays during the event. Figure 2.16 is a retrospective map of the event by Richards—no photographs of the performance exist.

Cage's incorporation of multiple events of indeterminate outcome in *Theater Piece No. 1* provoked a mixed response at its debut. Testimonies confirm that the event left some in the audience confounded and even hostile. Composer Stefan Wolpe, previously a Bauhaus student and currently teaching at the College, "bitched" about the chaos and left in protest; some thought it was "quite boring" to sit through though, while others claimed it was "an interesting experiment"; still others conceded that "you weren't supposed to understand it literally."[84] The seating arrangement discouraged a single vantage point, so contradictory accounts of the evening circulated as the many simultaneous and unrelated actions assailed spectators independently with several registers of sonic, literary, dancerly, and visual events. Spectators were required to turn their heads and move their bodies to see the actions taking place in a panorama above and around them, and to follow competing strains of aural information and coincident movement. In this sense, they were asked to become participants: by registering experiences in their bodies other than ones cued by visual perception, and by Cage's increasing phenomenological demands that audience members engage the broader sensorium of their bodies with acoustic, tactile, and even olfactory events.

Through its emphasis on simultaneity, the piece ostensibly revealed the unmotivated, untidy flow of life that concentration stifles and conscious design suppresses. As Cunningham reflected on the night: "Life itself is all these separate things going on at the same time. And contemporary society is so extraordinarily complex that way. Not only things going on right around you, but there are all the things that you hear instantly over the television, that are going on someplace else . . . they're happening at the same time."[85] That life involves a surfeit of difficult sensory information was its peculiar, splendid anarchy, according to the logic Cage set out in *Theater Piece No. 1*. The simultaneity of events was the indelible and inescapable fact of the modern world, and Cage's happening created a situation that intensified its pandemonium (all the while still framing the effect of randomness by a rigorously delimited score that contained defined time brackets and specific instructions).

As Cage was incorporating ambient and overlapping noises in musical composition and performance, he was also redefining what a music score could be. In his "score" for *Theater Piece No. 1*, for example, traditional musical notations of staffs, bars, keys, and notes were replaced with telegraphic durational segments to be interpreted by the performer. An existing fragment given to one of the performers (likely to Robert Rauschenberg or Nicholas Cernovich) reads, in Cage's hand (fig. 2.17):

> Projector:
> Begin at 16 min.
> play freely until 23 min.
> Begin again at 24:30
> play freely until 35:45
> Begin at 38:20
> play freely until 44:25[86]

De-skilling musical language beyond its notation in bars, notes, keys, and measures guaranteed that every event could be simply performed and would produce unique and unpredictable results (although the exacting, time-based constraints on the performer's freedom could inversely be interpreted as fussy and overbearing, not liberating). Whereas the quantity and length of the score's

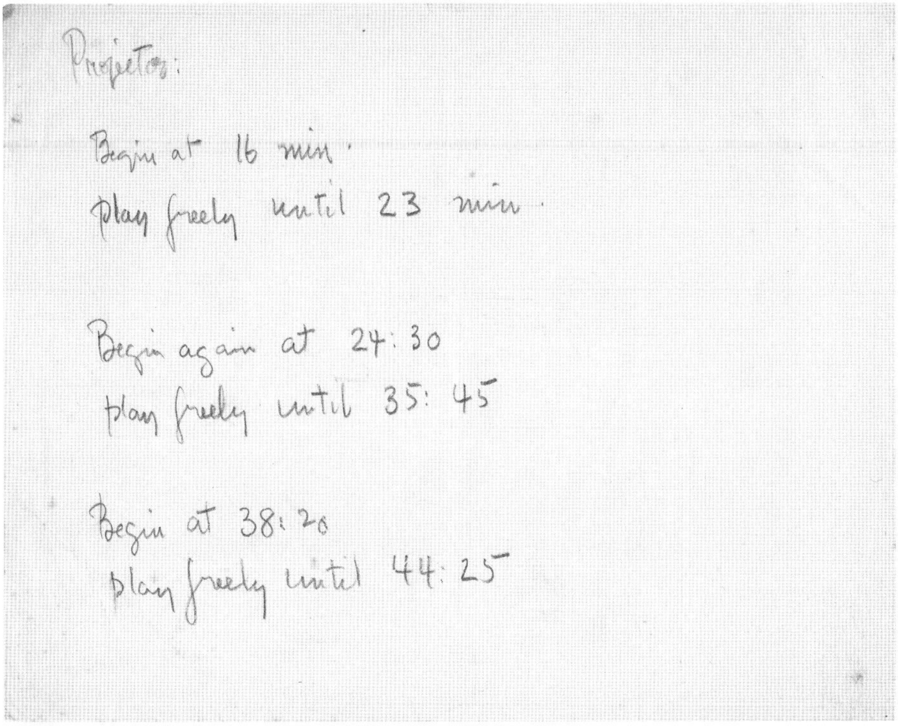
Projector:

Begin at 16 min.
play freely until 23 min.

Begin again at 24:30
play freely until 35:45

Begin at 38:20
play freely until 44:25

Figure 2.17
John Cage, Script for *Theater Piece No. 1*, 1952. 8½ × 11" paper. Music Division, The New York Public Library for the Performing Arts, Astor, Lenox and Tilden Foundations.

sections were generated by Cage's chance-derived use of the *I Ching*, the performers' interpretations of these instructional commands were ultimately unknown to him. The score, however, produced no reciprocal lack of mastery on the creator's part—it was not Cage's choices of which possibilities to put on the table, so to speak, that were chance derived, merely the questions about their specific details.

Because no photographic record or film footage of *Theater Piece No. 1* exists, to get a sense of its effect it is helpful to compare it to a surviving film recording of Cage's 1959 composition *Water Walk*, a work also based on timed segments, that he performed during a television appearance in 1960[87] (fig. 2.18). In *Water Walk* Cage is the sole performer, amid a field of some thirty-four items: domestic appliances and other household objects related to water or liquidity that are spread over various tables and the floor—a pressure cooker releasing steam, a rubber duck, a toy fish, an electric mixer, an ice cube tray filled with ice, a bottle of Campari, and a bathtub filled with water—as well as some objects related to music or timekeeping, including a piano, five radios, a Turkish cymbal, and

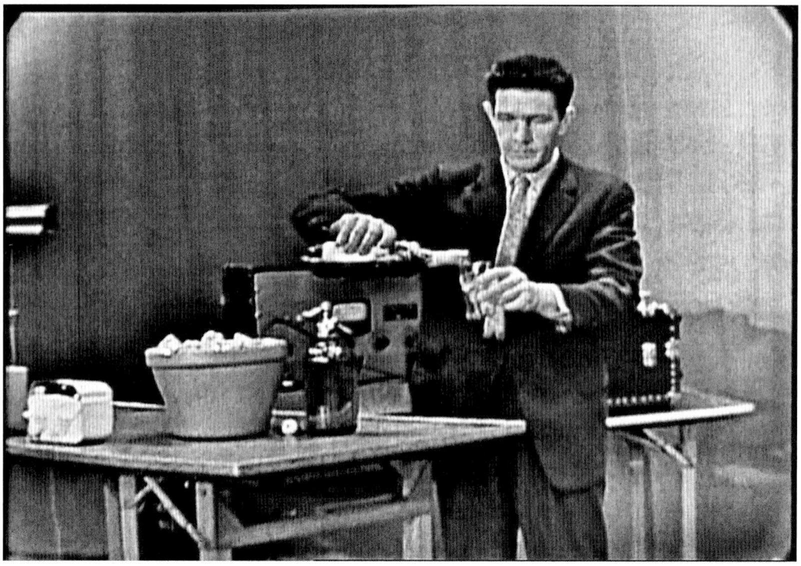

Figure 2.18
Still frame from performance of John Cage's *Water Walk* on *I've Got a Secret*, January 1960. Courtesy of FremantleMedia, North America.

a stopwatch. In the three minutes of *Water Walk*, Cage methodically moves among these objects: filling the blender with ice, slapping the radios, turning on the blender, squeaking the rubber duck, filling a glass with ice, pouring Campari, and later drinking from it, while periodically consulting his stopwatch. *Water Walk*'s first seconds begin with Cage slamming down the lid of the piano after putting the toy fish on its soundboard, and concludes with Cage knocking the radios to the ground, acts of physical and aural aggression that he manages to make appear calm and unemotional—premeditated—and even a bit slapstick-y.[88] The deliberation and calculation of the performance, despite its mild violence and cacophony, are surprising. During Cage's systematic movements through the space, he checks his watch like an athlete clocking pace. This element of precision is striking in many performances of Cage's works: the way the chance protocol—the fixed, clocked segments that produce seemingly aleatory results—lends a sense of dogged focus on time and duration to the performer's gestures (which can read as disinterestedness or obliviousness to audience members, an audience that may expect a virtuosic memorization of the score, as in "classical" music performances).

The score of *Water Walk* itself consists of a group of objects: a list of the "instruments"; a floor plan showing the placement of the props; three pages of a timeline (one minute for each page) with descriptions, pictographic diagrams, and notations of occurrence of events divided into five-second increments; and a list of notes "regarding some of the actions to be made in the order of occurrence" (fig. 2.19). Timings in the performed work are estimations: "Start watch and then time actions as closely as possible to their appearance in the score." *Water Walk* itself was therefore relatively fixed in its performance, but for the brisk yet unspecific tempo of the actions that were to be timed "as closely as possible."[89]

Water Walk's paper score relies on two earlier Cage works: *Water Music* (1952) and *Fontana Mix* (1958). Cage used the score of *Fontana Mix* (which, like many of his scores of the 1950s, employed the *I Ching* as a randomizing tool) to compose *Water Walk* and several other compositions; the former piece consists of ten transparencies containing various numbers of dots, ten sheets of paper with curved lines of various thicknesses, one transparency of a two-by-ten-inch grid, and another of a straight line. The *Fontana Mix* score was itself indeterminate (the performer was to superimpose the sheets to find "time units in which the event may take place").[90] According to Cage, the "graph units = any time units," thereby allowing the performance's duration and tempo to be conceived by the operator of the score. In its title and elements of pictorial scoring, *Water Walk* clearly resembles Cage's *Water Music*, which David Tudor premiered in May of 1952 at the New School for Social Research in New York before returning to Black Mountain—likely the work Tudor was playing during *Theater Piece*

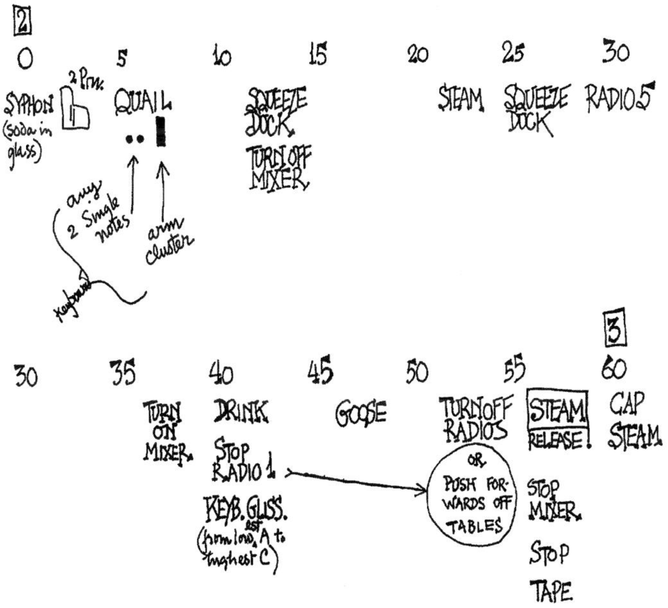

Figure 2.19
John Cage, Score for *Water Walk*, January 1959. Copyright © 1961 by Henmar Press, Inc. Used by permission of C. F. Peters Corporation. All rights reserved.

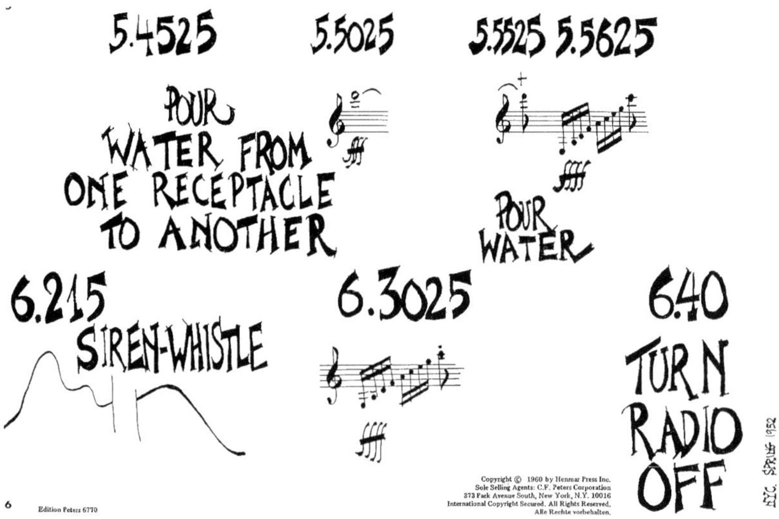

Figure 2.20
John Cage, Score for *Water Music*, May 1952. Copyright © 1960 by Henmar Press, Inc. Used by permission of C. F. Peters Corporation. All rights reserved.

No. 1.[91] Like *Water Walk*, the earlier *Water Music* emphasized the hybridity of the score as a visual document and aural experience. As Cage explained,

> *Water Music* wishes to be a piece of music, but to introduce visual elements in such a way that it can be experienced as theater. . . . I simply put into the chart things that would produce not only sounds but that would produce actions that were interesting to see.[92]

For example, in *Water Music*'s score, a descending tone of a steam whistle is depicted as a linear wave, and the instruction "Pour water from one receptacle to another" bears no musical notation whatsoever but is written in Cage's distinctive all-caps handwriting that is in essence a kind of calligraphic visual design (fig. 2.20).

In the sense that Cage described *Water Music* as introducing "visual elements" that could be "experienced as theater," one can begin to understand the chance protocol of *Theater Piece No. 1* as perhaps one part "chance" to several parts "protocol"—that the protocol's criterion of experimental innovation is a demand to "produce actions that were interesting to see." The staging of the Black Mountain College dining hall as a 360-degree panorama of competing aural and visual actions, often taking place simultaneously, was obviously not a random event; though the length of the time slots the performers were designated and the other questions Cage asked of the *I Ching* were subject to chance, they were organized by his framing of the questions. And if Cage's *Water Walk* television performance is any indication, it is likely that performers of *Theater Piece No. 1* utilized their time slots quite seriously, attempting, for example, to play the third projector segment for the *precise* six minutes and five seconds the score indicated—an officiousness distant from the reputation of "indeterminate" compositions as haphazard or non-intentioned.[93]

Similarly, in Cage's 1952 composition *4′33″*, created during his time at Black Mountain (though having percolated in his mind for several years), the piece's three time sections were chance-determined by use of the *I Ching* to be thirty-three seconds, two minutes and forty seconds, and one minute and twenty seconds apiece.[94] When Tudor first performed *4′33″*, he placed on the piano the several sheets of the handwritten score, which was notated conventionally on sheet music with blank measures (figs. 2.21, 2.22). Upon beginning each section, he closed the lid of the piano and, glancing at a stopwatch, turned the pages of the score as time passed. When each section ended, he opened the piano lid. Though the score indicates there should be no intentional sound on the performer's part, as with *Water Walk* a great deal of theatricalization surrounds actualizing the matrices of Cage's "non-matrixed" activity.

Cage's use of the *I Ching* was intertwined with his intensifying investigation of the revelatory possibilities of void-like events described in Zen Buddhist

Figures 2.21 and **2.22**
David Tudor's original version of John Cage's *4′33″*, pages 3 and 4, 1953. The John Cage Trust. Reproduced by permission of The Getty Research Institute, Los Angeles.

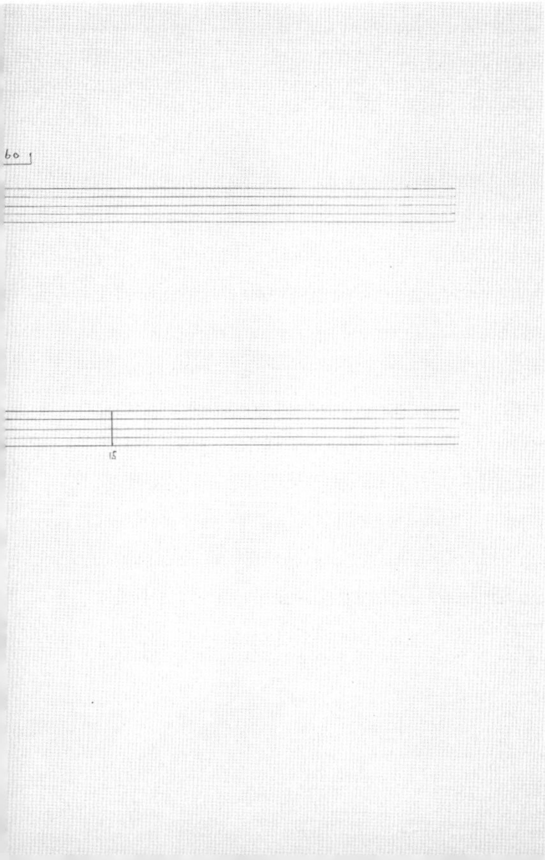

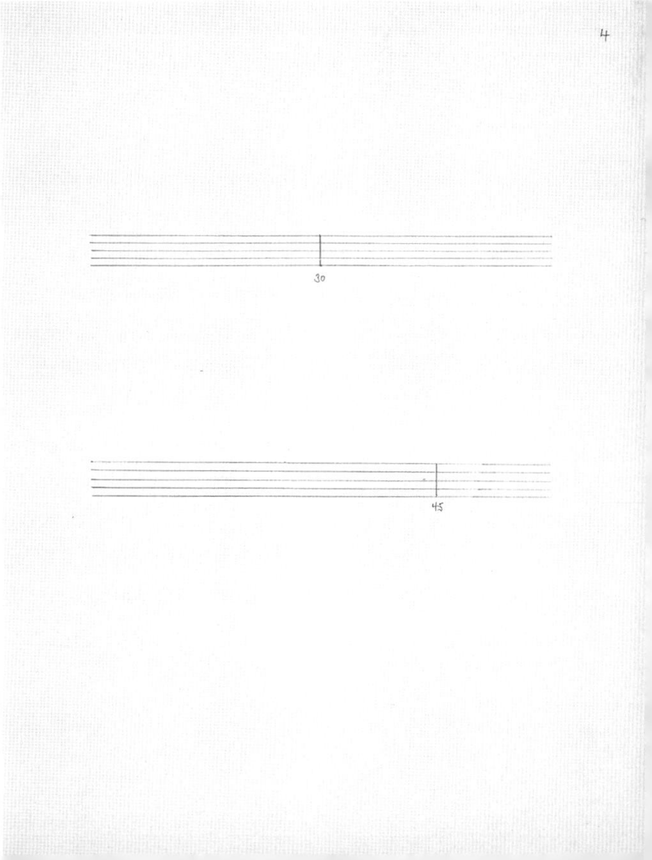

texts; he called these the "flow-through" of experiences that break down the ego's barrier.[95] Breaking down this barrier, for Cage, revealed the dominance of "no-mindedness," or non-intention, in the world, which could be accessed via an experience of the body as a vessel for sound.[96] This connection between sound and the "flow-through" of experiences followed his 1951 visit to an anechoic (an echoless, insulated, and therefore soundproof) chamber at Harvard University, during which his expectation of total acoustic withdrawal was overturned.[97] According to Cage, in the chamber he "heard two sounds, one high and one low. When I described them to the engineer in charge, he informed me that the high one was my nervous system in operation, the low one my blood in circulation."[98] Cage had gone to a place where he expected there to be no sound, and yet sound was nevertheless present and discernible. (He claimed that it was then that the composition of *4′33″* seemed possible; he realized that "until I die there will be sounds. And they will continue following my death. One need not fear about the future of music.")[99] Silence was in actuality a "walking concert" of the body; as Cage argued, "We call it 'silence' because it is free of *our* activity. It does not correspond to ideas of order or expressive feeling . . . [that] 'deafen' us to the sounds themselves."[100]

That the stimulation and plenitude of "no-mindedness" could be features of the ostensible void of an anechoic chamber Cage connected to ninth-century Buddhist sage Huang Po's *Doctrine of Universal Mind*.[101] In 1952, Cage began studying the text at Black Mountain, partly as a result of attending Daisetz Teitaro Suzuki's seminars on Buddhism in the mid-1940s, which Suzuki later taught at Columbia from 1952 to 1957 to great public acclaim.[102] Cage credited his investigation of Po's *Doctrine* as a central inspiration for the new directions his work at Black Mountain was taking, declaring,

> I had come through my study of Zen Buddhism with Suzuki to an appreciation of a particular text: I liked it more than the others connected with Zen Buddhism—it's called The Huang Po *Doctrine of Universal Mind*. So one evening at Black Mountain . . . we read the entire *Huang Po Doctrine* with all the notes and everything . . . after that experience . . . people told me their lives had changed.[103]

Po's text describes various paths to spiritual enlightenment, and advocates strategies of disengagement from action and withdrawal from the preoccupations of conscious thought. The doctrine of "no purpose" described therein suggests abandoning intentionality in order to avail the spirit to the true flux of experience. To Po, attaining enlightenment was an unpredictable and chancy process, though certain foundational steps could be undertaken in preparation. He advocated a form of non-attachment and quietism in which "you need study no doctrines whatever, but learn only how to avoid seeking for and attaching yourselves to anything."[104] Only when the mind and body were in a condition of harmonic balance, acting in concert with each other, could the "selflessness" of transcendence emerge. Po claimed that enlightenment may then arrive as an accident, as "a sudden self-realization" in a moment of utter dispassion.[105]

Cage was particularly impressed by Po's assurance that reducing the intentionality of conscious thought—what Po referred to as "conceptual thought"—laid a path to transcendence by way of bodily awareness. To Po, spiritual transcendence was possible for those who "would only eliminate all conceptual thought in a flash."[106] By rejecting the mind's demands toward reason, the spirit would recognize the transitory nature of material phenomena and physical stimuli; as Po asserted, "Every phenomenon that exists is a creation of thought; therefore I need but empty my mind to discover that all of them are void."[107]

Of special interest to Cage was Po's championing an empty, receptive mind—an emptiness or "void" alert to the greater flux and changeability of transitory events. The sense of the void as open possibility became the correlate to Cage's conception of an experiment as a protocol without predictable ends. As he explained,

> An *experimental* action, generated by a mind as empty as it was before it became one . . . does not move in terms of approximations and errors, as "informed" action by its nature must, for no mental images of what would happen were set up beforehand; it sees things directly as they are: impermanently involved in an infinite play of interpenetrations.[109]

Cage related the notion of the void as impermanence, as a play of unpredictable difference, to his study at Black Mountain of Antonin Artaud's work. Linking Po to Artaud, Cage saw similarities in their analyses of states of void-like instability in which the transcendence of routine and habit provided passage for unexpected events and flashes of inspiration. In this sense, *Theater Piece No. 1* was indelibly shaped by Black Mountain faculty member M. C. Richards's ongoing translation of Artaud's key texts, later compiled in the volume *The Theater and Its Double*, which called for forms of theatrical performance that were utterly immediate and therefore not reliant on scripting or literary interpretation.

Richards had been introduced to Artaud through her then partner Tudor's studies in contemporary French musical composers. In his attempt to puzzle through Pierre Boulez's 1948 *Second Piano Sonata* (confiding to Richards that though the sonata was complicated, he was actually "not having problems with the notes, but with the music"), Tudor had read Boulez's sources for the work: poet Stéphane Mallarmé and Artaud.[109] Richards, Tudor, and Cage discussed Artaud intensely at the College throughout the summer of 1952, and carefully studied chapters of *The Theatre and Its Double* as a companion to the *Doctrine*'s claims for the void-like elimination of intention.

Artaud's work, published first in France in 1938, collected essays and manifestos written throughout the previous two decades. It set forth a proposal for a "theater of cruelty" in which the effects of certain unpredictable actions onstage would shock viewers into a "new notion of space" when bombarded with many simultaneously occurring events.[110] This new perception of space was characterized by "overlapping images and movements" and the "collusion of objects, silences, shouts, and rhythms" which together perform an "extreme action" pushing the spectator's perception beyond its limits.[111] In breaking down the viewer's perceptual apparatus with overwhelming events, Artaud hoped to extend the effects of disorientation, "cruelty," and the difficulty of perception off the stage and into the world beyond theatrical performance. As he maintained, "There will be no unoccupied point in space, [and] there will be neither respite nor vacancy in the spectator's mind or sensibility. That is, between life and the theater there will be no distinct division, but instead a continuity."[112] It was an experience of shock in which the viewer's previous understandings of art—art as separated from life—would be overturned. These acts of disturbance returned art to the chaotic conditions of life veiled by traditional theater's codified techniques and habits of scripting, narrativity, and characterization. Those now moribund aspects of theater would thereafter be supplanted by events of the world outside theater, thus initiating a "new" art that looked remarkably like the flux, chaos, and cruelty of "external" life while prismatically allowing for a critical vision of that life. Rather than revolutionizing the observation of conditions of the world outside theater by setting up a counterpoint of illusory effects (or even altering those "external" conditions themselves), art for Artaud must collapse its pretensions to autonomy and separation into already existing "life" conditions, thus producing a radical, destructive, and shocking break in the minds and bodies of spectators accustomed to a theater of affectation and habit. In sum, only by destroying the separation between theater and life could an invigorated sense of theater *as* life catalyze viewers to become aware of their relationship with natural "life" forces.

To Cage, Artaud's description of a barrage of simultaneous events raised "the possibility of making a theatrical event in which the things that took place were not causally related to one another."[113] Interestingly, this is a claim Artaud himself never explicitly asserted. Cage, like Artaud, wanted to collapse the difference between theater and life, yet to Artaud the most radical feature of theater was its ability to compound visual and auditory effects in a dreamlike condensation of experience in which the spectator would lose a sense of the rules and conventions of the conscious mind. In viewing events as an endless accretion of disconnected moments, of different possible presents, Artaud felt the theater of cruelty mimicked the "internal world" of the spectator; the "true illusion" of theater was the manner in which it reflected the "truthful precipitates of dreams" (dreams which, after all, *do* have causal connections that represent the logic of the unconscious, however latent those connecting threads may be).[114]

In Cage's application of Artaud's theories of spectatorship to *Theater Piece No. 1*, theater would literally act on the audience, but not by the mediation of acting or plotting, or by employing the unifying field of vision that joined a costumed actor with the obviously constructed spaces surrounding him or her, as in Bauhaus theater. Instead, it would do so by an escape from the "rationalism" of premeditated, written theater performance. Artaud advocated a theater of "powerful feeling [that] produces in us the idea of the void . . . the real void of nature."[115] Effects of void-like states, what he claimed were the "deepest states of mind beyond thought," could be attained in a multisensory experience: it was "in the light of magic and sorcery that the *mise en scène* must be considered . . . as the burning projection of all the objective consequences of a gesture, word, sound, music, and their combinations."[116] Only then would the "sorcery" of theater spiral the spectator into the doubled world of his or her own unconscious.[117]

It is noteworthy that Oskar Schlemmer, Xanti Schawinsky, *and* Antonin Artaud invoked the notion of illusion as central to a new awareness and self-reflexivity they hoped to awaken in their audiences. Yet while Schlemmer saw the theater as a space of illusion, it was an illusion constructed through focused attention, not void-like states. In contrast to his and other Bauhaus figures' rational examinations of spaces, transacted in the controlled environment of the theater, to Artaud the immediacy of the present allowed spectators particular purchase on "void" experiences; any attempts to translate or express the void through the temporally "dissembling" process of scripting (in which thoughts, ideas, and intentions from the past hijacked the free expression of "feelings and passions" in the present) corrupted the truth of immediacy.[118] The chaos of the many simultaneous events onstage would induce experiences of shock in the audience, and for this reason Artaud insistently opposed the preeminence of dialogue in theater; as he stated in *The Theater and Its Double*, "Our purely verbal theater [is] unaware of everything that makes theater, of everything that exists in the air of the stage, which is measured and circumscribed by that air and has a density in space—movements, shapes, colors, vibrations, attitudes, screams."[119] This of course echoes Schlemmer's call for a theater exploring spatial arrangements in the context of bodily movement. Yet in contrast to the deliberate and ordered experimentation in Schlemmer's work (he often referred to his practice as "research experiment"), Artaud stressed the mutability and contingency of the theatrical space, stating that "the theater is the only place in the world where a gesture, once made, can never be made the same way twice."[120] In place of the Bauhaus idea of bodies oriented through calculated geometries of space, Artaud proposed a "total spectacle" in which "an intensive mobilization of objects, gestures, and signs" provided "sudden shocks to revive our understanding."[121] These shocks could be accomplished through immediacy and accident: theater should be as violent as "natural forces" that are subject to "interventions of chance."[122]

Cage adapted Artaud's sense of extrahuman "natural forces" as accidental and arbitrary; theater was a means to succumb to the greater chaos of those unintended, uncontrollable consequences. Such forces appear cruel or "tyrannous," in Cage's understanding of Artaud, only because attempts by human agents to organize and control them create friction between people and their environments. For Cage, the rational pseudo-order of the mind was to be abolished in favor of the real order of chance. He often invoked earlier Dadaist employments of chance to supplement his employment of Artaud's arguments. Marcel Duchamp's work in particular was a touchstone for Cage's notion of experimentation as the acceptance of accident and the elimination of conscious interference—those features of Cage's turn to chance that had so offended Albers. Cage advocated reconsidering Duchamp's uses of chance not only as a means to compose, but also as a tool to attain random or indeterminate results in experimental acts, boldly declaring, "One way to write music: study Duchamp."[123] In particular, he credited Duchamp with opening up a space of expanded, nonjudgmental awareness: his bottle racks and bicycle wheels underscored the dialogical experience of the art object, its recognition as art based on a community of understanding rather than any innate quality of the work. To Duchamp, the unsubjective or "casual" selection of a readymade was key; the work should be as randomly chosen and therefore as affectless as possible. As he wrote,

> It is necessary to arrive at selecting an object with the idea of not being impressed by this object on the basis of enjoyment of any order. However, it is difficult to select an object that absolutely does not interest you, not only on the day on which you select it, and which does not have any chance of becoming attractive or beautiful and which is neither pleasant to look at nor particularly ugly.[124]

To Duchamp, an artist's nominative act—the declaration itself regardless of the object—was itself the art. He could choose anything indifferent to, or even in spite of, its aesthetic merits. Thus began a conceptual leap of faith that continued to define the condition of art's intelligibility for Cage. Coupled with the disinterestedness of the selection of readymade, Duchamp's approach to chance also employed a paradox of intentional non-intention in its experimental method.

One would think that Duchamp's 1913 musical score *Erratum Musique* (which can be translated as "musical misprint"), in which twenty-five notes from F below middle C to high F were drawn from a hat by Duchamp and his two sisters, would have been pivotal to Cage. Yet Cage stated of the work, "I wouldn't be satisfied with that kind of chance operation in my work. . . . I enjoy details and like things to be more complicated."[125] Instead, of central importance was Duchamp's piece *3 Standard Stoppages* of 1913–14, in which he dropped a one-meter length of string three times and recorded the resulting forms (Cage apparently attempted to replicate the work)[126] (plate 13). In creating templates of the three trials, Duchamp transformed the "standard" of measure into an indexical reflection of a seemingly arbitrary event. Describing this as "canned chance," he underscored how the organizational protocol of the "experiment" resulted in repeatable, quantifiable, and measurable events, though each "finding" was ultimately unpredictable. As philosopher Ian Hacking has written, such a protocol can be said to use "chance devices to introduce a new level of control into experimentation. Control not by getting rid of chance fluxuations, but by adding some more."[127] Like a statistical study in which randomization and stochastic variation are harnessed to eliminate bias, Duchamp's "canned chance," in a most contradictory fashion, allowed each event's specificity to emerge by minimizing the subjective element in "human error."

The aleatory elements that Duchamp incorporated in the creation of *3 Standard Stoppages* stressed what he called the "chain of totally subjective reactions" the artist undergoes in planning and realizing a creative act.[128] The results of a chance operation, however, emphasized how chance in fact *minimized* the subjectivity of the artist:

> "Theory"
> 10 words found by opening the dictionary at random by A
> 10 words found by opening the dictionary at random by B
> These 2 sets of 10 words have the same difference of "personality" as if the 10 words had been written by A and B with an intention. Or else, it matters little, there would be cases where this "personality" may disappear in A and B. That is the best case and most difficult.[129]

To Duchamp, subjective "personality" could be effaced if chance events were not random at all—if arbitrary selections could somehow be made repeatable among a large-enough sample of chance events. The use of chance creates unique and diverse experiences that the human mind cannot predict, yet the mind is so varied and complex that after a few deliberative selections of words, a subjective and seemingly irrational range of possibilities and associations emerge that can be as difficult to causally explain as a chance event. Even samples generated by choice or intention produce seemingly chancy differences; to Duchamp, the ideal scenario—"the best case"—resulted when these two situations, randomness and intention, became coincident and when no distinction could be perceived between chance and design. Such a de-differentiation could null all forms of intention, though that remained only the "most difficult" and remote scenario.

Chance processes, to Duchamp, were paradoxically determinate in their composition (the control exerted by the creator in setting up the event), while producing indeterminate outcomes: "Your chance is different than mine."[130] Yet "canned chance"—the way in which chance generates results only as different as two different subjectivities—inserts elements of indeterminacy and randomness to create a wider range of possible outcomes, not capricious results.[131] Duchamp employed chance to refute habit and bias; he understood it as a practice with predictable operations though indeterminate results—in other words, as a chance protocol. No process of manipulating results, delineating beginnings and endings, or structuring propositions for chance activities wholly eliminates intentionality; chance protocols, as executed in Dada and later by Cage, do not reject motivated action. In fact, chance processes exemplify types of technique and control that are highly motivated and aspire to eliminate the emotional biases of both individuals and systems. As critic Ian Pepper has noted, Cage's "aesthetics of indifference" was in actuality a "'discipline' governed by the liquidation of intention, habit, and agency."[132] Indeed, Cage later rephrased his "questions not choices" formulation thusly: "Most people who believe that I'm interested in chance don't realize that I use chance as a discipline. They think I use it—I don't know—as a way of giving up making choices."[133] Chance in composition was a project predicated on assumptions that it produced new understandings of order. Chance is *always* laden with intention. In his years at and post-Black Mountain College, defining just *whose* intention reigned became the ground for mounting critiques of Cage's notion of the experimental act.

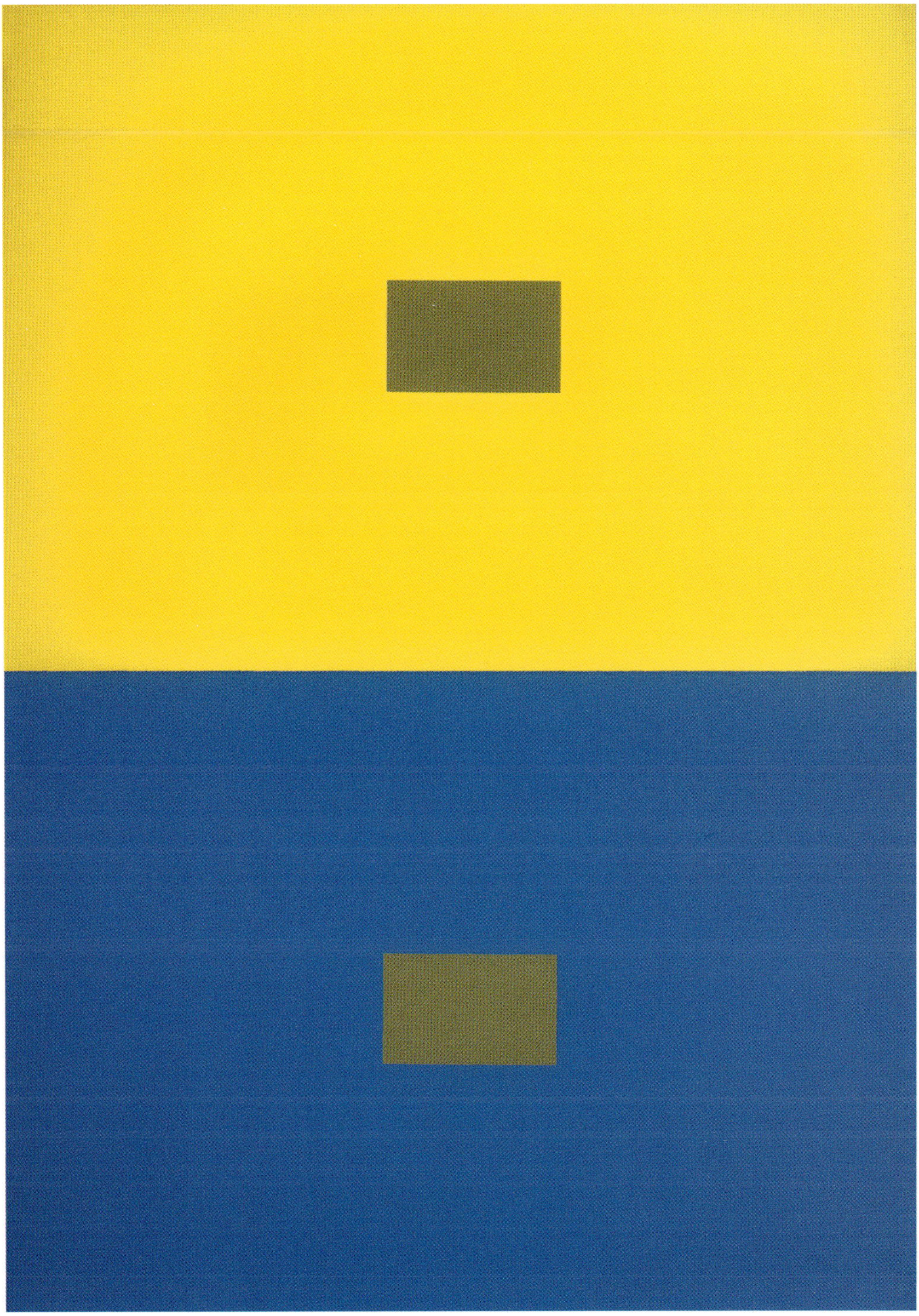

Plate 1
Color Study IV-3. From Josef Albers, *Interaction of Color* (New Haven, CT: Yale University Press, 1963/1971).

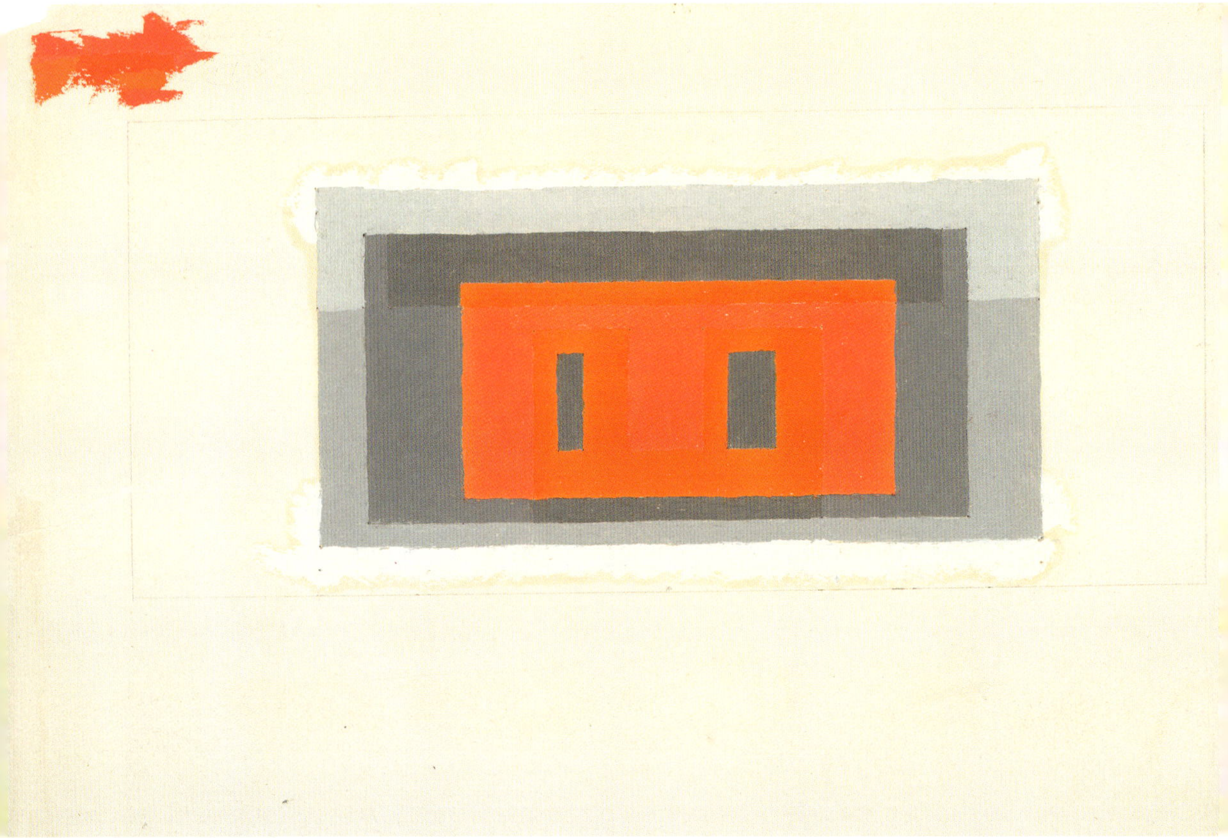

Plate 2
Josef Albers, template for a *Variant* study, n.d. 12 × 19".
Photograph by Tim Nighswander © The Josef and Anni Albers Foundation / Artists Rights Society, New York.

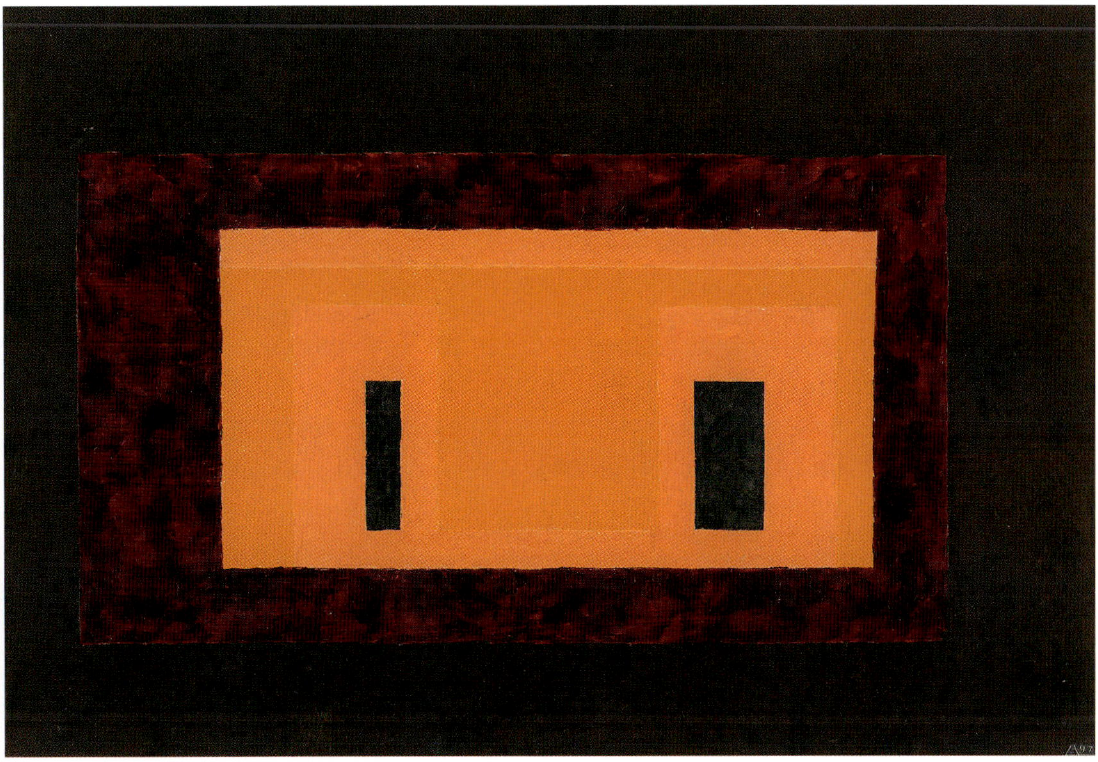

Plate 3
Josef Albers, *Variant*, 1947. Oil on Masonite, 12 × 18″. Photograph by Tim Nighswander © The Josef and Anni Albers Foundation / Artists Rights Society, New York.

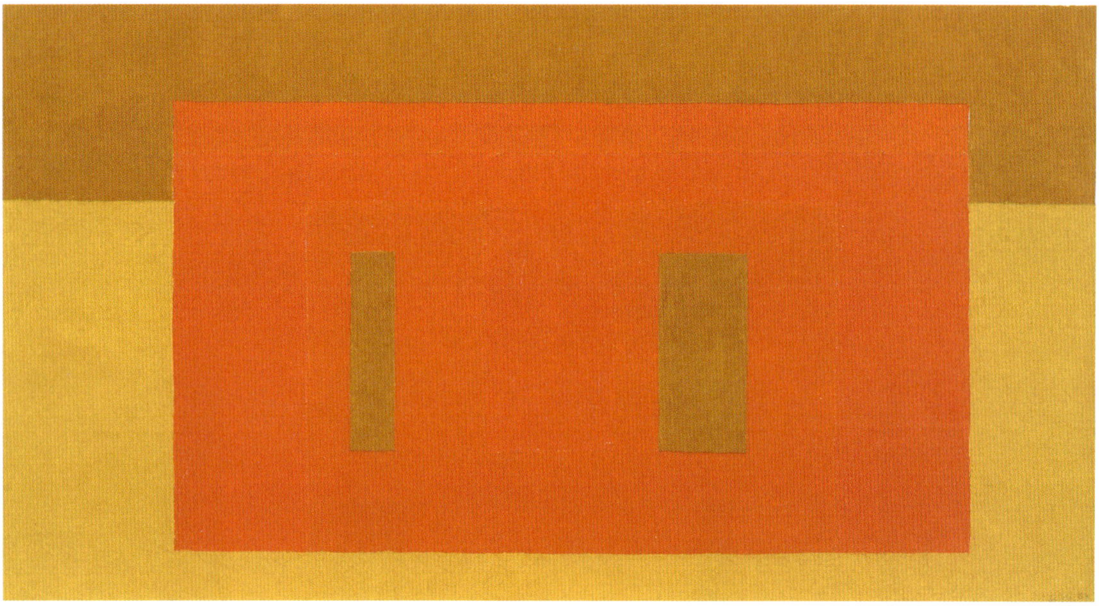

Plate 4
Josef Albers, *Variant: Southern Climate*, 1948–53. Oil on Masonite, 12¼ × 22½". Photograph by Tim Nighswander © The Josef and Anni Albers Foundation / Artists Rights Society, New York.

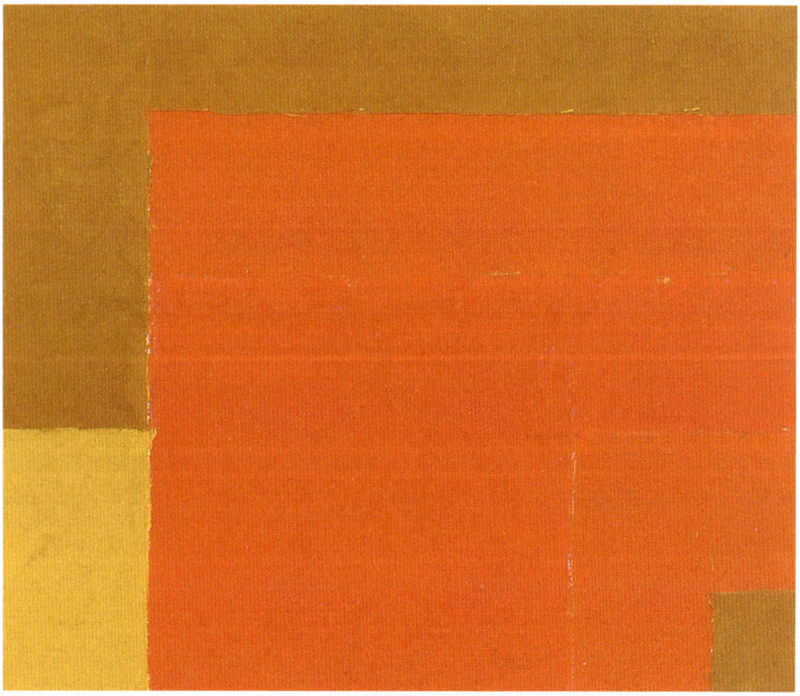

Plate 5
Josef Albers, *Variant: Southern Climate*, 1948–53, detail. Photograph by Eva Díaz © The Josef and Anni Albers Foundation / Artists Rights Society, New York.

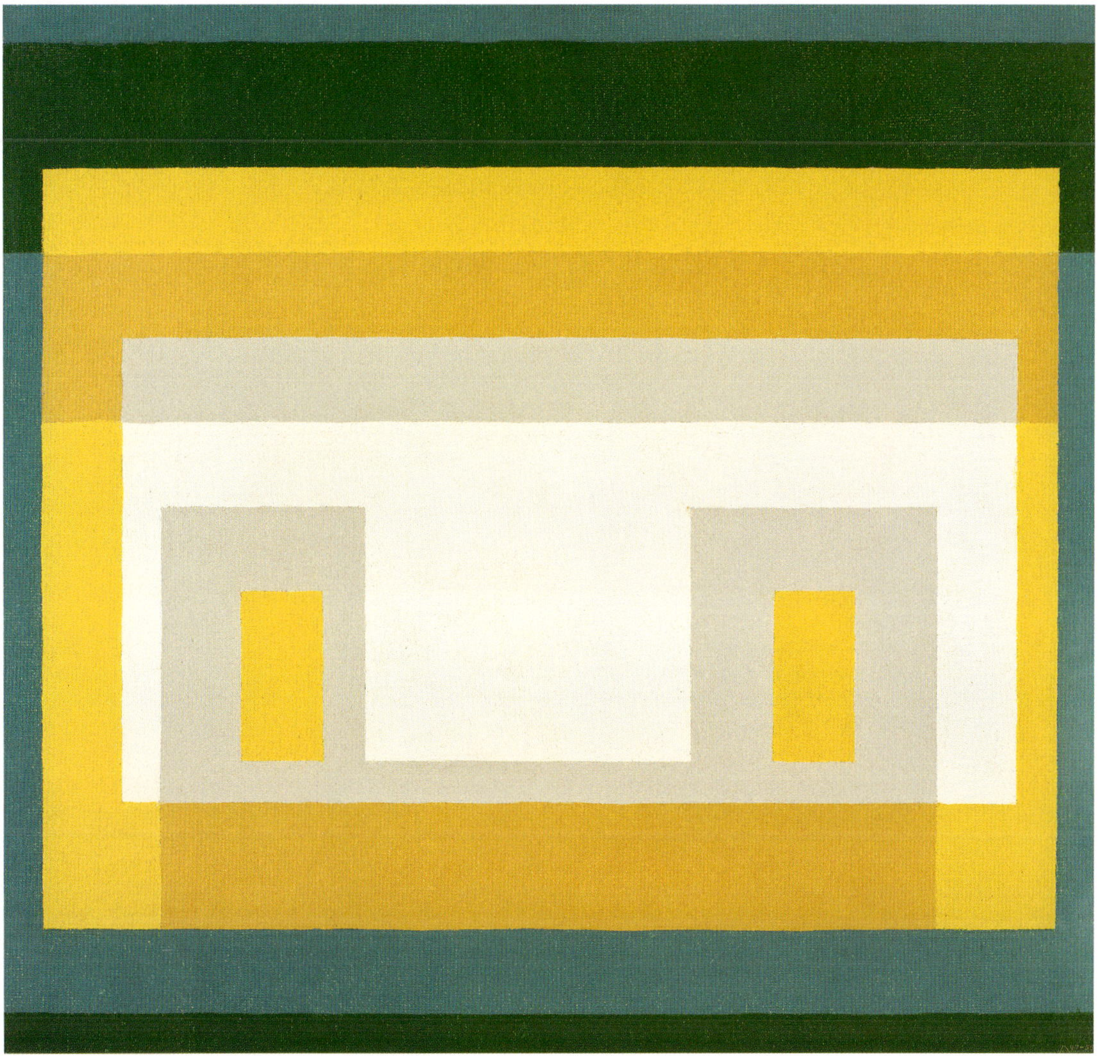

Plate 6
Josef Albers, *Variant*, 1947–55. Oil on Masonite, 26 × 28¼".
Photograph by Tim Nighswander © The Josef and Anni
Albers Foundation / Artists Rights Society, New York.

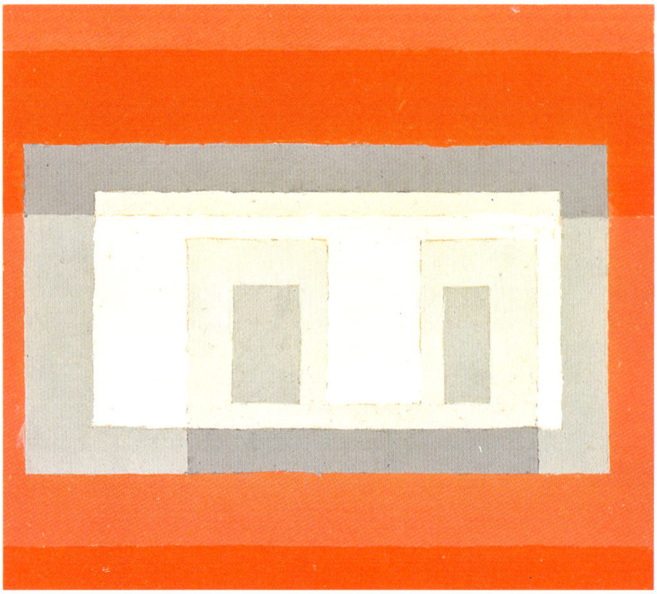

Plate 7
Josef Albers, *Study for a Variant (III), C*, 1947. Pencil and oil on paper, 9⅟₁₆ × 11⅞". Photograph by Tim Nighswander © The Josef and Anni Albers Foundation / Artists Rights Society, New York.

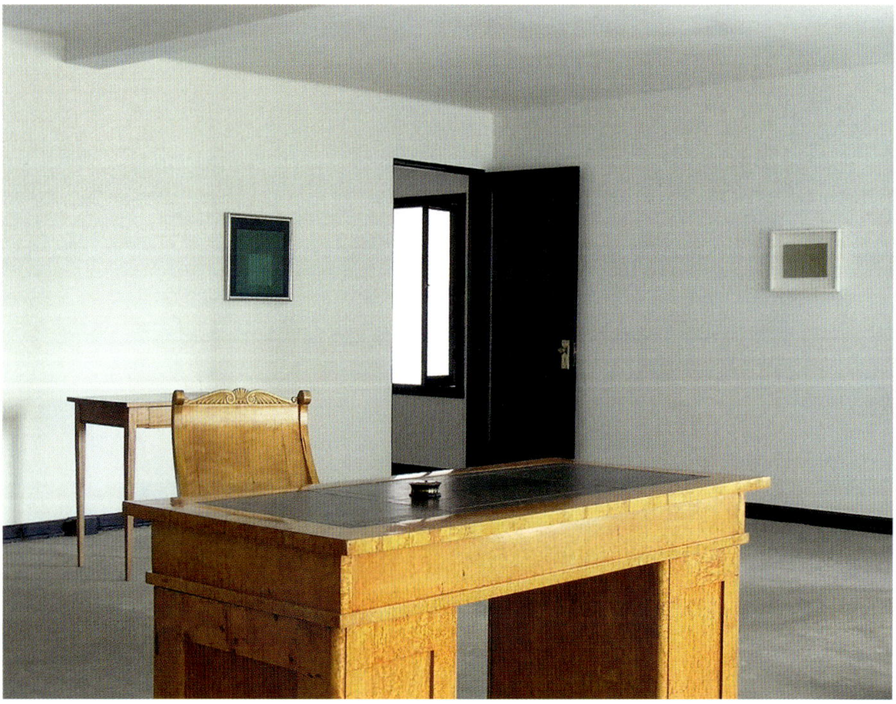

Plate 8
Josef Albers, *Homage to the Square*, 1958. Oil on Masonite, 18 × 18". Photograph © Judd Foundation. Courtesy Judd Foundation Archive.

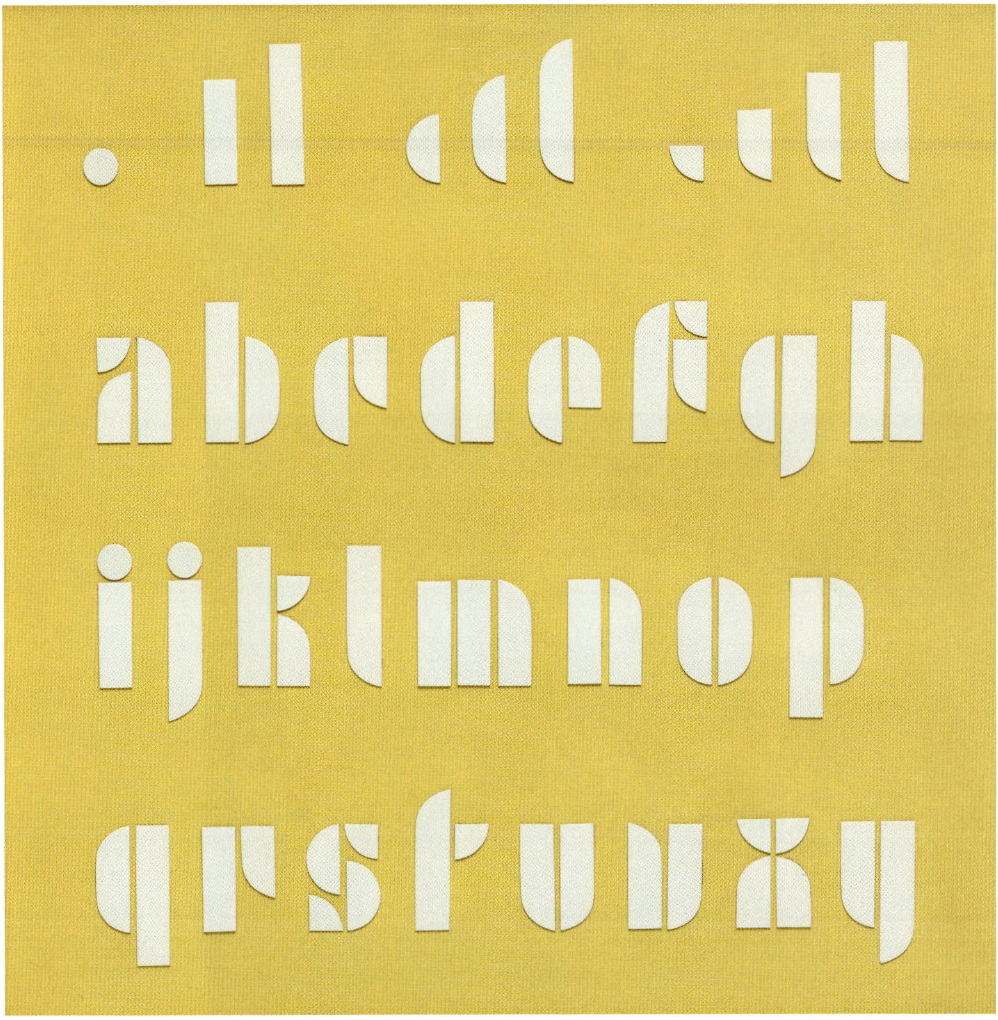

Plate 9

Josef Albers, *Lettering Set*, 1926–31. Milk glass on painted wood. The Josef and Anni Albers Foundation / Artists Rights Society, New York. Digital Image © The Museum of Modern Art/Licensed by SCALA / Art Resource, NY.

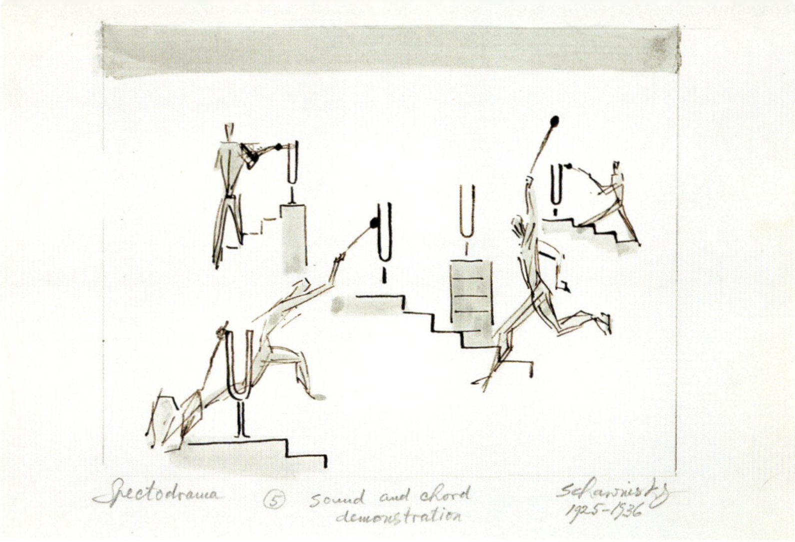

Plate 10
Xanti Schawinsky, *Sound and Chord Demonstration, Spectodrama Sketch #5*, 1936–37. The Xanti Schawinsky Estate.

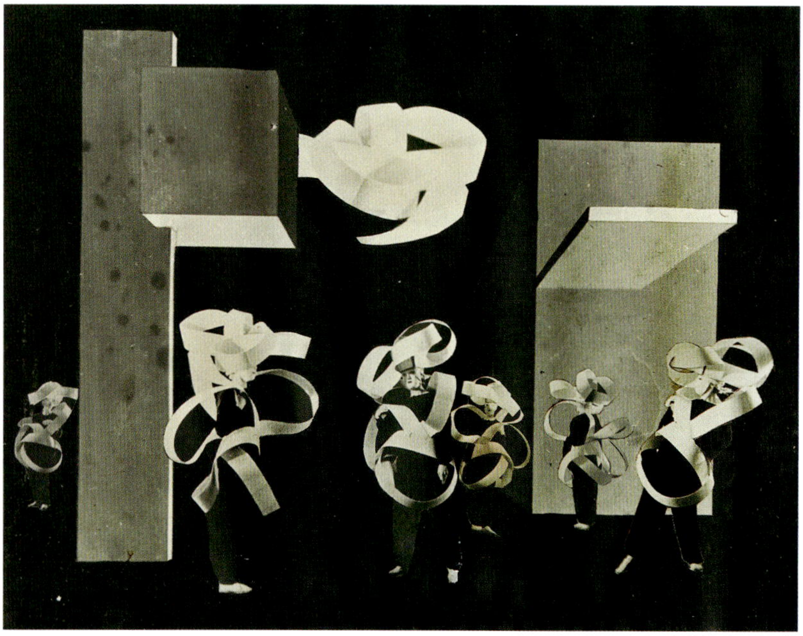

Plate 11
Xanti Schawinsky, *Spectodrama 8: Building (Tensional)*, 1936–37. Photocollage on paper, 16 × 21.1". The Xanti Schawinsky Estate.

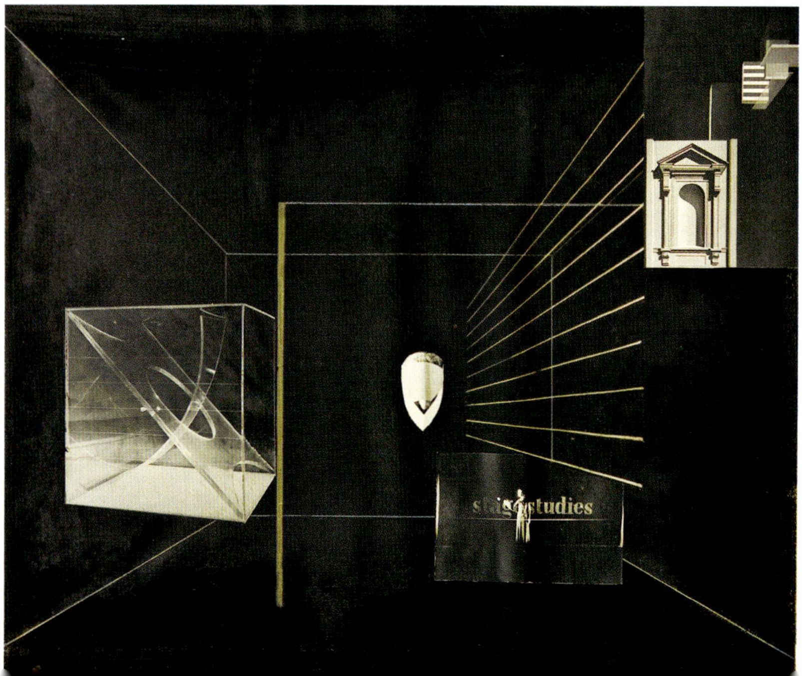

Plate 12
Xanti Schawinsky, *Spectodrama 5: Form and Language*, 1936–37. Photocollage and pen on paper, 16.6 × 20.4". The Xanti Schawinsky Estate.

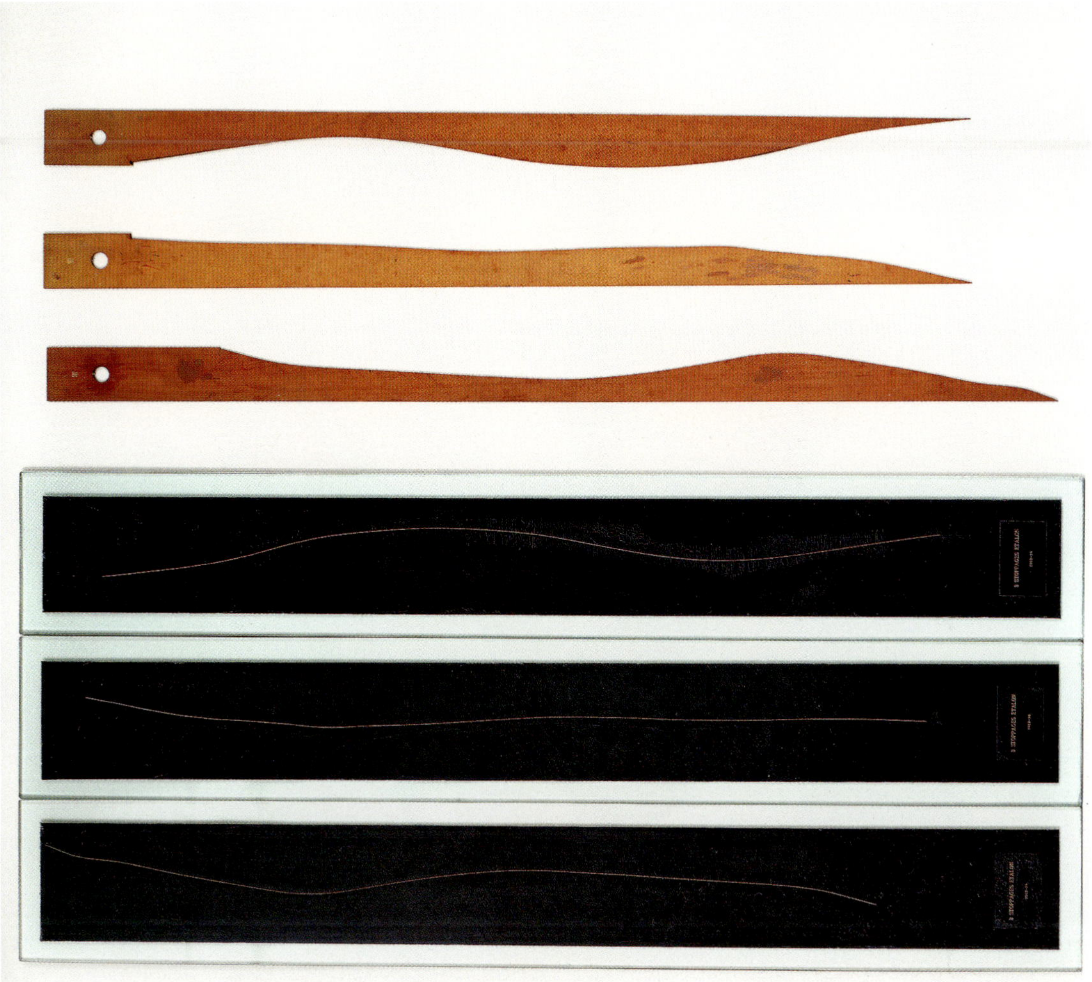

Plate 13
Marcel Duchamp, *3 Standard Stoppages*. Paris, 1913–14. Wood box 11⅛ × 50⅞ × 9", with three threads 39⅜", glued to three painted canvas strips 5¼ × 47¼", each mounted on a glass panel 7¼ × 49⅜ × ¼", three wood slats 2½ × 43 × ⅛", shaped along one edge to match the curves of the threads. © 2012 Artists Rights Society New York / ADAGP, Paris / Succession Marcel Duchamp. Digital Image © The Museum of Modern Art/Licensed by SCALA / Art Resource, NY.

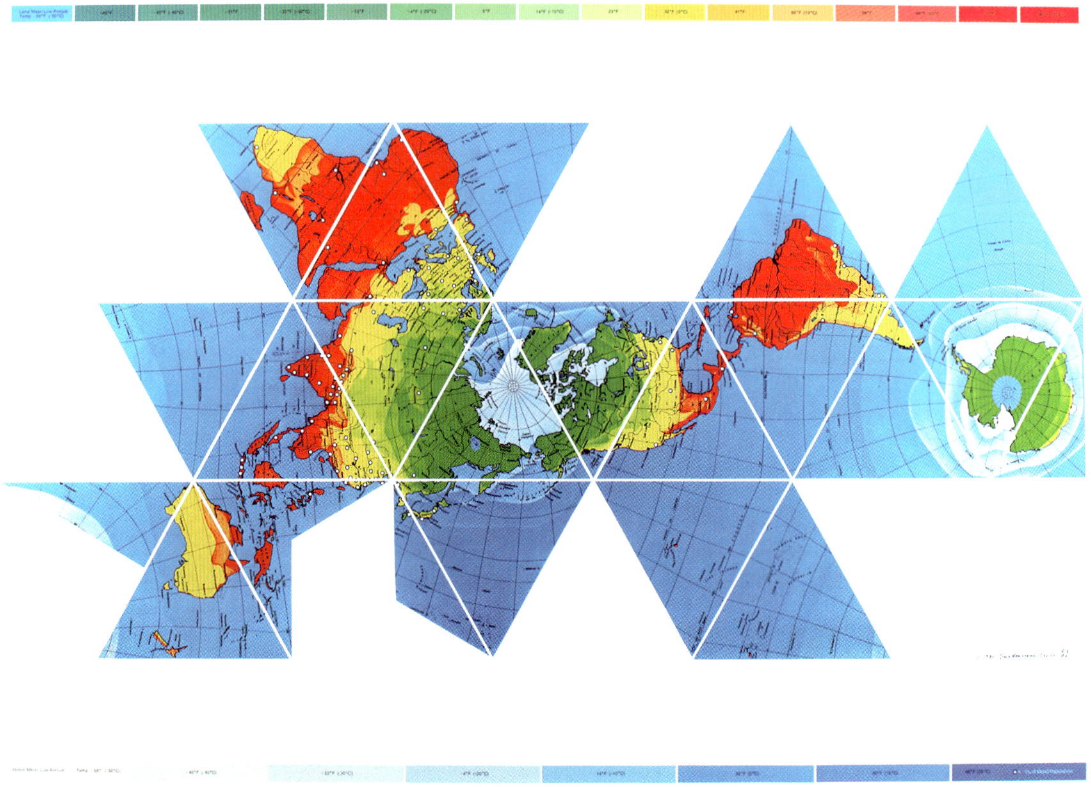

Plate 14
Buckminster Fuller, *Dymaxion Air-Ocean World Map*, 1954/1981. 29-color silkscreen on Arches 100% rag paper, 50 × 72". Edition of 85. Courtesy Carl Solway Gallery, Cincinnati, Ohio.

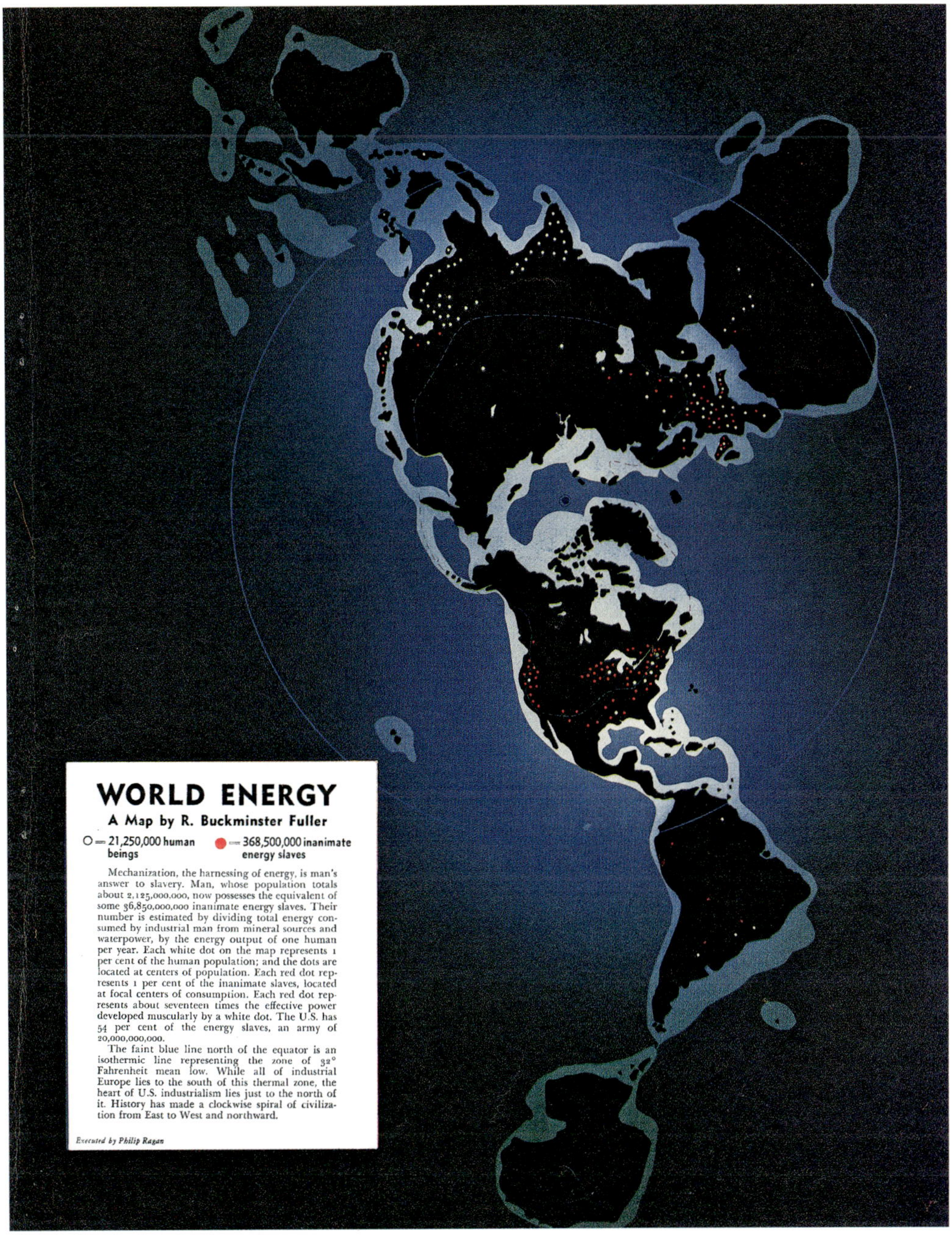

Plate 15

Buckminster Fuller, *World Energy*. First published in *Fortune*, February 1940. Courtesy The Estate of R. Buckminster Fuller.

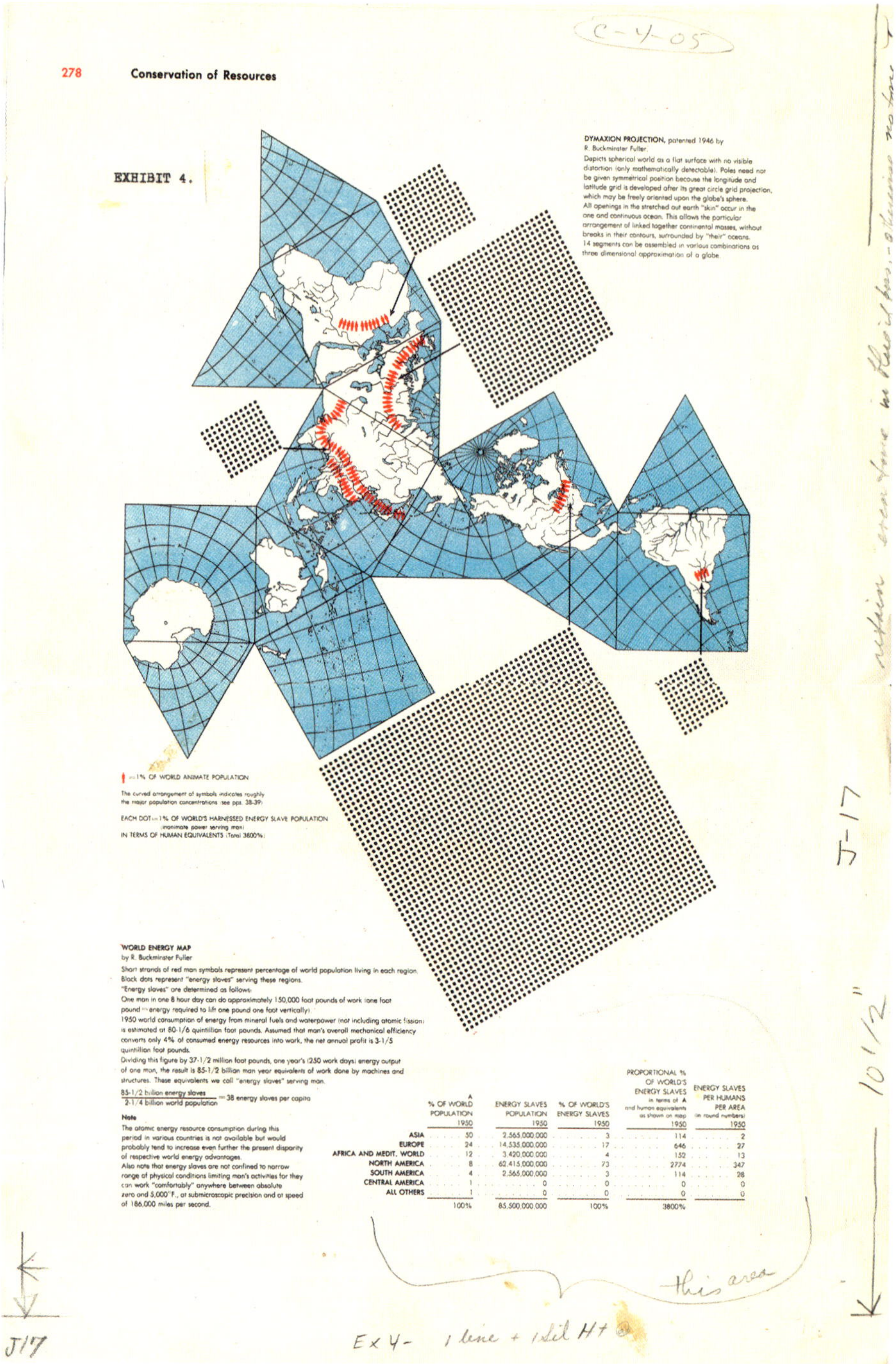

278 Conservation of Resources

EXHIBIT 4.

DYMAXION PROJECTION, patented 1946 by R. Buckminster Fuller.

Depicts spherical world as a flat surface with no visible distortion (only mathematically detectable). Poles need not be given symmetrical position because the longitude and latitude grid is developed after its great circle grid projection, which may be freely oriented upon the globe's sphere.
All openings in the stretched out earth "skin" occur in the one and continuous ocean. This allows the particular arrangement of linked together continental masses, without breaks in their contours, surrounded by "their" oceans.
14 segments can be assembled in various combinations as three dimensional approximation of a globe.

= 1% OF WORLD ANIMATE POPULATION

The curved arrangement of symbols indicates roughly the major population concentrations (see pps. 38-39)

EACH DOT = 1% OF WORLD'S HARNESSED ENERGY SLAVE POPULATION (inanimate power serving man) IN TERMS OF HUMAN EQUIVALENTS (Total 3800%)

WORLD ENERGY MAP
by R. Buckminster Fuller

Short strands of red man symbols represent percentage of world population living in each region.
Black dots represent "energy slaves" serving these regions.
"Energy slaves" are determined as follows:
One man in one 8 hour day can do approximately 150,000 foot pounds of work (one foot pound = energy required to lift one pound one foot vertically).
1950 world consumption of energy from mineral fuels and waterpower (not including atomic fission) is estimated at 80-1/6 quintillion foot pounds. Assumed that man's overall mechanical efficiency converts only 4% of consumed energy resources into work, the net annual profit is 3-1/5 quintillion foot pounds.
Dividing this figure by 37-1/2 million foot pounds, one year's (250 work days) energy output of one man, the result is 85-1/2 billion man year equivalents of work done by machines and structures. These equivalents we call "energy slaves" serving man.

$$\frac{\text{85-1/2 billion energy slaves}}{\text{2-1/4 billion world population}} = \text{38 energy slaves per capita}$$

Note
The atomic energy resource consumption during this period in various countries is not available but would probably tend to increase even further the present disparity of respective world energy advantages.
Also note that energy slaves are not confined to narrow range of physical conditions limiting man's activities for they can work "comfortably" anywhere between absolute zero and 5,000°F., at submicroscopic precision and at speed of 186,000 miles per second.

	A % OF WORLD POPULATION 1950	ENERGY SLAVES POPULATION 1950	% OF WORLD'S ENERGY SLAVES 1950	PROPORTIONAL % OF WORLD'S ENERGY SLAVES in terms of A and human equivalents as shown on map 1950	ENERGY SLAVES PER HUMANS PER AREA (in round numbers) 1950
ASIA	50	2,565,000,000	3	114	2
EUROPE	24	14,535,000,000	17	646	27
AFRICA AND MEDIT. WORLD	12	3,420,000,000	4	152	13
NORTH AMERICA	8	62,415,000,000	73	2774	347
SOUTH AMERICA	4	2,565,000,000	3	114	28
CENTRAL AMERICA	1	0	0	0	0
ALL OTHERS	1	0	0	0	0
	100%	85,500,000,000	100%	3800%	

Plate 16
Buckminster Fuller, *World Energy Map*, 1953. Published in Herbert Bayer's *World Geo-Graphic Atlas*. Courtesy The Estate of R. Buckminster Fuller.

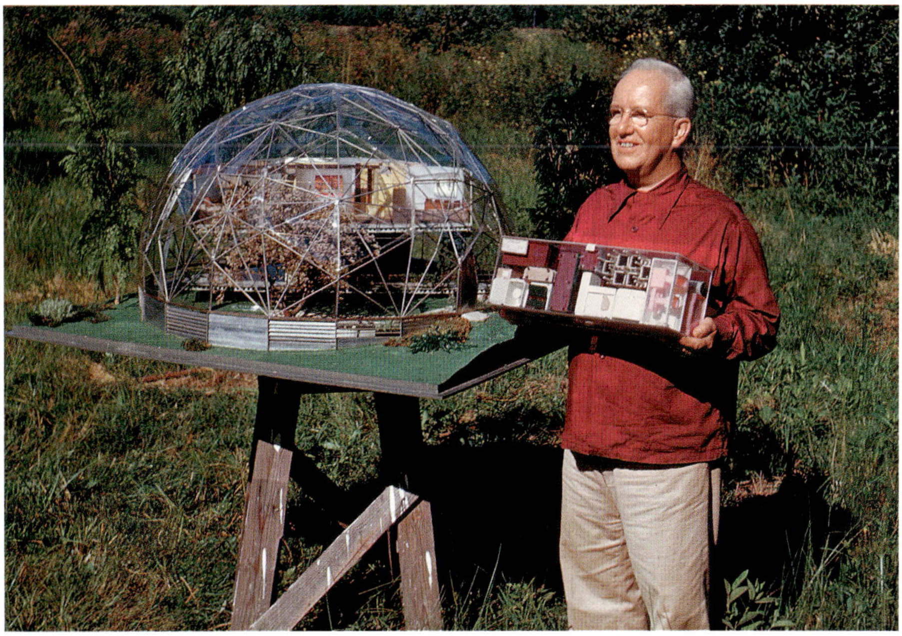

Plate 17
Buckminster Fuller holding model of *Autonomous Dwelling Machine*, 1947, next to model of same, assembled and housed inside geodesic dome, ca. 1950s. Courtesy The Estate of R. Buckminster Fuller.

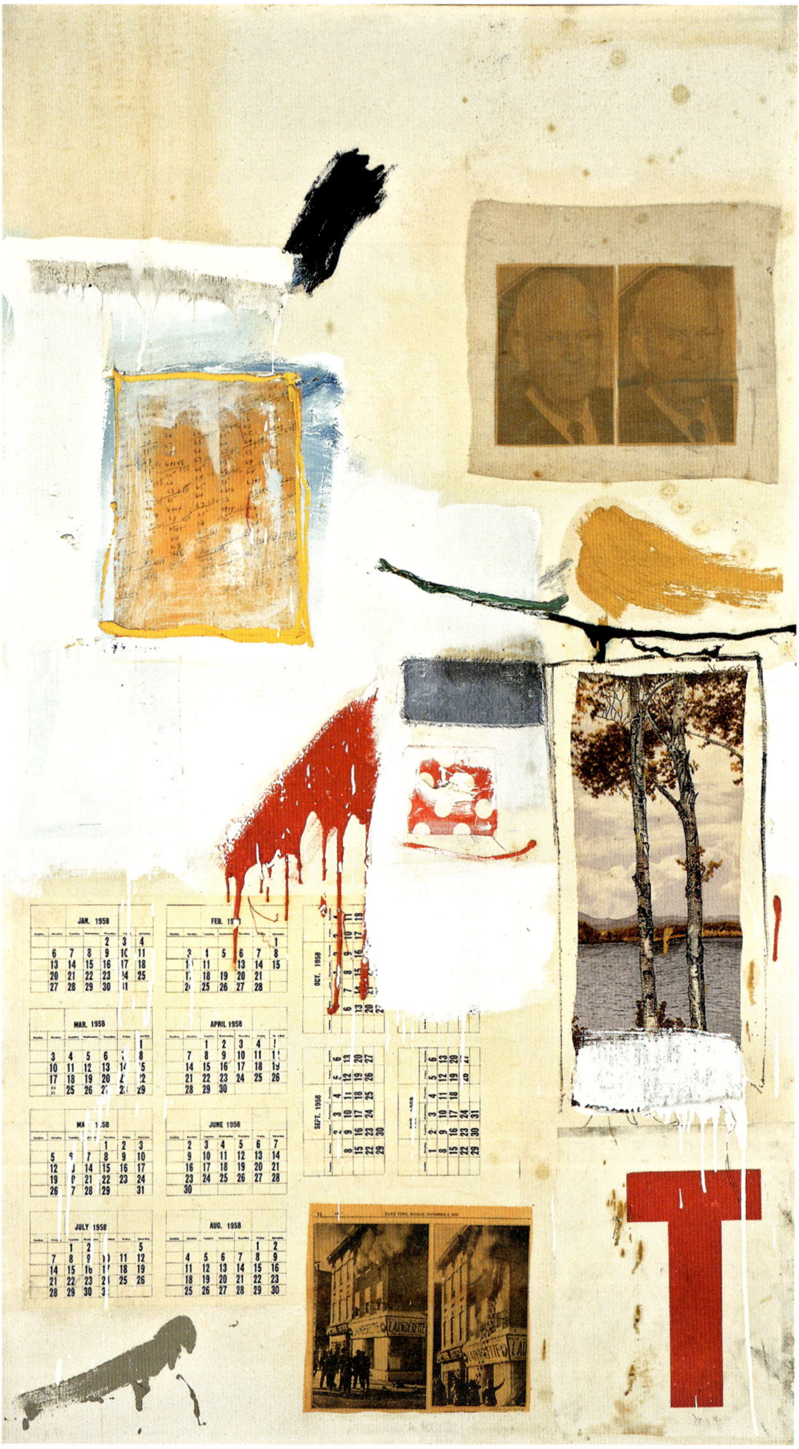

Plates 18, 19

Robert Rauschenberg, *Factum I* and *Factum II*, 1957. Both: Oil, ink, pencil, crayon, paper, fabric, newspaper, printed reproductions, and painted paper on canvas, 61⅜ × 35½" each. © Robert Rauschenberg Foundation/Licensed by VAGA, New York, NY.

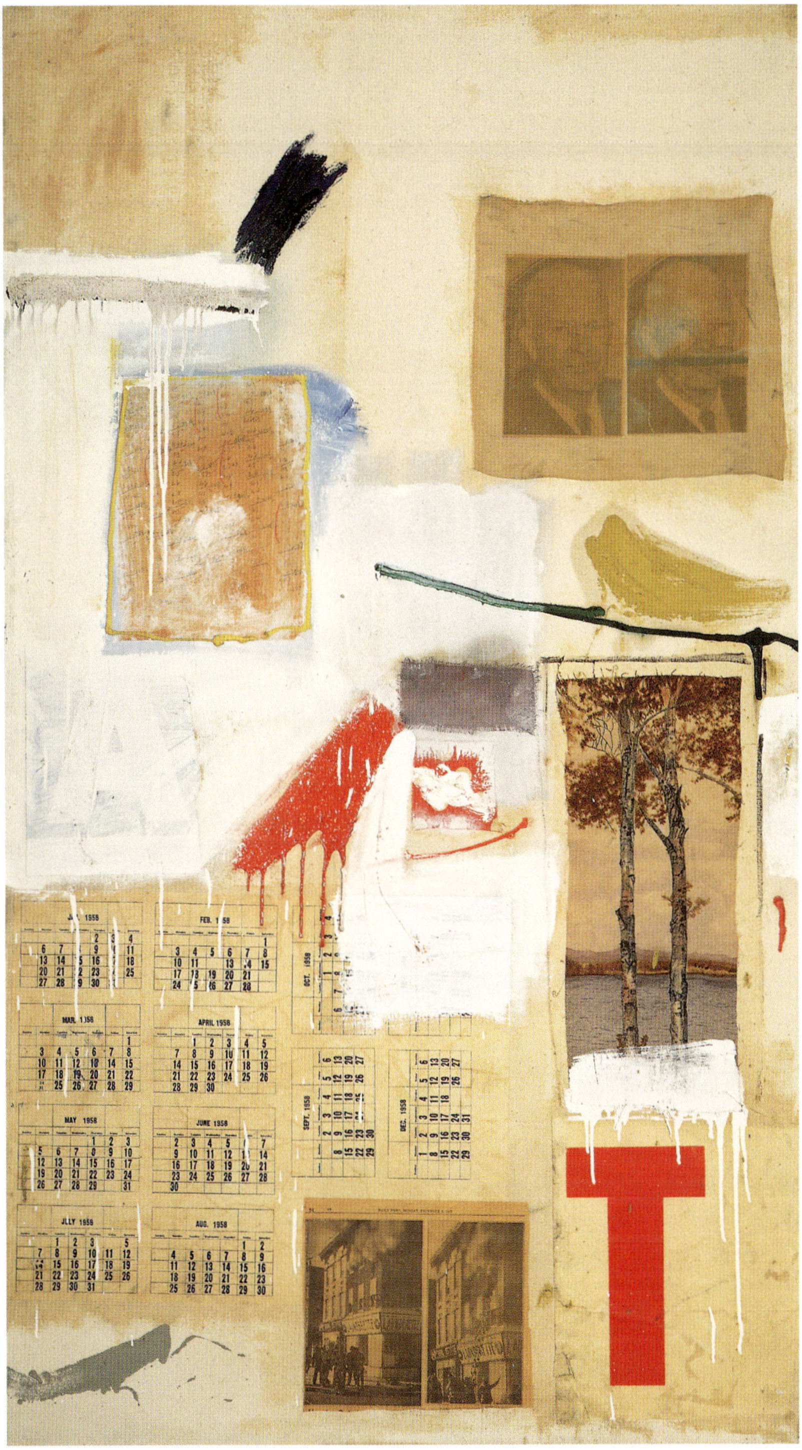
FEB. 1958
MAR. 1958
APRIL 1958
MAY 1958
JUNE 1958
JLLY 1958
AUG. 1958
OCT. 1958
SEPT. 1958
DEC. 1958
T

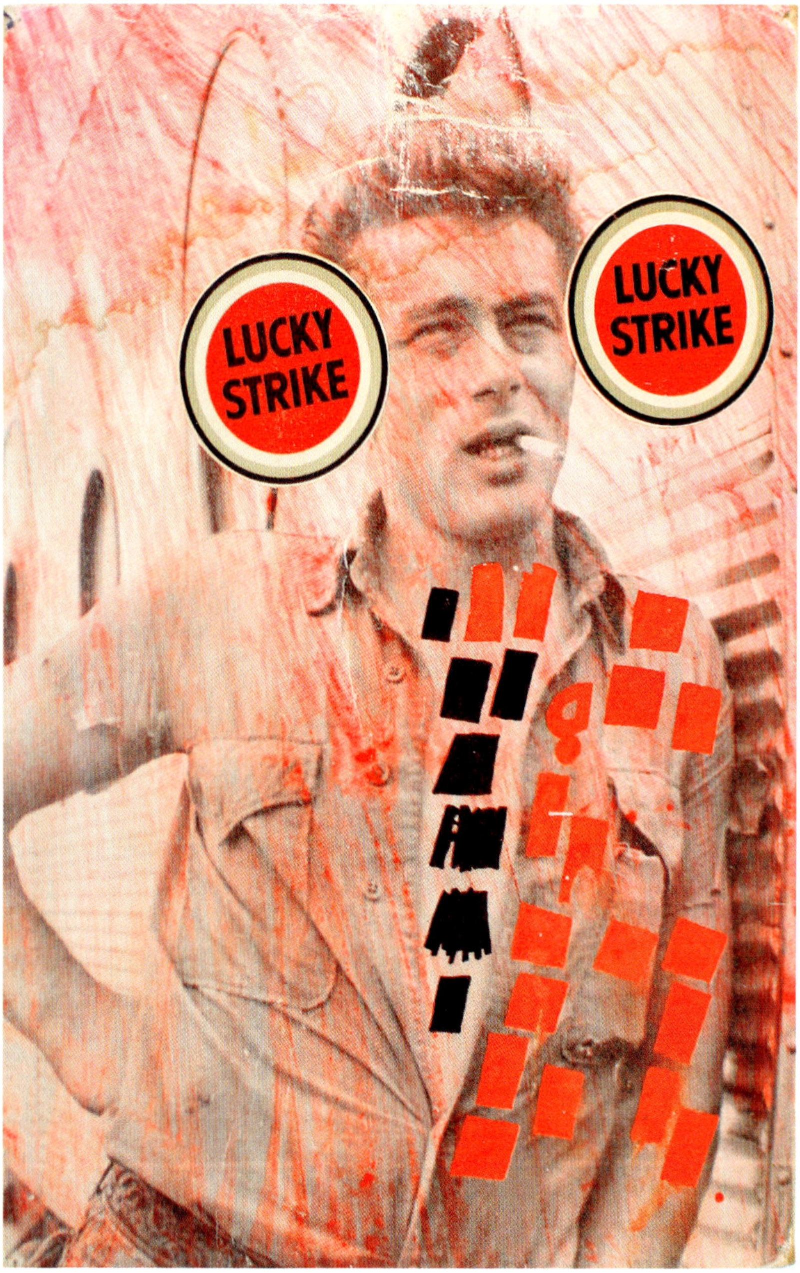

Plate 20

Ray Johnson, *James Dean (Lucky Strike)*, 1957. Ink, collage, and paper on cardboard, 18 × 15.375". © Ray Johnson Estate. Courtesy Richard L. Feigen & Co.

One way to understand the chance-protocol experiment is as a proposition that produces indeterminate results that must be accepted rather than judged—not as the production of material evidence to be evaluated, as Albers had argued. Cage's model of experimentation minimized purposeful communication between artist and audience, positing such exchanges as the obsolete habit of imposing predictable regularity on both the audience's interpretive freedom and on the underlying, fundamentally unknowable organization of nature. In these proposals of chance and indeterminacy, Cage argued that a new dimension of perception could be revealed outside human faculties of organization, assessment, and intention: "Not an attempt to bring order out of chaos nor to suggest improvements in creation, but simply a way of waking up to the very life we're living, which is so excellent once one gets one's mind and one's desires out of its way and lets it act of its own accord."[134]

In Cage's turn to a chance-protocol version of experimentation, his work received degrees of public exposure and notoriety that eclipsed nearly all other practices at Black Mountain College. In contrast to Albers's largely unpublished writings, Cage's discussions about his influences, and his commentaries on the development of procedures he was terming "experimental" as early as his first public talks in 1937 at age twenty-five, were widely published. By 1961, they were compiled in *Silence*, his influential collection of essays and lectures.[135] Cage's methodology of experimentation underwent many transformations in his long life, but what is pertinent to a study of him at Black Mountain—why he is such a vital case study of experimentation there—is the way he used his relatively brief time at the College to test rapidly maturing ideas about prolonging the creative *process* of experimentation in order to generate unpredictable compositions, and extending this new process to a work's *reception* in performance situations of unfixed outcome.

Moreover, in contrast to Albers's long association with the College as a teacher *and* artist, Cage's own work in this vein overshadowed his pedagogical strategies, which at least during his Black Mountain years were quite underdeveloped. When, for example, he found students unwilling to enroll in his summer 1952 class at the College, the stated goal of which was to apprentice helpers to do the tedious work of cutting and splicing bits of magnetic tape for his composition *Williams Mix*, Cage canceled all formal teaching for the term. His tenure at the College is most closely associated with his key performance events, and the way he formulated arguments about them into a new and persuasive experimental model that only *later* became the basis of an influential pedagogy (in his Experimental Composition classes at the New School for Social Research and elsewhere).

Ultimately, Cage attributed his split with Albers to the issue of chance as ratifying a new and uniquely American, as opposed to European, hence traditional, aesthetic; he declared that he "was more interested in a mediocre thing that is being made now, which is avant-garde, than . . . in the performance of a great masterpiece of the past."[136] In this he distanced himself from existing European (that is, German) artistic, musical, and theatrical currents at the College; yet as we have seen, he did this by linking his work with Far Eastern, particularly Chinese, as well as French models. In repudiating the dominant German harmonic tradition of Beethoven through Schoenberg, Cage supplanted that canon with overlooked French composers such as Satie, Claude Debussy, and Edgard Varèse (as he bemoaned, "No Germans take French music seriously").[137] In contrast to the German precedents reverberating in the work of Albers and other émigrés at the College, he abandoned their attentive examination of the structure and serial organization of form, though he continued to pursue their familiarly modernist goal of changing audiences' relationships to established patterns of perception. In this, Cage's model of experimentation paradoxically attempted to script, or rather to score, what he perceived as the eternal and underlying randomness of life rarely apparent in the rules and discipline of art and other cultural systems of order.

Cage sought greater indeterminacy so as to prove the fundamental uselessness of forms of human intervention in the order of nature. He saw his work as promoting the "disappearance of power politics" as part of a new, holistic "total system" existing outside human determination.[138] Freewheeling riskiness—the underlying order of the world as he perceived it—was too often impeded by the imposition of false order (political, artistic, or otherwise). One should, in Cage's words, "experiment endlessly" to unfix determinations of all sorts and rid the world of all manner of social and artistic habits, including the habit to think about the world as susceptible to change.[139] In this last respect, the title of Cage's essay from which the previous quotes are drawn is quite telling: "Diary: How to Improve the World (You Will Only Make Matters Worse)."

Threaded with his study of Duchamp, Antonin Artaud, and Zen precedents, Cage framed his experiments with chance and indeterminacy at Black Mountain as an expansion of performance toward the incorporation of simultaneously occurring and happenstance events.[140] In this, he linked his ideas to Robert Rauschenberg's works. Rauschenberg was in 1951 exploring the ultimate "anti-art" provocation, the monochromatic canvas, and his varied and prolific output during his years at Black Mountain included his so-called *Black Paintings*, in which he layered dirt and paint over newsprint, and his entirely *White Paintings*, shown during *Theater Piece No. 1*. These works tested the boundaries of an image's legibility by exploring the limits of minimal denotation, and flirted with the possibility of void-like emptiness. Cage referred to the *White Paintings* series as "airports for lights, shadows and particles," and attributed to Rauschenberg a passivity against composition and order that he himself advocated[141] (fig. 2.3). Cage claimed that in the *White Paintings* "there is the same acceptance of what happens and no tendency towards gesture or arrangement."[142]

Cage was intrigued with how the white canvases seemed to enhance the experience of typically overlooked events—the way, for example, the paintings amplified shadows, or how their color and appearance varied according to light conditions. Cage credited Rauschenberg with opening up a space of apparent emptiness and revealing it to be in fact full of diverse activity and experience. Indeed, during *Theater Piece No. 1*, if we are to believe some accounts, Rauschenberg's works oscillated between acting as paintings and operating as screens for slides or films—deployed as scenography within a theatrical situation rather than functioning as singular artworks.

In part, Cage attributed his 1952 composition of *4′33″* to Rauschenberg's challenge of empty openness. The score's "silence" was in actuality full of "sound"—the coughs, fidgets, and whispers of the audience, in addition to any other ambient noises. Cage argued that just as there was no emptiness in the *White Paintings*, there was also no silence in life. He felt that the "unfocused attention" of the paintings, like the voids advocated by Po and Artaud, was an attack against the separation of thought and experience, intention and immediacy, and in particular, art and life.[143] As Cage proclaimed, "Art's obscured the difference between art and life. . . . Where there's a history of organization (art), introduce disorder."[144]

As historian Branden Joseph has noted, Cage equated "intentional action" with a defense of the category of art, a schema that posited disorder as the underlying process of life, and chance as a "purer perception of reality."[146] Awakening the mind to the infinite and ultimately unknowable indeterminacy of nature was the objective, if such an interest in revealing the workings of nature can be said to have a goal at all. Herein lies the paradox at the center of Cage's chance protocol, a paradox of which he was well aware: he exerted control in fostering situations of greater indeterminacy because he believed that the world was fundamentally contingent and its possibilities indeterminate. As Cage proclaimed, "It's what you might call a 'music of contingency,' which means that you're necessary but not in control."[146]

It can be argued, however, that though indeterminate outcomes permit the appearance of freedom, they may in fact mistake the nature of the order they seek to sidestep. In a 1981 text that apostatizes the Cagean methods she had been associated with in early 1960s Judson Dance Theater, artist Yvonne Rainer contended that chance strategies were deployed "to equalize and suppress hierarchical differentiations of meaning."[147] In trying to reshuffle predictable outcomes without creating intentional alternatives, Cage's posture of dispassionate quiescence attempted to stifle the desire to influence at all—a stance that is remarkably amenable to a meek acceptance of the status quo. Challenging Cage, Rainer argued, "To have no desire—for 'improvements on creation'—is necessarily co-equal to having no quarrel with God-given manifestations of reality." For Rainer, Cage ultimately ignored that "we are surrounded by manifestations of reality that are not God-given but all fucked up by human society and that must be contested and reordered."[148] Attempting to transcend conditions of determination in the interest of greater contingency, Cage's chance protocol may serve to rationalize the chance operator's "questions" as though it were a whole new experience of a world without control that is being offered. In this space of relativism, judgments concerning interpretation are withheld, and an implicit trust is placed in "all answers answer[ing] all questions," as Cage claimed.[149]

Though *Theater Piece No. 1* made the space of performance beyond the stage a part of the "event" in a more aggressive way, such a move may, on the one hand, imply making audience members into participants. Or, on the other, it can indicate that spectators are mere props to the action. As historian Judith Rodenbeck has pointed out, the word "happening . . . also implies a kind of passivity—'it is happening to me'; in this respect it implies, too, an interesting desubjectification: the presence at an event of an objectified person."[150] The instructional logic of Cage's *Theater Piece No. 1* stimulated many future artists, particularly his students in his Experimental Composition classes at the New School, but has been criticized for the manner in which happenings' directives could sometimes only be narrowly interpreted.[151] Does one actually *participate* in the "non-matrixed" or nonarranged activity Cage described if, as in the case of *Theater Piece No. 1*, one follows a time-notated script or watches someone doing so? Or does one merely passively follow instructions (as a performer), or submissively let the many simultaneous events flow over oneself (as a spectator)?

The connection of the experimental chance protocol to arguments about spectatorial empowerment in this analysis should indicate how working "experimentally" offers models to test and to organize new forms of collective agency. For Cage, indeterminacy in musical composition mirrored his idea of a fundamentally uncontrollable and anarchical world. Conversely, in attempting to break down the intentions and order of society to emulate the chaotic character of nature, he was perhaps trying to fix a target that's always moving. The attempt by avant-gardists to conceive of a rigid social order, to set points of opposition and fixed codes to transgress (reason, order, intention, and so on), may misrecognize the intractable problem of the symbolic order: that it's always changing, and sometimes with a perverted rationality. Perhaps Cage set up order as a straw man, as a foil for his negations, thereby mistaking the at best distorted forms of rationality that characterize modernity's instrumental reason. Or was he exposing the contingency of practices and discourses—aesthetic, social, political, or other—that are otherwise pledged to convention, continuity, and order?

Cage perceived nature as accidental and arbitrary, and saw experimentation as a window onto the greater chaos of those unintended, uncontrollable consequences. The rational control of the mind was to cede to the real order of chance; Cage's chance-protocol experimental procedure harnessed conditions of indeterminacy as though chanciness were the order of nature. Chance is deployed, paradoxically and somewhat aporically, as a way to mimic the unintelligible (dis)order of nature. But, as Duchamp's "canned chance" questioned: Is nature *that* disordered; is it not also characterized by pattern, repetition, structure, and design?

If Cage sought to collapse the distinction between art and life, such a project could only be accomplished by dissolving art into what he perceived as the greater chaos of life. As he declared, "Let life obscure the difference between life and art."[152] Yet the question can and should be posed: What really *is* the benefit of the sensory overload that Cage evoked in the dissolve of art into life? As his chance-derived phenomenological overload aimed to unfocus attention and broaden the boundaries of perception, to many it may ever more closely resemble entertainment, diversion, and a subject immersed in a wash of confounding effects that to many is the experience of "life" in late-capitalist modernity.

In Cage's chance protocol, he fostered situations of greater indeterminacy because he believed that acts in the world should be detached, as much as possible, from fixed or predetermined outcomes. Similar to what philosopher Louis Althusser, in a series of late essays reexamining aleatory events, once described as a "unity of a conjuncture" in which many planned and unplanned events coalesce into unpredictable, immediately experienced presentness, Cage's chance protocol intended to unfocus viewers' attentiveness and diffuse their concentration in a field of simultaneously occurring events, thereby disrupting preconceived understandings of the role of causality in maintaining social and other orders.[153]

Although it is important, as Althusser writes, to "think the openness of the world to the event, [to] the as-yet-unimaginable," it may not be possible to prize Cage's chance protocol from the quietism about the openness of the world to chance with which his work is sometimes associated.[154] This is a "Zen" quietism with which Albers, Rainer, and many others have long struggled. In exploring greater contingency, perhaps Cage can be seen as working in Althusser's space of the conjectural, a space of experimentation, openness to the other, and openness to the unknown. That is to say, though the order of the world is fraught with radical instability, there is the *fact* of order. But that order is provisional, and only from a medley of various contingent possibilities comes the necessity of any one particular order.

Although both the Bauhaus tradition and Cage's French- and Chinese-inspired turn at Black Mountain willfully subordinated subjective expression, Cage instituted an experimental process based on the investigation of arbitrary structures and the exploration of extrarational experiences. In contrast, the model of theatrical experimentation proposed by the Bauhaus—with its techniques of reappraising the conditions of spatial perception, its attention to the organization of forms and their relations to one another, its careful investigation of the visual effects of bodily movement, and its charge to spectators that the rigor of attention in theatrical situations could bring a similar focus to circumstances outside a performance—was superseded by the one he put forward. Between these disparate models exist a range of performance strategies, the legacies and stakes of which continue to be contested today.

chapter three

r. buckminster fuller's design revolution

You succeed when you stop failing.

R. Buckminster Fuller, 1948[1]

By the late 1940s, Josef Albers's version of experimentation, which had come to define Black Mountain College's pedagogy in its first two decades, was beginning to be overshadowed by new and sometimes contradictory proposals. The Alberses' departure in 1949 left something of a vacuum that gave those alternatives traction and urgency.[2] As the previous chapter explored, John Cage's visits in 1948 through 1953 introduced a "chance protocol" in which experimentation was redefined as unleashing outcomes that were not previously foreseen, thereby supplanting Albers's model of testing attention through serial variation. Simultaneously, another, third proposition about the important stakes of experimentation was being hatched by Buckminster Fuller (known familiarly at Black Mountain and beyond as "Bucky"). His model of the test leveraged the creativity of the artist and the technological innovativeness of the scientist to completely rethink acts and objects of design. The test was not a means to reconfigure visual perception as much as a process of entirely re-envisioning (in all, including transcendental, senses of the word) postwar technocratic society.

Fuller's formulation of experimentation as "comprehensive design" was introduced and subsequently sharpened at Black Mountain College—in fact, he first penned the phrase as the title of the course he taught there in 1948.[3] His model, which involved experimentally questioning received ideas about artistic and architectural form, constituted a persuasive argument against specialization that at least superficially aligned with the College's Bauhaus-derived

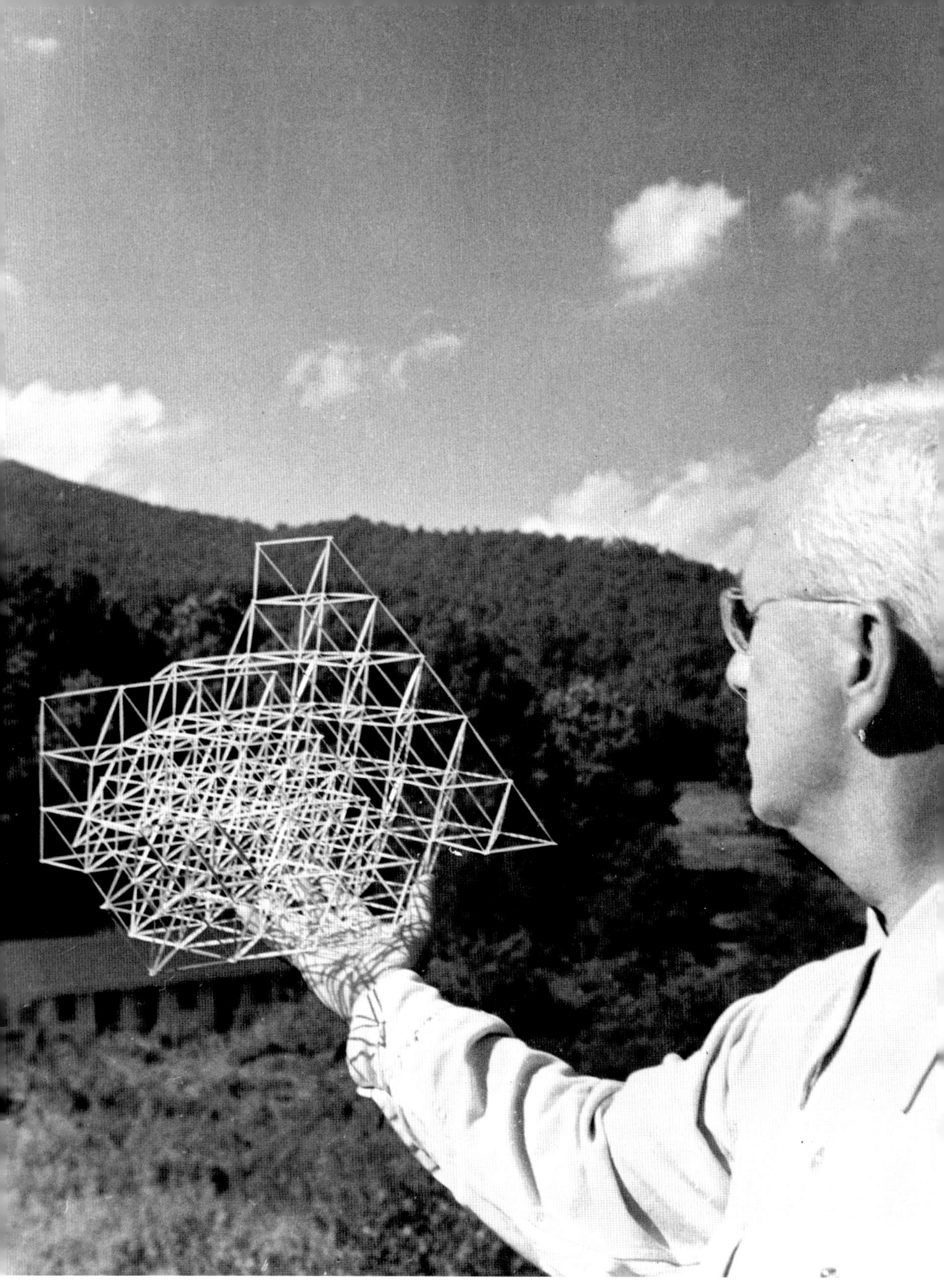

Figure 3.1
Masato Nakagawa, *Buckminster Fuller with Model*. Black Mountain College, summer 1949. Courtesy of the State Archives of North Carolina.

notion of visual art understood contextually to its surrounding environment by way of collaborations with shoulder disciplines such as theater, architecture and shelter design, and graphic and product design. In Fuller's case, however, interdisciplinarity was tied even more tightly to utilitarian social and political ends. For him, comprehensiveness was a process of moving design toward specific, functional goals. Experimentation tested existing, inefficient forms to arrive at a more complete picture of true, universal knowledge, and was far from being a practice of elaborating the greater contingency of perception (such as in the Albersian proposition that everything in the world has form, the appearance and structure of which can be unendingly tested in variation).

In this claim, Fuller joined Cage in further clouding the waters of Albers's pedagogical project at Black Mountain, a project that only very subtly moved from the artist's role in testing form to larger social ends (and those always described as an enrichment of a viewer's perceptual awareness). In a most contradictory fashion, the chance-protocol model of experimentation articulated by Cage united with Fuller's proposition of "total thinking" (the title of an essay he wrote while at the College) to shape powerful arguments against the Albersian model.[4] Cage's explorations of indeterminacy as a process to override or exceed human agency formed an unlikely partnership with Fuller's arguments about comprehensive design as an end beyond political means.[5] Fuller's vision of total design aimed to eventually eliminate contingency entirely, paradoxically by producing situations that embraced short-term failures—failures that looked like Cage's chaotic-seeming chance protocols—as proof of the farsightedness of his comprehensive, utopian vision.

This chapter addresses Fuller's work and writings of the 1940s and 1950s when he was elaborating his idea of experimentation as a technophilic and teleological form of design. Analysis of his methodology of experimenting, a method honed in the two halcyon and productive summers he taught at Black Mountain College while beginning to engineer plans for large-scale geodesic domes, will elucidate how an acceptance of passing failures in the interest of a deductive model of total design formed a potent argument against the vulnerability of experimental testing to microspecialization. Indeed, Fuller proclaimed that tests toward efficient design could prevent sociopolitical stagnation; according to him, he was "solving problems by design competence instead of by political reform."[6] His version of an experiment as a test and proof of total systems found company with many postwar iterations of pattern, network, and systems theories emerging from the Institute of Design (ID) in Chicago, where he taught after his first summer at Black Mountain (and, somewhat more obliquely, with cybernetics theories of corrective feedback coming out of MIT in Cambridge).[7]

The middle portion of this chapter takes up Fuller's relation to his ID colleagues László Moholy-Nagy and Gyorgy Kepes. Design for these men was not a product but a social process; experimentation proved that "structures are not *things*" but patterns.[8] As architect Lindy Roy claims of Fuller's methodology, "Form can no longer, even in design disciplines, be said to be a *thing* but at the very least a set of variable relations held in dynamic equilibrium."[9] Specifically, Fuller proposed that a radical and equitable redistribution of global resources (including natural and existing technological resources used to house, feed, move, and clothe the world's population) could be accomplished through an empirical study of dynamic patterns of consumption. Design processes could uncover underlying, universal truths hidden in patterns and networks, but only by emphasizing the structural constitution of form, not its surface appearance. As it will become clear, Fuller claimed his emphasis on structural engineering separated him from Bauhaus precedents, yet the importance of thinking design as process and action, not as a single object, remained the shared concern of all the models of experimentation emerging from Black Mountain College.

The final section of this chapter addresses the role of political agency in Fuller's proposal of experimentation as "comprehensive design." To Fuller, the universal application of comprehensive design—the study and design of the total human environment, including shelter, infrastructure, communication, transport, and other networked systems—could efficiently allocate the sufficient resources of the planet, "Spaceship Earth." In his scheme, as design substitutes for politics, so, too, would personal consumption replace production. The design and implementation of efficient technologies, in a teleological model, posited a technocratic utopia of postpolitical, postscarcity, postlabor subjects as its horizon of postwar potentialities. To some, that seemed like tomorrow's totalitarian post*agency* package wrapped in the mantle of today's experimental verification, and Fuller's complicated perspective on political action was frequently remarked on by others—somewhat jokingly by architectural critic Reyner Banham, and more sharply, as we will see, by art historian Meyer Schapiro.

Yet Fuller's call, for example, for portable and nomadic structures responsive to users' needs, or for the participation of wider groups, including college students, in design decisions, always implied that holistic theses subject to experimental verification would be pressured by contentious and possibly incompatible desires. In attempting to tease clarity from the bundle of contradictions in Fuller's model of total design, it is immediately apparent how radically he politicized experimentation by claiming it as a palliative to, or substitution for, electoral politics. Further sets of concerns are at stake here, too: the relationship between architecture and art, permanence and innovation;

between originality and repetition, control and freedom, chance and design, collectivity and singularity; between modernism's symbols of progress and its perceived symptoms of decay. (In discussing these contradictions, these paired relationships, let us not understand them as antinomies, binaries, or oppositions. Each term can and should be seen through the lens of its couple, as a dynamic, mutually informing relationship, as part of a dialectic whose terms collaborate to produce a synthesis.)

The tension between total, "anti-entropic" design and consumer choice-as-agency therefore hinges on Fuller's understanding of design as a dynamic process.[10] Though he sought to purge design of contingency in a quest for empirically verifiable facts, he recognized that experimental processes were rich with unexpected results in their short-term scenarios. Likewise, it is crucial to acknowledge how Fuller's proposal of experimentation recognized subjects' potential agency as too frequently limited by inefficient design and economic necessities—and how enthusiastically his alternative of activating design's social responsibility was received, at Black Mountain College and beyond.

THE INVENTION OF "TOTAL THINKING"

When Albers invited Fuller to teach at the College in the summer of 1948, the architect was beginning initial research on geodesic geometries (defined as the arcs of great circles), and he came to Black Mountain with a plan to test a prototypical large-scale dome constructed from such forms. By the time he returned to the campus in 1949 and successfully erected a freestanding geodesic structure, he was arguing his project of dome assembly as essential and essentially utopian: the dome was an articulation of "comprehensive, anticipatory design science" that tests traditional artistic and architectural forms (square, heavy, fixed buildings) in order to teleologically progress toward a utopia of efficiently managed resources (lightweight, portable domes that, like the earth, are spherical and therefore inherently more "natural," according to what he later termed the "cosmic evolution" of form).[11] Ever indefatigable, throughout 1948 and 1949 Fuller wrote eager letters about geodesic engineering to advertising agencies and press associates, proselytized to students in long lectures repurposed as even longer position papers, and sent peppy memos and production plans to various branches of the military and to contacts in the private building trades.

With a euphoric conviction that his latest research in geodesics represented an important and quite possibly definitive fix to the world's ills, by the 1950s Fuller was tirelessly advocating the adoption of the geodesic dome as the state-of-the-art shelter solution for the postwar consumer, as well as championing its use as a structure revolutionizing commercial and military construction. The proposal of the dome as a universally applicable form is thus chronologically and philosophically coincident with his developing argument about experimentation as the tireless prototyping of holistic design solutions in order to overturn conventional, inefficient habits of specialization and inequitable resource allocation. To understand how radically Fuller's concept of "the experiment" developed and transformed in his time at Black Mountain, and how substantially he, in turn, altered the rhetoric of experimentation at the College, it is helpful to contextualize these shifts. To grasp how Fuller arrived at the geodesic engineering his 1948–49 dome assemblies employed, it is necessary to understand his prior inventions: their effects in the period leading up to the Black Mountain domes, and their continuities and dissimilarities with the work he was doing in shelter design by the mid-1940s.

In the decades before coming to Black Mountain, Fuller had embarked on numerous ventures pitched as radical remedies to key problems in housing, automotive engineering, aeronautics, and cartography. Together, this body of inventions he termed "Dymaxion" constructions, in which portable, mass-produced goods and shelters efficiently delivered "the maximum gain of advantage from the minimal energy output."[12] Throughout the 1930s and 1940s, Fuller produced a variety of prototypical cars, houses, maps, and even bathrooms. Based on his initial 1927 "4-D House," to which a Marshall Field's advertising man had lent the "Dymaxion" moniker (a neologism derived from Fuller's predilection for the words *dynamic*, *maximum*, and *tension*), the Dymaxion constructions emphasized the efficient deployment of resources through mass production. Encouraging portability, they used the weight and cost of the completed structures as central design criteria.

The Dymaxion designs innovated in a variety of ways. The original 4-D House, a circular structure with a flexibly arranged internal wall scheme organized around a central supporting "mast" rather than load-bearing walls, weighed one hundred times less than conventional structures of similar scale, and in today's pricing could be purchased for approximately forty thousand dollars.[13] The 1932–33 Dymaxion Car adopted the streamlined appearance of airplane design with unique three-wheel engineering[14] (fig. 3.2). Prototypes reportedly reached speeds of 120 miles per hour, and the large twenty-foot-long body comfortably seated eleven passengers.[15] Fuller's 1944–46 Wichita House, sometimes called the Fuller House, finessed the mast support of the 4-D House with a new skin. Designed in collaboration with a Beech Aircraft engineering team, it featured a curved, sheet-metal aluminum exterior with continuous 360-degree windows encasing its radial plan, and was promoted as an easily transported, quick-assembly, affordable suburban home. In 1944,

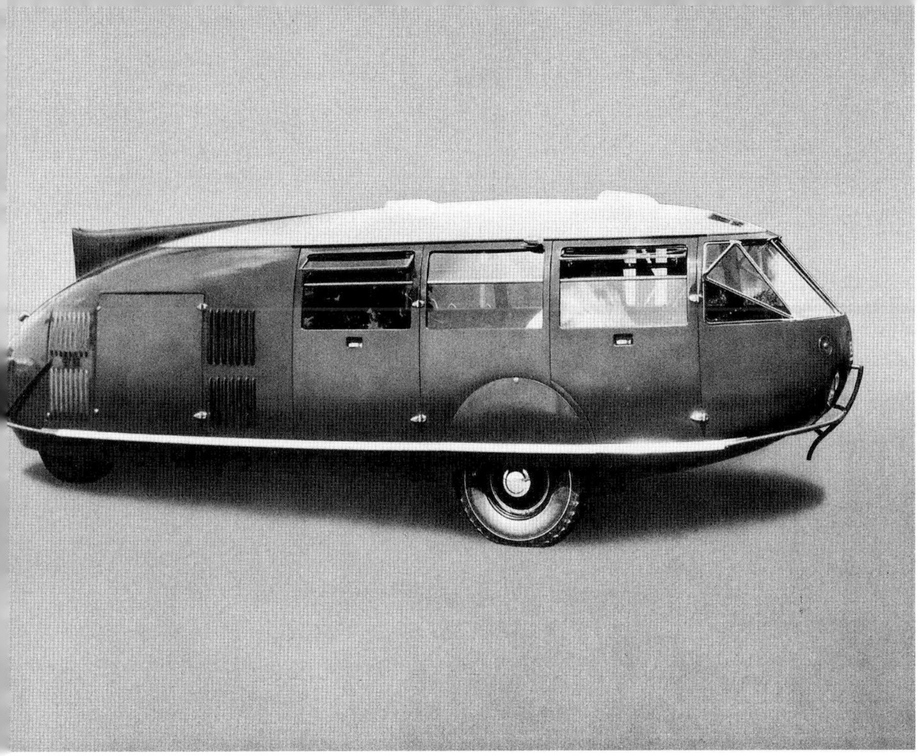

Figure 3.2
Buckminster Fuller, *Model of Dymaxion Car*, 1932–33. Screenprint on Lennox paper, 30 × 40". From *Inventions: Twelve Around One* (Cincinnati: Carl Solway Gallery, 1981). Edition of 60. Courtesy Carl Solway Gallery, Cincinnati, Ohio.

Fuller patented a low-distortion projection of the earth and called it—what else?—the Dymaxion Map. A two-dimensional plan, the map folded into various orientations and assembled into a three-dimensional, globe-like shape. When viewed as a flat projection, the map could be organized according to various strategic schemes—with all landmasses grouped together, for example, or the seas oriented in one broad oceanic route (plate 14). Soon after he developed the projection, Fuller was touting it as a template for networked information display: it permitted a global comparison of shifting economic and social data on energy use and natural resource management, and it could be used to chart, for example, the unequal consumption of raw resources in industrialized versus underdeveloped nations[16] (plates 15–16).

Despite his reputation as a prolific inventor, however, Fuller was hardly the top candidate for the position of architecture instructor at Black Mountain's 1948 summer session—the faculty had run through a list of several nominees too booked to attend, and he was a last-minute substitution for Harvard architect Bertrand Goldberg, a former Bauhaus student. His unflagging self-promotion aside, Fuller didn't have the greatest track record in 1948. Several criticisms were dogging him by the late 1940s, raising a chorus of dissent he attempted to outshout with the tenacity of a carnival barker. Once featured in influential and popular-culture magazines such as *Fortune, Time,* and the *Saturday Evening Post,* his inventions tended to languish soon after the prototype development stage.[17] Advance publicity for the Wichita House generated numerous serious buyers—from among approximately thirty thousand inquiries—throughout the mid-1940s, yet production had stalled as Fuller struggled with his backers at Beech. (In fact, his Black Mountain invitation had followed closely on the heels of a spring 1948 article in *Fortune* revealing the collapse of his plans to mass-produce the Wichita House design. Coincidentally, some years earlier a College faculty member had proposed purchasing one for the campus.)[18] The Dymaxion Map was intended as an educational distribution for elementary school students, but the project foundered when costs proved prohibitive for mass distribution. A fatal accident involving the Dymaxion Car at the 1933 Chicago World's Fair led automotive engineers to note that the car's emulation of aeronautic airstream capabilities encouraged dangerous drift on city roads. Fuller's projects all seemed so speculative, unrealizable, or downright dangerous that by 1948 a profile on him proposed for *Science Illustrated* generated the following internal queries: "Can you include in the piece some of the reasons why Fuller's plans and projects have failed. . . . Shouldn't there be some mention of the fact that Fuller never seems to carry things through? Doesn't look as though he ever will. Why?"[19] Grumblings of increasing frequency and intensity were voiced about Fuller's inability to shepherd a project beyond the realm of conjecture, thereby undermining his claims to efficiency through the mass production and distribution of his inventions.[20]

Fuller had long faced criticisms about the wider applicability of his designs, and his rhetoric of experimentation as an acceptance of failure was also ambivalently received. To critics, flaws in his inventions were exacerbated by his cultivation of a self-consciously prophetic breadth of thought, which permitted him to deflect specific criticisms of his projects by attacking his skeptics' narrow vision. To Fuller, because his projects were "evolutionary," they could be adequately realized only years or decades after his initial insights, an assertion that some found convenient, if not downright proleptic. Equally alienating to others was Fuller's style of argumentation—self-aggrandizing and portentous statements written with an autodidact's proclivity toward showcasing largely irrelevant information, evidenced in his epic lectures and notoriously lengthy digressions. Willfully falling between the two chairs of visionary design and practical execution, engineers found Fuller's proselytizing unserious, quaint, or fantastical, and dismissed his (frequently patented) schemes to mass-produce his inventions as being as difficult to implement as those of any backyard tinkerer.[21]

In Fuller's mind, his work demonstrated a form of predictive holistic thinking that by its very nature confounded specialists. As a result, his discoveries were subject to especially jealous and vehement critique, or so he alleged. When his 1927 plan for airlifted "4D Towers" high-rises was ridiculed as utterly unworkable and consigned by critics to the realm of science fiction, Fuller waved off disparagements of himself as a "radical" as quibbles from an establishment fearful of visionary design. He declaimed that critics beholden to the familiar would be refuted by the "highest order" of his "instrumental science":

> The blinders of habit persuaded man to accept the ignorant "reality." . . . "Fixed" brains will apprehend as "radical and revolutionary" every discovery.[22]

It would be no understatement to say that Fuller thrived on criticism, using it to fashion a myth of himself as the world's *most* forward-looking innovator. The malfunction of his inventions, both practically and according to their potential for mass distribution, to him paradoxically demonstrated the prescience of their design. It was up to someone *else* to make them workable and to accomplish global implementation. His vision was too prophetic for immediate gains, his productivity too great to bother with final production. To Fuller, failures were incidental given the scope and force of his greater program. By embracing failure, and positioning it as a defining characteristic of his practice, he cloaked himself with a Teflon-like invulnerability to his critics' dismissals.

However, Fuller's embrace of the sleek styling of airliners *did* foster a trend toward aerodynamic, cost-efficient automotive designs, and his notion of lightweight (and possibly airborne) portable housing *was* taken up as an alternative shelter design, at least initially by the US military. As he roamed through various disciplines, he blamed the turf battles and animosity his work engendered on wary specialists, who, corrupted by the narrow and incremental procedures of traditionally conceived science, rejected the foresight of his synthetic vision of shelter design as operating across the fields of art, design, urban and regional planning, structural engineering, and architecture. The totalizing vision of "anticipatory design science" as holistic and altruistic problem solving—an idea always contentiously received in architectural and planning communities—contributed to the tremendous receptiveness of students at Black Mountain and elsewhere to Fuller's demand that they scale up design to the level of a social practice. To him, the strength of any design innovation was inextricably linked to its potential common applications in mass distribution.

Yet the efficiency, either functionally or in terms of consumer interest and widespread consumption, of Fuller's Dymaxion designs was never tested in the crucible of mass production. Fuller brushed off criticisms about his inability to mass-produce Dymaxion products with a claim that his type of testing required prophetic design, which he could offer; marketing, promotion, and commercial distribution, though important, were secondary concerns. To him, experimentation was a form of "total thinking," which he defined as "experimental strategies which embrace potentially powerful forecasting capabilities."[23] Uncovering the universal principles of form could allow him to *anticipate* future problems and test provisional solutions; ultimately, his forecasting vision would always outpace implementation. In Fuller's model, experimental procedures were those by which the "valid data" of "what is really going on in nature" could be formulated conceptually by artists (also known as "comprehensive designers"), thereby making possible a higher standard of living for all people through effective resource management.[24] In attempting to think comprehensively about society, Fuller advocated inferring future experiments from existing postulates: as he proclaimed, "the design grew out of the philosophy."[25] Experimentation, to him, was the process of aligning specific failures of a method with the regularities of holistically conceived systems, a process not unlike a deductive application of the scientific method, in which a general hypothesis is offered and its merits then tested. In his model of experimentation, apparent complexities or impasses were subject to the skepticism of a holistic-thinking mind, with exposure of general underlying rules the result of the experimental protocol.[26] Anticipatory design science, as he defined it, demanded that findings be "generated by experimental discovery of the natural laws involved."[27]

The comprehensive designer's project of rendering technology less specialized and more efficiently and humanely distributed was one by which Fuller intended to bring "generalized principles into unique experimental control patterns."[28] Design was the revelation of heretofore hidden global codes: "By 'design' I mean: conscious employment of experimentally discovered principles governing pattern modulation."[29] To him, "design science" did this work of pattern recognition using a process of simplification "arrived at by separation of constituent factors of the problem . . . [so as] to deduce and classify the fundamental principles involved."[30] Reducing situations to basic principles revealed underlying truths, shaping a positivist endeavor to think empirically about everything on earth. As Fuller noted, "The progress of knowledge has been essentially a matter of separating things out very carefully from a matrix of confusion and isolating these pure, simple facts."[31] Simplifying, observing, and ordering the manifestations of a "problem" to discover underlying and universal patterns demonstrated that "science is the antithesis of chaos."[32]

Fuller's conception of design envisioned that postwar technocratic society would enrich the role of the artist, while the artist-as-generalist could in turn benefit society. (And, as we will see later, an artist played a decisive role in the development of Fuller's thinking at Black Mountain.) In 1927, he had an epiphany about the scope of this responsibility: as he described it, he "set about deliberately to be a comprehensivist in an era of almost exclusive trending and formal disciplining towards specialization," and "gave up forever society's general economic dictum that every individual who wants to survive must earn a living, substituting instead a search for the tasks that needed to be done that no one else was doing or attempting to do, which if accomplished, would physically and economically advantage society and eliminate pain."[33] These were lofty ambitions to be sure, but executable by an elite cadre of comprehensive designers (after Fuller's time at Black Mountain, they also came to be called "artist-scientists"), "an emerging synthesis of artist, inventor, mechanic, objective economist, and evolutionary strategist."[34] The important contribution of artistic practice toward this hybrid role would be to "formulate conceptually . . . all of the as-yet unknown or unproven" in preparation for a process of experimental verification.[35]

In a most idealizing fashion, the role of the "artist" represented the unfettered freedom to pursue broad-minded investigations of society against a culture of professionalization and specialization, and the example of artists' labor was the privileged model of autonomy. As Fuller asserted,

> The artist . . . is a predominantly non-frustrated individual holding vigorously to his innate freedoms of exploration, evaluation, self-expression, and . . . his appreciation of liberty of inquiry and initiative is precisely what we hold most valuable.[36]

The conception of artists' "innate freedoms" and "liberty" as exterior to the power structures of the status quo rehearses one of Fuller's common tendencies to see in design an uncorrupted "outside" to social processes, a place of dissent from which to attack and colonize the "center" and transform its moribund values. His heady proposition of artist-scientists seeking truths beyond organized politics was a self-described "design revolution," the parameters of which could be understood only years into the future.[37] A new hybrid role for creative producers—joining features of many professions for the greater good—would also necessarily involve a closer and more supervisory role for designers vis-à-vis capitalist production. In a 1949 letter to media magnate Henry Luce, Fuller explained that the "reinspiration of the individual" required that "artists . . . become the capital patrons of initial enterprise."[38] If engineers and industrial designers became "artists" and initiates to creative production, according to Fuller, their creativity would in turn benefit society in economic terms: "The community looks to the artist for this function of upping its standards."[39] His technocracy presented a picture of total design transacted in a world of self-sacrificing nonspecialists risking failure in order to improve unproductive habits in society. The artist's license to think creatively could fuse with the competence of the engineer to revolutionize shelter design in particular—the traditional province of the architect that, to Fuller, was unfortunately too often merely "traditional architecture." (In the early 1940s Fuller coined the term *debunk*, as one contemporary noted, in order to "point out the flaws in traditional architecture which his type of housing was intended to correct.")[40]

Fuller actively cultivated such a "debunker" persona, having dedicated the previous twenty years to separating himself from "the conventional way of doing things," particularly with respect to how housing resources were traditionally allocated.[41] His sense of the historic implications of the Black Mountain dome projects was likewise informed by his well-rehearsed renegade biography that emphasized his lifelong fascination with shelter as well as air-, land-, and sea-vessel design. Born to a well-situated and culturally active New England family, Fuller had little success as an undergraduate at Harvard University and quit to join the US Navy.[42] Engaged in various capacities in the building trades (his wife's family business) following World War I, he found himself disaffected by the conventions and inefficiencies of housing construction. He began to explore prefabricated housing options and briefly managed a corporation producing modular building materials. Various personal crises during the mid-1920s, most notably the death of his eldest child and a layoff from his corporate directorship, galvanized Fuller to act on his dissatisfaction by setting forth an alternative to existing ideas about architecture, shelter, and design.

To Fuller, home design was *the* essential field for innovation; not only was it a basic and universal requirement, it demanded a high premium on scarce land, labor, and material resources. Taking as his example the aeronautic and maritime industries, he realized that structures on land had a tremendous implicit advantage that encumbered greater efficiency: an almost complete avoidance of the factors of mass and mobility. Both air and sea vessels were preeminently concerned with weight, for purposes of either buoyancy or lift. This factor separated more vulnerable constructions for flight and sailing from the fixed, overbuilt, and inefficient architecture on land. As Fuller lamented, "No architects even know what buildings weigh. . . . Buildings are being built as fortresses, historically, really, the heavier, bigger the better."[43]

His first proposal for lightweight shelter design, the 4-D House, anchored a cylindrical tower with a single enormous mast from which the walls and floors would be hung using high-tension wires rather than being supported from below. Suspending the shell permitted the enclosure of the structure in a series of innovative, easily adaptable, screen-like glass panels. Hence, understanding weight as a previously unacknowledged factor in building construction enabled greater flexibility in designing prototypes and experimenting with new designs. As Fuller noted, "You can't make many experiments with big stone blocks, they're going to kill you. So heavy that it's really dangerous to experiment."[44]

Traditional construction compresses a great deal of a structure's weight in load-bearing beams or walls requiring significant reinforcement to remain upright. Fuller's successive Dymaxion houses in fact underscored this element by relying on a massive central post to support the structure's cylindrical skin. In contrast, his explorations of geodesics in cartographic projections and schematic representations of the globe stimulated a shift in his research toward the smooth and continuous tension of spherical surfaces as opposed to the rigid stress points created by right angles in post-and-lintel structures.[45] Because spheres emulate the form of the earth itself, to Fuller they epitomized the universal form of nature that was "Spaceship Earth." Indeed, according to historian Mark Wigley, "reconfiguring the relationship between structure and image" motivated his topological plotting of the sphere-as-earth onto the facets of a polyhedron, a geometric solid composed of multiple plane faces: "Fuller's spheres are always surrogate planets."[46] In analyzing spherical forms, Fuller extracted the tetrahedron—a pyramid with four sides—as the fundamental element, the *ur*-form, from which one could then extrapolate the structural behavior of all spheres.

Though superficially different in appearance, tetrahedrons and spheres share certain characteristics: in regular tetrahedrons each joint of a triangular plane forms a point of contact upon which even pressure is exerted (by the edges of three planes converging to one point), thereby distributing weight in a dynamic and continuous manner as a sphere does. A series of regular and irregular tetrahedrons could be combined to constitute a near-spherical form, thereby distributing load through multiple points spaced throughout the structure. These innovations in geodesic construction Fuller termed "energetic geometry," and he made several models in which combinations of polyhedrons were utilized to create circular hinged forms (fig. 3.3). Because the sum of the components performed better than the constituent parts (in terms of load distribution and overall strength), he termed this increased tensile and load-bearing capacity "synergetic."

Yet the methodology of experimentation Fuller termed comprehensive design—with its tests of synergetic and energetic geometries—was only be-

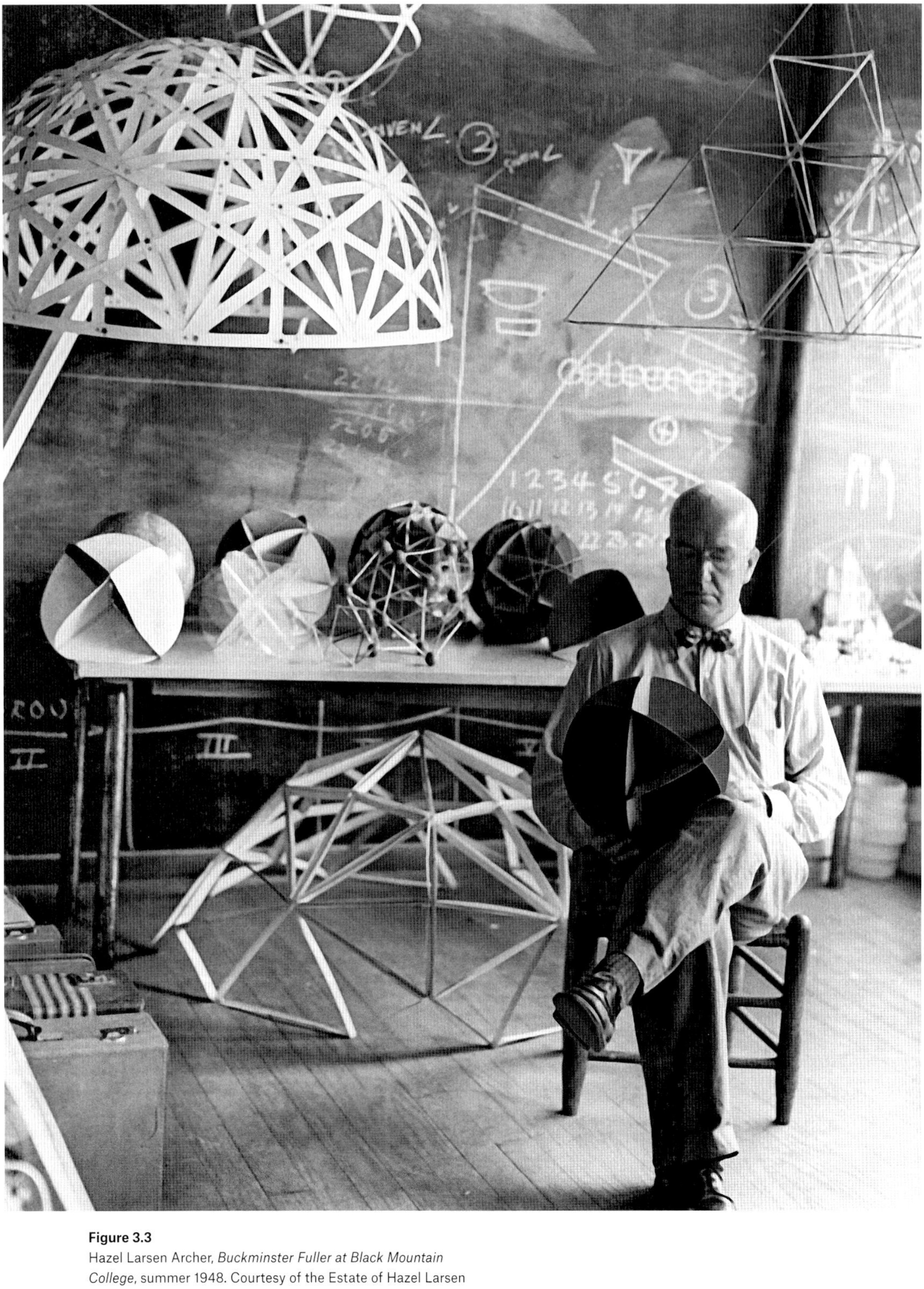

Figure 3.3
Hazel Larsen Archer, *Buckminster Fuller at Black Mountain College*, summer 1948. Courtesy of the Estate of Hazel Larsen Archer and the Black Mountain College Museum + Arts Center.

ginning to be articulated as he accepted his first-ever teaching commission in the summer of 1948; the invitation to Black Mountain provided respite at a time when his career was beset by setbacks and criticism.[47] Upon his arrival at the campus in June, in a three-wheeled Dymaxion motor home filled with energetic geometry models, his unfailing optimism and capacity for charming audiences by the sheer force of his ebullient personality won converts immediately.[48] Faculty and students were invigorated by his impish enthusiasm, which he unleashed in marathon lectures on topics ranging from global resource management to industrialization by way of military innovation, with "our dear friend, the hypotenuse" among the asides he'd sneak in.[49] Fuller had the sort of avuncular, mad scientist personality that nearly everyone on campus found endearing, and at Black Mountain he received his most enthusiastic reception to date—at least until he became a countercultural phenomenon at other colleges and universities by the early 1960s, and a veritable pop-science guru by the end of that decade. And after his time at the College, as we will see, education became a major prong of Fuller's public self-definition, with pedagogy's role in initiating the reorganization of social life a chief preoccupation of his extensive writings.[50]

When he arrived at the campus in 1948, Fuller met sculpture student Kenneth Snelson, who became excited by the new instructor's ideas. The next summer, in 1949, Snelson showed Fuller *X-Piece*, an approximately one-foot-tall column he had constructed of wood and plastic (fig. 3.4). In the work, two wooden cruciform shapes of equal size are perpendicularly oriented to each other, one above the other. They are supported by nylon wires connecting the center and the upper arms of both X forms, suspending the topmost wood form in midair while the lower form acts as a strut. Load is distributed through the wires' high tension, rigging both figures to balance upright as thin wires boxing the exterior of the Xs keep the forms oriented at an exact right angle to each other. The top form is therefore held aloft by a wire support system mirroring that of the base, implying that further iterations could rise up out of the same system. The sculpture therefore disperses compressive forces, creating what Snelson termed a "floating compression," an engineering principle of discontinuous compression and continuous tension that uses the mass of the structure to generate tension, which strengthens synergistically with the addition of further elements.

Snelson's unique concept inspired Fuller, who saw in it a new and efficient engineering principle. He asked Snelson to build a modified version, to which he later assigned the name "tensegrity"—short for tensional integrity, the way the work's int*egrity* (its structural stability) was maintained through a pervasive *tens*ional force. Fuller declared that tensegrity would eventually transform the

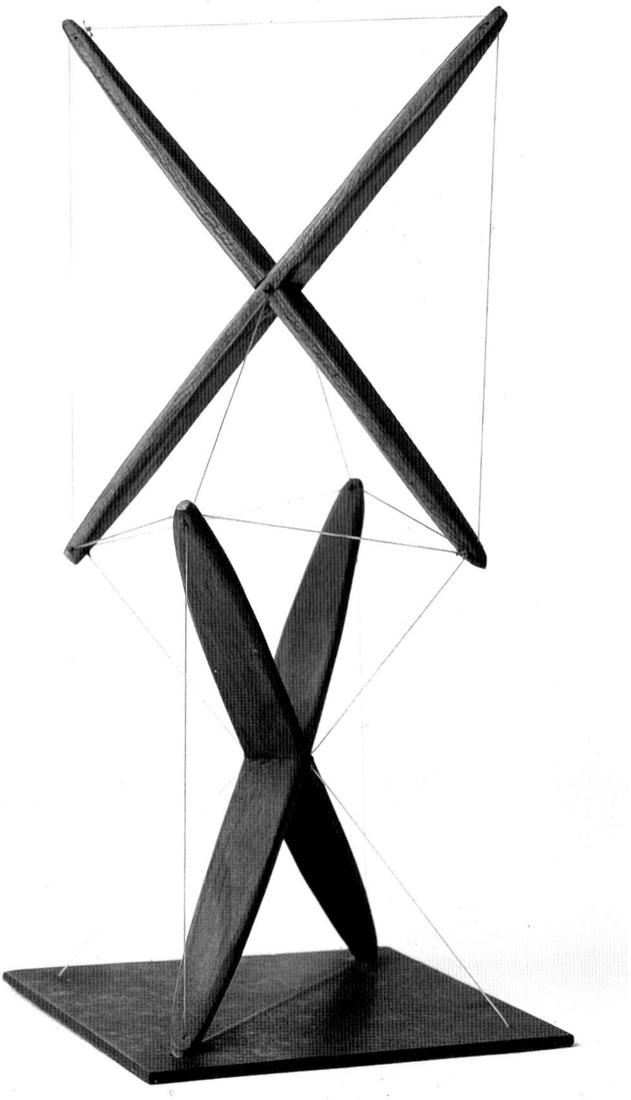

Figure 3.4
Kenneth Snelson, *Early X-Piece*, tensegrity structure, 1948–49. Wood and nylon, 11½ × 5⅜ × 5⅜". Collection of the artist. Photograph by Kenneth Snelson. © Kenneth Snelson. Courtesy Marlborough Gallery, New York.

building industry; for example, it would allow towers to rise to great heights without external buttresses, deep anchors, or foundations. Separately, each man patented his version of the tensegrity principle.

Fuller and Snelson's developments in tensegrity can be seen as a response to Fuller's plan to construct a large-scale, twenty-two-foot-high geodesic dome at the College (figs. 3.5, 3.6). One damp morning, after an extensive series of (pre–computer era) calculations, dozens of cheap, flexible, commercially available Venetian-blind slats were assembled as the dome's armature.

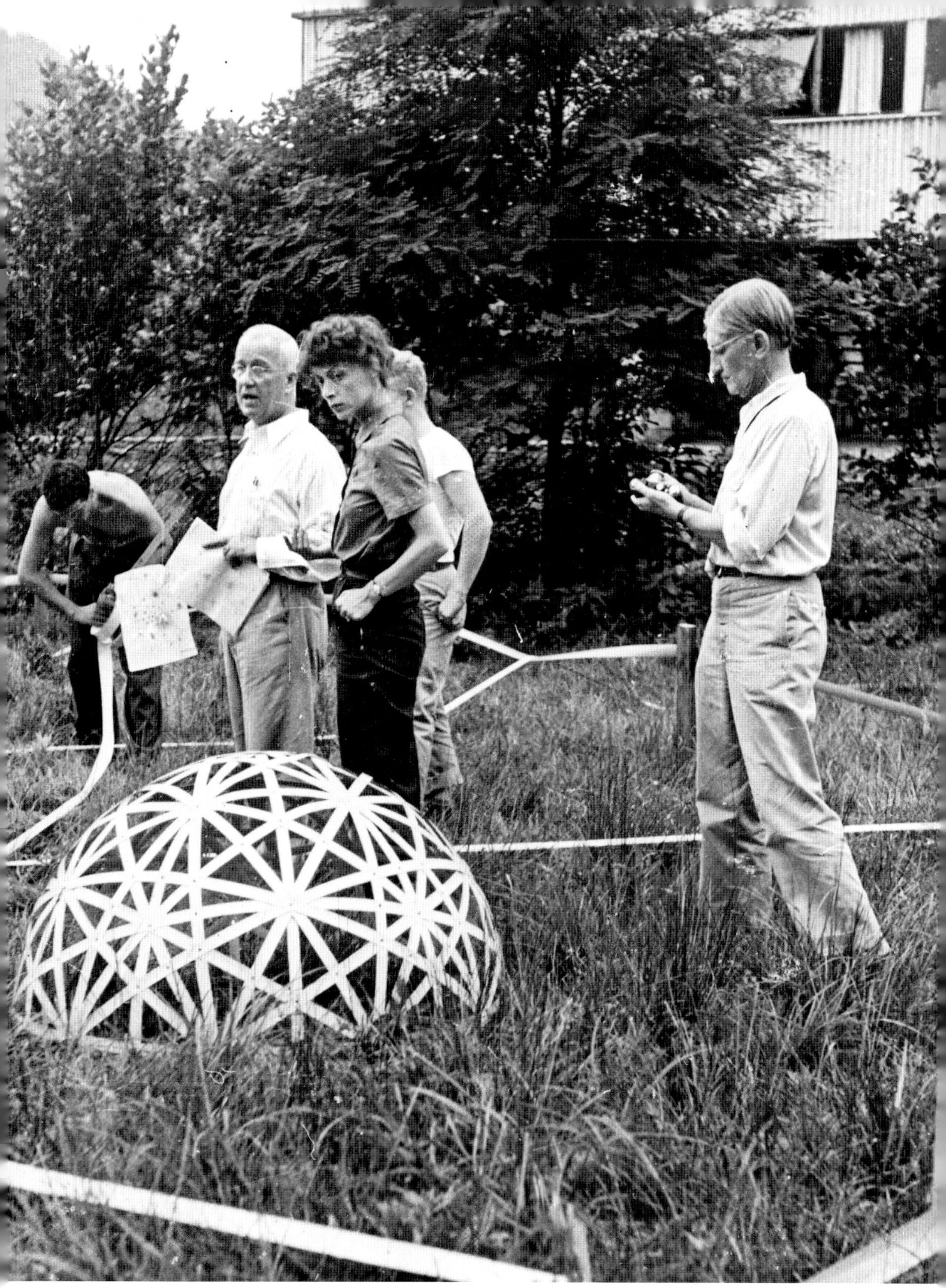

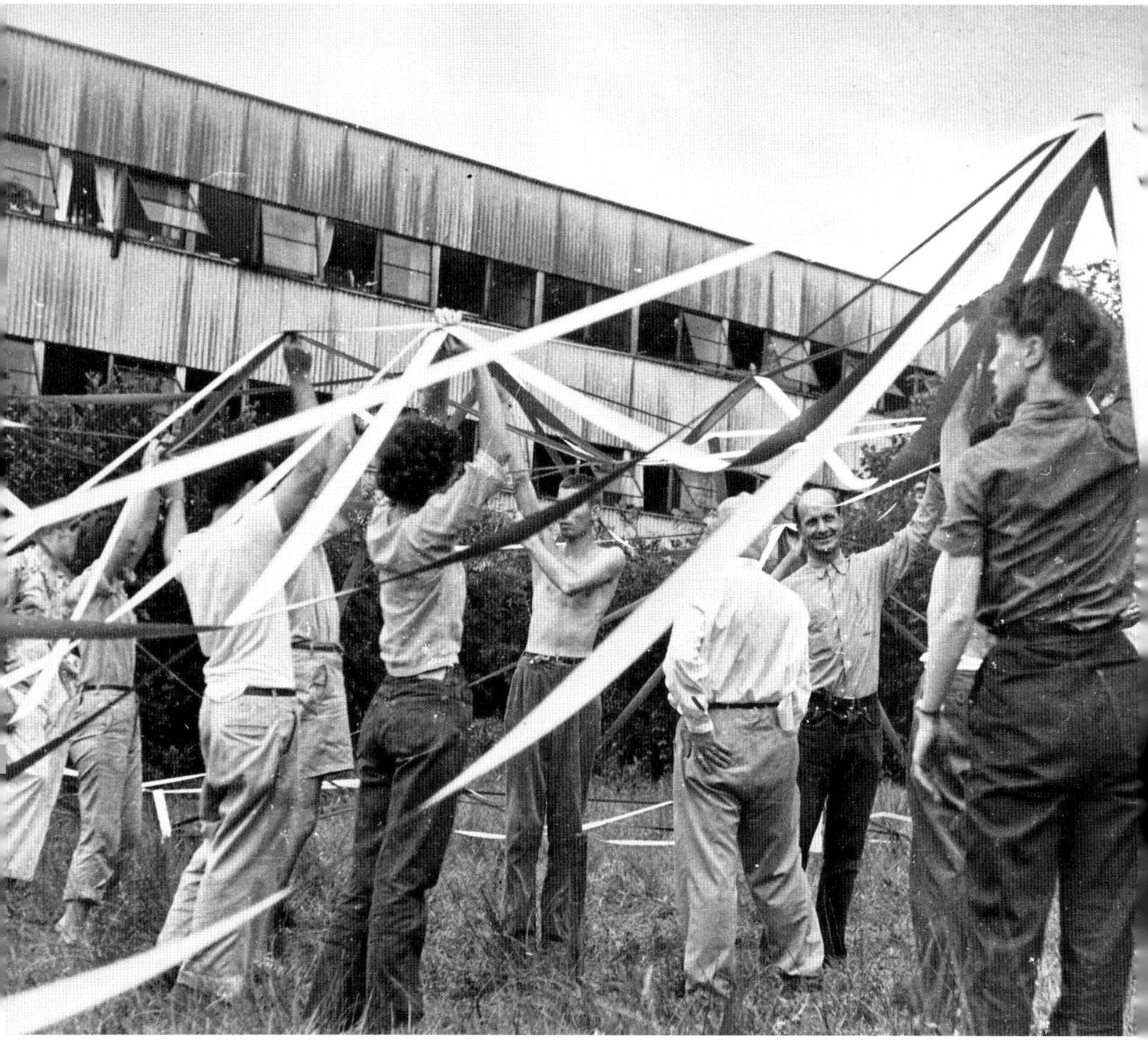

Figures 3.5 (previous page) and **3.6** (above)
Beaumont Newhall, *Buckminster Fuller Constructing Dome from Venetian Blinds at Black Mountain College*, 1948 (*pictured in fig. 3.5*: Buckminster Fuller, Elaine de Kooning, Josef Albers). © 1948 Beaumont Newhall; © 2012 the Estate of Beaumont and Nancy Newhall. Permission to reproduce courtesy of Scheinbaum and Russek Ltd., Santa Fe, New Mexico.

Not surprisingly, the dome failed to rise, and was good-naturedly named the Supine Dome[51] (fig. 3.7). According to Fuller, though he was aware that the slats needed to be doubled up in order to have sufficient strength and tensile capability to elevate the dome, he decided to push ahead with insufficient materials so as to demonstrate that structures could be gradually built up to the point of standing, thereby creating materially and economically efficient

Figure 3.7
Beaumont Newhall, *Buckminster Fuller Constructing Dome from Venetian Blinds at Black Mountain College*, 1948 (*pictured,* Elaine de Kooning). © 1948 Beaumont Newhall; © 2012 the Estate of Beaumont and Nancy Newhall. Permission to reproduce courtesy of Scheinbaum and Russek Ltd., Santa Fe, New Mexico.

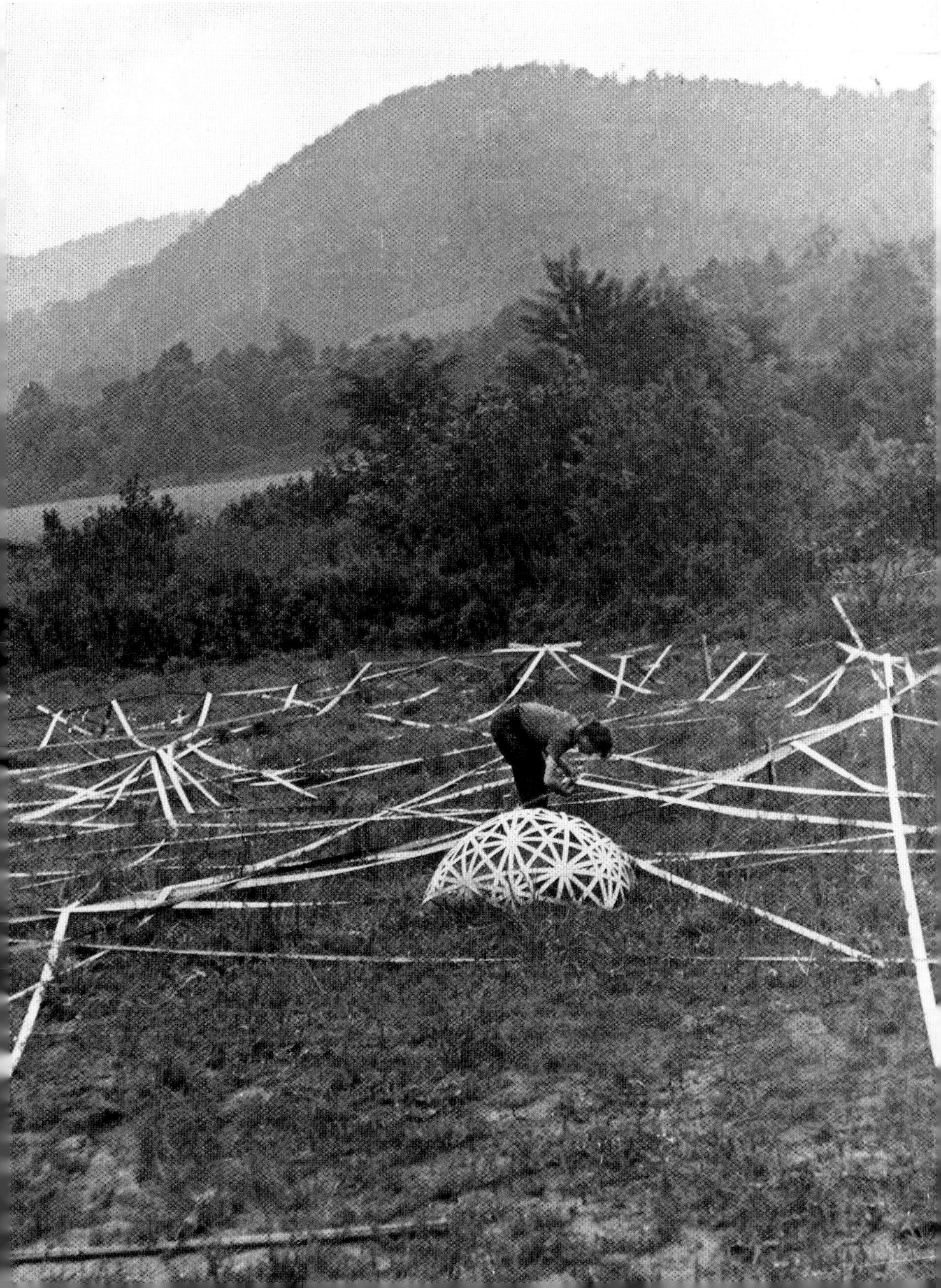

buildings. Lightness was a prime feature of the dome's design; as he stated, "I want to build a building that they're not afraid of having it collapse because it's so light it can't hurt anybody, it's like confetti . . . [you] stop having it fall down . . . [to] make it stand up. . . . So you start with this supine thing, and then keep fortifying until now . . . it's standing up."[52]

To Fuller, investigational prototyping was inextricably part of any experimental method—"I designed this thing so it would deliberately fall down, would not stand." As disorderly as the process of constructing the dome may have appeared to participants—wet Venetian blinds scattered throughout the

Figure 3.8
Clemens Kalischer, *Buckminster Fuller in "The Ruse of Medusa,"* 1948.
Gelatin silver print. © Clemens Kalischer. Courtesy the artist.

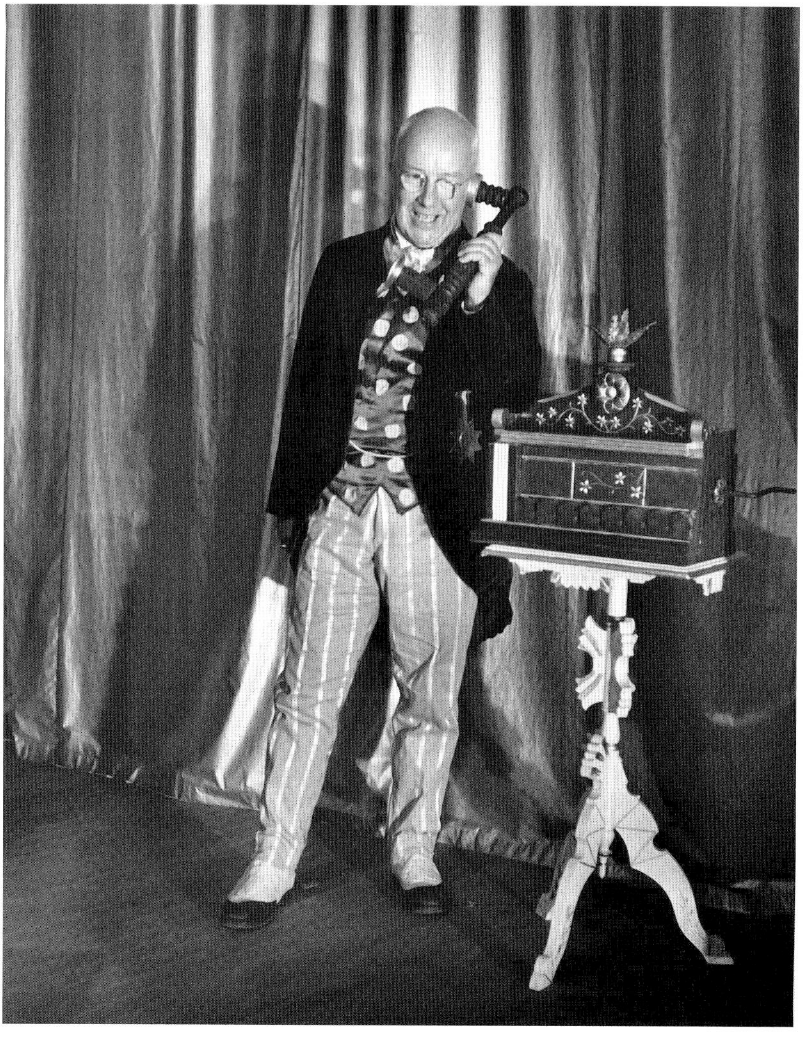

landscape of Black Mountain's Lake Eden campus—the dome was, according to him, engineered and "measured by comprehensive and strict practices of calculation and test."[53] Fuller wanted students to think structurally about buildings, questioning underlying engineering principles without accepting formal architectural conventions. He excoriated the way most art and architecture programs "teach otherwise innocent students to make pathetic attempts to out-Mies Mies while overlooking the energetic and economic fundamentals governing development of truly evolutionary design initiative, and design responsibility."[54] His emphasis on the engineering principles that uphold structures, rather than the manipulation of buildings' superficial appearances, added radical new focus on the material constitution and structural considerations of architecture. Innovations in the appearance of structures should follow tests of new engineering principles, as opposed to older architectural methods that modified surfaces, only later to ascertain their structural integrity. (This would become the central tenet of his developing critique of Bauhaus design, to which I'll return.)

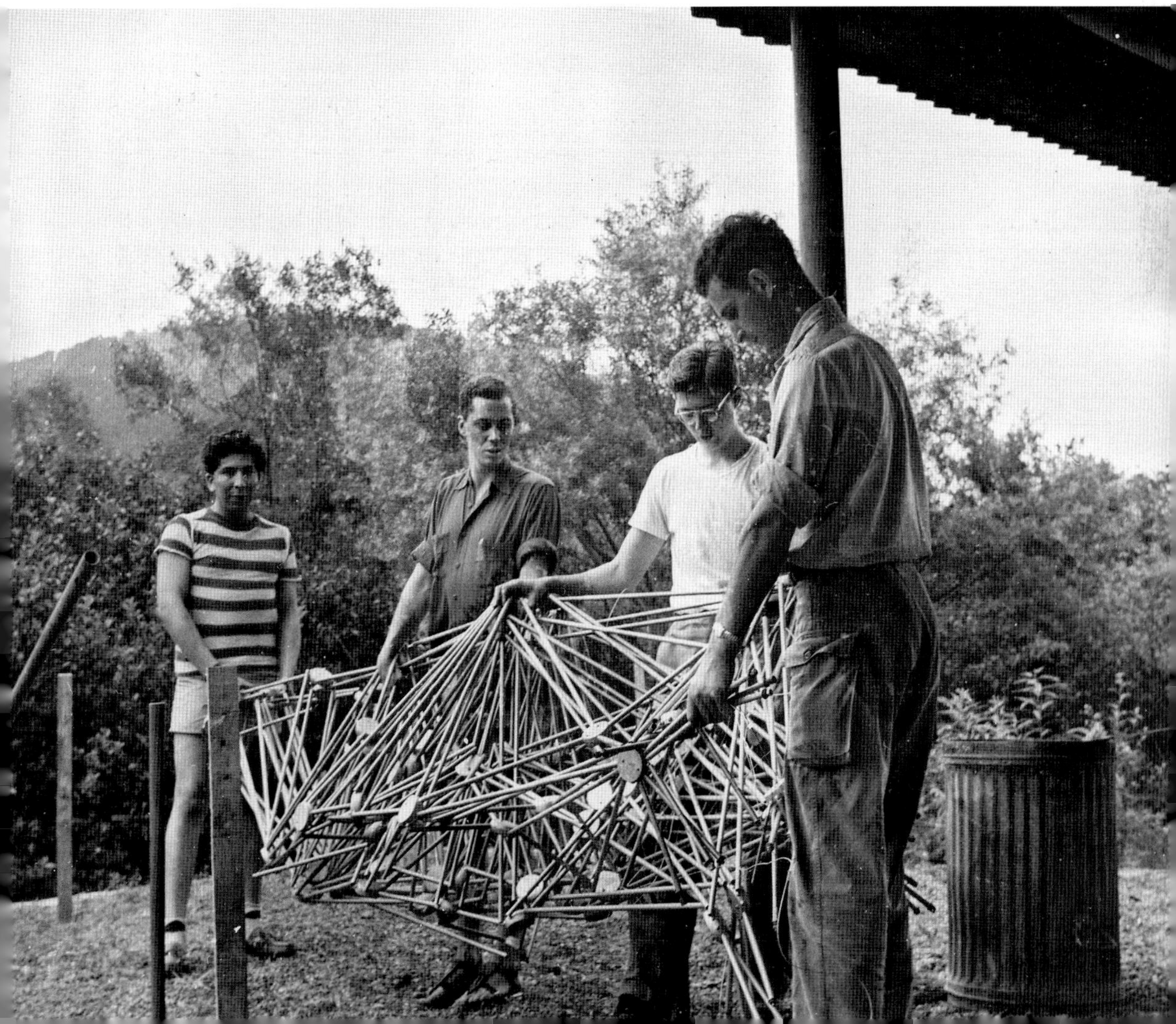

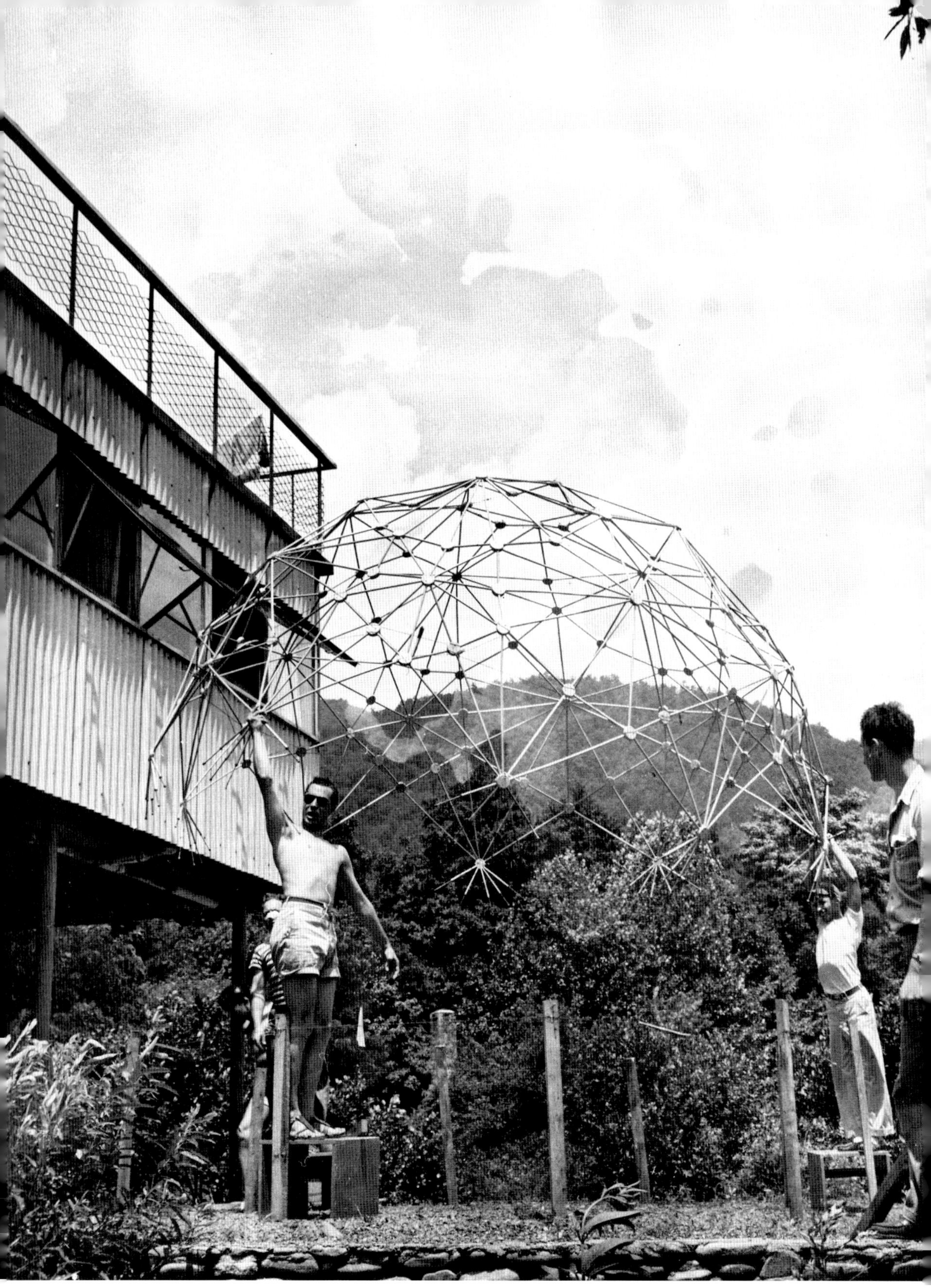

Figures 3.9 (previous page) and **3.10** (above)
Masato Nakagawa, Buckminster Fuller's dome of thirty-one great circle necklace structure of tubular beads and continuous internal cable with double heat-sealed, pneumatic, transparent skin. Designed and constructed at the Institute of Design, Chicago, 1948–49. Plastic skin tested at Black Mountain College, summer 1949. Courtesy of the State Archives of North Carolina.

Fuller's presence—and his memorable performance as the Baron Medusa in John Cage's production of Erik Satie's play *The Ruse of Medusa* (fig. 3.8)—so electrified the campus that upon Josef Albers's resignation in the spring of 1949, he was offered the vacant rectorship of the College. Although he refused the position, Black Mountain, particularly its enthusiastic students such as Snelson and Ruth Asawa, provided Fuller with the unique opportunity to continue conducting what he termed "exploratory work."[55] That year he returned to the College as Director of the Summer Institute, accompanied by a dozen or so ID students from Chicago. He also brought along a newly manufactured prototypical dome influenced by the cable engineering of Snelson's *X-Piece*, this one more modestly scaled than the earlier Venetian-blind model and composed of flexibly constructed aluminum tubing with an internal cabling system[56] (figs. 3.9, 3.10, 3.11). The second dome was erected successfully (it had been prepared

Figure 3.11
Kenneth Snelson, *Buckminster Fuller's Dome, Demonstration of Strength*. Black Mountain College, summer 1949. © Kenneth Snelson. Courtesy Marlborough Gallery, New York.

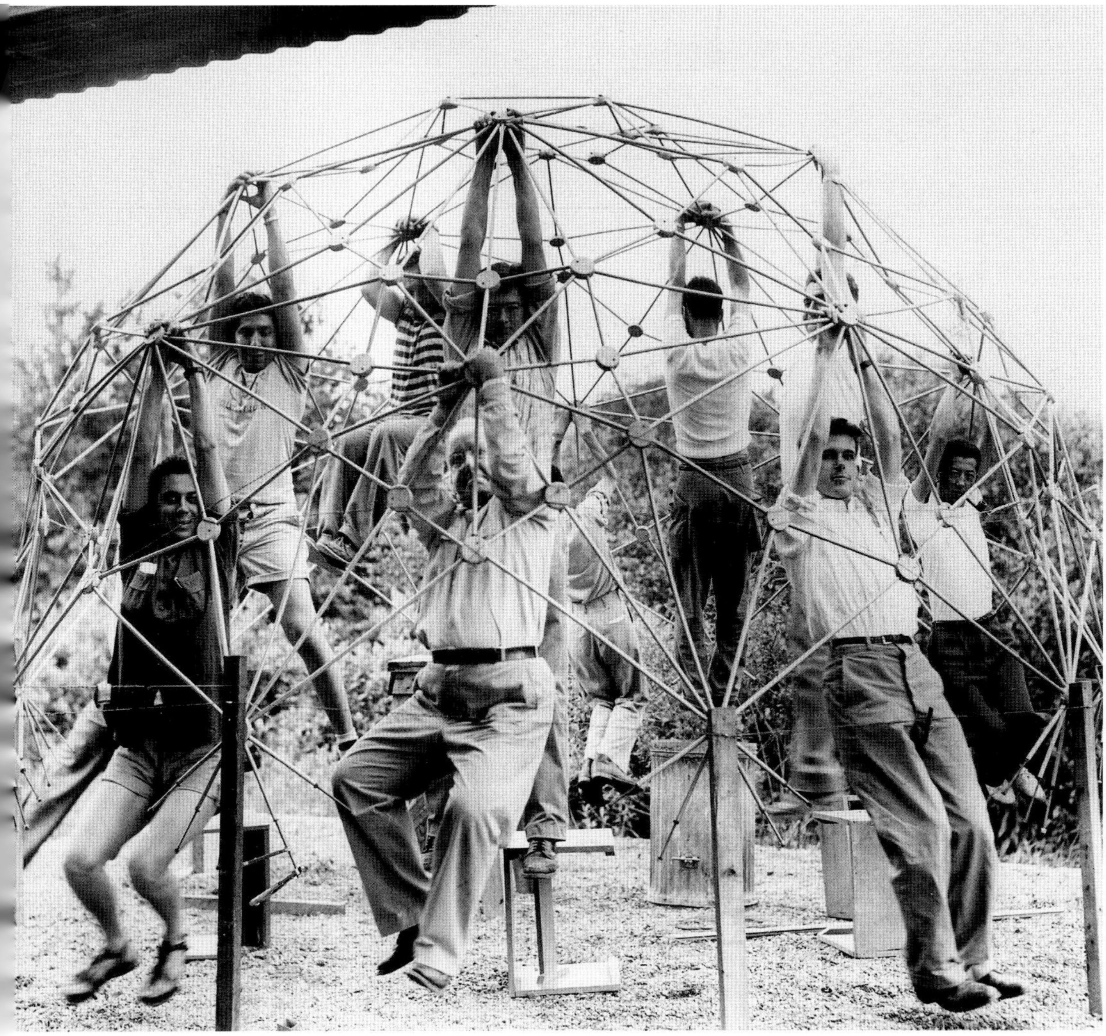

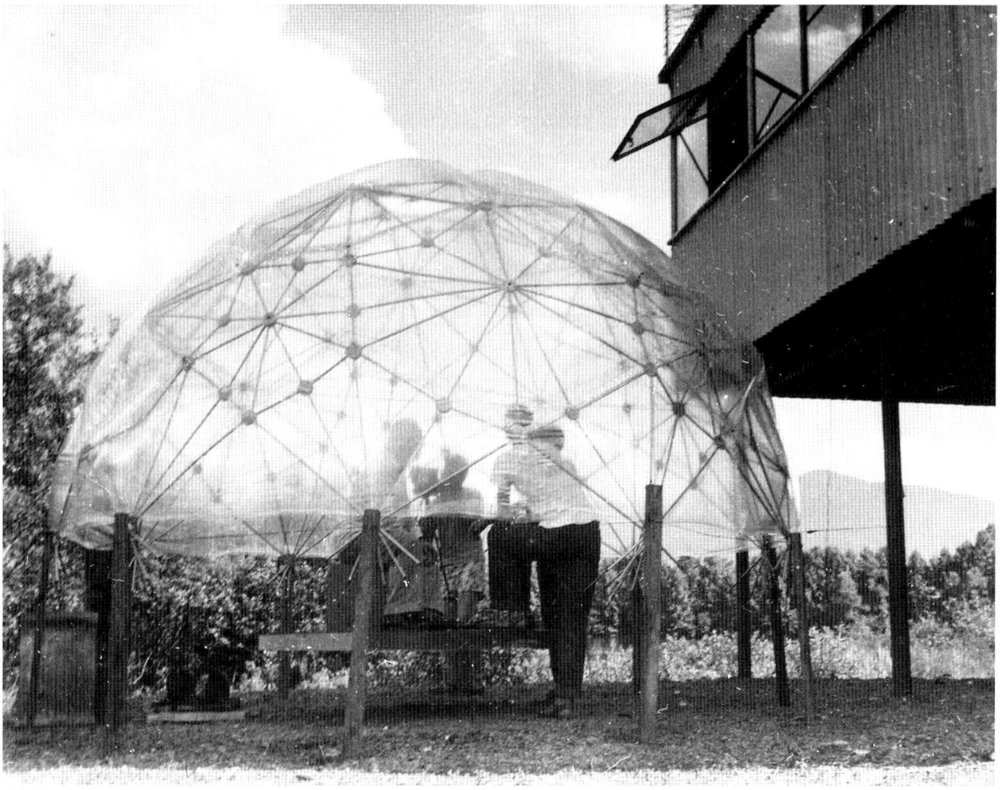

Figure 3.12
Masato Nakagawa, *Buckminster Fuller's Dome, Demonstration of Plastic Skin*. Black Mountain College, summer 1949. Courtesy of the State Archives of North Carolina.

months earlier for a demonstration at the Pentagon in Washington, DC), and a new plastic weather-insulating skin was tested[57] (fig. 3.12).

The success of the second dome assembly reflected the achievement of a "synergetic" process, but not only in the sense that the lattice structure, when erected, became stronger than its constitutive parts. To Fuller, when an entire system's or holistic theory's synergy (in this case, the theory of tensegrity) was experimentally validated, it reinforced the presuppositions supporting the entire method, and therefore strengthened the total system. Synergy was "evolutionary"—it compelled progressive improvements of knowledge from a state of chaos to one of order (unlike evolution understood non-teleologically, as biologists in the legacy of Darwin such as Jacques Monod would see it).[58] The success of synergetic thought was, Fuller believed, an indication of the "inherent success" of humanity, or what he termed human beings' role as "the most comprehensive anti-entropy function of the Universe."[59] He viewed "total thinking" as a model of scientific speculation that had been confirmed by the success of the dome assembly. Paradoxically, it was the *failure* of the initial dome construction that supported his claim to be, in fact, a comprehensive experimentalist with the vision to undertake large-scale dome constructions, not a mere technician tweaking small modulations. Thus, Fuller's main preoccupations were encapsulated in the Black Mountain dome experiments: his focus on shelter as the primary site of innovation; his emphasis on the central role of artists in accomplishing design advancements; his concern that designers challenge problems creatively while risking short-term failures and possible ridicule by the "Establishment"; and his demand that single experiments support larger, systemic planning.[60]

THE EXPERIMENTAL FINISHING SCHOOL

Fuller found an unlikely ally at Black Mountain in John Cage, and in the summer of 1948 they began articulating a model of risk and failure in experimentation that discouraged incremental change in the interest of a nearly libertarian freedom from restraint. Cage, after his first encounter with Fuller, deemed experimentation an American individualist "utilitarianism" as distinguished from purposeful, collective (read: European), and ultimately failed politicizations of form.[61] Superseding that decline, the men jointly proposed a new model of the test as an act of radical transformation by renegade experimentalists, quite unlike the systematic testing of variables characterizing Albers's method. "Comprehensive design"—Fuller's terminology—or "indeterminacy"—Cage's—were couched in language directed against the system of methodically varied modifications in Albers's pedagogy and artistic process. (And yet both men, like Albers, were quite methodical in their approaches to formulating "experiments," and singularly regimented in their daily lives.)

As Fuller recalled of his first summer at Black Mountain,

> John Cage and Merce [Cunningham] and I had breakfast every morning together out under the trees. And we really did have a very great deal of fun because I spent that summer with them on a fun schematic new school, and I called it "the finishing school." We would finish anything. In other words, we would really break down all of the conventional ways of approaching school. And "the finishing school" was going to be a caravan, and we would travel from city to city.[62]

It's hard not to read Fuller and Cage's iconoclasm about the "finishing school"—itemizing "all of the conventional ways of approaching school"—as both triggered by and directed against the existing experimentation models endorsed by German émigrés at Black Mountain. Though Fuller was sympathetic to Albers, calling him a fellow "experientialist," he found Bauhaus architectural design misleading in its claims of engineering structural innovations.[63] When in 1955 Fuller was asked by John McHale of the London Independent Group if Bauhaus ideas had influenced his work, he testily replied, "I must answer vigorously that they have not."[64] He isolated two major methodological differences separating him from Bauhaus predecessors. First, he believed in the teleological nature of technological innovation as an "absolute principle"—as he claimed, "The more you used technology, the more it improved."[65] Second, his model of experimentation emphasized the construction and operation of structures as opposed to buildings' aesthetic appearances. He decried the "international style thus brought to America by the Bauhaus innovators," which operated "without . . . knowledge of the scientific fundamentals of structural mechanics and chemistry."[66] In sum, "they only looked at problems of modification of the surface of end products."[67]

Upon his first visit to Black Mountain, Fuller's distance from Bauhaus precedents was immediately noted. As Elaine de Kooning commented, "Bucky, with his emphasis on how things *worked* and his total disregard for the Bauhaus concern with design—with how things *looked*—was a bit of an irritant to the regular faculty."[68] Snelson, for his part, soon realized that the geometric models Fuller was testing—experiments that had emerged from close study of the structural properties of tetrahedrons and spheres—would produce architectural forms very different from the basic Bauhaus unit of the cube. He credited Fuller with demonstrating that in most design, "how you occupy space with architecture . . . has nothing to do with structure. And it became clear to me what kinds of experiences or experiments you had to conduct before you know what a structure really is . . . because it's a result of forces which can form stable systems. . . . That's what I got from Bucky, quite opposite to the loose notions of structure that the Bauhaus ideas were involved with."[69] For all Bauhaus members' interests in axonometric projections and dynamic geometric perspectives, to Fuller these were merely static representations; instead, he foregrounded architectural forms as embedded in systems (transportation, energy, mediatic communication, and so on) seen holistically and as functions of society's total needs.[70]

Upon closer examination, Fuller's emphasis on the "experimental" as tests of total systems can be situated within a cultural lexicon that had in fact emerged at the Bauhaus just a few years earlier. His philosophy of efficiency, and the economy of resources and labor, echoes that of Bauhaus practitioners, much like what Albers had earlier called the "ratio of effort to effect."[71] In Albers's version of experimentation, reduction to the fundaments of form (and form was always understood in its structure *and* appearance, despite Fuller's stereotyping of Bauhaus methods otherwise) was a way to induce complex comparisons between subtle variations often overlooked in "macro" judgments. Yet to Fuller, the goal was not reduction and economical presentation—"less is more," one could say—but rather the effective employment of existing resources to appear and function greater than their parts—that is, synergistically. As he wrote, "The whole strategy of [the] artist-engineer initiative comes under the head of progress by comprehensive simplification, by constantly *doing more with less*."[72] "Doing more with less" implied efficiency at the level of labor-saving technologies and in the interest of ever-increasing technological productivity, not in order to think of production processes themselves as human endeavors worthy of close study and complex attention. In this, Fuller's emphasis on systemic rather than formal concerns can be clarified by comparison with the work of László Moholy-Nagy, Albers's partner (and sometimes antagonist) in teaching the required foundation course at the Bauhaus.[73]

Moholy-Nagy had been a member of the Bauhaus faculty from 1923 to 1928 and went on to found the New Bauhaus in Chicago (ID, where Fuller himself taught during the academic year between his summers at Black Mountain). Exact contemporaries (both were born in 1895), Moholy-Nagy died of leukemia in 1946, two years before Fuller arrived at ID. Though they never worked together directly, in important ways Fuller's deductive experimental model, which edged design toward a vision of a new technological utopia, overlapped with Moholy-Nagy's ambitious project of experimentation as radical technological innovations undertaken by artist-designers.

Moholy-Nagy called for a culture of artistic production, driven by scientific advancements, that would reject disciplinary specialization while understanding the designer's responsibility to the total system of society. Like Fuller, he wanted to reclaim science from its misapplication by specialists; as he wrote in his 1938 book *The New Vision: Fundamentals of Bauhaus Design, Painting, Sculpture, and Architecture*, "Specialists—like members of a powerful secret society—obscure the road to all-sided individual experiences."[74] Instead, Moholy-Nagy saw design as "an integration of intellectual achievements in politics, science, art, technology, in all the realms of human activity. . . . Our time is one of transition striving toward a synthesis of all knowledge."[75] His emphasis on cross-disciplinarity was similar to what Fuller would soon be defining as comprehensive design. To Moholy-Nagy, this disciplinary fusion could be accomplished by the universal application of technological innovations. As he contended,

> The possibilities of the machine—with its abundant production, its ingenious complexity on the one hand, its simplification on the other, had necessarily led to a mass production which has its own significance. The task of the machine—satisfaction of mass requirements—will in the future be held more and more singly and clearly in mind. . . . Invention and systematization, planning and social responsibility must be applied in increased measure to this end.[76]

Systematization allowed designers to categorize the structure and function of materials, as opposed to manipulating superficial characteristics that might in fact be quite subjectively understood. Altering the mere appearances of forms facilely disregarded the complexities of production; Moholy-Nagy claimed that the artist "today knows usually very little of engineering problems . . . nothing about statics, mathematics, technology, although an understanding of these would be more helpful than aesthetic rules in suggesting an efficient working method."[77] In art, for example, dynamic, not static elements of forms should be accentuated, a result Moholy-Nagy referred to as "equiposed sculptures," in which volume and material were unified in balanced yet mobile systems. With such objects, "the path to the freeing of a material from its weight" could be found.[78] The equiposed sculpture not only brings "more and more new single pieces into relation," it expands the notion of sculpture into its environment, and "demonstrates the whole borderland lying between architecture and sculpture."[79]

The second-to-last image of Moholy-Nagy's *The New Vision* is striking in how it posits structural lightness—material freed from weight—as an inherently positive social value (fig. 3.13). The photograph, taken in 1926, depicts a dozen or so men balanced on a soaring, intricate lattice of triangular struts; the caption indicates that they are constructing the framework for the Carl Zeiss planetarium in Jena, Germany.[80] The description continues: "A new phase of our victory over space: men poised in a swaying open network, like airplanes flying in a formation."[81] As was the case for Fuller, Moholy-Nagy's vision of lightness as the new, universal property of modern construction linked engineering innovations to unified yet networked social design. The ability of technologically advanced structures to represent, metaphorically, the interconnected matrix of social systems was key. Like Fuller's dome designs, whose shape simultaneously referenced the enclosure of domestic life, kiosk-like community shelters, and the networked systems of Spaceship Earth, Moholy-Nagy's networked forms could inspire a "universal outlook" that would posit design improvements as part of a pattern of growth applicable to the whole of society.[82] The artist-designer would deal above all with information and its representation; in an issue of the journal *ANY* devoted to Fuller it was noted, "The ability to gather and

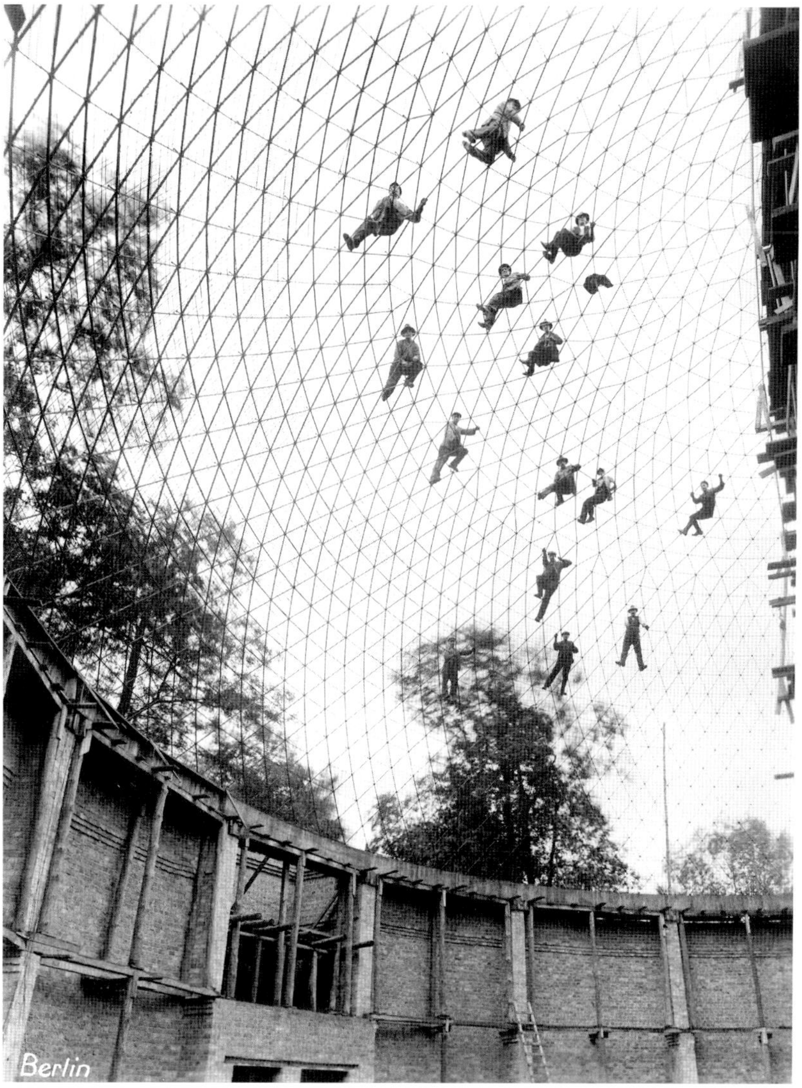

Figure 3.13
Network Lattice-Framework for a Zeiss Planetarium, n.d. Reprinted in László Moholy-Nagy, *The New Vision: Fundamentals of Bauhaus Design, Painting, Sculpture, and Architecture* (Mineola, NY: Dover, 1938/2005), 203. Source: Zeiss Archiv.

coordinate vast amounts of information enables the designer to deal once again with the 'design of the whole.'"[83]

To Fuller and Moholy-Nagy, architecture was hybrid in many ways, most essentially so when it provided shelter while managing the representation of networked resources. In particular, Fuller envisioned the dome as itself a networked building—a site connected to real-time information feeds updated in various media. One can see this sensibility encapsulated in his 1962 "Geoscope" proposal, a precursor to today's "digital globes." The Geoscope was envisioned as a two-hundred-foot-diameter spherical display covered with colored lights.

Fuller planned to have the enveloping space—literally, the environment—of the Geoscope updated with networked information, data that would allow individual spectators to visualize, study, and possibly redesign the total human ecology in order to quickly and efficiently apportion resources globally.

In contrast to Fuller, Moholy-Nagy envisioned planning on a centralized and collective level, and called for workers' control of industrial capital for the benefit of all.[84] Yet like his American counterpart, he believed that the benefits of technological gains could be extended to many more individuals through socially transformative educational experiences. Training subjective awareness about perception through group exercises and individual assignments could make the larger public proficient in complex visual and structural phenomena. Education could therefore allow students to understand the components of form in order to rethink the structural constitution of problems, rather than letting solutions be executed from habit or tradition. Additionally, education was a process in which outcomes were unfixed (as they would not be in industry) and therefore allowed for greater experimental freedom. Both Moholy-Nagy and Fuller invested heavily in their respective pedagogical efforts, and in some ways one could consider design for these men as a polemical project of shaping minds.

Gyorgy Kepes, Moholy-Nagy's colleague at ID, also believed design pedagogy was the key to representing complicated variables as intelligible patterns rather than as static objects, so as to train a new and unique breed of designer. As historian Reinhold Martin has commented, for Kepes this new designer "was, in effect, a new social type, bearing a humanistic, universal outlook, an evolutionary adaptation capable of managing the reorganization of vision for the benefit of humanity as a whole."[85] Encouraging this universal outlook while teaching at ID and later at MIT, Kepes connected design with other visual systems, increasingly, marketing and product design. Thus, for both Kepes and Moholy-Nagy, systems-based analysis depended on the training of visual perception, which linked their models to Albers's and others from Bauhaus. This perceptual emphasis recedes in Fuller's model, as the focus on structure over appearance produces judgments of dynamism linked more to engineering than to vision.

In 1956, Kepes invited Fuller to contribute to *The New Landscape in Art and Science*, a book he was assembling that set out to synthesize and systematize the whole of scientific and aesthetic knowledge around the concept of organizational patterning. Primarily a visual compendium, *The New Landscape* featured images of Fuller's geodesic dome and other recent inventions, along with objects by Charles and Ray Eames, Le Corbusier's modular figure, and all manner of microscopic and magnified images from nature, such as snails' tongues and the Crab Nebula—examples of the harmonious unity of nature organized around morphologies of repetition and networked structure. Kepes later invited Fuller to submit an article to a collection of essays he was editing titled *Structure in Art and in Science*; according to Kepes, the volume would provide a "structure of structures" in order to focus "the power to see our world as an interconnected whole."[86] In Fuller's contributed essay, "Conceptuality of Fundamental Structures," he argued, after musing on the complex math of bubbles and other closely packed spheres, that nature does not "do what we call fudging of her design which means improvising." Instead, it is the artist who could reveal that mathematical constants such as *pi*—an irrational (not fractional), transcendental (without end) number—are merely models to help us understand the world, and that patterns beyond calculation exist in nature.[87] Kepes characterized Fuller's essay as providing "an inspiring bridge between our comprehension of the structural principles of nature and the potential application of this knowledge to creation of man-made forms."[88] It was this potential for detecting and understanding patterns shared by natural forms and artistic and architectural constructs that Kepes viewed as the communicative prospect of experimentation and a vital educational tool in Fuller's work.

In his post–Black Mountain College writings, Fuller increasingly emphasized design pedagogy, but for him a student's understanding of dynamic structures and the way they relate to social problems could emerge only through heuristic experimentation rather than the focused perceptual training advocated by Moholy-Nagy and Kepes. In contrast to the deductive (and predictive) methods of his own comprehensive teleological social planning, Fuller believed that laboratory teaching methods ought to involve a freedom to try out responses to problems without regard for success—what he termed "intuitive probing" in his Kepes essay. To achieve this, he discouraged students from concentrating on surface appearances; as he wrote in 1948, "I am particularly anxious *not* to 'picture' in advance the nature of logical solutions (à la Beaux-Arts programs), thus leaving the student only those superficial tasks of decoration or assemblage of preconceived components."[89] He derogated the language of visual form (note the deployment of "pictur[ing]" as a negative value leading to rote "superficial" and "decorative" work). To him, open-ended experimentation without repeated trials allowed students to invent a variety of possibilities that a narrower focus—as Josef Albers required—would foreclose, while still demanding the intense examination of a problem in which the stakes were as high as people's lives: "[As] in aircraft technology, *nothing* is taken for granted."[90] Free experimentation was encouraged because Fuller's system was so encompassing, so universal, that its operations required wide-ranging tests to keep pushing toward a horizon of complete and finite knowledge. As he explained, "Instead of a teaching methodology successfully employed in the past, I assume that all past undertakings are in some degree obsolete, as the total environment of the technical frontier is constantly providing improved means."[91] By discouraging study of the visual appearance of form, in his pedagogy he emphasized the benefit of leaping to connect form to its social utility.

In this sense, too, failure became the essential feature of experimental pedagogy and design; failure represented the freedom to stumble on the unforeseen. As Fuller declared,

> *Design* must imagine and discern . . . in as informed a manner as possible. *Design*, however, cannot guarantee its results. Failure . . . provides pivotal data for the efficient designer. . . . Failure in *design* is honourable, in science and engineering it is found to be mark of incompetence and failure in politics and finance is ruinous.[92]

He regarded the ethos of speculative experimentation, and its risks of failure, as reflecting the process of personal growth and transformation possible in education itself, and to some extent as helping to shed preoccupations about immediately determining a work's success. Every experimental failure yielded data and therefore revealed the rules and patterns underpinning the test. The Supine Dome typified his experimentation model; it allowed tactical failures as part of a larger strategy and emphasized the dynamic process of educational risk, not the success or failure of the discrete form of a single dome. For Fuller, alleviating struggles for scarce resources demanded uncovering the principles of a perfectly ordered world of predictable outcomes that could be revealed through experimental verification. As he remarked in 1949, the "integration of a complex series of failures represents the only means of attaining from nature" a plan about where to go next.[93] "Nature" would reveal its elusive secrets only after a prolonged campaign of discovery, each failure reinforcing the experimental methodology and yielding more data about the overarching system.

In Fuller's sometimes overweening confidence about the inevitable acceptance of his Dymaxion and dome designs, an important pedagogical precedent is found, despite and sometimes because of these inventions' often spectacular and highly publicized failures. His work represented an influential model for how students could—before they were tracked into disciplinary specializations—think holistically about their own roles in shaping a better and more just society. Although his methodology was cloaked in the flamboyant, self-important, and sometimes baffling rhetoric of his verbose written tracts and pseudoscientific neologisms, Fuller's inventions, and his discursive construction of experimentation as not incompatible with failure, continue to influence a diverse array of practitioners in art, architecture, design, engineering, and science (a class of dome-shaped carbon molecules has even been named for him).[94] He sensed dangerous cultural decline in specialists' inability to act in concert toward macro-level planning, and spent his long lifetime proposing alternative collaborative models between disciplines. His justification for risk, and the acceptance of failure as contributing to "systems-level" thinking, proved irresistible to those attending the 1948 and 1949 summer sessions at Black Mountain College. As John Cage paraphrased Fuller, "I learn much more when I have a failure than when I have a success."[95] Beyond Black Mountain, his "failure-as-risk" formulation influenced students of future generations as he became a sought-after speaker on the college lecture circuit by the 1960s. Yet instead of his dream of a technological utopia, it was the paradox of self-declared success in the face of apparent failure, of an experimentation model accommodating individual setbacks for the good of the larger holistic program, that is perhaps Fuller's greatest contribution to pedagogy and design teaching. To accomplish this holistic program, his "design revolution" had to be cleaved from political connotations, and technologically determined functionalism substituted for the vicissitudes of political action.

THE POLITICS OF THE DESIGN REVOLUTION

Fuller's yoking of pedagogy with risk meant that *anyone* could join the ranks of the comprehensive designers:

> What impressed me about me in making the experiment with me was that I was so very average. . . . I knew when I started in 1927 that I could not jump very high and I could not swim very fast and I hadn't earned the best marks in the class, and I was very obviously very average and inasmuch as I was interested in what the average individual could do, I was a very good case for experimentation.[96]

Fuller's universalization of experimentation—his sense that all students could participate in total thinking as comprehensivists because nature's universal laws were true and unchanging—was attractive at Black Mountain, to Cage in particular. Fuller's acceptance of accidents and failures demystified the role of the artist; as Cage noted, "I would like to make it, as Bucky Fuller does in his talks, where he says 'I'm just an average human being'—and to make it clear that anybody can do marvelous things."[97]

Cage credited Fuller's zeal for technological innovation as the necessary practical foundation for greater social and artistic freedom, linking it to his own belief in anarchy: "You see what anarchy needs in order to be practical is that all the utilities work. . . . If, in other words, the water works, the food works, and if there's money, and so on, if people have what they need, then anarchy gets along beautifully."[98] Despite the apparent differences between their experimental models, one deductive in the name of total design, the other at times mechanistic in the name of aleatory processes, Cage felt his view of apolitical experimentation was closely aligned with Fuller's:

> Bucky . . . agreed that there was no conflict between us. He said he was trying to make a world through his ideas that would work so well for everyone that they could live as I was suggesting. In other words, without intention, he was using his intention to make a world in which there could be the presence of non-intention. It would be organized so well that it could be, so to speak, without government.[99]

How two disparate approaches to experimentation could make such happy bedfellows at Black Mountain College reflects an underlying homology in their seemingly conflicting systems. Cage and Fuller were mutually suspicious of electoral politics, which they associated with the powers of governmental or other organizational authority over individuals' freedoms and creative independence. In a budding friendship that became a lifelong alliance, they proclaimed the distance of their respective experimental models from any political agendas, and shared a discomfort with organized political acts of any form. As was common in postwar, nascent McCarthyite America, they also claimed that the diminishing relevance of such acts, and their replacement by "total" planning and design, foreshadowed the decline of European culture, with its protracted history of political revolutions.[100]

Cage noted that despite the evident paradox of such an alliance, their parallel visions of a highly efficient utilitarianism anticipated a world emancipated from the human struggles technology would soon render obsolete. The great distance between this and perceptual formalisms such as Albers's turns on this very issue, perhaps more so than any other. What is Viktor Shklovsky's proposal to "make forms difficult" but a demand to uphold the intensity of art, as an ethical claim, in order to educate subjects about the complexity of art with respect to other social relations?[101] For Cage, the possibility of perceptual intensity remained open, if one can call an openness to the non-intention of void-like events "involvement," but only *after* Fuller's comprehensive designers had stitched up the logistical difficulties hampering social progress. To Albers, in contrast, art had special purchase in developing better attentiveness, by and through the complexity of form; this attentiveness could itself produce a better culture.

"I can't see much hope in the political solutions," Fuller announced in a 1948 talk at ID.[102] His pessimism was evident on the micro and local levels at Black Mountain College: he saw the changes in College leadership, changes that resulted in his assuming a more prominent role there in 1949, as an epic and deleterious political battle of left- versus right-wing Cold War ideology that comprehensive design and total thinking would resolve. The departure of the Alberses and Ted Dreier, the latter one of the College's original founders and a chief financial supporter (by way of his wealthy family), was, to Fuller, a result of a Communist plot to take over the College by purging the old guard; as he stated, "One of the places where cold psychological warfare probably first [started] was right at Black Mountain."[103] (Fuller's anti-Communism was *always* hyperbolic, to be sure; in actuality, that schism at the College resulted from debates about whether practical arts training or liberal arts courses should be emphasized.) Disdaining the power struggles that characterized the campus administration, Fuller claimed that in his tenure "I had a very free field on my comprehensivity at Black Mountain."[104]

Because Fuller felt himself to be above the political fray, in an interview he distinguished his position throughout the internecine battles at the College thusly: "I'm certainly not a Communist but I'm certainly not a capitalist, I'm really very transcendental to political—I think that politics is now irrelevant and obsolete so I don't belong to any of the camps."[105] Rather than participating in skirmishes at the College, he aligned himself with Cage, Merce Cunningham, and others he considered to be separate from or agnostic to political conflicts. In this, he repeatedly invoked "democracy" as a blanket form of counter-Communism, but his could be said to be a most quixotic form of democracy, applied speedily and efficiently from above as a kind of universal value whose main purpose was to ensure a population's free and equal access to technological improvements—less direct democracy than direct design.[106] Comprehensive designers would buck "traditional" electoral politics, acting instead as techno-gurus or omniscient cosmologists selflessly plotting global change in the interest of a radical, egalitarian dissemination of technology—the key example being Fuller's own advocacy of the geodesic dome as a comprehensive design solution to many if not all the world's problems.

After the success of the second geodesic dome assembly at Black Mountain, Fuller set about promoting it as a design revolution with a strenuous public relations campaign; the benefit of domes was touted to journalists, military strategists, and students alike. Lightweight and portable, geodesic domes could

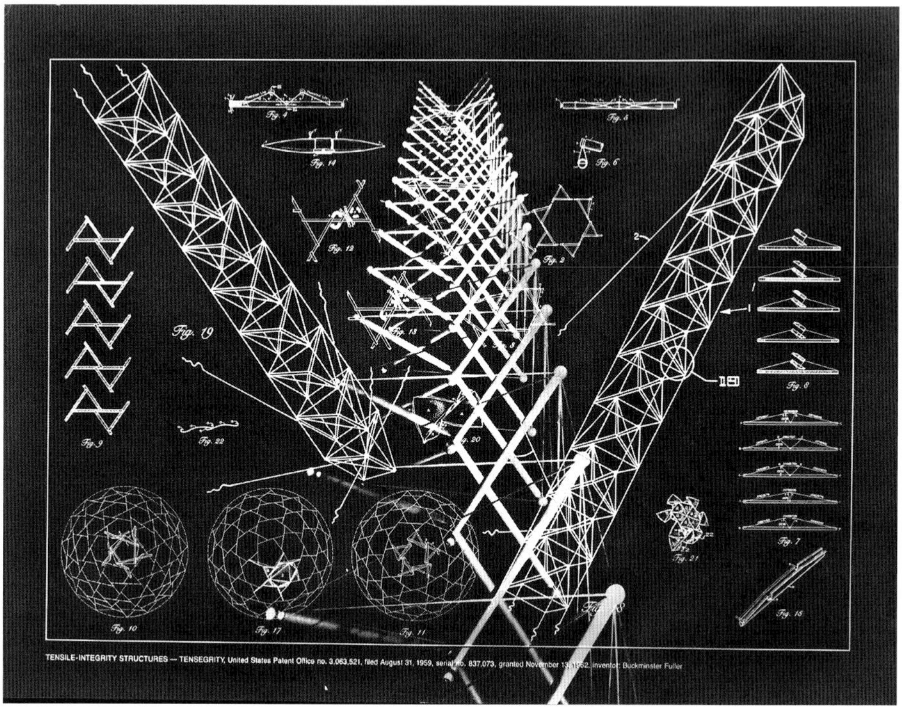

Figure 3.14
Buckminster Fuller, *Tensile Integrity Structures—Tensegrity*, technical drawing for 1959 patent filing. Screenprint in white ink on clear polyester film overlaid on a screenprint on Lennox paper, 30 × 40". From *Inventions: Twelve Around One* (Cincinnati: Carl Solway Gallery, 1981). Edition of 60. Courtesy Carl Solway Gallery, Cincinnati, Ohio.

be airlifted to sites previously inaccessible to construction, and their use of inexpensive building materials such as aluminum meant that large structures such as airplane hangars could be manufactured cheaply. Featuring Fuller's newly developed octet truss (a lattice-like system of triangular struts braced in 60-degree configurations) that utilized the tensegrity principle, domes became exponentially stronger as their surface area increased[107] (fig. 3.14). The dome's curved exterior profile reduced external wind drag, and its circular shape encouraged internal heat circulation. Precise factory prefabrication would facilitate speedy on-site assembly and keep labor and construction costs low. Moreover, the large internal volume of the dome could be effectively utilized by suspending multiple decks from its frame, thereby adding further square footage. And because the surface area of the enclosing dome skin equals twice the area of its base (in contrast to traditional rectilinear housing construction, in which the outer area is between three to five times as large as the enclosed

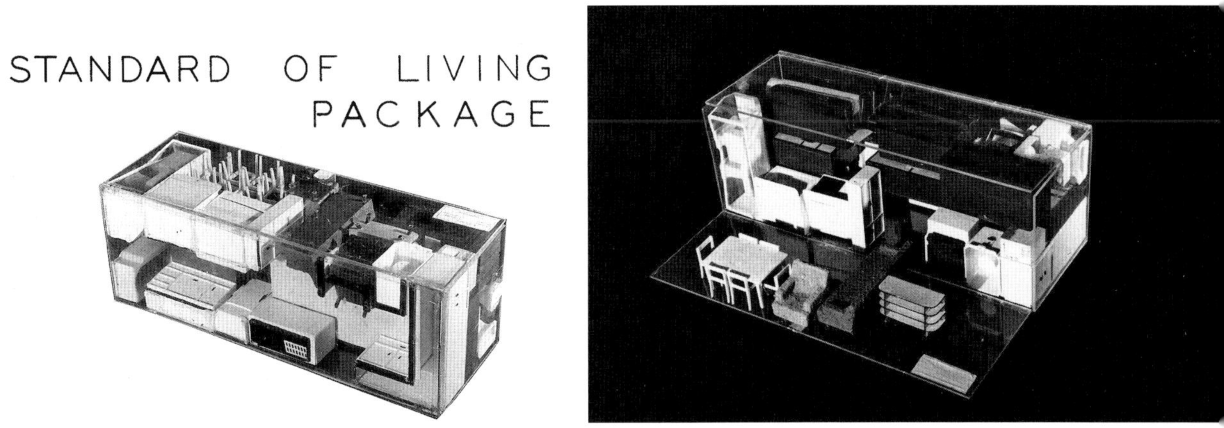

Figure 3.15
Buckminster Fuller, *Standard of Living Package*, 1947.
Courtesy The Estate of R. Buckminster Fuller.

square footage), domes required less material and energy resources to construct than other buildings of equivalent size.

Not content with merely industrial applications, Fuller envisioned the dome as an easily transported shell for a prepackaged home system he termed the "autonomous dwelling machine" (fig. 3.15; plate 17). Shipped via freight container, the dwelling machine already contained all infrastructural elements (plumbing, refrigeration, heat, electrical wiring) in addition to all appliances and furniture that occupants generally purchased separately, what he called the "standard of living package." Yet he contrasted such a dwelling with the range of prefabricated homes then popular in the housing market.[108] To Fuller, in prefabrication "the box is primary," that is, a set of rectilinear panels are perched on a preexisting foundation. Additionally, the contents of the house—furniture, appliances, and fixtures—are rarely supplied. Though the prefab house is originally mobile, once it finds its platform it remains fixed and permanent. Even before his successful dome assembly, in other words, Fuller was contending that the notion of the house as a static object was outmoded: "'Prefabricated' houses represent the latest phase of treating with the obsolete concept that the individual and the family are identified with only one spot on this earth's surface."[109] A lattice dome's collapsible and mobile aspect presented a new, "evolutionary" prospect of shelters that could be as peripatetic as human beings' own ambulatory character, and would use postwar innovations in containerization to treat homes as cargo. But beyond humanity's history of migration and nomadic patterns, movement was perhaps the single most defining quality of the universe itself, its universal law, so to speak. This was a strikingly prescriptive sense of architecture literally moving humanity toward its technologically enriched destiny: as Fuller wrote in 1945, it was nothing less than "the emancipation of society from its shackled environment."[110] Indeed, according to historian Antoine Picon, "Fuller dreamed of a fluid society in the universe's own image with all of its components in radiation and flow."[111]

By connecting architectural structure to dynamic energy flows, the dwelling machine responded to patterns of nomadism Fuller believed should and would supersede the fortress/mansion model of home construction. The dwelling machine's integrated and portable network of infrastructure knit together "a tight but neat assembly of various mechanical units," permitting the "shell"—the form and façade of the home—to remain secondary to the "dwelling activities" within.[112] Aiming to mass-produce the entire house package, Fuller hoped to make a standard version available to lower-income groups while enticing wealthy customers with deluxe editions. In the immediate postwar period, he predicted, housing would be the most "outstanding demand" globally.[113] Yet fragmented and localized housing construction markets encouraged short-term profits and static design considerations rather than a dynamic reconsideration of the industry's goals and potential. As Fuller wrote, "I am dubious of any good coming from those who promote for the sake of making money instead of for the sake of mass producing up-standard housing."[114]

Selling the mobile dome as a bundled package, however novel a sales gimmick, failed for several important reasons. The dwelling machine package did not allow for much customization, and neglected that many potential buyers had invested heavily in existing possessions and appliances, most of which were duplicated or made superfluous by a bundled purchase. And though hypothetically several size options were available, in effect the dome was a standardized silhouette; in art historian Branden Joseph's words, for Fuller "universal accessibility [was] gained at the cost of rendering the world universally similar."[115] Moreover, the shape of the dome itself was not amenable to customary furniture—its curved interior walls were unsuitable for most existing interior designs—and the affordable costs Fuller publicized presupposed high-volume mass production, though in reality each single package was prohibitively expensive. Additionally, domes as "autonomous dwelling machines" were envisioned as single-family homes in suburban land tracts or rural areas, atomized and disconnected from existing, occupied central-city areas.

Perhaps it is not surprising that Fuller's view of architecture as dispersed through the extra-urban frontier found its greatest fiscal patronage in US military agencies that sporadically used his geodesic domes for remote Arctic utility outposts and as helicopter hangars. And though the dome later found its broadest nonmilitary audience in countercultural communities of the 1960s and 1970s who adopted it in part due to Stewart Brand's advocacy of Fuller in the *Whole Earth Catalog*, even in these manifestations the structure was a symptom of decentralized, low-density sprawl. Some have argued that "dropping out" and living in a dome became a subcultural alternative to active participation in urban society.[116] And yet, with their "access to tools" ethos, the *Whole Earth Catalog* and its other do-it-yourself satellite publications and organizations were particularly important forums for exploring, testing, and propagating Fuller's demand to think of experimentation as an often absurdly impractical prototyping.[117] It was this freedom to fail that had been an immensely liberating lesson at Black Mountain, too.

In the case of Fuller's propagation of the dome, can we see both a libertarian individualism *and* a messianic technocratic determinism at play? As Mark Wigley has commented, in Fuller's world "a quasitheological view underpins the questionable sense of the beauty of 'natural order,' the 'harmony' of the cosmos, and so on. Ecology is a barely disguised form of theology."[118] Fuller had argued that designers were the ultimate apolitical seers: "My envisioned transcendental world design plan would be inherently non-political, because it would be utterly independent of any need for authority beyond that [necessary] for initiation of its study and development."[119]

In positing a utopian place outside politics, some have suggested that Fuller misrecognized social rule as the repression of individuals' creative initiative, thereby dismissing political participation as a confusing cacophony of inefficient, conflicting interests.[120] Comprehensive designers were ultimately responsible to that abstraction called democracy else they appear as Communist master planners, yet actual democratic processes remained sidelined in a vision of society as a hyperefficient architecture of networked domes outfitted with "standard living packages."[121]

Fuller's suspicions about politics as a collective social process ran deep. What he viewed as the most advanced political system—America's multiparty representative democracy—he simultaneously accused of having intractable structural flaws, and he was deeply skeptical of the slow pace and retrograde pluralism he attributed to postwar mass elections. He was even more distrustful of the politicians such a process voted into power, and dismissed voting outright, claiming of his own "preventative pathology,"

> *Ipso facto* this is a technical rather than a political scheme. Therefore the referendum cannot be initiated by politics. Political referendums have become

negative referendums in which the lesser antipathy is registered. However, our industrial-consumer referendum, which is proposed here, can and will be ultimately recognized and incorporated by politics as mandatory.[122]

Fuller condemned political leaders of all stripes for the slow pace of change, and denied them praise for any successes in improving living standards.[123] To him, humanity had been raised from material deprivation by technological improvements, not by the political gains of revolutions. He argued that with a closer relationship to capitalism, scientific design could unleash greater freedoms for individuals. But as "clients" of industry, public will conversely could be seen as subordinated, and supervision remained firmly in the hands of designers. As Fuller crowed, "Comprehensive anticipatory design science assumes that the client knows absolutely nothing about what he needs or what should be done about it."[124]

To Fuller, experimentation itself was a profoundly altruistic though nonpartisan enterprise. Society's tendency toward specialization was anathema; it dispersed accountability for global concerns through a field of compartmentalized political agencies in competing nations. The charge to designers, then, was to convert reactive and compensatory political thinking into "anticipating and laboratory experimenting."[125] The problem was politics, and the solution was more technology, distributed in a more equitable fashion. Thus, Fuller's universalist proposals aimed to redistribute access to global resources, including the resource of design thinking itself, in the name of the public good. Yet rather than redistributing existing *wealth*, he proclaimed that the pace of development could be accelerated so that those without technological advantages could soon be raised up into the "natural world equilibrium" of a universal class.[126] What Fuller advocated was nothing less than "a design revolution and not a political revolution."[127] He insisted as much:

> All previous revolutions have been designed where the vast majority of the underprivileged pulled down the undeserving few. In a design revolution you don't pull anything down; we elevate not only the previously underprivileged but [also] those who thought they were privileged to something really good. We get equality attained at the top, and not at the bottom. We've never had a revolution like that before.[128]

As he pointed out, the "design revolution . . . this was an entirely new idea, and was not political. And it simply took the initiative away from politics."[129] The transformation from pointless voting to economic Easy Street could be accomplished after a "critical point" was reached—when more than 50 percent of the global population would equally benefit from access to all available technologies (estimated by Fuller in 1952 to occur in 1972; peak industrialization and commodity distribution were to be attained in the year 2000). At that time, "everybody will realize that their physical success is in terms of man as consumer instead of man as a producer (because very rapidly in a technical sense, we are transferring from man as a muscle machine to man as a prototyping and reorganizing, redesigning initiator)."[130]

Technology should be equitably distributed, Fuller maintained, but it also should be applied scientifically. In a key statement of his goals, he wrote a memo to the J. Walter Thompson Company, a leading advertising agency, seeking to inform it of his "plan for reconversion of a major portion of the war aircraft industry to mass production of dwelling machines."[131] Dome structures, made of the same lightweight aluminum as airplanes, of course fit the bill splendidly for such a project. For Fuller, the way total thinking tested "practical principles" demonstrated "a preventative philosophy of living instead of a now excruciatingly curative psychology of necessity," the results being "far greater than will ever be manifested by politics or lip service."[132] He regarded this preventative work of comprehensive design as "a sociological science of precisely definable and equatable mechanics."[133] Here emerges a key paradox of Fuller's claims to total planning—and indeed the limitation of all technocratic thinking—that social desires can be "precisely definable" and mechanical. It can be argued that he succumbed to a deterministic functionalism in which social agency is subject to "all-pervasive laws" discernible by designers alone.[134]

In this vein Reyner Banham, inspired by the spirit of language play that coined the "Dymaxion" slogan, christened Fuller a "dymaxicrat."[135] By joining the already compound *Dymaxion* with *technocrat*, he underscored Fuller's contradictory position in design circles—as both a technological innovator *and* a (prolix) spokesperson for technology (and Banham humorously remarked on the problem of writing around Fuller's neologisms and linguistic animations: "Comprehensibility survives into print, if the text is Bucky's own, but if it is written by another hand . . . trouble!").[136] He recognized that Fuller's confidence in technology was a kind of blind trust, in that "he operationally demonstrate[d] a true hot-rodder's faith that when he want[ed] a component or adapter, one [would] pop out of the cornucopia of U.S. technology."[137] Perhaps this faith was in fact a kind of hubris, if the "technocrat" part of Banham's formulation is given equal weight with "Dymaxion." The comprehensive designer—"the artist"—in effect becomes a kind of redeemer, elevating society out of the quagmire of inefficiency and stagnation that to Fuller characterized indecisive political processes.[138] The faith in technological solutions and the broad application of his design principles were undertaken in the name of public good, yet without the public's participation. In effect, Fuller had substituted techno-boosterism for democracy, experimentation for politics. His emphasis on comprehensive design implied that only exceptional individuals could save the masses from themselves, and his criteria for who in fact qualified as a designer were never clearly defined or transparent.[139]

In sum, Fuller's "total thinking" experimental model is open to several possible criticisms. The first stems from a tautological fallacy at the heart of many totalizing justifications for technocratic social planning: that in thinking holistically about the "big picture," failures today will assuredly be credited later as deferred proofs. The second relates to Fuller's attempts to liberate design from the tyranny of short-term expediency caused by ineffective political stewardship with a promise of smoothly functioning and equitably distributed technological solutions for all. In the wholesale adoption of a totalizing system, however, modifications and actions beyond the prescribed architectural program were unaccounted for, and the agency of those individuals in whose names he acted were subsumed in large-scale master-planning initiatives. Claiming to facilitate the "body politic" being given a "controlling voice," Fuller instead acted as if emancipation from poverty, hunger, and material want were *absolutely*, not merely routinely, neglected by the "special interests" of democratic squabbling.[140] As he declared, liberation from the "monopoly" of majority rule "will be provided only by scientific organization."[141] Was there room for contingency, change, and individual agency in Fuller's "total process"?[142] Or was "total thinking" a scheme of paternalistic oversight—or worse yet, a regime of totalitarian design?

The answer might be: *both*. Fuller was perhaps the postwar period's most enthusiastic technophilic utopian; he believed that the world's population could be fed and housed with existing global resources, but only if master planners were allowed to efficiently allocate them. He saw the tremendous benefits of technological development—for example, in raising standards of living worldwide—but few of its pitfalls. Those problems he patly attributed to an inequitable distribution of technology on the part of governments. He disavowed technocracy by name, distancing himself from the concept by claiming that technocracy was political and because he was apolitical, he was "not a technocrat . . . there is no political aspect to my talk." Yet technology was in effect an electric messiah, and he its prophet promising the end of labor and material want: "When the environment is scientifically conceived and rendered, the human occupants can then divest themselves of the necessity of onerous and Puritanic hardship."[143]

Postulating a world of voluntary or unalienated labor has been a hallmark of utopian thinking from Jonathan Swift to Karl Marx to László Moholy-Nagy, yet Fuller's vision had several distinct characteristics. Historian Reinhold Martin has noted of Fuller's predictive and deterministic logic that "he sought to reconcile disunities into a contrived unity in the service of 'the future.'"[144] Additionally, Fuller believed that technology was at heart universally positive: "Technology was a basic resource that improved, or self-multiplied, with each repeated opportunity of its application."[145] Although he was critical of the munitions industry, for example, he supported developments in war technology because of the many practical applications in the civilian sector; such applications, he felt, justified the research and its devastating effects.[146] Nor did he view technological development as selective in its applications when driven by financial considerations.

Criticisms of Fuller's relationship to profit-driven development gained momentum in subsequent decades; indeed, many found his uncompromising endorsement of capitalism problematic and discomfiting. To some, Fuller's design revolution was willfully naïve regarding technological advancement, neglecting that the competitive economies for research and the distribution of technology were frequently controlled by capitalist, not magnanimous, imperatives. Instead, he believed that industrialization was at root a process of extending the benefits of scientific innovation throughout the world.[147] To Fuller, private industry was the main engine of technological progress, and he believed it had the public good as its primary interest. Countering this thinking, in an epistolary debate from the 1930s Meyer Schapiro upbraided Fuller's shelter designs for several forms of disingenuousness.[148] Schapiro's essay pointedly criticized Fuller for his

> faith in an automatic evolution of society through improved housing techniques, irrespective of the conflict of class-interests. For how can one suppose that a new device for manufacturing cheaper houses, controlled by the corporations, which are, by their very nature, party to overproduction, competition, wage-slashing, unemployment speculation, will by itself work any appreciable change in the structure of capitalist society?[149]

In positioning citizenship within a consumer model, the capitalist economy became for Fuller the engine running civic participation. Admitting that the current organization of capitalist production was inadequate and perpetuated patterns of unequal access to housing and other basic resources, he could not, however, overcome his optimistic belief that industry would "evolve" of its own goodwill. As Schapiro remarked: "Precisely how technology will yield this result [a less wasteful industry] is never stated. . . . Capitalism, it seems, will simply wither away. The ruling class will awaken one morning and discover that its holdings are valueless, but that its services to humanity will continue on a more noble technological level."[150] That the private sector never fully accepted or financially underwrote Fuller's schemes was due perhaps to this fundamental misapprehension about the ostensibly unselfish objectives and charitable goals of profit-driven technologies.

Additionally, Fuller thought scientific innovation could be applied more justly by encouraging scientists to reflect generally on society's problems as opposed to working narrowly as specialists. But in assuming that society's problems are coextensive with the problems of science, Fuller was committing the common error of seeing the social benefits of innovation as the primary factor motivating scientific discovery. As many philosophers of science from Karl Popper to Thomas Kuhn have noted, scientific progress is sometimes driven by internal protocols having more to do with professionalization and the buttressing of confirmed postulates on which career successes are based than any notion of scientific altruism as an interest in progressive social change.

In sum, Fuller provided few insights as to how the *structure* of society could be transformed; functionalism does tend to avoid asking such questions in its pursuit of mapping existing systems. In scorning political action, he placed no faith in the pace of democratic change. To him, it was a matter of exceptional individuals stepping up to the task of envisioning social problems holistically. Fuller clearly wanted inequalities ameliorated, but he did not mean for the underprivileged to take matters into their own hands in any other way than to become trained as comprehensive designers. He foreswore mass political action as mass populism, or what he termed "mob outburst."[151] In 1952 he wrote, in words that echo the rhetoric of present-day right-wing pundits, that it was "historically easy for insurgent politicians to excite the 99% who were have-nots against the few 'privileged' men."[152] Nor did he ever question the sanctity of private property or private enterprise. Equality was simply a matter of capitalism waking up to its inefficiencies.

Never is it explored that capitalism might *produce* class and other inequalities as an effect of its rampant technological development. Fuller believed that social problems could be isolated from the fabric of systemic inequality, prototypes generated that could attempt to solve such problems, and finally a "testing thereof under both theoretical and working conditions, in all ways consistent with the best technical practices in late phases of industry."[153] He was experimenting with refining the veneer of capitalist production to encourage a wider distribution of technology's boons, yet he never questioned the structure of class inequity. His positivist fixation with facts led Fuller to reduce experience to its quantifiable features: as he claimed, "One of the most important contributions of science to society is its development of the ability to consider all of the wonders of the physical universe as measurable and rational and of immediate practical significance."[154] To borrow from Max Horkheimer's description of this sort of positivist empiricism, Fuller's instrumentalized reason never "[rose] above the consideration of immediate utilitarian values . . . [to] devote itself to reflections about the social order as a whole."[155]

Though he may have neglected "the social order as a whole," Fuller's underlying argument that shelter was a crucial problem, and that inadequate housing for the poor could be redressed on a global scale, was a persuasive one in its time and into the present. The limitation of politics, in his view, was its inability to see beyond compensatory fixes to pressing concerns. Such expedient thinking occasioned a crisis-response pattern that foreclosed long-term strategic planning, which in turn triggered a series of avoidable emergencies that required extensive resources to ameliorate. The comprehensive, anticipatory designer could alleviate this pattern of inefficient short-term spending. As Fuller stated, "It is up to the creative pioneer to see to it in advance that his good life-saving equipment has been carefully designed and tested and made ready to hand against the certain coming of the emergency."[156] Moreover, his "creative pioneer" of technocracy would ostensibly "render the total tonnage of world resources effectively distributable to the physical advantage of the total world population."[157] In these claims, Fuller was part of a larger "post-scarcity" technocratic utopianism claiming that the tools for such a redistribution were available, and only needed to be systematically applied by social planners.[158] But justifying such means-ends rationalisms is more difficult—in Fuller's capitulation to a quasi-autocratic design process of total thinking, only very few individuals, in practice, were able to see the big picture and deduce the appropriate problems to test.

His skepticism about political action was in part tied to wider cultural fears pervasive in the post–World War II nuclear age, and his work stands at the crossroads of a period in which war's destruction was frequently attributed to political shortsightedness, not to overinvestment in a limited range of (often military) technologies. One of the comprehensive designer's main tasks was anticipating the effects of an imminent, devastating nuclear episode, an event Fuller portrayed as yet another indictment of the political misapplication of technology, in no way connected to munitions profiteering and the interpenetration of science research with military spending. In 1949, his lectures at the Institute of Design presented his students with the following problem of apocalypse-cum-homework assignment: "The city is to be evacuated. All residential and industrial concentrations of 50,000 persons or more are in immediate danger of annihilation. Consumable goods now directed towards these areas will be diverted to smaller decentralized communities. . . . Everything

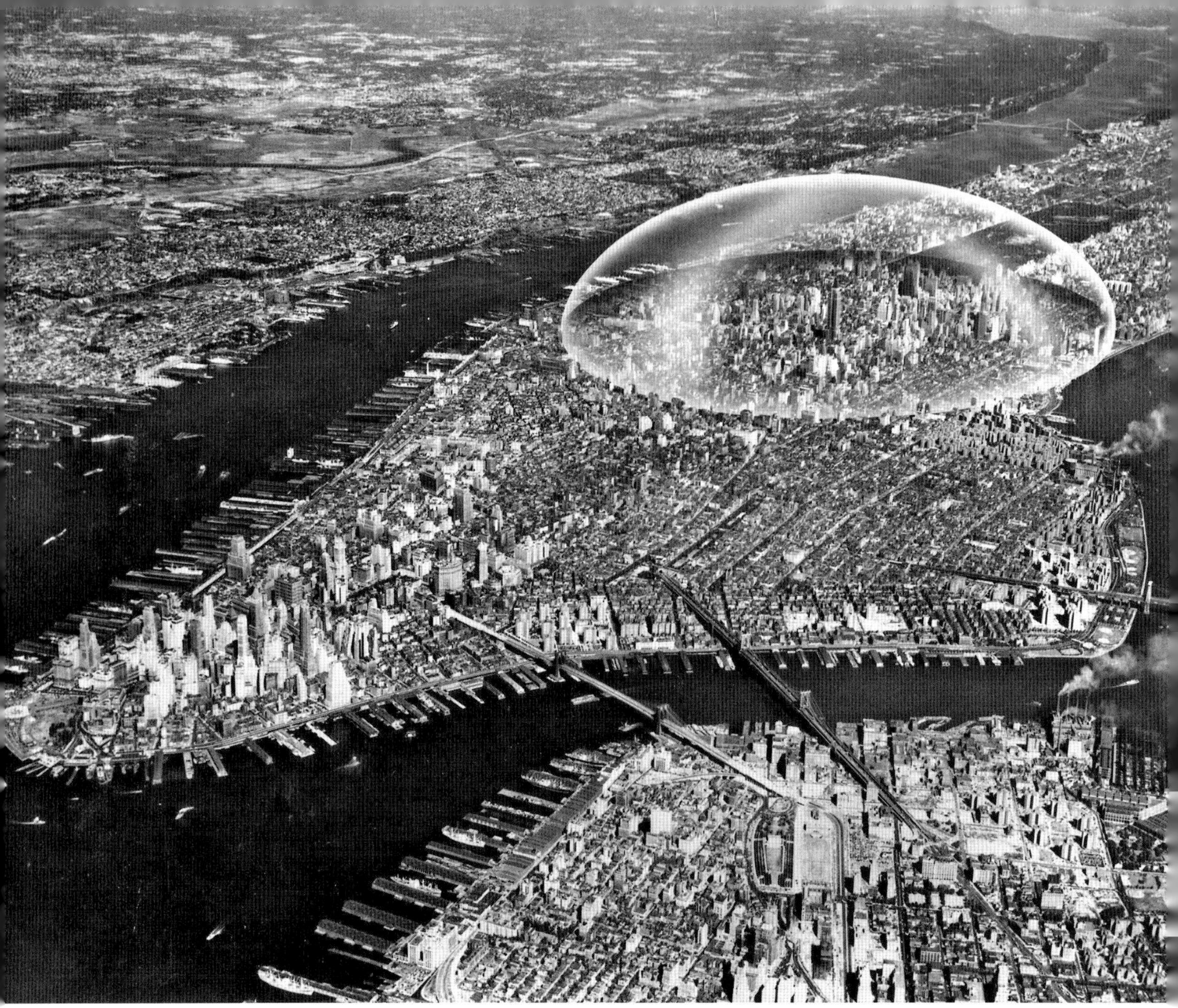

Figure 3.16
Buckminster Fuller and Shoji Sadao, *Dome Over Midtown Manhattan*, 1960. Courtesy The Estate of R. Buckminster Fuller.

not decentralized will be destroyed."[159] To Fuller, suburban dispersal was the optimal response to the threat of nuclear attack; existing urban centers could, however, be selectively shielded. One of his most ambitious proposals was for the construction of a giant transparent dome covering Midtown Manhattan: a colossal fallout protection device[160] (fig. 3.16). Such eschatological musings lent urgency to his projects in much the same way that totalitarian impulses have often traded in fear and insecurity.

Fuller attempted to move beyond specialization—artistic, political, or otherwise—toward a unity of technological progress and industrial design. His call for a comprehensive approach to mass housing and emergency planning, and

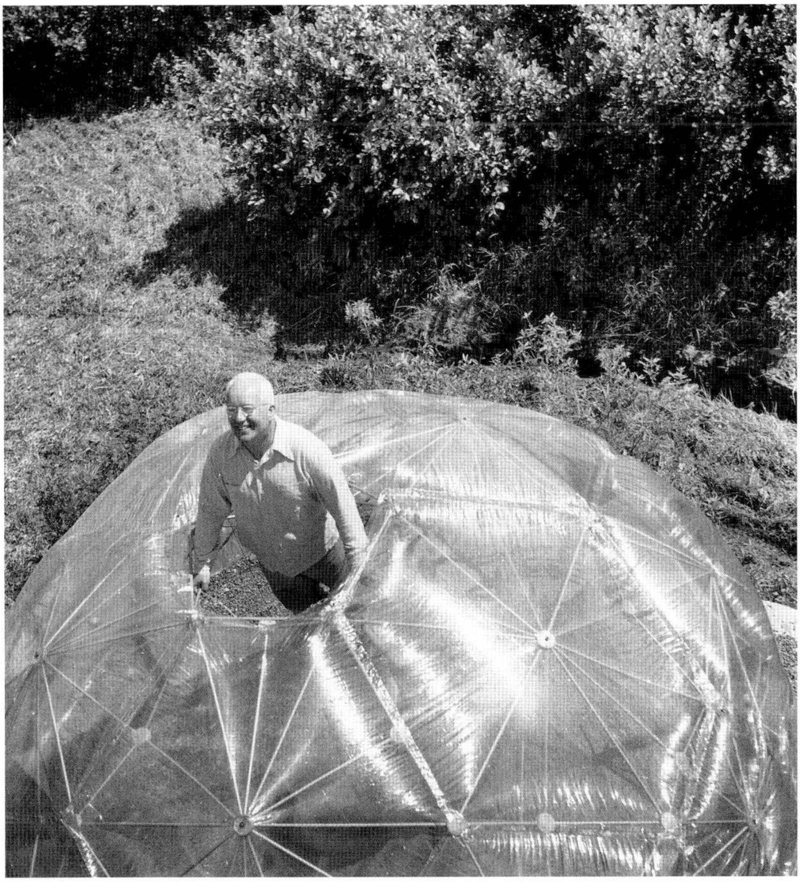

Figure 3.17
Hazel Larsen Archer, *Buckminster Fuller with Dome, Black Mountain College*, summer 1949. Courtesy of the Estate of Hazel Larsen Archer and the Black Mountain College Museum + Arts Center.

his prototyping of viable alternative structures in the absence of robust governmental initiative or private patronage, represent an important ad hoc ethic to solving problems of unequal access to shelter. His time at Black Mountain coincided with the optimistic moment before the escalation of Cold War military spending, similar to the recent *post*–Cold War one, in which a reallocation of global resources to social justice ends seemed possible.

Yet Fuller's language of experimentation was coextensive with a midcentury cultural lexicon emphasizing scientificity in a spirit of American technological optimism and exceptionalism. Design would henceforth be the central element of social planning, superseding political processes: design toward the telos of efficiently distributed technology. Fuller believed that technological development stimulated progress beyond politics along a "great circle course of transition from absolute ignorance to absolute technical knowledge."[161] His design revolution—technocracy by another name—advocated the efficient distribution of resources in a society reoriented toward the complete acceptance of scientific authority. His idea of the dome as a manifestation of the patterns of nature to him proved the infallible truth of his discoveries, in which alternatives and the unknown gradually fell away as the universal order of total design was revealed. Fuller's experimental method may be best understood as design striving for the elimination of unpredictability, contingency, and chance, so as to allow art to remain open to those self-same concerns.

epilogue legacies of black mountain college

The category of the experimental in art is a porous one. Experimentation can encompass practices that are incongruous, even fundamentally irreconcilable, and its very porosity has often elided competing visions about spontaneity and rationality, improvisation and discipline, order and chaos, or the relationship of art and life that charged midcentury discussions about it.

At Black Mountain College in the immediate post–World War II period, experimentation was adopted by some faculty and students who rejected the drift toward expressionism.[1] One could even call experimentation, in its diversity, *the* Black Mountain College idea, marking an important, yet relatively overlooked episode in the history of midcentury American art practices, pedagogy, and modernism more generally. What emerged from this episode was not a single alternative to expressionism. The models of experiment Josef Albers, John Cage, and Buckminster Fuller proposed—in Albers's case, the methodical testing of the various appearances and constructions of forms in the interest of designing new aesthetic experiences; in Cage's example, an exploration of how aleatory processes can be organized in order to anarchically generate indeterminate outcomes; and in Fuller's paradigm, a type of "comprehensive, anticipatory design science" that tests traditional artistic and architectural forms in order to teleologically progress toward a utopia of efficiently managed resources—represent a set of disparate directions for postwar art, music, and architecture.

Though it would be beyond the purview of this project to trace the considerable repercussions of Albers's, Cage's, and Fuller's models of experimentation into the present, it is worthwhile to sketch some directions for future research. Despite their different definitions of experimentation, the intensity of these men's Black Mountain dialogues and the intersection of their various efforts at an arts education institution consequently mapped Black Mountain–era debates onto later artistic practices. This emphasis on pedagogy lent a designer like Fuller and a composer like Cage tremendous influence in art practices and discourses of the 1950s and 1960s: Neo-Dada, Fluxus, Judson Dance Theater, the Independent Group, Experiments in Art and Technology, and Land Art, as well as art ventures associated with the *Whole Earth Catalog* and the journal *Radical Software* such as Ant Farm and Drop City, can be traced to their inspiration or direct participation. Yet practices of experimentation at Black Mountain in the late 1940s and early 1950s should themselves always be situated within the larger historical context of artistic experiment or laboratory-based production—of the Bauhaus in Albers's case, or Francophone Dada in Cage's, or interdisciplinary applications of scientistic methods in Fuller's.

Albers's influence at Black Mountain College and Yale University on students such as Ray Johnson, Kenneth Noland, Robert Rauschenberg, Eva Hesse, and Richard Serra has been broached in recent scholarship, but would profit from further analysis.[2] In particular, how and why does Albers's rhetoric of experiment and contingency, in the vocabulary of Hesse's and Serra's work, increasingly become a phenomenological argument about the conditions under which art objects are tested and made contingent by forces such as gravity, and put in a relational field with other objects and bodies? Also, Albers's emphasis on process led some of his students to perceive art objects as artifacts of rehearsed performances, but in ways that pushed the logic of variation toward a concern with the serialized mark—Robert Rauschenberg's *Factum I* and *Factum II* of 1957 are perhaps the best examples of this, but Ray Johnson's painting-collage *Moticos* also repeated motifs increasingly divorced from their source material, as in his 1957–58 series using images of James Dean[3] (plates 18–20).

The secondary reception of Albers in the mid-1960s by those who were not his students is also relatively underanalyzed. The recovery by minimalists of early twentieth-century formalisms foregrounded the relativity of perception at the level of color and proportion, and heightened concern about the contextualization of works by situating their seriality in relation to the environments in which they were displayed.[4] Albers's model of experimentation was revisited, by artist-critic Donald Judd, artist Sol LeWitt, and particularly by critic John Coplans, as a progenitor to serial practices as they shifted from explorations of sequentiality (works on consistent subjects, themes, or forms) to works based on systems.[5]

Albers did not cultivate disciples, and it would be too simple to see his influence merely in works that refer to his idea of the relativity of color, such as those presented in the 2008 contemporary art exhibition at the Museum of Modern Art, *Color Chart: Reinventing Color from 1950 to Today*, or to register the effect of his work on painters that continue practices of geometric abstraction.[6] Like Albers, many artists today deploy a language of experimental testing and variation toward understanding how the visual appearance and material constitution of form represent the foundational elements of artistic practice, in large part because Albers's students trained further generations by adopting his teaching methods as faculty at Yale, the University of Pennsylvania, and the Cooper Union, in particular.[7]

In moving from a midcentury modernist project to the present, it is worth probing the relevance today of the Albersian notion of art as attentiveness to form, as a strategy of carefully attending to, and possibly altering, habits of perception.[8] To Albers, the better "vision" of art that attentive perception would trigger is an awareness of the ways in which the individual is sited in the larger field of social relations. Everything in the world has form, he claimed; training the eye in the composition of form was a precondition for understanding and possibly transforming the world. Today, this idea of the function of art as opening eyes wide to the phenomena of the world might offer a criterion by which to distinguish artistic practices from other types of visual or sensory experiences. The Albers pedagogical tradition, with its emphasis on illuminating viewers about the fundamental (and often overlooked) elements of form by demanding a close attention to their own perceptual stimuli, is rich with potential for both artists and art historians today.

Albers's strenuous emphasis on order and disciplined work was frequently cast as dogmatic and single-minded at the College and elsewhere, but it must be remembered that his vision of a diverse art curriculum was the impetus behind his invitations to Cage and Fuller to join the Black Mountain faculty. In contrast to this rigorous emphasis on pedagogy, experimentation for Cage and Fuller was less rooted in a codified teaching practice in their years at the College, which in some ways explains the different reception their ideas received in subsequent years. The thoroughness of Albers's model was sometimes chafing for more advanced students; for others, the parameters for contingency were too narrowly conceived as painstaking trial-and-error experimentation. In contrast, Cage's emphasis on indeterminate outcomes, and Fuller's acceptance of failure, often allowed for more risky and complex ventures that brought artistic practices into a more immediate relationship to their audiences.

Although figures such as Cage and Fuller were in residence for relatively brief periods, the events they initiated at the College colored their future work and the reception of their careers. It is no coincidence that Cage staged the chance-derived happening and several of his other early groundbreaking experimental performances at the same Black Mountain that was home to Albers's pioneering tests of perception in design. Cage's work was a crucial new element taking its place among various tendencies of performance already present at the College that charted a spectrum of possibilities about order, chance, and design. In the case of performance-specific events, these new explorations focused on the body—its relation and perception in space, its interactions with objects and audiences, its movement in time, its intelligibility (or not) within narrative structures, and its role in fabricating illusions or, conversely, stressing quotidian gestures—in ways that reemerged in Cage's influential Experimental Composition courses taught at the New School in New York from 1957 to 1959. There, Cage introduced future Fluxus-bound students Jackson Mac Low, Allan Kaprow, Al Hansen, George Brecht, and Dick Higgins to the possibility of contingency in scoring and performance, which they expanded and reworked.

Of course, even a quick summary of Cage-inspired art would far exceed the scope of this discussion, yet it is worth noting that tracing and comparing the shifting reception of his work by his students—first at Black Mountain by Rauschenberg, Johnson, and Cy Twombly, and later by those that took his New School courses—would be fertile ground for research.[9] For example, at least three directions were taken up by his students in response to the provocation of Cage's experimental model developed at Black Mountain: explorations of the minimal denotation of form and monochromatic painting stemming from his arguments about Zen, silence, and void-like experiences; the scripting of simultaneously occurring events in the form of happenings; and the notion that quotidian events could be fodder for artistic practices in the development of the "event score."[10]

Cage's institution of a chance protocol fundamentally altered the landscape of possibilities for performance art in postwar America, as is particularly evident in its adoption by Fluxus and Judson Dance Theater performers in the early 1960s. But, as we have seen, certain precedents were overshadowed in its preeminence. In particular, the mapping of the body in terms of its architectonic relations championed by Oskar Schlemmer, Walter Gropius, and László Moholy-Nagy offers underrecognized though vital precedents for thinking gesture: the body's effects in specific environments and its determinations by preexisting conditions in those environments. It is worth rethinking the benefits of the disorienting sensory overload that Cage (through Antonin Artaud) evoked, and questioning how he plotted the dissolution of art into life through indeterminate events.

As opposed to the rationalist and focused visual illusions of Albers and other Bauhaus figures, Cage's chance-derived phenomenological overload and unfocused attention broadened the boundaries of perception by using control and reason to arrive at unreason, flux, and disorder. Yet in this, it may come to resemble entertainment, diversion, and a wash of confounding effects that immerse the subject. Cage proposed "letting sounds be themselves."[11] This implies that not only is the composer abdicating control over final results, but that the spectator is asked to remain a relatively passive observer of a score's "infinite play of interpenetration."[12] As Merce Cunningham Company dancer Carolyn Brown has commented, such an approach may present a "philosophy . . . of reluctance, even refusal, to let *people* be *themselves*."[13] Cage's chance protocol was compelled by a much deeper philosophical critique of non-intention and "carelessness" that posited experimentation beyond verbal intention, redefining it as attention scattered through a field of independently transacted and seemingly unrelated events.[14]

In the case of Fuller's work, many today are stimulated by his postwar dome technologies to radically rethink architectural structures, both as a practical solution to urban housing crises (proposing ad hoc, lightweight, portable, and efficient shelters), and as a key historical trope of innovative "guerilla"—decentralized and possibly unauthorized—architecture. Fuller's rambling, sometimes haranguing exhortations can be distilled to a basic set of claims that have subsequently proved immensely influential: he proposed that a radical and equitable redistribution of global resources (including natural and existing technological resources used to house, feed, and clothe the world's population) could be accomplished through an experimental study of dynamic patterns of consumption. In turn, the universal application of pattern knowledge would use the criterion of efficiency in design to allocate the sufficient resources of the planet, "Spaceship Earth." In these claims, Fuller was part of larger "post-scarcity" technocratic arguments claiming that the tools for such a redistribution were available, but simply needed to be applied more fairly.

Probing the influence of Fuller on art practice today and understanding how his ideas of equitable resource management and holistic planning—what he termed "comprehensive design"—are received in the present will always be mediated by his reception in the 1960s and 1970s. Of particular importance in exploring, testing, and propagating Fuller's ideas during that period were the "access to tools" ethos of the *Whole Earth Catalog* and other DIY satellite publications and organizations; the examples in practice of the network of intentional communities such as Libre, Drop City, and Red Rockers profiled by the *Whole Earth* books that were constructing domes and deploying other Fuller-inspired alternative technologies throughout this time; and finally, the challenge of radical art and architectural collectives such as Ant Farm, bent on politicizing the libertarian logic of Fuller's theories often embraced by his acolytes.

In Fuller's case, his reception by artists has been pronounced from the 1960s into the present, and many explicitly cite him in ways that very nearly constitute a revival. A wide array of contemporary artists and collectives are today reassessing the legacy of his work with mass shelter solutions and just resource management.[15] So many more are interested in or inspired by the Bucky Fuller–*Whole Earth*–Drop City–Ant Farm constellation that it would be impossible to detail each invocation of Fuller, or every exploration of the geodesic dome or its related alternative architectures, undertaken by contemporary artists. Instead, the task would be to investigate how artists have inherited and reexamined Fuller's experimental model of total design, even though their interest is often mediated by suspicions about teleological "anti-entropic" utopian forms—particularly as this critique was articulated by one of his most astute critics in the 1960s and early 1970s, Robert Smithson.[16]

Yet the articulation of "total thinking," culminating in the invention of the geodesic dome, was not the lasting consequence of Fuller's time at Black Mountain. It was his proposal of an experimentation model that accommodated failure in the name of the larger holistic program that proved to be Fuller's greatest contribution to Black Mountain and beyond. Dropping the totalizing, holistic, technocratic program, while picking up the practical demand to think of experimentation as an often preposterously impractical or absurd prototyping, is a means by which artists today engage Fuller's utopian imagination, just as Cage did at the College.

In this vein, an in-depth study of the aftereffects of the Cage-Fuller friendship nurtured at Black Mountain would be tremendously generative. Just as Black Mountain found an important precursor in the Bauhaus, so did the mid-1960s collaborative movement Experiments in Art and Technology (EAT) look to Black Mountain as a touchstone of its interdisciplinary approach to considering methodologies of experiment.[17] This key offspring of the College, heavily influenced by Fuller's argument about networks as comprehensive systems, was composed of a broad array of ex–Black Mountain faculty and students such as John Cage, Robert Rauschenberg, and pianist David Tudor, as well as scientists, dancers, and artists such as Billy Klüver, Yvonne Rainer, and Robert Whitman. EAT sought to collapse the distinction between technology and everyday life by using concepts of experimentation and laboratory testing that had earlier been debated, and provisionally defined, at Black Mountain in the late 1940s and early 1950s. Its legacy is crucial in understanding hotly contested notions of experiment in science and aesthetics, then and today. Similarly, a study of the impact on artistic practices of John Cage's wholehearted embrace of Fuller's (and Marshall McLuhan's) technopolitics by the 1960s would be a productive avenue for approaching this research.

From the 1960s Cage-Fuller nexus arises a related question: *why* did Albers's methods, once so dominant at Black Mountain, lose out to the more enthusiastically received Cage and Fuller models? That Albers was a master teacher with dedicated students is obvious. Yet his experimental methodology largely circulated within a network characterized by degrees of personal connection; Cage and Fuller are now, and have been for some time, about as close to household names as twentieth-century cultural figures could ever be.[18] Albers's demand for artistic discipline and his emphasis on the specific conditions of perceptual awareness, which he held would generate situations of greater contingency, were often considered rigid and lacking in spontaneity. Perhaps his modernist model of order and design, birthed in the 1920s in Weimar, Germany, and nurtured in a small village in western North Carolina between the wars, isn't what people expected or even wanted from art by the 1960s. His example has none of Fuller's visionary, utopian romanticism; it lacks Cage's sense of freewheeling freedom and anarchy.[19]

Cage "won out" by inverting the Albersian formulation: design would henceforth be subordinate to chance in the deployment of protocols toward indeterminacy. Fuller, however outrageous his rhetoric, tried to connect Bauhaus concerns about the appearance and structure of form to the proposition that an efficient allocation of global resources could induce social responsibility. Among Black Mountain's explorations of chance and design lie a great many possibilities for addressing how artistic experimentation might be defined today.

As much as the concept of experimentation has been understood as a methodological practice shared by artists and scientists, similar common ground can be found between works of visual art, musical composition, and architectural design by using the notion of experiment proposed here.[20] That is to say, if experiment can be understood as *both* a test of tradition and a search for innovative outcomes more generally, we can begin to see the work of a composer, an artist, and an architect as organized by a shared methodology, albeit with very different results. Invoking the test as a primary procedure of modernist culture and practice underscores the central role played by experimentation, which alters the limits of representation to depict in form—whether visual, theatrical, or architectural—conditions of process, change, and contingency.

notes

INTRODUCTION

1. Kenneth Kurtz, "Black Mountain College, Its Aims and Methods," *Black Mountain College Bulletin*, no. 8 (1944): 3 [NC State Archives]. Reprinted from *Haverford Review* 3, no. 1 (Winter 1944).

2. It is important to note that Black Mountain College was founded very rapidly during a low point of the Great Depression. Rice was dismissed from Rollins in March 1933, and Theodore Dreier, who left Rollins in July, raised nearly $15,000 throughout the summer months. Black Mountain College was open to students by September 1933. The College's institutional organization was peculiar and problematic. It was wholly owned by the faculty and students, with a governing Board of Fellows (headed by an elected rector) composed of eight faculty members and one student member culled from their respective constituencies. Nonbinding recommendations were made by an external Advisory Board that met infrequently. A work program was required of all College members, although in practice students executed most of the duties. Admissions decisions were made by a committee composed of faculty and students. No grades were awarded, and graduation was effectuated by an examination performed by an outside scholar. A community council representing faculty, staff, and students considered problems and proposed solutions relating to the entire community. For more information about the founding of Black Mountain College, see Mary Emma Harris, *The Arts at Black Mountain College* (Cambridge, MA: MIT Press, 1987), 2–7.

3. On the topic of European émigrés at Black Mountain, particularly those coming from the Bauhaus, please see Hal Foster, "The Bauhaus Idea in America," in *Albers and Moholy-Nagy: From the Bauhaus to the New World*, ed. Achim Borchardt-Hume (London: Tate, 2006), 92–102; Carl Goldstein, "Teaching Modernism: What Albers Learned in the Bauhaus and Taught to Rauschenberg, Noland, and Hesse," *Arts Magazine* 54, no.

4 (December 1979): 108–16; Margret Kentgens-Craig, *The Bauhaus and America: First Contacts 1919–1936* (Cambridge, MA: MIT Press, 1999); and Charles Darwent, "From Bauhaus to Black Mountain," *Modern Painters* 14, no. 4 (Winter 2002): 48–49. For more information about intentional communities, see Martin Duberman's *Black Mountain: An Exploration in Community* (New York: W. W. Norton, 1972), which charts the history of the College within a legacy of American communitarian experiments. He assesses individuals' roles in generating and maintaining community structures in the highly charged atmosphere of an artistic experimental cooperative such as Brook Farm or Black Mountain College. (Brook Farm was an experimental agricultural community near Boston, Massachusetts. Founded in 1841, it was inspired by Charles Fourier's utopian socialism and was associated with American transcendentalism. Ralph Waldo Emerson and Margaret Fuller were visitors while Nathaniel Hawthorne and Amos Bronson Alcott were inhabitants of the relatively short-lived community.) For further information about Black Mountain and racial integration, see Camille Clark, "Black Mountain College: A Pioneer in Southern Racial Integration," *Journal of Blacks in Higher Education*, no. 51 (Spring 2006): 46–48; Duberman, *Black Mountain*, 175–85, 213–18; and Harris, *Arts at Black Mountain College*, 70–71. For an exploration of the role of Black Mountain College in a history of progressive education in the United States, see John Andrew Rice, *I Came Out of the Eighteenth Century* (New York: Harper and Brothers, 1942); and Katherine Chaddock Reynolds, *Visions and Vanities: John Andrew Rice of Black Mountain College* (Baton Rouge: Louisiana State University Press, 1998). Martin Duberman's and Mary Emma Harris's books are good on this topic as well.

4. Anni Albers, "Work with Material," *Black Mountain College Bulletin*, no. 5 (November 1938), 3 [NC State Archives]. Reprinted in *College Art Journal* 3, no. 2 (January 1944): 51–54.

5. From a selection of the literature from and on the College: "Black Mountain: An Experiment in Education"; "Report from the Academy: The Experimental College"; *Black Mountain College: Experiment in Art*; "Art as Experiment." Louis Adamic's essay "Black Mountain: An Experiment in Education" is from his book *My America* (New York: Harper and Brothers, 1938), 612–45. An earlier version of the essay was published in *Harper's* as "Education on a Mountain: The Story of Black Mountain College" in April 1936, 516–30. College faculty member Eric Bentley's article on the College, "Report from the Academy: The Experimental College," is from *Partisan Review* 12, no. 3 (1945): 422–30. Vincent Katz's exhibition catalog, *Black Mountain College: Experiment in Art*, was recently published (2003) by MIT Press. "Art as Experiment" is a chapter title from Harris's *Arts at Black Mountain College*, 140.

6. As Zygmunt Bauman has written, words such as *experiment* may have denotative meanings, but "some words . . . also have a 'feel.'" A feel-good word, in Bauman's sense, partakes in a complex relation to desire and nostalgia, and evokes several meanings, "all of them promising pleasures, and more often than not the kinds of pleasures we would like to experience but seem to miss." See Bauman, *Community: Seeking Safety in an Insecure World* (Cambridge: Polity Press, 2001), 1. The often-invoked notion of experiment in today's art world (and hardly a day goes by that it doesn't grace a press release or a critical piece about contemporary art) is similarly subject to aspirations and retroactive appraisals stemming from its flurry of articulations in the pre- and immediate post–World War II period, and at Black Mountain specifically. Experiment embodies the longing for types of cultural and social production that are flexible and capable of change, that are responsive to the needs of individuals, including complex needs for cultural growth and social stability, and that satisfy ambitions for egalitarian interaction and artistic innovation.

7. For a further discussion, see my essay "Experiment, Expression, and the Paradox of Black Mountain College," in the exhibition catalog *Starting at Zero: Black Mountain College, 1933–1957*, ed. Caroline Collier and Michael Harrison (Bristol, England: Arnolfini Gallery; Cambridge: Kettle's Yard Gallery, University of Cambridge, 2005): 39–61.

8. Raymond Williams, *Keywords: A Vocabulary of Culture and Society* (New York: Oxford University Press, 1976), 126.

9. Albers quoted in Eugene Gromringer, *Josef Albers* (New York: George Wittenborn, 1990), 171.

10. John Cage, "Experimental Music: Doctrine," in *Silence* (Hanover, NH: Wesleyan University Press, 1961), 13.

11. Buckminster Fuller, "I Figure" [1942], in *The Buckminster Fuller Reader*, ed. James Meller (Middlesex, England: Penguin Books., 1972), 102.

12. Or what Fuller termed "experimentally unproveable myths." *Buckminster Fuller: Anthology for the New Millennium*, ed. Thomas T. K. Zung (New York: St. Martin's Press, 2001), 107, 120.

13. Technically the weaver Gunta Stölzl was the only female master appointed in the Bauhaus's fourteen-year history, as her former student Anni Albers provisionally headed the workshop after Stölzl's departure (the latter resigned when her interfaith marriage to a Jewish former Bauhaus student was protested by increasingly rabid anti-Semitic factions within and without the school).

14. Albers quoted himself saying this at his welcome ceremony at Black Mountain in Martin Duberman's interview with Josef and Anni Albers on November 11, 1967, 13 (typescript) [NC State Archives].

15. Transcript of taped Josef Albers lecture (handwritten in Martin Duberman's hand "At Yale; from Barry Cohen"), n.d., probably late 1950s, 6 [NC State Archives].

16. Albers stated that it was necessary to see "*action* as the aim of education." "Tradition and Experiment in Contemporary Art," n.d., 10 [Yale Papers].

17. Albers, "Seeing Art," n.d. [Yale Papers].

18. Dewey, a member of Black Mountain College's advisory board, visited the College several times throughout the 1930s. After one of his visits, he wrote approvingly of the College, stating that it was "a living example of democracy in action," and that "the College exists at the very 'grass roots' of a democratic way of life." Letter from Dewey to Ted Dreier, dated July 18, 1940 [NC State Archives].

19. This is what Ray Johnson called, somewhat facetiously, a "galaxy of talent." See Johnson, "Norman Soloman's Doberman Interviews Ray Johnson," n.d. [ca. 1968] [NC State Archives]. Johnson's often parodic text was sent to historian Martin Duberman in lieu of an interview when Duberman was conducting the research on Black Mountain College that resulted in his book *Black Mountain College: An Exploration in Community.*

20. "Firsts" are always tricky historical constructions, however; as Cage himself demurred when asked about the event, "Present histories for some reason give me credit for all sorts of things, and that of course could change in the future if someone creates another version." Cage interviewed by Martin Duberman, April 26, 1969, 15 [NC State Archives]. My project in taking up how the chance-protocol experimental model culminated in the happening is not to perform the debunking Cage's words invite. Geoffrey Hendricks, speaking from the later perspective of Fluxus and Happenings, terms *Theater Piece No. 1* a "proto-happening." See Hendricks, *Critical Mass: Happenings, Fluxus, Per-*

formance, Intermedia, and Rutgers University, 1958–1972 (New Brunswick, NJ: Rutgers University Press 2003), 129n23.

21. Cage interviewed by Duberman, 15.

22. Cage in Richard Kostelanetz, *Conversing with Cage* (New York: Routledge, 1987, 2003 [2nd ed.]), 231.

23. For more on this change, see RoseLee Goldberg's *Performance Art: From Futurism to the Present* (London: Thames and Hudson, 2001).

24. Fuller's tactical failures were, generally, technical failures. Interestingly, his emphasis on strategy inverts the logic of Michel de Certeau's now well-known "tactics" versus "strategies" formulation. As de Certeau writes of a strategy, "When a subject of will and power (a proprietor, an enterprise, a city, a scientific institution) can be isolated from an 'environment' . . . and thus serve as a basis for generating relations with an exterior distinct from it (competitors, adversaries, 'clientèles,' 'targets,' or 'objects' of research). Political, economic, and scientific rationality has been constructed on this strategic model." A tactic, on the other hand, "insinuates itself into the other's place, fragmentarily, without taking it over entirely. . . . It has at its disposal no base where it can capitalize on its advantages, prepare its expansions, and secure independence with respect to circumstances." To Fuller, in contrast, the fragmentary nature of tactical thinking was precisely the limitation of traditionally defined architecture, and artists pursuing larger strategic goals could help isolate a problem from its environment so it could be prototyped and tested. Michel de Certeau, *The Practice of Everyday Life* (Berkeley: University of California Press, 1984), xix.

25. Fuller, "Influences on My Work" [1955], in *The Buckminster Fuller Reader*, ed. James Meller (London: Jonathan Cape, 1970), 56.

26. Fuller was vague on who would fill the ranks of comprehensive design. At one point, he understood the field as constituted by graduate students in universities. As he wrote of such students, "A science of comprehensive design can be developed through the initiative of those who are custodians of [the] cumulative intellectual and technical resources of man. These custodians are the universities. The task of developing graduate students in comprehensive design (as comprehenders of the principles permeating the plurality of sciences and arts and of the principles operative in the logistics of world resources processing) is superficially formidable, but clearly subject to solution." Fuller, "Considerations for a Curriculum," n.d., 3 (labeled "p. 16" in Fuller's hand) [Fuller Papers].

27. Fuller often referred to "universal laws," and in the late-career autobiographical book *Guinea Pig B: The 56 Year Experiment* ("B" stands for Bucky) he summarized his many attempts to uncover them. See in particular the introduction to the volume, released by Critical Path, Clayton, California, 1983/2004. Fuller first coined the phrase "Spaceship Earth" in 1951, according to Claude Lichtenstein. See Joachim Krausse and Claude Lichtenstein, eds., *Your Private Sky: R. Buckminster Fuller, Discourse* (Baden, Switzerland: Lars Muller, 2001), 279. The phrase later found its way onto the cover of Fuller's book *Operating Manual for Spaceship Earth* (New York: E. P. Dutton, 1963).

28. "Doing More with Less: Excerpts from an Interview with Buckminster Fuller," 1978, 5 [Fuller Papers]. The identity of the interviewer is not mentioned in the typescript.

29. Fuller, "Conceptuality of Fundamental Structures," in *Structure in Art and in Science*, ed. Gyorgy Kepes (New York: George Braziller, 1965), 66.

30. Fuller, "Bulletin of the Fuller Research Foundation: Exhibit 1—Airocean [*sic*] World Plan," June 1955, 4 [Fuller Papers]. Fuller wrote that the march to what he termed "right-makes-right" is a "teleologic processing of experience-into-design," that is to say, a process that proceeds toward an inevitable resolution; quoted in *Buckminster Fuller Reader* (1970 ed.), 55.

31. Charles Olson as quoted by Jonathan Williams, in Duberman, *Black Mountain*, 406.

32. Olson, in ibid., 393.

33. Charles Olson's "Projective Verse" as quoted in Daniel Belgrad, *The Culture of Spontaneity: Improvisation and the Arts in Postwar America* (Chicago: University of Chicago Press, 1998), 29.

34. The rooting first of Bauhaus and later of French modernist traditions in the United States is a central focus of this project, though such an emphasis must be seen contextually with respect to the growing prominence of abstract expressionism at the College in the work of painters such as Willem de Kooning, Franz Kline, and Robert Motherwell, as well as against the backdrop of a strong, US-based realist painting and muralist tradition important at Black Mountain in the 1930s and 1940s. In the latter case, painters such as Jean Charlot (a French-born, Mexico- and Colorado-based muralist who was formerly an assistant to Diego Rivera), Jean Varda (a Greek-born collagiste based in California), and New York–based realist painters such as Jacob Lawrence and Ben Shahn were in residence during this period, and the cofounder of the purist movement in France, painter Amédée Ozenfant, had embarked on an influential series of realist paintings about Black Mountain during his stay in 1944. Yet, as will be discussed in chapter 1, John Dewey's ideas of experimentation as "learning by doing" sometimes traveled to Black Mountain by way of the Bauhaus, a seemingly improbable transatlantic move. Dewey, *Democracy and Education: An Introduction to the Philosophy of Education* (New York: Free Press, 1916), 184.

35. For further discussion of politically motivated schisms at the College, see Duberman's *Black Mountain College*, particularly pp. 172–211 and 281–331.

36. In a series of late essays from the 1980s, Louis Althusser addressed criticisms that his concept of determination overemphasized the reproduction of existing structures of domination, thereby diminishing the role of human agency in effecting structural change. In his reassessment of this necessitarian logic, Althusser introduced the idea of a "fact of contingency." Expanding on the concept, he maintained that in each event there are singular uncertain and unforeseeable elements that result in a "void essential to any aleatory encounter." That is to say that the order of the world is fraught with radical instability; that though there is a *fact* of order, that order is provisional, and only from a medley of various contingent possibilities comes the necessity of any one particular order. It is therefore important to "think the openness of the world to the event, [to] the as-yet-unimaginable." Althusser, *Philosophy of the Encounter, Later Writings, 1978–1987* (London: Verso Press, 2006), 170, 202, and 264.

CHAPTER ONE

1. From a speech by Josef Albers, given at the first general meeting of Black Mountain College (at the beginning of the new college year), September 22, 1941, 5 [Albers Foundation]. The full statement is "Experimentation means learning by experience, the most lasting way of learning."

2. This phrase is a frequent refrain in the Albers literature. He quoted himself saying this upon arriving at the College in his and Anni Albers's interview with Martin Duberman,

November 11, 1967, 13 (typescript) [NC State Archives].
3. For a discussion of the centrality of vision in Bauhaus theory, see Foster, "Bauhaus Idea in America."
4. Albers stated it was necessary to see "*action* as the aim of education." "Tradition and Experiment in Contemporary Art," n.d., 10 [Yale Papers].
5. Albers, *Search Versus Re-Search* (Hartford, CT: Trinity College Press, 1969), 49.
6. Ibid., 4.
7. Albers, "Truthfulness in Art" (in Albers's writing: "Talk given at Harvard Graduate School of Design about 37–38"), 1 [Yale Papers].
8. Albers, untitled handwritten manuscript with the heading "September 11, 1948 BMC," 6 [Albers Foundation].
9. M. Norton Wise, "Making Visible," *Isis* 97 (2006): 75–82.
10. Molly Nesbit, "Readymade Originals: The Duchamp Model," *October* 37 (Summer 1986): 59.
11. Howard Singerman, *Art Subjects: Making Artists in the American University* (Berkeley: University of California Press, 1999).
12. Albers, "Address for the Black Mountain College Meeting at New York," June 12, 1940, 3 [Albers Foundation]. At Black Mountain, in contrast, Albers believed art education was "at the center of all activity." However, this was an issue of contention within the faculty (art training vs. a liberal arts education), leading to a schism in 1948–49 and the eventual resignation of the Alberses in 1949. Quote is from Duberman's interview with Josef and Anni Albers, 8. See note 14 below for discussion of the schism.
13. Albers, "Address for the Black Mountain College Meeting at New York," 3.
14. College founders John Andrew Rice and Theodore Dreier quoted in Harris, *Arts at Black Mountain College*, 16. The Alberses' departure from the College was due in large part to disputes about its mission as it pertained to the importance of art education, although a complicated set of factors reduceable to the College's financial difficulties also contributed. The schism of 1948–49 that led to the Alberses' final break with the College was aggravated by a move on the part of certain faculty members to shift focus away from art instruction. Social sciences faculty member Bill T. Levi (then married to the College English professor M. C. Richards) angered Albers by declaring, in Albers's words, "Economics are more important than art." But, as Anni Albers pointed out, she and Josef left "because . . . of constant tension and the constant lack of privacy and constant lack of money and the constant friction with every faculty member in having the same voice that you had . . . that you didn't have enough stability to—the members who had built it up, that every new one could topple it over, like Mr. Levi's coming proved." The precarity of the Alberses' financial situation was a decisive factor in the final break (they lacked guaranteed retirement funds at Black Mountain); Josef was sixty-two during the final crisis, and he and Anni had more seniority than nearly any other faculty member. Both quotes are from his interview with Martin Duberman (with Anni present), 43, 47. Josef went on to teach at the University of Mexico (summer 1949), Pratt Institute (spring 1950), and Harvard University (summer 1950), and by the fall of 1950 his appointment was finalized as chairman of the reorganized Department of Design in the School of Fine Arts at Yale.
15. Albers, "Speech at Black Mountain College luncheon at the Faculty Club," Cambridge, Mass., April 29, 1938, 2 [Albers Foundation].
16. Ibid.
17. Albers, "Tradition and Experiment in Contemporary Art," 2. This in no way implies

that art is thoughtless or completely intuitive. As Albers stated, "I believe that thinking is necessary in art as everywhere else and that a clear head is never in the way of genuine feelings." This is a form, one could argue, of John Dewey's "thinking in situations." Albers, one-page typed note dated "ca '50" which begins "The ratio of effort to effect" [Yale Papers]. Or, put another way, for Albers, "*Life*, not school, is the goal," and "the best proofs are the results in later life." Albers, "Speech at Black Mountain College luncheon at the Faculty Club," 1, and Albers, "Concerning Art Instruction," *Black Mountain College Bulletin* 2 (1934): 7.

18. Speech by Josef Albers, given at the first general meeting of Black Mountain College, September 22, 1941, 2.

19. Gropius, lecture on August 28, 1944, at Black Mountain College [Albers Foundation].

20. Albers, "Concerning Art Instruction," 6.

21. Peter Galison, "Aufbau/Bauhaus: Logical Positivism and Architectural Modernism," *Critical Inquiry* 16, no. 4 (Summer 1990), 710.

22. Albers often taught the courses simultaneously, but generally Basic Drawing preceded Color and Painting, and Basic Design was taught before his Structural Sculpture course; see the "Black Mountain College Tentative Program for 1949–1950" [Albers Foundation]. "Test of seeing" is from Albers, "Concerning Art Instruction," 4.

23. To Albers, "Our drawing is the study of objective representation." "Concerning Art Instruction," 5.

24. Albers interviewed by Duberman, 22.

25. In a telegrammed response to a request by Alfred H. Barr Jr., Albers explained: "I use 3 terms structure facture texture to describe surface appearances of materials as follows: firstly structure concerns the inherent character of raw material[,] that is how it grew or was formed[,] like the grain of wood or fiber of thread or crystalline structure of marble... secondly we speak of facture if the appearance is dominated by the effect of working the material[,] for example hammered metal[,] twisted yarn[,] or combed hair show the effect of treatment of the empression [*sic*] of tool used . . . thirdly we speak of texture if similar elements are combined in a constructive organ[;] these elements may show both structure and facture for instance woven[,] braided[,] or knitted material and masonry." Dated November 26, 1938 [Yale Papers].

26. An example of altering surface appearance was, according to Albers, "how can we make something [that] look[s] like bread . . . [from] stone." Interview with Duberman, 63.

27. Albers, "Concerning Art Instruction," 6.

28. Albers, "Truthfulness in Art," 7.

29. Ibid.

30. Ibid.

31. Ibid., 8.

32. Albers, "Concerning Art Instruction," 6.

33. Albers, "Report on a Course in Basic Drawing, Design and Color Given at the Hochschule für Gestaltung in Ulm," US Specialist Report submitted to Office of the High Commission for Germany, January 20, 1954, 5–6 [Yale Papers].

34. A brief prehistory of the break is necessary in order to understand its importance in Albers's subsequent understandings of expressionism and subjectivity. The Bauhaus was founded in 1919 in Weimar, Germany, under Walter Gropius's vision of "a universally great, enduring, spiritual-religious idea" of a *Gesamtkunstwerk*, the "cathedral of the future." Beginning in 1922, however, Gropius began to shift the school's mission from its original articulation to the model of design production. The engineer was the preferred type, and work "led more and more to the production of single prototypes (which will serve as guides to the craftsman and industry)." Gropius criticized the "wild romanticism" of "individualized" expressionism, which many felt was a pointed attack on Johannes Itten. Itten, feeling the threat, departed with several students, and in 1923 Albers and László Moholy-Nagy replaced Itten as instructors of the Preliminary Course. (Albers taught part of the then one-semester-long course from 1923 to 1925. In 1925, he taught the entire first semester of the two-semester course [Moholy-Nagy was responsible for the second semester]. From 1928 to 1933, Albers taught both semesters alone.) Gropius, quoted in Éva Forgács, *The Bauhaus Idea and Bauhaus Politics* (Budapest: Central European University Press, 1991), 36, 74–75.

35. Comments by the artist taken from the press release of Sidney Janis Gallery's January 7–26, 1952, exhibition, "New Work by Josef Albers—'Homage to the Square' and 'Transformation of a Scheme'" [Yale Papers].

36. Ibid.

37. Ibid.

38. All quotes John Locke, "An Essay Concerning Human Understanding," in *The Empiricists: Locke, Berkeley, and Hume*, comp. Jean Austin (New York: Anchor Press, 1974), 32–33.

39. Jonathan Crary, *Suspensions of Perception: Attention, Spectacle, and Modern Culture* (Cambridge, MA: MIT Press, 1999), 321.

40. Ibid., 317.

41. As James M. Curtis has argued, Viktor Shklovsky's notion of habituation in art is most certainly indebted to Henri Bergson. See Curtis, "Bergson and Russian Formalism," *Comparative Literature* 28, no. 2 (Spring 1976): 109–21.

42. Viktor Shklovsky, "Art as Technique," in *Art in Theory 1900–2000: An Anthology of Changing Ideas*, ed. Charles Harrison and Paul Wood (Oxford: Blackwell, 2003), 279–80.

43. Ibid., 280.

44. Albers, draft poem, n.d.; begins "Every perceivable thing has form," 1 [Yale Papers].

45. The possibility for change was the necessary precondition in Albers's understanding of design. If, as he wrote, "Life is continuous change," therefore potentials exist for a better articulation. Albers, "Tradition and Experiment in Contemporary Art," 1.

46. As mentioned, for example, in student Harry Seidler's notes from the color and design courses, dated Summer 1946, 8 [Albers Foundation].

47. Albers, "Concerning Art Instruction," 2.

48. Albers's language of form derives from the complex notion of "gestalt" in German. As Albers stated, "In Gestalt psychology the value of a form element is understandable only in relationship to the whole. . . . From the name Gestalt derives the verb 'gestalten.'" Albers, draft poem, 4.

49. Ibid., 1.

50. Albers, "Concerning Art Instruction," 2.

51. Albers, "Address by Josef Albers given at the Black Mountain College Meeting at the Museum of Modern Art, New York, January 9, 1940," 3 [Albers Foundation].

52. As Albers stated, "No educator has the right to demand from others what he is not able or willing to do himself . . . education is first self-education." Ibid.

53. Albers, "Speech given at the first general meeting of Black Mountain College in the beginning of the 7th College year," September 12, 1939, 3 [Albers Foundation]. Albers, like Dewey, wanted to diminish arbitrary hierarchies, but not to destroy them in an anarchical flourish. As he wrote, he was opposed to the "undecided laissez-faire of many so-called progressive schools." Speech by Josef Albers, Black Mountain College meeting at Mr. and Mrs. Wiener's, New York, n.d. (probably 1941), 4 [Albers Foundation].

54. Albers, "Address for the Black Mountain College Meeting at New York," June 12, 1940, 4 [Albers Foundation].

55. Albers interviewed by Martin Duberman, 34.

56. Ibid., 49.

57. Albers continues: "I have always said in my saying or teaching, 'Make the result of teaching a feeling of growing.' That is the greatest incentive to continue developing yourself. The feeling of growing. And today a little bit more than it was yesterday. And a little bit more than it was last year. You see? That you feel, I'm getting wider and deeper and fuller." Ibid., 57. To progressive educator Dewey, growth, too, was a central concept. As he stated, "The educative process can be identified with growth when that is understood in terms of the active participle, *growing*." John Dewey, *Experience and Education* (New York: Touchstone Books/Simon and Schuster, 1938/1997), 36.

58. Ilya Bolotowsky's course listing for painting, Fall Semester 1947–48, Black Mountain College, 1 [NC State Archives].

59. Ilya Bolotowsky and Henry Geldzahler, "Adventures with Bolotowsky," *Archives of American Art Journal* 22, no. 1 (1982): 23–24.

60. Albers, "Truthfulness in Art."

61. Bauhaus student Hannes Beckmann quoting Albers in Frank Whitford, ed., *The Bauhaus: Masters and Students by Themselves* (Woodstock, NY: Overlook Press, 1993), 224.

62. Albers, "Truthfulness in Art," 1.

63. From student Harry Seidler's notes on Albers's Basic Design course, 24.

64. Student Hannes Beckmann quoted in Rainer K. Wick, *Teaching at the Bauhaus* (Stuttgart: Hatje Cantz Verlag, 2000), 181.

65. Albers, "Concerning Art Instruction," 2.

66. Ibid., 3.

67. Albers, untitled list of work titles and descriptions, dated "ca. 50" (in Albers's hand: "Compiled for Leslie Cheek, Richmond, Va."), 7 [Yale Papers].

68. Albers, *Search Versus Re-Search*, 20.

69. Ibid., 21.

70. Yve-Alain Bois, *Painting as Model* (Cambridge, MA: MIT Press, 1990), xxi, writing on P. N. Medvedev and M. M. Bakhtin's *The Formal Method in Literary Scholarship* (1928), trans. Albert J. Wehrle (Baltimore: Johns Hopkins University Press, 1978).

71. Albers, *Search Versus Re-Search*, 21. Earlier, Albers had proposed "presentative art" as opposed to "non-representational" or "abstract" art, arguing that his art fostered "an immediate perception of all cognitive realities . . . meaning directly apprehending or apprehended by the mind." Albers, "Abstract—Presentational," in *American Abstract Artists* (New York: Ram Press, 1946), 2 [Yale Papers].

72. Albers, untitled list of work titles and descriptions. Second quote is from Albers, *Search Versus Re-Search*, 21.

73. Albers, "Abstract Art," speech made in Asheville, NC, 1935, 4 [Yale Papers].

74. Albers, *Interaction of Color* [1963] (New Haven, CT: Yale University Press, 1971), 74.

75. Albers interview with Duberman, 26. He continues, "So that form, whether we call it a line or a surface or a color, demands endless performances, endless. Using it again and again and again, so now I therefore make a thousand squares. You see? There is no end. I do not mean the square, I mean the color that is served in that dish—square."

76. Albers, "On my work," n.d., single page (probably 1940s), begins "When I paint and construct . . ." [Yale Papers].

77. Albers, *Interaction of Color*, 69.

78. Ibid., 71.

79. Albers, "Statements," in *Albers at the Cincinnati Art Museum*, an exhibition catalog (Cincinnati: Cincinnati Art Museum, 1949), 2 [Yale Papers].

80. It is difficult to attribute exact dates to the *Variants* series. This *Variant* is reproduced from a 2003 PaceWildenstein catalog and is dated 1947–55, and for consistency's sake I have preserved the broad date range. Yet Albers was showing *Homage to the Square*, as well as working on his *Structural Constellations* series, by 1952. A better attribution for the *Variants* series is 1947–50.

81. Svetlana Alpers, "The Studio, the Laboratory, and the Vexations of Art," in *Picturing Science, Producing Art*, ed. Caroline A. Jones and Peter Galison (New York: Routledge, 1998), 409.

82. Albers, draft poem, 4. See also note 48 above.

83. Reinhold Martin, in a parallel study of Albers's contemporary Gyorgy Kepes, has argued that positioning form as a process emphasizes the high stakes of organizing the visual field: Martin claims that Kepes, like Marshall McLuhan, believed that the "image is not the carrier of a message; it *is* the message." Martin, *The Organizational Complex: Architecture, Media and Corporate Space* (Cambridge, MA: MIT Press, 2003), 62. See my discussion of Kepes in chapter 3, section 2 of this book.

84. Donald Judd, "Josef Albers," in the exhibition catalog *Josef Albers* (Marfa, TX: Chinati Foundation, 1991). Essay is reproduced in *Chinati Foundation Newsletter* 11 (2006): 60–69, quotation is from p. 69.

85. Galison, "Aufbau/Bauhaus," 713.

86. Rudolf Carnap, annotations to Bertrand Russell's *Our Knowledge of the External World as Field for Scientific Method in Philosophy* (Chicago: Open Court, 1914), 97; quoted in Galison, "Aufbau/Bauhaus," 733.

87. In their modularity, Albers's language forms differed from his Bauhaus colleague Herbert Bayer's "universal" typography, in which Bayer designed a lowercase font based on circles and right angles. See Ellen Lupton, "Herbert Bayer: Designs for 'Universal' Lettering, 1925 and 1927," in *Bauhaus 1919–1933: Workshops for Modernity*, ed. Barry Bergdoll and Leah Dickerman (New York: Museum of Modern Art, 2009), 200–203.

88. For one example among many, in his 1961 essay "Modernist Painting," Greenberg argued for a strictly optical/visual reception of painting: "That visual art should confine itself exclusively to what is given in visual experience, and make no reference to anything given in any other order of experience, is a notion whose only justification lies in scientific consistency"; Greenberg, "Modernist Painting" [1961], in *Clement Greenberg: The Collected Essays and Criticism*, ed. John O'Brian (Chicago: University of Chicago Press, 1993), 4:91. As Caroline Jones has argued, "Purity, abstraction and the exclusion of unnecessary illusions" were the defining characteristics of Greenberg's formulation of modernism. See Caroline A Jones, *Eyesight Alone: Clement Greenberg's Modernism and the Bureaucratization of the Senses* (Chicago: University of Chicago Press, 2005), in particular chapter 4, which focuses on Georgia O'Keefe and Hans Hofmann.

89. Albers, "Art as Experience," *Progressive Education*, October 1935, first page.

90. Ibid., second page.
91. Albers, "Address by Josef Albers given at the Black Mountain College Meeting at the Museum of Modern Art," 2.
92. Albers, "Speech at Black Mountain College luncheon, Cosmopolitan Club, New York City," December 9, 1938, 6 [Albers Foundation].
93. Ibid., 5.
94. Albers, untitled handwritten manuscript with the heading "September 11, 1948 BMC," 4.
95. Albers, "The Educational Value of Manual Work and Handicraft in Relation to Architecture," in *New Architecture and City Planning*, ed. Paul Zucker (New York: Philosophical Society, n.d. [probably 1944]), 690.
96. Quoted from an untitled fragment that begins, "To me (so far) art is to present," n.d. [Yale Papers].
97. As Albers defined visual articulation, "To direct eyes in observation—know what you are seeing and know why you are seeing it." Interview with Duberman, 19. In the schema of observation informing articulation, articulation is both directed and purposeful: "I see that art essentially is purpose and seeing." Albers, "On my work," n.d.
98. Albers, "The Meaning of Art," lecture delivered at Black Mountain College, May 6, 1940, 1 [NC State Archives].
99. Preceding two quotes are from the speech by Josef Albers, given at the first general meeting of Black Mountain College, September 22, 1941, 4–5.
100. Albers, "Art as Experience," second page. Again, he linked the organization of society through education to well-ordered art: "Education just as art means order and therefore is [an] opposition to chaos. So against mess and dirt as well as against confusion." Albers, untitled handwritten manuscript dated September 11, 1948, 6.
101. Transcript of taped Josef Albers lecture (handwritten in Duberman's hand "At Yale; from Barry Cohen"), n.d., probably late 1950s, 1 [NC State Archives].
102. "In Gestalt psychology the value of a form element is understandable only in relation to the whole." Albers, draft poem, 4.
103. Transcript of taped Albers lecture, 5.
104. Albers, "Statements," 1.
105. Ibid.
106. Transcript of taped Albers lecture, 3–6.
107. Albers, *Search Versus Re-Search*, 20.
108. Albers, "Statements," 1.
109. Albers, untitled typewritten note dated January 1949, 2 [Yale Papers].
110. Albers, "Statements," 1.
111. Albers in Eugene Gromringer, *Josef Albers* (New York: George Wittenborn, 1990), 171.
112. From student Harry Seidler's notes on Albers's Basic Design course, 5.
113. Albers quoted in Wick, *Teaching at the Bauhaus*, 182. Emphasis in original.
114. Theodor Adorno, *Aesthetic Theory* (Minneapolis: University of Minnesota Press, 1997), 37.
115. Ibid.
116. Theodor Adorno, "Perennial Fashion—Jazz," in *Prisms* (Cambridge, MA: MIT Press, 1986), 123.
117. Adorno, *Aesthetic Theory*, 37.
118. Ibid., 37–38, 24.

119. Albers interview with Martin Duberman, 71.
120. Though an excellent and superbly written compendium about Albers's teaching, the publication by Frederick Horowitz and Brenda Danilowitz, *Josef Albers: To Open Eyes* (London: Phaidon, 2006), does not explore this central feature of his pedagogy.
121. Speech by Josef Albers, meeting at Mr. and Mrs. Wiener's, New York, 2.
122. The reform movement had a two-pronged agenda, although strictly speaking it never was cohesive. On the one hand, of crucial importance were the attainment of universal primary school education and the extension of mass education to higher grades. In particular, Georg Kerschensteiner's transatlantic dialogue with John Dewey and the notion of primary education as a work school were immensely important. On the other hand, of key influence was the establishment of the Deutscher Werkbund in 1907, an industrial design movement that attempted to accommodate the changes on handicraft wrought by the advent of industrial production. Walter Gropius was associated with the Werkbund in the mid-1910s (his mentor Peter Behrens was a founding member). The precursor to the Bauhaus, the School of Arts and Crafts in Weimar, was established by another Werkbund affiliate, Henry van de Velde. For more on the reform movement, see Marjorie Lamberti, *The Politics of Education: Teachers and School Reform in Weimar Germany* (New York: Berghahn Books, 2002). For a study of the Werkbund's influence on the Bauhaus, see Forgács, *Bauhaus Idea and Bauhaus Politics*.
123. Dewey, *Democracy and Education*, 294; a discussion of "learning by doing" can be found on page 184.
124. Albers, "Historical or Contemporary" (1924), quoted in Wick, *Teaching at the Bauhaus*, 173.
125. Ibid.
126. Ibid., 174.
127. Walter Benjamin, "Theses on the Philosophy of History" [1940], in *Illuminations* (New York: Schocken Books, 1968), 255.
128. Albers, "Tradition and Experiment in Contemporary Art," 2.
129. Ibid.
130. Though Albers counterposed the tendency of most education to concentrate on the past to progressive education's emphasis on changing the present for the sake of the future, he understood that any notion of a better future is dialectically informed by past experience and historical understanding. As he stated in 1941, "In education, any sensible historical contemplation is related to the future." Speech by Josef Albers, given at the first general meeting of Black Mountain College, September 22, 1941, 2. Yet he qualified this, noting that the goal was to produce a student "who knows that the present is only partly a result of the past." Albers, "Speech at Black Mountain College luncheon at the Faculty Club," 6.
131. Albers continued, "Contemporary art, today as yesterday and ever before, confronts us with a continual struggle for articulation of our sensations and emotions; in other words, it demands visual demonstrations of our changing 'seeing' and 'feeling.'" Albers, "Tradition and Experiment in Contemporary Art," 4. In an interview with George Heard Hamilton in 1957, Albers explained that "art exists because there is something which cannot be said in words." "The Teaching of Art II, Training in Visual Experience," broadcast on radio program *Yale Reports* no. 54, Sunday, January 20, 1957, transcript p. 3 [Yale Papers].
132. See note 18 of the introduction for more information about Dewey's involvement at the College.

133. Dewey, *Democracy and Education*, 276.
134. Raymond Williams, "Base and Superstructure in Marxist Cultural Theory," in *Problems in Materialism and Culture* (London: Verso Press, 1974), 39.
135. Pierre Bourdieu, "Cultural Reproduction as Social Reproduction," in *Power and Ideology in Education*, ed. Jerome Karabel and A. H. Halsey (New York: Oxford University Press, 1977), 487.
136. Ibid., 494.
137. Bourdieu's theory of cultural transmission rarely addresses the conditions of progressive education, concentrating instead on structured inequalities that reinforce existing class positions, generally due to the uneven coverage and outcomes of mass public versus exclusive private education. In fact, Bourdieu's notion of "the educational system" tends to elide education writ large with "dominant culture transmission."
138. Albers advocated for weakened divisions among disciplines and between art and craft, but not for eliminating them entirely. To him, the unity of purpose of all knowledge—observation in the interest of rearticulation—diminished distinctions between fine and applied arts, and between all fields of creative practice. Such a unity would occur in an educational environment in which art, that is to say active doing, was central and exchange between disciplines was encouraged: "A nearer connection, or better, an interpenetration, of all the art disciplines and artistic purposes in school life . . . showed that their problems are very much the same." The similar function of education in each discipline engendered close studies of form and created artists who have "the task of selecting the forms and of showing them in their highest quality, their greatest intensity." Albers noted that though a general training in vision was beneficial for everyone, in any given cohort "only two or three of these [students] want[ed] to become practicing artists." He also stated, "My greatest pride is that my students are not Albers." Quotes, in order, are from Albers, "Art as Experience," second page; Albers, "A Note on the Arts in Education," *American Magazine of Art* 29, no. 4 (April 1936): 233; Albers, "Speech at Black Mountain College luncheon at the Faculty Club," 3; and interview with Martin Duberman, 66.
139. Dewey, *Experience and Education*, 23.
140. Albers, "Address for the Black Mountain College Meeting at New York," June 12, 1940, 1.
141. Chantal Mouffe, *The Return of the Political* (London: Verso Press, 1993), 69.
142. Albers, untitled handwritten manuscript with the heading "September 11, 1948 BMC," 5.
143. Ibid.
144. Albers, draft poem, 1.
145. Clement Greenberg, "Review of Exhibitions of Adolph Gottlieb, Jackson Pollock, and Josef Albers" [1949], in *Clement Greenberg: The Collected Essays and Criticism*, ed. John O'Brian (Chicago: University of Chicago Press, 1986), 2:286.
146. Robert Rauschenberg quoted in Calvin Tomkins, *The Bride and the Bachelors: Five Masters of the Avant-Garde* (New York: Viking Press, 1965), 199.
147. In the same interview, Anni Albers continued: "We were at a party . . . and Rauschenberg was there and he came to me when we were leaving and maybe he had several drinks or something, but anyway he came and said, 'Tell Albers that I love him and I still think he's the greatest teacher.' And I said, 'You know it doesn't help if a wife tells him, write him a note,' but he never did." Albers (with Anni Albers) interview with Duberman, 62–63.

148. Albers, *Interaction of Color*, 70.
149. Albers, "Seeing Art," n.d. [Yale Papers].
150. Please see my essay, "Experiment, Expression, and the Paradox of Black Mountain College."
151. Cage, "Experimental Music," 13.

CHAPTER TWO

1. Cage, "Experimental Music," 12.
2. The faculty of the 1946 Summer Art Institute joining Anni and Josef Albers included painters Jacob Lawrence and Jean Varda, sculptor Leo Amino, architect Bertrand Goldberg, formerly of the Bauhaus (invited to teach when Walter Griopius could only visit that summer for a lecture), and photography historian Beaumont Newhall, recently of the Museum of Modern Art. As an addition to a film series Albers organized that summer with Newhall, filmmaker Maya Deren was asked to teach for the summer, though she could not attend. Students present that summer who would go on to future art careers included Ruth Asawa, Joseph Fiore, and Ray Johnson. The April 1946 issue of *Design* magazine was devoted to Black Mountain College and greatly increased interest in and enrollment at the College, particularly for the Summer Art Institute—over sixty students enrolled in it that year.
3. Elaine de Kooning, "De Kooning Memories: Starting Out in the 1940s," in *Black Mountain College: Sprouted Seeds; An Anthology of Personal Accounts*, ed. Mervin Lane (Knoxville: University of Tennessee Press, 1990), 251–52. Originally published in *Vogue*, December 1983.
4. It would be interesting to trace the development of artistic "freedom" as a form of libertarian anarchism in Ab Ex, developing as it did out of a particular and quixotic reading of surrealist painting in the 1940s, and sharing some of that movement's Dada-inspired radical attack on the institution of art and its institutions of pedagogy. Please see Serge Guilbaut, *How New York Stole the Idea of Modern Art: Abstract Expressionism, Freedom, and the Cold War*, trans. Arthur Goldhammer (Chicago: University of Chicago Press, 1983). Contrast de Kooning's antipathy to school to Albers's appeal as a teacher to a later generation; for example, Donald Judd's reconsideration of the centrality of art pedagogy and Albers's model in particular: "I underestimated the usefulness for others, not [of] Albers, [but] of his color theory. First, something that might be useful and relevant must be taught, which is certainly the color theory. Second, real thought about recent and past art is always relevant. Third, mainly, since attitudes and generalizations are part of the nature and the level of quality of art, it's absolutely necessary that beginning artists, who are not really students, be taught by first-rate artists, who like what they do and like their activity as a whole and assume that art is meant to be first-rate. The students of Albers were smart to have chosen him and lucky he was there." Judd, "Josef Albers," 11.
5. Mary Emma Harris, interview with Clement Greenberg, quoted in her book *Arts at Black Mountain College*, 214.
6. Please see Howard Singerman's discussion of abstract expressionism, education, and self-expression in *Art Subjects*, 149–54. In particular, Singerman argues that Ab Ex was preeminently concerned with talking about art—"a university style"—as opposed to formal or technical studies like those undertaken in an art school such as Black Mountain College. Interestingly, the model of the informal artist's group was not subject to

such criticisms, and many Ab Ex artists, including de Kooning, were associated with the Artists' Club, founded in 1949. For examples of recent debates on the topic of pedagogy versus practice, see Singerman's "A History of the Whitney Independent Study Program—In Theory and Practice," *Artforum* 42, no. 6 (February 2004): 112–17, 170–71.

7. Cage saw his work at the time—his *Sonatas and Interludes* composed from February 1946 to March 1948—as characterized by a "marriage of form and content. . . . Those were my views at the time that I went to Black Mountain. And they were fairly Germanic. . . . And this kind of thinking was just perfect from Albers's point of view." Cage, quoted in Martin Duberman, "Phone Interview with John Cage," April 26, 1969, 5–6 [NC State Archives].

8. Cage in Kostelanetz, *Conversing with Cage*, 231.

9. For more on Bauhaus theater's current of interdisciplinarity, see Juliet Koss's "Bauhaus Theater of Human Dolls," *Art Bulletin* 85, no. 4 (December 2003): 724–45. See also Susanne Lahusen, "Oskar Schlemmer: Mechanical Ballets?" *Dance Research* 4, no. 2 (Autumn 1986): 65–77.

10. Interestingly, Brecht's concept of *Verfremdungseffekt* is a translation of Viktor Shklovsky's *ostranerie*, "estrangement" or "defamiliarization." For a discussion of Shklovsky's concept with respect to Josef Albers, see chapter 1 of this book. For more information on *Verfremdungseffekt*, see Eric Bentley's translation of Brecht's "The Alienation Effect" in *Theater Arts* 33, no. 1 (January 1949): 38–40. For a discussion of the reception of Brecht in the United States, please see Philip Glahn, "Estrangement and Politicization: Bertolt Brecht and American Art, 1967–79" (PhD diss., City University of New York, 2007), and his article "The 'Brecht Effect': Politics and American Postwar Art," *Afterimage* 24, no. 3 (November–December 2006): 29–32.

11. One could say that Bauhaus theater found its greatest public expression in the band New Order's *True Faith* music video (1987), produced by French choreographer Philippe Decouflé, which was inspired by Oskar Schlemmer's *Triadic Ballet*. Marianne Hasting restaged *Triadic Ballet* in 1970, and Debra McCall began recreating Schlemmer's dances, including *Triadic Ballet*, in the early 1980s. See McCall's essay "Reconstructing Schlemmer's Bauhaus Dances: A Personal Narrative," in *Oskar Schlemmer* (Baltimore: Baltimore Museum of Art, 1986), 150. Sound artist Laurie Anderson also credited Schlemmer as an influence (she'd seen restagings of his work in 1984). As she said in an interview, "Steve Martin once said, 'Talking about music is like dancing about architecture.' But you can do that. Recently, I saw an Oskar Schlemmer revival of some Bauhaus dance work, and you actually can dance about architecture—volume, space, and construction." From "Laurie Anderson Interview with Charles Amirkhanian" [1984], in *Theories and Documents of Contemporary Art: A Sourcebook of Artists' Writings*, ed. Kristine Stiles and Peter Selz (Berkeley: University of California Press, 1996), 420.

12. See Branden Joseph's article "White on White," *Critical Inquiry* 27, no. 1 (Autumn 2000): 90–121, for an argument about Cage's relationship to Henri Bergson. Joseph notes that Cage's fluency in reading French connected him to many primary sources of the French prewar avant-garde.

13. In 1947, Cage named one of his compositions "Music for Marcel Duchamp."

14. Cage, "On Robert Rauschenberg, Artist, and His Work," in *Silence*, 100.

15. Ibid., 106.

16. Ibid., 100.

17. Though Cage studied with Arnold Schoenberg in Los Angeles in the 1930s for two years, he developed a lifelong antipathy to the Germanic musical legacy Schoenberg's work represented. For example, when Schoenberg criticized Cage's lack of feeling for harmony, he replied, "In that case I will devote my life to beating my head against that wall." Cage, "Indeterminacy," in *Silence*, 261.

18. Cage quoted by Duberman in his book *Black Mountain College*, 288. According to Duberman, "Cage can't recall if BMC ever replied to his letters, but 'if they did, it was negative.'" Ibid., 512n18. Cage had been working for years to establish such a music center. When he met László Moholy-Nagy while working as Merce Cunningham's accompanist at Mills College in Oakland, Moholy-Nagy was enthusiastic about bringing the center to the interdisciplinary Institute of Design he had founded in Chicago (known as ID, and later the New Bauhaus), and in 1941–42 he invited Cage to teach there. Unfortunately, ID had little money and few assets. Cage later reflected on the disappointing experience: "I spent two years trying to establish a Center for Experimental Music, in a college or university or with corporate sponsorship. Though I found interest in my work I found no one willing to support it financially." See "Oral History with John Cage," May 2, 1974; Archives of American Art, Smithsonian Institution, available at http://www.aaa.si.edu/collections/interviews/oral-history-interview-john-cage-12442.

19. Cage, interview with Duberman, 10. Cage had taught music performance at various schools, including Mills College and the Institute of Design in Chicago. His attempt to teach a course titled "Sound Experiments" at ID in 1941–42 was aborted when he realized that all classes were being held in a common room.

20. As Cage recalled, "The school was largely German-minded. So the fact that I was . . . devoting the whole summer not to modern music in general but to Erik Satie in particular, was somewhat irritating. And Albers, in order to lessen the irritation, and to make the thing seem reasonable, required me to give talks before each concert. . . . These went fairly well until the central point, in the middle of the Summer Session, where I—to express the views of Satie (which were anti-Beethoven)—gave a talk, a rather long talk relative to the other talks, in which I denounced Beethoven. . . . This lecture produced a kind of—it was like a bomb falling in the place." Cage, interview with Duberman, 3–4.

21. Willem de Kooning, quoted in John Elderfield et al., *De Kooning: A Retrospective* (New York: Museum of Modern Art, 2011), 61.

22. Erik Satie, *The Ruse of Medusa*, translated as *Medusa's Snare*, in *A Mammal's Notebook: Collected Writings of Erik Satie*, ed. Ornella Volta (London: Atlas Press, 1996), 77.

23. Ibid., 75–76.

24. Cage, "Erik Satie," in *Silence*, 79.

25. Ibid., 78.

26. Ibid., 82.

27. Ibid., 79, 76.

28. Ibid., 81.

29. Despite its relative simplicity, *Vexations* was notated in unusual enharmonic spellings—when notes, intervals, or keys are designated by different letter names in spite of their similar pitches—that are difficult to read immediately. Cage organized a performance of *Vexations* at the Pocket Theater in Manhattan on September 9, 1963, that lasted over eighteen hours.

30. Cage, "Erik Satie," in *Silence*, 82.

31. Oskar Schlemmer, "Man and Art Figure," in *The Theater of the Bauhaus*, Oskar Schlemmer, László Moholy-Nagy, and Farkas Molnar (Middletown, CT: Wesleyan University Press, 1961), 18.

32. This dance was also known as "Man and Mask." Quote is from Oskar Schlemmer,

"Abstraction in Dance and Costume" [1928], in *The Bauhaus: Weimar, Dessau, Berlin, Chicago*, by Hans Wingler (Cambridge, MA: MIT Press, 1969), 472.
33. Oskar Schlemmer, "Stage" [1927], in Wingler, *The Bauhaus*, 474.
34. Schlemmer, "Man and Art Figure," 17.
35. Ibid., 21.
36. Under director Hannes Meyer at the Bauhaus, Xanti Schawinsky had actually led the Stage Design course in 1928, taking over from Schlemmer, who eventually left in 1929. Schlemmer had insisted on remaining in Germany under conditions of increasing deprivation until his death in 1943. In 1933, the Nazis dismissed him from his position at the Vereinigte Staatschulen in Berlin, and in 1937 his work was shown in the Degenerate Art exhibition in Munich.
37. Among Schawinsky's other pursuits: he developed an architectural practice, collaborating on projects with Gropius and Marcel Breuer, and later turned to painting.
38. Margret Kentgens-Craig points out that Hans Dreier, the head of Paramount Pictures' art department in Hollywood, was influenced by Bauhaus ideas, though he was never a student of Schlemmer's. See her book *Bauhaus and America*, 46. Though he was known mainly for his photography, some of Lux Feininger's visual record of his studies with Schlemmer traveled with him to the United States when he emigrated in 1936, though many of his negatives remained in Germany, where they subsequently disappeared.

Schawinsky's publications on Black Mountain include "Spectodrama: Contemporary Studies," *Leonardo* 2, no. 3 (July 1969): 283–86; "From the Bauhaus to Black Mountain," *Drama Review: TDR* 15, no. 3 (Summer 1971): 30–44; and "My 2 Years at Black Mountain College, N.C.," 1973 [North Carolina Museum of Art, BMC Research Project, NC State Archives].
39. Schawinsky, "Spectodrama: Contemporary Studies," 286.
40. Ibid., 283.
41. László Moholy-Nagy, "Theater, Circus, Variety," in Schlemmer, Moholy-Nagy, and Molnar, *Theater of the Bauhaus*, 60.
42. L. Moholy-Nagy, *The New Vision: Fundamentals of Bauhaus Design, Painting, Sculpture, and Architecture* (Mineola, NY: Dover Publications, Inc., 1938/2005), 13, 18.
43. Ibid., 138.
44. L. Moholy-Nagy, *Malerei, Photographie, Film* (Munich: Albert Langen Verlag, 1925); English translation in Victor Margolin, *The Struggle for Utopia: Rodchenko, Lissitzky, Moholy-Nagy, 1917–1946* (Chicago: University of Chicago Press, 1997), 140.
45. L. Moholy-Nagy, "The Coming Theater—the Total Theater," in Wingler, *The Bauhaus*, 132.
46. Ibid.
47. Schlemmer, "Abstraction in Dance and Costume," 472, and L. Moholy-Nagy, "The Coming Theater—the Total Theater," 132.
48. Walter Gropius, introduction to Schlemmer, Moholy-Nagy, and Molnar, *Theater of the Bauhaus*, 10.
49. Construction of the theater was undertaken in Berlin in 1926 but abandoned when the Nazis assumed power.
50. Gropius, introduction to Schlemmer, Moholy-Nagy, and Molnar, *Theater of the Bauhaus*, 12.
51. Ibid.
52. Ibid.

53. Oskar Schlemmer, "Theater," in Schlemmer, Moholy-Nagy, and Molnar, *Theater of the Bauhaus*, 95.
54. Ibid., 92, and Schlemmer, "Man and Art Figure," 32.
55. Schlemmer, "Theater," 82, 85.
56. Schawinsky, "From the Bauhaus to Black Mountain," 44.
57. Schawinsky, "My 2 Years," 7.
58. Ibid.
59. Xanti Schawinsky in Harris, *Arts at Black Mountain College*, 40.
60. Xanti Schawinsky, Description of Stage Studies Class, 1936–37 Course Catalogue, Black Mountain College [NC State Archives].
61. Schawinsky, "My 2 Years," 4.
62. Schlemmer, "Theater," 82, 94.
63. This implies no judgment about whether these concerns *should* be part of visual art, and I do not mean to say that Albers would have argued a kind of medium specificity designating these concerns as beyond art and instead properly theatrical. Nor does it mean that Cage was innovative strictly because he was attempting to blur the distinctions between vision, experience, and motion.
64. Satie, *A Mammal's Notebook*, 79.
65. Ibid., 191.
66. Sandra Skurvida, e-mail exchange with the author, August 20, 2008.
67. Liz Kotz, "Post-Cagean Aesthetics and the Event Score," *October* 95 (Winter 2001): 57.
68. Elaine de Kooning and Buckminster Fuller credited Arthur Penn, the student-director of *The Ruse of Medusa* production, for loosening them up as performers. Fuller noted that Penn's direction helped him develop as a public speaker. Fuller interviewed by Mary Emma Harris, October 3, 1971, 3 [NC State Archives].
69. Michael Kirby and Richard Schechner, "An Interview with John Cage," in *Happenings and Other Acts*, ed. Mariellen R. Sandford (New York: Routledge, 1995), 56.
70. Cage quoted in Harris, *Arts at Black Mountain College*, 146.
71. Ibid.
72. Anarchy to Cage was envisioned as a social, not a political, program. As he wrote, "The chance operations of the *I Ching* . . . permitted the writing of a music which was not based on harmony, but it permitted harmonies to enter into such a nonharmonic music. How could you express that in political terms? It would permit that attitude expressed socially. It would permit institutions or organizations, groups of people, to join together in a world that was not nationally divided." Cage quoted in Kostelanetz, *Conversing with Cage*, 91.
73. Albers, "Statements," in *Albers at the Cincinnati Art Museum*, an exhibition catalog (Cincinnati: Cincinnati Art Museum, 1949), 1 [Yale Papers]. As Cage summarized, "Art in my opinion is not self-expression"; quoted in Kostelanetz, *Conversing with Cage*, 284.
74. Cage, interview with Martin Duberman, 5.
75. Ibid., 6. Prior to the break in 1952, Cage explained, "Albers I think was responsive to my views. He was an amazing man. Because he combined the strictness of German thinking . . . and the ability to inspire people with the possibility of their own individual freedom." Ibid., 4.
76. Pete Jennerjahn quoted in V. Katz and Brody, eds., *Black Mountain College*, 187.
77. Kostelanetz, *Conversing with Cage*, 17. See also Steve Marshall's article, "John Cage's

I Ching Chance Operations: The Visual Art of John Cage," n.d. www.biroco.com/yijing/cage.htm (accessed September 12, 2013).

78. John Cage, "An Autobiographical Statement" [1990], *Southwest Review* 76 (Winter 1991): 59–76. Available on johncage.org/autobiographical_statement.html (accessed September 30, 2013).

79. Cage, Duberman interview, 15.

80. M. C. Richards quoted in William Fetterman, *John Cage's Theater Pieces* (New York: Routledge, 1996), 101.

81. Cage in Kostelanetz, *Conversing with Cage*, 109.

82. Antonin Artaud, *The Theater and Its Double*, trans. Mary Caroline Richards (New York: Grove Press, 1958), 96, 125.

83. In an interview with Martin Duberman, David Weinrib said that Tudor played *Water Music*, though other accounts have him playing a prepared piano composition by Cage. See Duberman, *Black Mountain College*, 374. In his book *John Cage's Theater Pieces*, William Fetterman writes that "David Tudor vaguely recalls playing *Water Music* in the untitled event" (97).

84. Francine du Plessix Gray (quoting Wolpe), David Weinrib, and Katherine Litz are quoted in Duberman, *Black Mountain College*, 373–76. "Quite boring" is composer Lou Harrison quoted in Fetterman, *John Cage's Theater Pieces*, 104.

85. Cunningham quoted in Duberman, *Black Mountain College*, 377.

86. Because of disparate and contested accounts of the event, it is difficult to ascertain exactly to whom Cage gave this script. Both Cernovich and Rauschenberg later worked for the Merce Cunningham Dance Company, in whose archives this existing fragment was found. Cage, script for *Theater Piece No. 1* (1952), provided to the author by David Vaughan [Merce Cunningham Archives].

87. The show was an American comedy game show called *I've Got a Secret*.

88. Slapping and knocking over the radios were last-minute adaptations when CBS union rules prevented the radios from being plugged into the wall.

89. All quotes are from the score for *Water Walk* (London: Edition Peters, 1959).

90. *Fontana Mix* score (London: Edition Peters, 1958).

91. Cage later (erroneously) claimed that "*Water Music* comes from 1952 . . . the same year as the Black Mountain show—and was my immediate reaction to that event." Cage in Kostelanetz, *Conversing with Cage*, 113.

92. Ibid.

93. The issue of a performer's seriousness was a major one for Cage; he hated when performers hammed during his works.

94. *4′33″* premiered in Woodstock, New York, on August 29, 1952, at the aptly named Maverick Music Hall as a Benefit Artists' Welfare Fund event. See Larry J. Solomon's essay "The Sounds of Silence: John Cage's *4′33″*" (1998) for a detailed history and analysis of Cage's influences in composing this work; it is available at http://solomonsmusic.net/4min33se.htm.

95. Cage in Kostelanetz, *Conversing with Cage*, 14.

96. Ibid.

97. Ibid.

98. Cage, *Silence*, 8.

99. Ibid.

100. Cage in Kostelanetz, *Conversing with Cage*, 244–45. Emphasis in original.

101. Ibid., 14. Cage was initially exposed to Buddhism in the 1930s after attending a lecture on Zen and Dada at the Cornish School in Seattle; it was given by Nancy Wilson Ross, a Bauhaus alumna and Buddhist scholar. He attributed his sharpening interest in Eastern philosophy during the 1940s as the pursuit of an alternative to psychoanalysis following his separation from his wife Xenia.

102. Suzuki was an early translator of the *I Ching* into English and a key popularizer of the texts and theologies of various Buddhist, Hindu, and Gnostic sects; his teachings introduced Cage to mystics such as the medieval theologian Meister Eckhart. Both Suzuki and Eckhart would prove to be lifelong points of reference in Cage's speeches and writings.

103. Cage in Kostelanetz, *Conversing with Cage*, 57.

104. Huang Po, *The Zen Teaching of Huang-Po: On the Transmission of Mind*, with a preface by P'ei Hsiu (New York: Grove Press, 1994), 40.

105. Ibid., 34.

106. Ibid., 36.

107. Ibid., 72.

108. Cage, "Experimental Music," 15. Emphasis in original.

109. David Patterson, "Celebrating a Life" [on David Tudor], *Musicworks*, no. 67 (January 1997): 57–58.

110. Artaud, *Theater and Its Double*, 124.

111. Ibid. As historian Will Rockett has noted, "Artaud's lesson is of the cruelty and tyranny of unpredictable, unfathomable forces that transcend the reasoned limits of reality as humanity understands them. The methods used to deliver this brutal lesson are based on a theory of generating a series of shocks, effected by the collision of images, sounds, and savage acts conveyed in a primarily non-verbal, synaesthetic language." Will H. Rockett, *Devouring Whirlwind: Terror and Transcendence in the Cinema of Cruelty* (Westport, CT: Greenwood Press, 1988), 57ff.

112. Artaud, *Theater and Its Double*, 126.

113. Cage, interview with Martin Duberman, 15.

114. Artaud, *Theater and Its Double*, 92.

115. Ibid., 71.

116. Ibid., 73.

117. Ibid.

118. Ibid., 71.

119. Ibid., 56.

120. Schlemmer's "research experiment" is found in "The Stage and the Bauhaus" [1926], in Wingler, *The Bauhaus*, 117. Artaud is from *Theater and Its Double*, 75.

121. Artaud, *Theater and Its Double*, 86–87.

122. Ibid., 123.

123. John Cage, *A Year from Monday: New Lectures and Writings* (Middletown, CT: Wesleyan University Press, 1963), 72.

124. Marcel Duchamp in a 1932 letter quoted by Octavio Paz, "The Ready-Made," in *Marcel Duchamp in Perspective*, ed. Joseph Masheck (Englewood Cliffs, NJ: Prentice-Hall, 1975), 88.

125. Cage in Kostelanetz, *Conversing with Cage*, 234.

126. It is claimed that in attempting to duplicate the *3 Standard Stoppages*, Cage found that the twine bunched up each time, unlike the nearly meter-length results of Duchamp's original trials. See Rhonda Roland and Stephen Jay Gould, "Hidden in Plain

Sight: Duchamp's 3 *Standard Stoppages*, More Truly a 'Stoppage' (An Invisible Mending) Than We Ever Realized," *Tout-fait*, no. 1 (April 1999), http://www.toutfait.com/issues/issue_1/News/stoppages.html.

127. Ian Hacking, *The Taming of Chance* (Cambridge: Cambridge University Press, 1990), 205.

128. This is Duchamp's description of "the personal 'art coefficient'" he devised. Quoted in Harriet Ann Watts, *Chance: A Perspective on Dada* (Ann Arbor, MI: UMI Research Press, 1980), 40–41.

129. Marcel Duchamp, quoted in *Salt Seller: The Writings of Marcel Duchamp*, ed. Michel Sanouillet and Elmer Peterson (New York: Oxford University Press, 1973), 79.

130. Duchamp quoted in Watts, *Chance*, 40.

131. The use of stochastic actions to produce indeterminacy has been misrecognized by some commentators as a liberatory gesture, as eliminating "all established perceptual patterns for experience and neutralizing [them] in one's habitual mode of interpreting the world, [calling] upon chance as a new, totally unpredictable unit of measure." Similarly, the *motivation* for introducing chance processes has been explained as an emancipation of art from the predictability and stultifying conformity of bourgeois rationalism: Robert Pincus-Witten has written in this vein, "Arbitrary and imaginative methods began to be adopted as a means of liberating a shackled idealism . . . the arbitrary, the fortuitous—sheer chance itself—seemed a desirable means of realizing an art of free and pure spirit." See Robert Pincus-Witten, "Against Order: Poetical Sources of Chance Art," in *Against Order: Chance and Art*, an exhibition catalog (Philadelphia: Institute of Contemporary Art and University of Pennsylvania, 1970), 5. Harriet Watts goes further in positioning chance as the liberator of fettered experience: "Chance is the force that can ultimately menace all ideas of order" (Watts, *Chance*, 49). These aggrandizing portrayals depict the use of chance as a quest for types of artistic production and human agency untainted by instrumentalized reason and social determination. Chance is thus represented as successfully prying art from its embeddedness in the matrix of sociopolitical context, in a move toward personal and aesthetic autonomy.

132. Ian Pepper, "From the Aesthetics of Indifference to Negative Aesthetics: John Cage and Germany, 1958–1972," *October* 82 (1997): 46.

133. Cage in Kostelanetz, *Conversing with Cage*, 17.

134. Cage, "Experimental Music," 12.

135. In contrast, Albers's *Interaction of Color* was not released as a paperback until 1971, when Albers was eighty-three (the 1963 volume was a limited edition). "Experimental" from 1937 is from Cage, "The Future of Music: Credo," in *Silence*, 6.

136. Cage in Kostelanetz, *Conversing with Cage*, 221. For more on Cage's anti-European views, see Caroline A. Jones, "Finishing School: John Cage and the Abstract Expressionist Ego," *Critical Inquiry* 19, no. 4 (Summer 1993): 628–65.

137. Cage in Kostelanetz, *Conversing with Cage*, 52.

138. For more on this, see my discussion of Cage and Buckminster Fuller's relationship in chapter 3 of this book. Quotes are from Cage, *A Year from Monday*, 2–4.

139. Ibid., 10.

140. In fact, Cage made his affiliation with these precursors, and an eclectic canon of modernist renegades such as Henry David Thoreau, James Joyce, Marshall McLuhan, and Buckminster Fuller (as well as more historically distant sources such as Meister Eckhart and Po), into a very public pantheon of citation and intertextual commentary throughout his life. Parsing his process of "working through" these sources will help reveal the theoretical and practical touchstones to which he constantly returned when he defined experimentation.

141. Cage, "On Robert Rauschenberg, Artist, and His Work," 102. It has been claimed by some, quite persuasively, that their passivity was a defensive posture in the face of postwar homophobia. See Jonathan Katz, "John Cage's Queer Silence or How to Avoid Making Matters Worse," *GLQ: A Journal of Lesbian and Gay Studies* 5, no. 2 (April 1999): 231–52 (reprinted in *Writings through John Cage's Music, Poetry, and Art*, ed. David W. Bernstein and Christopher Hatch [Chicago: University of Chicago Press, 2001]), 41–61, as well as Jones, "Finishing School."

142. Cage, "On Robert Rauschenberg, Artist, and His Work," 102.

143. Ibid., 100.

144. Cage, *A Year from Monday*, 19.

145. Joseph, "White on White," 115.

146. Cage quoted in Kostelanetz, *Conversing with Cage*, 27.

147. Yvonne Rainer, "Looking Myself in the Mouth," *October* 17 (Summer 1981): 73.

148. Ibid., 73–74.

149. John Cage, *I–VI*, Charles Eliot Norton Lectures, 1988–89 (Hanover, NH: Wesleyan University Press, 1997), 6.

150. See Judith Rodenbeck's discussion of happenings' treatment of their audiences in *Radical Prototypes: Allan Kaprow and the Invention of Happenings* (Cambridge, MA: MIT Press, 2011), 164.

151. Happenings can be interpreted as issuing commands or directives to participants, in contrast to Fluxus event scores that allow more ambiguity in their performances.

152. Cage, *A Year from Monday*, 19.

153. Althusser undertook these late-career essays in large part to address criticisms of his work as overly deterministic. Althusser, *Philosophy of the Encounter*, xli; though the phrase is Althusser's reworking of concepts first articulated in Althusser and Etienne Balibar's *Reading Capital* [1965] (London, Verso Press, 1998), 279.

154. Althusser, *Philosophy of the Encounter*, 170, 202, 264.

CHAPTER THREE

1. Quote is from *Buckminster Fuller: Anthology*, 201. According to student Albert Lanier, Fuller said this after the failure of his first dome assembly at the College in 1948; Lanier quoted in an interview with Harris, *Arts at Black Mountain College*, 151.

2. For more on the Alberses' final year at Black Mountain and the schism that led to their departure, see note 14 in chapter 1 of this book.

3. Fuller outlined his methodology of "comprehensive design" in a version of the course of the same name that he taught at the College in the summer of 1948 and later that year at the Institute of Design, Chicago. Please see "Comprehensive Design: Synopsis of course to be conducted by Buckminster Fuller at the Institute of Design, Chicago, Ill. Oct. 4, '48-Jan. 29, '49," pp. 1–1h, Spring 1948 [Fuller Papers]. His course description was later adapted and turned into the essay "Comprehensive Designing," published in his book *Ideas and Integrities: A Spontaneous Autobiographical Disclosure* (Englewood Cliffs, NJ: Prentice Hall, 1963), 173–82. That essay is reproduced in *Buckminster Fuller: Anthology*, 69–76.

4. "Total thinking" became a touchstone phrase in Fuller's rhetorical repertoire, and was used earlier in his career in the essay "I Figure," written in 1942. See Fuller, "I Figure," 102; and Fuller, "Total Thinking" [1949], in *Buckminster Fuller Reader* (1972 ed.), 310–28. He brought his secretary from the Institute of Design to Black Mountain in 1949 to transcribe the "Total Thinking" essay. See Harris, *Arts at Black Mountain College*, 158.

5. A 2006 conference in Illinois took as its theme the unlikely compatibility between Fuller's and Cage's ideas: "Geodesic Mathematics and Random Chaos: John Cage and Buckminster Fuller," September 16, 2006, Northern Illinois University. A description of the program is available at h-net.msu.edu/cgi-bin/logbrowse.pl?trx=vx&list=H-ArtHist&month=0608&week=c&msg=ctBzqhF%2BHa59invU90/dTw&user=&pw= (accessed September 12, 2013).

6. Fuller, "2-Way TV & Geoscopes," from *Education Automation: Freeing the Scholar to Return to His Studies* (Carbondale: Southern Illinois University Press, 1962), 38–46 (quotation is from p. 38); republished as "Education" in *Buckminster Fuller: Anthology*, 54.

7. It could be argued, however, that Fuller's holistic program of deductive comprehensive design is in fact diametrically opposed to a cybernetic vision of adaptive, and one could say inductive, technologies. Fuller said he hadn't read Norbert Wiener's *The Human Use of Human Beings: Cybernetics and Society* (1948) when he wrote "Total Thinking" in 1949, though he claimed his own ideas provided "a broad view of computer-programming conceptions and experimental strategies which embrace potentially powerful forecasting capabilities." Fuller, introduction to "Total Thinking," 310.

8. Fuller, "Conceptuality of Fundamental Structures," 66.

9. Lindy Roy, "Geometry as a Nervous System," *ANY*, no. 17 (1997): 27. Emphasis in original.

10. Fuller was using the term *anti-entropic* as early as 1927, according to James Meller. See Fuller's "Universal Requirements for a Dwelling Advantage" [1927/1949], in *Buckminster Fuller Reader* (1972 ed.), 261.

11. Fuller, *Critical Path* (New York: St. Martin's Press, 1981), xxxviii.

12. Fuller, "Emergent Humanity: Its Environment and Education," in *R. Buckminster Fuller on Education* [1965], edited by Peter H. Wagschal and Robert D. Kahn (Amherst: University of Massachusetts Press, 1979), 86–113; republished in *Buckminster Fuller: Anthology*, 101–21; quotation is from p. 119.

13. In 1929, Fuller estimated the cost of the 4-D House at three thousand dollars. See "The Dymaxion House," *Architecture* (Chicago), June 1929; reproduced in Krausse and Lichtenstein, *Your Private Sky*, 137. Adjusting for inflation, I generated a figure of approximately $39,900 using the Consumer Price Index relative value calculator at www.usinflationcalculator.com.

14. Isamu Noguchi designed various models of the car, and wind-tunnel tests honed the vehicle's aerodynamic performance.

15. For further information about the car, see Michael John Gorman, "Dymaxion Timeline," accessed September 12, 2013, hotgates.stanford.edu/bucky/dymaxion/timeline.htm.

16. Fuller writes that the each dot on the *World Energy Map* is an "energy slave" that can be redistributed: "1% of World's harnessed energy slave population (inanimate power serving man) in terms of human equivalents." Text from Fuller, *World Energy Map*, reproduced as plate 16.

17. Fuller's Wichita House was featured in an article in the April 1946 issue of *Fortune*. An article on Fuller and his inventions also appeared in *Architectural Forum*. Often, profiles emphasized his failings—for example, the *Saturday Evening Post*, October 18, 1944:

"Some people say the inventor of the 3-wheel automobile and the 'dwelling machine' is an authentic 18-carat genius. Others just laugh and laugh." Quoted in Krausse and Lichtenstein, *Your Private Sky*, 14.

18. "What Became of the Fuller House," *Fortune* 37 (May 1948): 168. It was Fritz Hansgirg who had proposed buying a couple of the structures for the campus. See Harris, *Arts at Black Mountain College*, 146.

19. Edward Hutchings Jr. quoted in Beaumont Newhall's letter to John R. Whiting, editor of *Science Illustrated*, August 11, 1948 [Fuller Papers].

20. See the final sections of Robert W. Marks, "Man of Science: Bucky Fuller's Dymaxion World," *Science Illustrated*, November 1948, 30–31.

21. Fuller obtained patents for twenty-five inventions in his lifetime, and enforced them doggedly. Certifying his students as "Dymaxion designers" allowed them to produce no more than one geodesic dome after graduation before paying licensing fees—see, for example, his "Dymaxion License" inscribed to an Institute of Design student dated May 27, 1949 [Fuller Papers]. He chased down unauthorized dome assemblies on college campuses, underscoring his copyright. (A form letter to "Mr. X" of "X School of Art" dated February 11, 1955, describes the royalties Fuller requested to avoid filing a lawsuit if more than one dome had been assembled on the offending campus [Fuller Papers].) One could attribute such tight proprietary control over his patents to greed or overmonitoring, as licensing his ideas as inventions is hardly commensurate with a comprehensive designer's ostensibly altruistic impetus. Years later, Fuller realized that enforcing his patents appeared ungenerous, and he seemed contrite when he stated, "I did not take out the patents to make money but only to document and demonstrate what the inventive little individual can accomplish, and to prove documentably [*sic*] the socio-economic existence of such unique industrialization lags. . . . Now that I have proven that an individual can be world-effective while eschewing either money or political advantage-making, I do my best to discourage others from taking patents, which almost never 'pay-off' to the inventor. My patent taking was to effect a 'bridgehead' accreditation to more effective employment of humanity's potentials." From Fuller, *Critical Path*, 149.

22. Fuller, "Preview of Building," April 1, 1949, 3 [Fuller Papers].

23. Fuller, "Total Thinking," 310.

24. This is what Fuller termed "experimentally unproveable myths." Fuller, "Emergent Humanity," in *Buckminster Fuller: Anthology*, 107, 120.

25. Fuller, letter to Deborah Allen, associate editor, *Interiors*, May 8, 1949, 1 [Fuller Papers].

26. As Fuller claimed, it was necessary to take "the phenomena [of] life as we are given it as an experiment, exploring it thoroughly and fulfilling the given problem." Fuller, lecture, n.d. (immediately follows lecture dated December 2, 1948, part 2. It begins "I'm anxious at the point to eliminate . . ."), likely presented at the Institute of Design, Chicago, 2 [Fuller Papers].

27. Fuller, "Bulletin of the Fuller Research Foundation," June 1955, Exhibit 1, 3 [Fuller Papers].

28. Fuller, "Influences on My Work," 43.

29. Fuller, "Design Definition," typed and handwritten note by B. F. appended to T. S. Jones's memo to Aspen Design Conferences of 1951 and 1952, subject "Design Definition" [Fuller Papers]. See also a similar formulation in his "Considerations for a Curriculum," n.d. [Fuller Papers].

30. Fuller, "Designing a New Industry" [1945–46], in *Buckminster Fuller Reader* (1972 ed.), 185.
31. Fuller, lecture dated Saturday, November 6, 1948, likely presented at the Institute of Design, Chicago, 2 [Fuller Papers]. To Fuller, a proper emphasis on facts was too often overlooked: "So-called practical man . . . has lost all contact with actual facts." Ibid., 11.
32. Fuller, "Designing a New Industry," 185.
33. Fuller, "Emergent Humanity," in *Buckminster Fuller: Anthology*, 120, 118.
34. Fuller, "Comprehensive Designing," in ibid., 75, 71.
35. Fuller, "Emergent Humanity," 114–15.
36. Fuller, "Yale Collaborative," n.d., 7 [Fuller Papers].
37. "Doing More with Less: Excerpts from an Interview with Buckminster Fuller," 1978, 5 [Fuller Papers]. The identity of the interviewer is not mentioned in the typescript.
38. Fuller, letter to Henry Luce of Time, Inc., October 20, 1949, 1 [Fuller Papers].
39. Ibid.
40. Leigh White, "Buck Fuller and the Dymaxion World," *Saturday Evening Post*, October 14, 1944; republished in Krausse and Lichtenstein, *Your Private Sky*, 132.
41. The full statement by Fuller is: "People should think things out fresh and not just accept conventional terms and the conventional way of doing things." Quoted in Laurence J. Peter, *The Peter Plan: A Proposal for Survival* (New York: W. Morrow, 1976), 108.
42. His great-aunt, Margaret Fuller, had been a member of the transcendentalist circle with Emerson and Thoreau, and an influential women's rights activist. Fuller, proud of her historical influence, wrote, "She predicted the public's ripening ability to appreciate its responsibility to the regenerative functioning of the individual artists." See Fuller, "Margaret Fuller's Prophecy" [1932], in *Buckminster Fuller Reader* (1972 ed.), 40. Perhaps the family resemblance extended to their reputations for loquaciousness; as he remarked, "Her genius was as a rule revealed only in conversation." Letter from Fuller to his sister Rosamund Fuller, n.d., in Krausse and Lichtenstein, *Your Private Sky*, 69.
43. Fuller interviewed by Martin Duberman, June 26, 1969, 13 [NC State Archives].
44. Ibid.
45. Mark Wigley similarly sees links between cartographic projection using polyhedrons and Fuller's invention of the geodesic dome. See page 21 of Wigley's "Planetary Homeboy," *ANY*, 16–23.
46. Ibid., 18.
47. According to sculpture student Kenneth Snelson, "Professor Fuller arrived for the summer session as a substitute for an architecture professor who withdrew at the last minute. It was Fuller's first teaching job." http://www.kennethsnelson.net/faqs/faq.htm, accessed September 12, 2013.
48. As Elaine de Kooning later reflected, "Bucky's eyes . . . had us all mesmerized. They were, to us [his students at Black Mountain in the summer of 1948], the eyes of a visionary, a saint, all-comprehending, all-forgiving. We loved him and hung on every word." See de Kooning, "De Kooning Memories," 247.
49. Elaine de Kooning quoting Fuller, ibid.
50. For example, Fuller later propagated a large-scale version of his Dymaxion Map as a pedagogical tool in what he termed the "World Game" in the 1960s. The World Game was a participatory geographical model of the earth to assist college students in rethinking global resource management. See "Emergent Humanity," in *Buckminster Fuller: Anthology*, 117.

51. As Fuller said, "I called it the Supine Dome." Fuller interview with Duberman, 14.
52. Ibid., 15, 16.
53. Fuller, letter to Jake Butts, January 11, 1948, 1 [Fuller Papers].
54. From a form letter Fuller wrote to "Mr. X" at "X School of Art," February 11, 1955, 4 [Fuller Papers].
55. Fuller, letter to Seymour Goldstein, May 22, 1950, 5 [Fuller Papers].
56. In a letter Fuller wrote to Kenneth Snelson dated December 22, 1949, he gave credit to his student's innovation: "In all my public lectures I tell of your original demonstration of discontinuous-pressure (com-pressure) and continuous tension structural advantage . . . that you were excited by the later E. G. [Energetic Geometry]. . . . The name Kenneth Snelson will come to be known as a true pioneer" [Fuller Papers].
57. The second dome, according to Fuller, was a "small geodesic structure of fourteen-foot diameter erected in [the] garden of [the] Pentagon Building in Washington, D.C. March 13, 1949." Letter to Dean Wells Bennett, School of Architecture and Design, University of Michigan, May 14, 1949 [Fuller Papers].
58. See Jacques Monod's book *Chance and Necessity* (New York: Alfred A. Knopf, 1971).
59. First two quotes are Fuller, "Influences on My Work," 46, 48; third is Fuller, "Emergent Humanity," in *Buckminster Fuller: Anthology*, 120.
60. For more on how Fuller's conception of the "Establishment" developed in the 1960s, see "Thoughts of Buckminster Fuller," *Whole Earth Catalog*, Winter 1968, 3.
61. Cage commended Fuller's stance in the following terms: "It seems to me that Fuller's solutions are not political in any sense but are based upon utility, a utility to individuals, a utility to the society, and a utility to nature. . . . I like to think of them as being utilitarian." Cage's remarks were from a recording of the TV film *Birdcage* on April 7, 1972. Quoted in "Reconsidering John Cage, Part Two," special issue, *October* 82 (Fall 1997): 81–82.
62. Fuller interviewed by Mary Emma Harris, October 3, 1971, 34 [NC State Archives].
63. Speaking fondly of Albers, Fuller credited him with "removing . . . an insurmountable mystery of universities, and he was removing the unnecessary mysteries of it, that you can't do it, and make it possible that you can do that much. And this is what I certainly tried to do. I found that there is an enormous obscurationism [*sic*] in people who know the tricks, and they try to make it seem difficult. . . . But I try to make it go exactly the other way, to make it really seem easy to do things, so the individual can really accomplish and get to some real mysteries and not just a nonsense mystery. . . . I felt Albers to be akin to that way of thinking and doing. He was what I call an 'experientialist.' . . . That you really didn't just talk about it theoretically." Fuller interview with Harris, 28.
64. Fuller, "Influences on My Work," 43.
65. Fuller, "Designing a New Industry," 163.
66. Fuller, "Influences on My Work," 62.
67. Ibid., 64.
68. De Kooning, "De Kooning Memories," 248.
69. Kenneth Snelson interviewed by Mary Emma Harris, March 25, 1972, 10 [NC State Archives].
70. Recently reconsidered projects by Bauhaus director Hannes Meyer can also be seen as attempting to understand spaces as total systems. Meyer for years fell outside the canon of the Bauhaus as historicized by émigrés such as Walter Gropius, particularly in the MoMA's 1938 catalog for the exhibition Bauhaus 1919–1928. That project, organized by Gropius in collaboration with Herbert Bayer and Isa Gropius, had excised the contradictions of the post-Gropius years, during which directors Meyer and later Mies van

der Rohe each took the school in radically different directions. In particular, see Detlef Mertins's discussion of Meyer's holistic, "total" design for the German Trade Unions School in Bernau, "Hannes Meyer: German Trade Unions School, Bernau, 1928–30," in Barry Bergdoll and Leah Dickerman, eds., *Bauhaus 1919–1933: Workshops for Modernity* (New York: Museum of Modern Art, 2009), 256–61.

71. Albers, "Concerning Art Instruction," 6.

72. Fuller, "Comprehensive Design: Course synopsis" (version 2, n.d., likely 1948), 3, emphasis in original [Fuller Papers].

73. For a discussion of the split between the two men's concepts of Bauhaus education, see Achim Borchardt-Hume's essay "Two Bauhaus Histories" in *Albers and Moholy-Nagy,* in particular pages 70–71 and footnote 21.

74. L. Moholy-Nagy, *New Vision,* 10.

75. Ibid., 16–17.

76. Ibid., 13.

77. Ibid., 113.

78. Ibid., 132.

79. Ibid., 115.

80. This image is fig. 220 in the 2005 reprint of the 1938 edition of L. Moholy-Nagy's *New Vision,* 203.

81. Ibid.

82. Ibid., 20.

83. Wigley, "Planetary Homeboy," 19. See also Wigley's "Network Fever," *Grey Room* 4 (Summer 2001): 82–122.

84. In contrast to Fuller, Moholy-Nagy held that "technical progress should never be the goal, only the means" to release workers from exploitation of their labor. L. Moholy-Nagy, *New Vision,* 13.

85. Martin, *Organizational Complex,* 53.

86. Gyorgy Kepes, introduction to his *Structure in Art and in Science,* ii.

87. Fuller's typically dense prose in the essay reads: "Artists who . . . tried to follow the scientists into 'nonconceptuality' with their 'non-representational' quasi-abstractions are now proven to have been intuitively sound in their conviction that they could really follow or even lead science in the game of intuitive probing." Fuller, "Conceptuality of Fundamental Structures," 66, 80–81.

88. Kepes, *Structure in Art and in Science,* v.

89. Fuller, letter to Serge Chermayeff, May 26, 1948, 1 [Fuller Papers]. Emphasis in original.

90. Ibid., 2. Emphasis in original.

91. Fuller, letter to Carl Koch, May 25, 1949, 1 [Fuller Papers].

92. Fuller, "Design for Survival—Plus," talk given before the Illinois Institute of Technology, January 26, 1949, 9 [Fuller Papers]. Emphasis in original.

93. The original, prolix quote: "The integration of a complex of series of failures represents the only means of attaining from nature the original data essential to realization of *evolutionary tactical events.*" Ibid., 3. Emphasis in original.

94. Fullerenes are molecules composed entirely of carbon, and form hollow spheres, tubes, or ellipsoids. The spherical Buckminsterfullerene (formula C60) exists in shapes resembling soccer balls, which are known as "buckyballs."

95. John Cage interview with P3 (Takashi Serizawa, Rumiko Kanesaka, Michiko Takagishi), January 9, 1989, 1; provided to the author by Shoji Sadao.

96. He often referred to himself as "Guinea Pig B." See, for example, Fuller, "The R.I.B.A. [Royal Institute of British Architects] Discourse, 1958: Experimental Probing of Architectural Initiative," reprint from the *Journal of the Royal Institute of British Architects*, October 1958, 6 [Fuller Papers].
97. Cage, interview with Duberman, 5–6.
98. Ibid., 23–24.
99. Cage interview with P3, 4.
100. See Branden Joseph, "Hitchhiker in an Omni-Directional Transport: The Spatial Politics of John Cage and Buckminster Fuller," *ANY*, no. 17 (1997): 43–44.
101. See my discussion of Albers and Shklovsky in chapter 1 of this book. Shklovsky, "Art as Technique."
102. "Talk by B. F. to the Institute of Design, Feb. 1948 (with [Serge] Chermayeff's reworkings)," 15 [Fuller Papers].
103. Fuller interview with Duberman, 5.
104. Ibid., 37.
105. Ibid., 6.
106. For example, take this fairly typical obfuscation: "Democracy is in great trouble today. . . . The Communists and dictatorships scoff at democracy—saying it doesn't work. I am sure that democracy is inherently more powerful and capable and appropriate to man's needs than any other form of government, but it needs proper updated implementation to a one-to-one velocity correspondence in respect to each and every stimulation-and-response, and then democracy can work—magnificently." Fuller, "2-Way TV & Geoscopes," reprinted as "Education," 53–54.
107. Alexander Graham Bell was the actual inventor of the octet truss, but Fuller claimed to have tested it independently. See "Interview with R. Buckminster Fuller" in the preface of Dorothy Harley Eber's *Genius at Work: Images of Alexander Graham Bell* (New York: Viking Press. 1982). The interview can also be found online at http://www.grunch.net/synergistics/docs/bellnote.html (accessed September 17, 2013).
108. Coincidentally, architect Lawrence Kocher, who designed Black Mountain's second Lake Eden campus and helped erect it in 1940, collaborated with fellow architect Albert Frey on several influential prefab homes—1931's Aluminaire most famously, in addition to publishing a series of texts on prefabrication in *Architectural Record*. See also Barry Bergdoll and Peter Christensen, eds., *Home Delivery: Fabricating the Modern Dwelling* (New York: Museum of Modern Art, 2008).
109. Fuller, letter to Virginia Thorndike, J. Walter Thompson Co., July 17, 1944, 2 [Fuller Papers].
110. Fuller, "Designing a New Industry," 178.
111. Antoine Picon, "Fuller's Promised Land," *ANY*, no. 17 (1997): 29.
112. Fuller, letter to Thorndike, 3.
113. Fuller, letter dated August 14, 1944, no addressee indicated [Fuller Papers].
114. Fuller, letter to Otis Winn, Architect Consultant, UAW Housing Department, Detroit, Michigan, March 3, 1947, 1 [Fuller Papers].
115. Joseph, "Hitchhiker in an Omni-Directional Transport," 41.
116. For a discussion of dome constructions following Fuller's precedent such as Drop City, Red Rockers, and Libre in Colorado, see Felicity Scott's "Acid Visions," *Grey Room* 23 (Spring 2006): 22–39, and the discussion of the influence of Fuller in the 1960s and into the present in my "Dome Culture in the Twenty-First Century," *Grey Room* 42

(Winter 2011): 80–105.
117. See, for example, the *Whole Earth Catalog* "shelter" editor Lloyd Kahn's influential compendium *Shelter* (Bolinas, CA: Shelter Publications, 1973/2000) and his *Domebook* series: *Domebook One* (Bolinas, CA: Pacific Domes, 1970) and *Domebook Two* (Bolinas, CA: Pacific Domes, 1971), as well as his repudiation of dome construction in *Refried Domes* (Bolinas, CA: Shelter Publications, 1990).
118. Wigley, "Planetary Homeboy," 22.
119. Fuller, "Influences on My Work," 58.
120. See Joseph, "Hitchhiker in an Omni-Directional Transport," 43.
121. Giving lip service to the concept, Fuller wrote that "democracy alone can authorize experiment," though it should not interfere in its protocols. Fuller, "How to Make Democracy Work," April 29, 1948, 2 [Fuller Papers].
122. Fuller, "Earth, Inc." [1947], in *Buckminster Fuller Reader* (1972 ed.), 246.
123. See, for example, Fuller's "The Designers and the Politicians" [1962], in *Ideas and Integrities*, 302–8. Reprinted in *Buckminster Fuller Reader* (1972 ed.), 370–76.
124. Fuller, "The R.I.B.A. [Royal Institute of British Architects] Discourse, 1958," 7 [Fuller Papers].
125. Fuller, "Influences on My Work," 56.
126. Fuller, "The Next Two Billion Customers," February 7, 1952, 5 [Fuller Papers].
127. "Doing More with Less: Excerpts from an Interview with Buckminster Fuller," 1978, 5 [Fuller Papers].
128. Ibid.
129. Fuller interview with Harris, 26.
130. Fuller, "The Next Two Billion Customers," 6.
131. Fuller, letter to Thorndike, 1.
132. Fuller, letter to Butts, 2.
133. Fuller, letter to Albert Gotlieb, Council on Atomic Implications, University of Southern California, March 15, 1948 [Fuller Papers].
134. Fuller, "Comprehensive Design: Synopsis of course," 2 (document numeration p. 1a) [Fuller Papers].
135. Reyner Banham opens his essay with clever praise of Fuller: "Buckminster Fuller needs no introduction—at last! It comes as a real relief to us foundation members of the Dymaxion Fan Club." From Banham's "The Dymaxicrat," in *A Critic Writes* (Berkeley: University of California Press, 1996), 91–95; reprinted from *Arts Magazine* 38 (October 1963): 66–69.
136. Ibid., 93.
137. Ibid., 94.
138. As Fuller proclaimed in 1949, "It is now possible that the artist is abandoning his hope that politicians can legislate and subsidize society . . . the artist above all men can see that the generation of new wealth of advantage for man . . . constitutes the only effective transition from a curative to an anticipatory social pathology." Letter to Henry Luce, 2.
139. See note 26 in the introduction for a discussion of who could be a comprehensive designer.
140. The full quote: "Net earnings in standard of living will accrue if and when democratic body politic is given the controlling voice over its industrially organized and mechanically implemented commonwealth." Fuller, "I Figure," 112.

141. Ibid., 119–20.
142. Fuller, "Comprehensive Design: Synopsis of course," 4 (document numeration p. 1c) [Fuller Papers].
143. Fuller, "I Figure," 125.
144. Reinhold Martin, "Forget Fuller?," *ANY*, no. 17 (1997): 15.
145. Fuller, "Influences on My Work," 45.
146. One could include his Dymaxion Deployment Unit, a portable, corrugated-steel bunker he designed for the US Army during World War II. As Fuller stated, "War promotes major technical advances of civilization." Fuller, "Earth, Inc.," 245. Though he believed that the advances of his "design science" would make war itself obsolete: "Ergo [the] Design revolution will constitute [an] alternative to [the] next phase of open world warring." Fuller, "Comprehensive Design: Course synopsis" (version 2, n.d., likely 1948), 5 [Fuller Papers].
147. As he noted, "Industrialization does constitute the direct evolution of man." Fuller, lecture dated Saturday, November 13, 1948, part 2, likely before the Institute of Design, Chicago, 5 (of second section) [Fuller Papers].
148. Meyer Schapiro was incensed that Fuller had rejected one of his essays for publication in *Shelter*, a magazine Fuller was then publishing and editing, while simultaneously printing an attack on the very essay that was declined.
149. In this case, Meyer Schapiro was writing under the pseudonym John Kwait. Schapiro, "Looking Forward to Looking Backward: A Dossier of Writings on Architecture from the 1930s," ed. Felicity Scott; compiled in *Grey Room* 6 (Winter 2002): 71.
150. Ibid., 73.
151. Fuller, "Universal Requirements of a Dwelling Advantage," 1949, 4 [Fuller Papers].
152. Fuller, "The Next Two Billion Customers," February 7, 1952, 4 [Fuller Papers].
153. Fuller, "Comprehensive Design: Synopsis of course," 2 (document numeration p. 1a) [Fuller Papers].
154. Fuller, "Preview of Building," April 1, 1949, 2 [Fuller Papers]. He continues by claiming that "instrumented science" is the "progressive augmentation of the faculties of the highest order," 3.
155. Max Horkheimer, *Eclipse of Reason* (New York: Continuum, 1947), 4.
156. Fuller, letter to Otis Winn, 1.
157. Ibid.
158. Murray Bookchin's *Post-Scarcity Anarchism* (Berkeley, CA: Ramparts Press, 1971) perhaps best encapsulates the argument, popular in the period, that the liberatory potential of recent technological advances would soon allow all goods to be free and readily available.
159. Fuller's anxiety is perhaps understandable given the climate of fear in late-1940s America generated by the possibility that the Soviet Union would obtain the atom bomb, which it eventually detonated on its soil in August 1949. Quote is from "Group Project, Architecture 7, R. Buckminster Fuller, Instructor, Institute of Design, Chicago," spring semester 1949, 2 [Fuller Papers]. See also his mention of catastrophic decentralization in "Preview of Building," 10.
160. Though nuclear war hovers as the obvious spur to such a design, Fuller and Shoji Sadao's dome over Manhattan ostensibly provided a controlled climate to economize on snow-removal costs.
161. Fuller, "Earth, Inc.," 239.

EPILOGUE

1. For a discussion of this topic, see my essay "Experiment, Expression, and the Paradox of Black Mountain College."
2. Serra arrived after Albers retired, and assisted Albers on the preparation of *Interaction with Color*. For more about Albers's legacy at Yale, see Jeffrey Saletnik, "Josef Albers, Eva Hesse, and the Imperative of Teaching," *Tate Papers*, Spring 2007 (available at www.tate.org.uk/research/tateresearch/tatepapers/07spring/saletnik.htm), and Horowitz and Danilowitz, *Josef Albers*. For a general treatment of Albers's pedagogy on selected students, see Goldstein, "Teaching Modernism."
3. This interest in performance should be distinguished from the manner that Jackson Pollock's work in particular, and gestural abstraction more generally, were being reinterpreted in the late 1950s by Allan Kaprow in his important essay "The Legacy of Jackson Pollock," collected in Kaprow's *Essays on the Blurring of Art and Life*, ed. Jeff Kelley (Berkeley: University of California Press, 1993), 1–9. Regarding Ray Johnson's *Moticos*, artist Nayland Blake describes their process: "Early on, in works he dubbed 'moticos,' Johnson worked directly, cutting and pasting images from magazines and newspapers. As time went on, however, each gesture became more considered and distanced from the source material. He would draw a squiggle and then photocopy the drawing, paste the result onto board, and sand the image until it nearly disappeared. This procedure would be repeated over and over until the gesture and the chronology of the piece became impossible to disentangle. Johnson would work and rework his collages, which ultimately left many of them airless in their intricacy." Quote is from Blake's review of the exhibition *Ray Johnson: Correspondences* at the Whitney Museum of American Art in *Artforum*, March 1999, 107–8.
4. For example, speaking about an Albers work he owned (discussed on p. 18), Donald Judd claimed, "The change of color provides changes in proportion, which is unusual in recent art, and which I am interested in my own work." Judd, "Josef Albers," 10.
5. See John Coplans, "Serial Imagery," *Artforum* 7, no. 2 (October 1968): 34–43. For a discussion of the import of this essay today, see Brian O'Doherty, "Critically Literate; Provocations: Writings by John Coplans," *Artforum*, February 1998, 11–12. For further reading on discussions of seriality in the 1960s, see Lawrence Alloway, introduction to *Systemic Painting*, an exhibition catalog (New York: Solomon R. Guggenheim Foundation, 1966), 11–21; and Mel Bochner, "Systemic," *Arts Magazine* 41, no. 1 (November 1966): 40; "Serial Art, Systems: Solipsism," *Arts Magazine* 41, no. 8 (Summer 1967): 39–43; and "The Serial Attitude," *Artforum* 6, no. 4 (December 1967): 73–77.
6. Organized by curator Ann Temkin, *Color Chart* ran from March 2 to May 12, 2008. Interestingly, Temkin's exhibition toggled between treating color as a readymade—emphasizing the artist's use of unmixed paint and paint chips (in this vein Frank Stella's quip, "I tried to keep the paint as good as it was in the can," was mentioned in the show's press release and subsequently quoted in the *New York Times* review of the exhibition)—and Albers's notion of the relativity and relationality of color perception. Karen Rosenberg, "Primary Season at the Modern," *New York Times*, March 4, 2008.
7. For example, Albers's student William Bailey went on to teach painting and sculpture at Yale and served as the dean of the School of Art there. Richard Lytle, Albers's student at Yale, taught painting there from 1960 until very recently, and continued to teach from

Albers's *Interaction of Color*. Another of Albers's students at Yale, Neil Welliver, taught painting there (1955–65) and at the University of Pennsylvania Graduate School of Fine Art (1966–89). Robert Slutzky also studied with Albers at Yale and went on have a great influence as a teacher at the Cooper Union from 1968 to 1990. Julian Stanczak, associated with Op Art, studied under Albers at Yale and taught at the Art Academy of Cincinnati from 1957 to 1964, and was a professor of painting at the Cleveland Institute of Art from 1964 to 1995. For a discussion of the legacy of Albers's teaching, see page 95 of Fred Horowitz's essay "Albers the Teacher," in Horowitz and Danilowitz, *Josef Albers*, 72–97. Horowitz was himself a student of Albers's at Yale.

8. The notion of creative experimentation as the primary legacy of the Bauhaus was embraced by artists such as Asger Jorn, who criticized functionalist design practices associated with the School of Design in Ulm founded by Bauhaus alum Max Bill. For a discussion of Jorn and the International Movement for an Imaginist Bauhaus, see Jörn Etzold's essay "Honoring the Dead Father? The Situationists as Heirs to the Bauhaus," in *Bauhaus Conflicts, 1919–2009: Controversies and Counterparts*, ed. Philipp Oswalt (Ostfildern, Germany: Hatje Cantz Verlag, 2009), 152–70; and McKenzie Wark, *The Beach Beneath the Streets* (London: Verso, 2011).

9. Some of this work has begun: see, for example, Branden Joseph's *Random Order: Robert Rauschenberg and the Neo-Avant Garde* (Cambridge, MA: MIT Press, 2003).

10. For more on the event score, please see Liz Kotz, "Post-Cagean Aesthetics and the Event Score"; and Julia Robinson, "The Brechtian Event Score: A Structure in Fluxus," *Performance Research* (UK) 7, no. 3 (September 2002): 111–23.

11. Cage, "Experimental Music," 10.

12. Cage, "Composition," in *Silence*, 59.

13. Carolyn Brown, *Chance and Circumstance: Twenty Years with Cage and Cunningham* (Evanston, IL: Northwestern University Press, 2007), 239.

14. Kirby and Schechner, "An Interview with John Cage," 56.

15. Some of these include Caitlin Berrigan, Matt Bua, Molly Corey, Fritz Haeg and the Sundown School, Dave Hardy, Heather and Ivan Morison, N55, Nils Norman, Sarah Oppenheimer, Nosey Parker, Plastique Fantastique, Marjetica Potrc, Raumlabor, Michael Rakowitz, Tomas Saraceno, Oscar Tuazon, and Holly Ward. See also Marta Herford and Markus Richter, eds., *We Are All Astronauts: The Universe of Richard Buckminster Fuller Reflected in Contemporary Art* (Bielefeld, Germany: Kerber Verlag, 2011).

16. See chapter 3, page 124, for more discussion about anti-entropy. For more information about Robert Smithson's view of Fuller, see his interview with Alison Sky, "Entropy Made Visible" [1973], in *Robert Smithson: The Collected Writings*, ed. Jack Flam (Berkeley: University of California Press, 1996), 301–9; and Dana Miller, "Thought Patterns: Buckminster Fuller the Artist/Scientist," in *Buckminster Fuller: Starting with the Universe*, ed. Dana Miller and Michael Hays (New Haven, CT: Yale University Press, 2008), 21–43.

17. A dissertation by Michelle Kuo is currently in progress at Harvard University on this topic, and is titled "'To Avoid the Waste of a Cultural Revolution': Experiments in Art and Technology (E.A.T.), 1966–1979."

18. This argument is not about degrees of fame and notoriety but about those of influence—always more difficult to discuss.

19. Although, as Carolyn Brown has written, "The by-products of anarchy made [Cage] extremely uncomfortable." His anarchy could appear hypocritical given his demand that performers interpret his work soberly. The quote is from page 264 of her memoir *Chance* *and Circumstance*; see also the passages on pages 198–99, 239, 264–67, and 334 for more discussion of the topic.

20. On thinking about experimentation as a process of research shared by art and science, see my article "Futures: Experiment and the Tests of Tomorrow," in *Curating Subjects*, ed. Paul O'Neill (London: Open Editions, 2007), 92–99; Alpers, "The Studio, the Laboratory, and the Vexations of Art"; and Hans Ulrich Obrist and Barbara Vanderlinden, eds., *Laboratorium*, an exhibition catalog (Antwerp, Belgium: Provincial Museum of Photography, 1999).

bibliography

ABBREVIATIONS

Albers Foundation
Josef Albers Archives
The Josef and Anni Albers Foundation, Bethany, Connecticut

Cage Papers
John Cage Collection
Music Library, Northwestern University Library, Evanston, Illinois

Cunningham Foundation
Merce Cunningham Archives
Cunningham Dance Foundation, New York, New York

Fuller Papers
R. Buckminster Fuller Collection
Department of Special Collections, Stanford University Libraries, Stanford, California

NC State Archives
Black Mountain College Records, 1933–56
North Carolina Museum of Art, Black Mountain College Research Project, 1933–73
Martin Duberman Collection, 1933–80
North Carolina State Archives, Division of Historical Resources, Raleigh, North Carolina

Yale Papers
Josef Albers Papers
Manuscripts and Archives, Sterling Memorial Library, Yale University Library, New Haven, Connecticut

Adamic, Louis. "Black Mountain: An Experiment in Education." In *My America*, 612–45. New York: Harper and Brothers, 1938.
Adorno, Theodor. *Aesthetic Theory*. Minneapolis: University of Minnesota Press, 1997.
———. "Perennial Fashion—Jazz." In *Prisms*, 119–32. Cambridge, MA: MIT Press, 1986.
———. "Vers une Musique Informelle." In *Quasi una Fantasia: Essays on Modern Music*, translated by Rodney Livingstone, 269–322. London: Verso, 1994.
Albers, Anni. *Selected Writings on Design*. Edited by Brenda Danilowitz. Hanover: Wesleyan University Press, 2000.
Albers, Josef. "Abstract—Presentational." In *American Abstract Artists*, 2 pp. New York: Ram Press, 1946 [Yale Papers].
———. "Art as Experience." *Progressive Education*, October 1935. 3 pp.
———. "Concerning Art Instruction." *Black Mountain College Bulletin* 2 (1934): 2–7.
———. "The Educational Value of Manual Work and Handicraft in Relation to Architecture." In *New Architecture and City Planning*, edited by Paul Zucker, 688–94, n.d. [ca. 1944].
———. *Interaction of Color*. New Haven, CT: Yale University Press, 1963/1971.
———. "A Note on the Arts in Education." *American Magazine of Art* 29, no. 4 (April 1936): 233.
———. *Search Versus Re-Search*. Hartford, CT: Trinity College Press, 1969.
———. "Statements." In *Albers at the Cincinnati Art Museum*, 4 pp. Cincinnati: Cincinnati Art Museum, 1949. Exhibition catalog [Yale Papers].
Albers, Josef, and Donald Judd. *Josef Albers, Donald Judd: Form and Color*. New York: PaceWildenstein, 2007. Exhibition catalog.
Alloway, Lawrence. Introduction to *Systemic Painting*, 11–21. New York: Solomon R. Guggenheim Museum, 1966. Exhibition catalog.
Alpers, Svetlana. Review of Vincent Katz, ed., *Black Mountain College: Experiment in Art*. *Key Reporter* 68, no. 3 (Fall 2003): 14–15.
———. "The Studio, the Laboratory, and the Vexations of Art." In *Picturing Science, Producing Art*, edited by Caroline A. Jones and Peter Galison, 401–17. New York: Routledge, 1998.
Althusser, Louis. *Philosophy of the Encounter, Later Writings, 1978–1987*. London: Verso Press, 2006.
Althusser, Louis, and Etienne Balibar. *Reading Capital* (1965). London, Verso Press, 1998.
Aronson, Arnold. *American Avant-Garde Theatre: A History*. London: Routledge, 2000.
Artaud, Antonin. *The Theater and Its Double*. Translated by Mary Caroline Richards. New York: Grove Press, 1958.
Auslander, Philip. *Liveness: Performance in a Mediatized Culture*. New York: Routledge, 1999.
———. "The Performativity of Performance Documentation." *PAJ: A Journal of Performance and Art* 28, no. 3 (2006): 1–10.
Ball, Hugo. *Flight Out of Time*. Berkeley: University of California Press, 1996.
Banes, Sally. "The Birth of Judson Dance Theatre: 'A Concert of Dance' at Judson Church, July 6, 1962." *Dance Chronicle* 5, no. 2 (1982): 167–212.

———. *Democracy's Body: Judson Dance Theater, 1962–1964*. Durham, NC: Duke University Press, 1993.
———. *Greenwich Village 1963: Avant-Garde Performance and the Effervescent Body*. Durham, NC: Duke University Press, 1993.
Banham, Reyner. "The Dymaxicrat." In *A Critic Writes*, 91–95. Berkeley: University of California Press, 1996.
———. *Theory and Design in the First Machine Age*. Cambridge, MA: MIT Press, 1980.
Bauhaus-Archiv Berlin, Museum für Gestaltung, Stiftung Bauhaus Dessau, and Klassik Stiftung Weimar. *Bauhaus: A Conceptual Model*. Ostfildern, Germany: Hatje Cantz Verlag, 2009.
Bauman, Zygmunt. *Community: Seeking Safety in an Insecure World*. Cambridge: Polity Press, 2001.
Baxandall, Lee. "Spectacles and Scenarios: A Dramaturgy of Radical Activity." In *Radical Perspectives in the Arts*, edited by Lee Baxandall, 371–88. Harmondsworth: Penguin, 1972.
Beck, Julian. *The Life of the Theatre: The Relation of the Artist to the Struggle of the People*. San Francisco: City Lights, 1972.
Belgrad, Daniel. *The Culture of Spontaneity: Improvisation and the Arts in Postwar America*. Chicago: University of Chicago Press, 1998.
Benjamin, Walter. *Illuminations*. New York: Schocken Books, 1968.
Bentley, Eric. "Report from the Academy: The Experimental College." *Partisan Review* 12, no. 3 (1945): 422–33.
———. Translation of Bertolt Brecht, "The Alienation Effect." *Theater Arts* 33, no. 1 (June 1949): 38–40.
Bergdoll, Barry, and Peter Christensen, eds. *Home Delivery: Fabricating the Modern Dwelling*. New York: Museum of Modern Art, 2008.
Bergdoll, Barry, and Leah Dickerman, eds. *Bauhaus 1919–1933: Workshops for Modernity*. New York: Museum of Modern Art, 2009.
Berghaus, Günter. "Neo-Dada Performance." In *Neo-Avant-Garde*, edited by David Hopkins, 75–96. Amsterdam: Editions Rodopi BV, 2006.
Bernstein, Sheri. "Josef Albers at Black Mountain College, 1933–45." In *Exiles and Emigrés: The Flight of European Artists from Hitler*, edited by Stephanie Barron with Sabine Eckman, 259–60. Los Angeles: Los Angeles County Museum of Art; New York: Abrams, 1997.
Bird, Jon. "Indeterminacy and (Dis)order in the Work of Cy Twombly." *Oxford Art Journal* 30, no. 3 (2007): 486–504.
Bittman, Arnold. *To Open Eyes*. Albany: ACI Films, State University of New York at Albany, 1971 [Albers Foundation].
Black Mountain College Museum and Arts Center. *Hazel Larsen Archer: Black Mountain College Photographer*. Asheville, NC: BMCMAC, 2006.
———. *The Shape of Imagination: Women of Black Mountain College*. Asheville, NC: BMCMAC, 2008.
Blake, Nayland. Review of the exhibition *Ray Johnson: Correspondences*. *Artforum* 37, no. 7 (March 1999): 107.
Bochner, Mel. "Serial Art, Systems: Solipsism." *Arts Magazine* 41, no. 8 (Summer 1967): 39–43.

———. "Futures: Experiment and the Tests of Tomorrow." In *Curating Subjects*, edited by Paul O'Neill, 92–99. London: Open Editions, 2007.

———. "We Are All Bauhauslers Now." *Art Journal* 70, no. 2 (Summer 2011): 115–18.

Drucker, Johanna. "Collaboration without Object(s) in the Early Happenings." *Art Journal* 52, no. 4 (1993): 51–58.

Duberman, Martin. *Black Mountain: An Exploration in Community*. New York: W. W. Norton, 1972.

Duchamp, Marcel. *Salt Seller: The Writings of Marcel Duchamp*. Edited by Michel Sanouillet and Elmer Peterson. New York: Oxford University Press, 1973.

Duve, Thierry de. *The Definitively Unfinished Marcel Duchamp*. Halifax: Novia Scotia College of Art and Design; Cambridge, MA: MIT Press, 1991.

———. *Kant after Duchamp*. Cambridge, MA: MIT Press, 1996.

Eber, Dorothy Harley. *Genius at Work: Images of Alexander Graham Bell*. New York: Viking Press. 1982.

Eisenstein, Sergei. "The Cinematographic Principle and the Ideogram." In *Film Theory and Criticism*, edited by Gerald Mast et al., 127–38. 4th ed. New York: Oxford University Press, 1992.

Elderfield, John, et al. *De Kooning: A Retrospective*. New York: Museum of Modern Art, 2011. Distributed in North America by D.A.P./Distributed Art Publishers.

Etzold, Jörn. "Honoring the Dead Father? The Situationists as Heirs to the Bauhaus." In *Bauhaus Conflicts, 1919–2009: Controversies and Counterparts*, edited by Philipp Oswalt, 152–70. Ostfildern, Germany: Hatje Cantz Verlag, 2009.

Fesci, Sevim. "An Interview with Ray Johnson" [April 17, 1968]. *Archives of American Art Journal* 40, nos. 3, 4 (2000): 17–27.

Fetterman, William. *John Cage's Theater Pieces*. New York: Routledge, 1996.

Flam, Jack, ed. *Robert Smithson: The Collected Writings*. Berkeley: University of California Press, 1996.

Flavin, Dan. ". . . on an American artist's education. . . ." *Artforum* 6, no. 7 (March 1968): 28–32.

Forgács, Éva. *The Bauhaus Idea and Bauhaus Politics*. Budapest: Central European University Press, 1991.

Foster, F. A. "Black Mountain College." Unpublished, May 1987. Typed brochure.

Foster, Hal. "The Bauhaus Idea in America." In *Albers and Moholy-Nagy: From the Bauhaus to the New World*, edited by Achim Borchardt-Hume, 92–102. London: Tate, 2006.

———. "Dada Mime." *October* 105 (Summer 2003): 166–76.

———. *The Return of the Real: The Avant-Garde at the End of the Century*. Cambridge, MA: MIT Press, 1996.

Fuller, R. Buckminster. *Buckminster Fuller: Anthology for the New Millennium*. Edited by Thomas T. K. Zung. New York: St. Martin's Press, 2001.

———. *The Buckminster Fuller Reader*. Edited by James Meller. London: Jonathan Cape, 1970. Reprint, Middlesex, England: Penguin, 1972.

———. "Comprehensive Designing." In *Ideas and Integrities* [1969], 178–82. Reprinted in Zung, *Buckminster Fuller*, 69–76.

———. "Conceptuality of Fundamental Structures." In Kepes, *Structure in Art and in Science*, 66–88.

———. *Critical Path*. New York: St. Martin's Press, 1981.

———. "Design Definition." Typed and handwritten noted by B. F. appended to T. S. Jones's memo to Aspen Design Conferences of 1951 and 1952, subject "Design Definition" [Fuller Papers].
———. "Design for Survival—Plus." Talk given before the Illinois Institute of Technology, January 26, 1949 [Fuller Papers].
———. "The Designers and the Politicians" [1962]. In *Ideas and Integrities*, 302–8. Reprinted in *Buckminster Fuller Reader* (1972 ed.), 370–76.
———. "Designing a New Industry" [1945–46]. Reprinted in *Buckminster Fuller Reader* (1972 ed.), 153–230.
———."The Dymaxion House." *Architecture* (Chicago), June 1929. Reprinted in Krausse and Lichtenstein, *Your Private Sky*, 137.
———. "Earth, Inc." [1947]. Reprinted in *Buckminster Fuller Reader* (1972 ed.), 231–51.
———. "Emergent Humanity: Its Environment and Education" [1965]. In *R. Buckminster Fuller on Education*, edited by Peter H. Wayschal and Robert D. Kahn, 86–133. Amherst: University of Massachusetts Press, 1979. Reprinted in Zung, *Buckminster Fuller*, 101–21.
———. *Guinea Pig B: The 56 Year Experiment*. Clayton, CA: Critical Path, 1983/2004.
———. *Ideas and Integrities: A Spontaneous Autobiographical Disclosure*. Englewood Cliffs, NJ: Prentice Hall, 1963.
———. "I Figure" [1942]. Reprinted in *Buckminster Fuller Reader* (1972 ed.), 98–129.
———. "Influences on My Work" [1955]. Reprinted in *Buckminster Fuller Reader* (1970 ed.), 43–66.
———. *Inventions: Twelve Around One*. Cincinnati: Carl Solway Gallery, 1981.
———. *I Seem To Be a Verb*. New York: Bantam Books, 1970.
———. "Margaret Fuller's Prophecy" [1932]. Reprinted in *Buckminster Fuller Reader* (1972 ed.), 39–43.
———. *Operating Manual for Spaceship Earth*. New York: E. P. Dutton, 1963.
———. "The R.I.B.A. [Royal Institute of British Architects] Discourse, 1958: Experimental Probing of Architectural Initiative." Reprinted from the *Journal of the Royal Institute of British Architects*, October 1958 [Fuller Papers].
———. "Total Thinking" [1949]. Reprinted in *Buckminster Fuller Reader* (1972 ed.), 310–28.
———. "2-Way TV & Geoscopes." In *Education Automation: Freeing the Scholar to Return to His Studies*, 38–46. Carbondale: Southern Illinois University Press, 1962. Reprinted as "Education" in Zung, *Buckminster Fuller*, 48–59.
———. "Universal Requirements for a Dwelling Advantage" [1927/1949] [Fuller Papers]. Reprinted in *Buckminster Fuller Reader* (1972 ed.), 252–69.
———. *Utopia or Oblivion: The Prospects for Humanity*. Baden, Switzerland: Lars Müller, 2008.
Galison, Peter. "Aufbau/Bauhaus: Logical Positivism and Architectural Modernism." *Critical Inquiry* 16, no. 4 (Summer 1990), 709–52.
"Geodesic Mathematics and Random Chaos: John Cage and Buckminster Fuller." Conference, Northern Illinois University, September 16, 2006. Program description accessed September 12, 2013, at h-net.msu.edu/cgi-bin/logbrowse.

pl?trx=vx&list=H-ArtHist&month=0608&week=c&msg=ctBzqhF%2BHa59in vU90/dTw&user=&pw=.
Glahn, Philip. "The 'Brecht Effect': Politics and American Postwar Art." *Afterimage* 24, no. 3 (November–December 2006): 29–32.
————. "Estrangement and Politicization: Bertolt Brecht and American Art, 1967–79." PhD diss., City University of New York, 2007.
Glimcher, Arne, ed. *Josef Albers: Homage to Color*. New York: PaceWildenstein, 2003.
Goldberg, RoseLee. *Performance Art: From Futurism to the Present*. London: Thames and Hudson, 2001.
Goldstein, Carl. "Teaching Modernism: What Albers Learned in the Bauhaus and Taught to Rauschenberg, Noland, and Hesse." *Arts Magazine* 54, no. 4 (December 1979): 108–16.
Gorman, Michael John. "Dymaxion Timeline." hotgates.stanford.edu/bucky/dymaxion/timeline.htm. Accessed September 12, 2013.
Greenberg, Clement. "'American-Type' Painting." In *Art and Culture*, 208–29. Boston: Beacon Press, 1961.
————. *The Collected Essays and Criticism*. Edited by John O'Brian. Vol. 2. Chicago: University of Chicago Press, 1986.
————. *The Collected Essays and Criticism*. Edited by John O'Brian. Vol. 4. Chicago: University of Chicago Press, 1993.
Griffiths, Paul. *Modern Music and After: Directions since 1945*. Oxford: Oxford University Press, 1995.
Gromringer, Eugene. *Josef Albers*. New York: George Wittenborn, 1990.
Gropius, Walter, ed. *Bauhaus 1919–1928*. New York: Museum of Modern Art, 1938.
————. Introduction to Schlemmer, Moholy-Nagy, and Molnar, *Theater of the Bauhaus*, 7–14.
————. *The New Architecture and the Bauhaus*. Cambridge, MA: MIT Press, 1965.
Groys, Boris. "On the New." In *Art Power*. Cambridge, MA: MIT Press, 2008.
Guilbaut, Serge. *How New York Stole the Idea of Modern Art: Abstract Expressionism, Freedom, and the Cold War*. Translated by Arthur Goldhammer. Chicago: University of Chicago Press, 1983.
————, ed. *Reconstructing Modernism: Art in New York, Paris, and Montreal 1945–1964*. Cambridge, MA: MIT Press, 1990.
Haas, Karen E., ed. *Josef Albers in Black and White*. Boston: Boston University Art Gallery; Seattle: University of Washington Press, 2000.
Hacking, Ian. *The Taming of Chance*. Cambridge: Cambridge University Press, 1990.
Hapgood, Susan. *Neo-Dada: Redefining Art, 1958–1962*. New York: Universal, 1994.
Hapgood, Susan, and Jennifer Rittner. "Neo-Dada: Redefining Art." *Performing Arts Journal* 17, no. 1 (January 1995): 63–70.
Harris, Mary Emma. *The Arts at Black Mountain College*. Cambridge, MA: MIT Press, 1987.
Hatton, E. M. *The Tent Book*. Boston: Houghton Mifflin, 1979.
Hayman, Ronald. *Artaud and After*. Oxford: Oxford University Press, 1977.
Hays, K. Michael. *Modernism and the Posthumanist Subject: The Architecture of Hannes Meyer and Ludwig Hilberseimer*. Cambridge, MA: MIT Press, 1992.
Hays, K. Michael, and Dana Miller, eds. *Buckminster Fuller: Starting with the Universe*. New Haven, CT: Yale University Press, 2008.

Hendricks, Geoffrey. *Critical Mass: Happenings, Fluxus, Performance, Intermedia, and Rutgers University, 1958–1972*. New Brunswick, NJ: Rutgers University Press, 2003.
Herford, Marta, and Markus Richter, eds. *We Are All Astronauts: The Universe of Richard Buckminster Fuller Reflected in Contemporary Art*. Bielefeld, Germany: Kerber Verlag, 2011.
Hines, Thomas S. "'The Not yet 'Cage': The Los Angeles Years, 1922–1938." In *John Cage: Composed in America*, edited by Marjory Perloff and Charles Junkerman, 65–99. Chicago: University of Chicago Press, 1994.
Hollier, Denis. "The Death of Paper Part 2: Artaud's Sound System." *October* 80 (Spring 1997): 27–37.
Hopps, Walter. *Robert Rauschenberg: The Early 1950s*. Houston: Houston Fine Art Press, 1991.
Hopster, Gene. *Illustrated Dome Building*. Monterey, CA: Domeplans Press, 2005.
Horkheimer, Max. *Eclipse of Reason*. New York: Continuum, 1947.
Horowitz, Frederick, and Brenda Danilowitz. *Josef Albers: To Open Eyes*. London: Phaidon, 2006.
Huyssen, Andreas. "Back to the Future: Fluxus in Context." In *In the Spirit of Fluxus*, edited by Elizabeth Armstrong and Joan Rothfuss, 142–51. Minneapolis: Walker Arts Center, 1993.
Innes, Christopher. *Avant Garde Theatre, 1892–1992*. London: Routledge, 1993.
James, William. *Pragmatism*. New York: Dover, 1907/1995.
Jameson, Frederic. *Archaeologies of the Future*. London: Verso Press, 2005.
———. "The Politics of Utopia." *New Left Review* 25 (January–February 2004): 35–54.
Jones, Caroline A. *Eyesight Alone: Clement Greenberg's Modernism and the Bureaucratization of the Senses*. Chicago: University of Chicago Press, 2005.
———. "Finishing School: John Cage and the Abstract Expressionist Ego." *Critical Inquiry* 19, no. 4 (Summer 1993): 628–65.
———. *Machine in the Studio: Constructing the Postwar American Artist*. Chicago: University of Chicago Press, 1996.
Joseph, Branden. *Beyond the Dream Syndicate: Tony Conrad and the Arts after Cage*. New York: Zone Books, 2008.
———. "Engineering Marvel: On Billy Kluver." *Artforum*, March 2004, 39, 42, 202.
———. "Hitchhiker in an Omni-Directional Transport: The Spatial Politics of John Cage and Buckminster Fuller." *ANY*, no. 17 (1997): 40–44.
———. "John Cage and the Architecture of Silence." *October* 81 (Summer 1997): 80–104.
———. "Modernism without Organs: Antonin Artaud." *Artforum*, September 2012, 494–501.
———. "'My Mind Split Open': Andy Warhol's Exploding Plastic Inevitable." *Grey Room* 8 (Summer 2002): 80–107.
———. *Random Order: Robert Rauschenberg and the Neo-Avant Garde*. Cambridge, MA: MIT Press, 2003.
———, ed. *Robert Rauschenberg*. Cambridge, MA: MIT Press, 2002.
———. "White on White." *Critical Inquiry* 27, no. 1 (Autumn 2000): 90–121.
Judd, Donald. "Josef Albers," in *Josef Albers*. Exhibition catalog. Marfa, TX: Chinati Foundation, 1991. Essay is reproduced in *Chinati Foundation Newsletter* 11 (2006):

60–69.
Judson, Ben. "Silence and Void: Cage, Fuller, and Urban Space." *Art Lies*, no. 58 (Summer 2008), texashistory.unt.edu/ark:/67531/metapth228023/m1/24/. Accessed September 12, 2013.
Kahn, Douglas. "Artaud in America." In *100 Years of Cruelty: Essays on Artaud*, edited by Edward Scheer, 237–62. Sydney: Power Publications and Artspace, 2000.
———. *Noise, Water, Meat: A History of Sound in the Arts*. Cambridge, MA: MIT Press, 1999.
———. "Silence and Silencing." *Music Quarterly* 81, no. 4 (Winter 1997): 556–98.
Kahn, Lloyd. *Refried Domes*. Bolinas, CA: Shelter Publications, 1990.
———. *Shelter*. Bolinas, CA: Shelter Publications, 1973/2000.
Kahn, Wolf. "Hans Hofmann's Good Example." *Art Journal* 42, no. 1 (Spring 1982): 22–23.
Kaprow, Allan. *Essays on the Blurring of Art and Life*. Edited by Jeff Kelley. Berkeley: University of California Press, 1993.
Katz, Jonathan. "John Cage's Queer Silence or How to Avoid Making Matters Worse." *GLQ: A Journal of Lesbian and Gay Studies* 5, no. 2 (April 1999): 231–52. Reprinted in *Writings through John Cage's Music, Poetry, and Art*, edited by David W. Bernstein and Christopher Hatch, 41–61. Chicago: University of Chicago Press, 2001.
Katz, Vincent, and Martin Brody, eds. *Black Mountain College: Experiment in Art*. Cambridge, MA: MIT Press, 2003.
Keller, Sean, et al. "Global Outlook: The Legacy of Buckminster Fuller." *Artforum* 47, no. 3 (November 2008): 280–97.
Kelly, Rob Roy. "Recollections of Josef Albers." *Design Issues* 16, no. 2 (Summer 2000): 3–24.
Kenny, Neil. "Changing the Languages of Theatre: A Comparison of Brecht and Artaud." *Journal of European Studies* 13 (September 1983): 169–86.
Kentgens-Craig, Margret. *The Bauhaus and America: First Contacts 1919–1936*. Cambridge, MA: MIT Press, 1999.
Kepes, Gyorgy, ed. *Structure in Art and in Science*. New York: George Braziller, 1965.
Kirby, Michael. *Happenings: An Illustrated Anthology*. New York: Dutton, 1965.
Kirby, Michael, and Richard Schechner. "An Interview with John Cage." In *Happenings and Other Acts*, edited by Mariellen R. Sandford, 51–71. New York: Routledge, 1995.
Kirk, Andrew W. *Counterculture Green: The Whole Earth Catalog and American Environmentalism*. Lawrence: University Press of Kansas, 2007.
Kooning, Elaine de. "Albers Paints a Picture." *Art News*, November 1950, 40–43, 57–58.
———. "De Kooning Memories: Starting Out in the 1940s." *Vogue* 173 (December 1983): 352–53, 393–94. Reprinted in Lane, *Black Mountain College*, 243–52.
Koss, Juliet. "Bauhaus Theater of Human Dolls," *Art Bulletin* 85, no. 4 (December 2003): 724–45.
Kostelanetz, Richard, ed. *Conversing with Cage*. New York: Routledge, 1987/2003 (2nd ed.).
———. *The Theatre of Mixed Means: An Introduction to Happenings, Kinetic Environments, and Other Mixed-Means Presentations*. New York: RK Editions, 1980.

Kotz, Liz. "Post-Cagean Aesthetics and the Event Score." *October* 95 (Winter 2001): 54–89.

———. *Words to Be Looked At: Language in 1960s Art*. Cambridge, MA: MIT Press, 2007.

Kotz, Mary Lynn. *Rauschenberg / Art and Life*. New York: Harry Abrams, 1990.

Krausse, Joachim, and Claude Lichtenstein, eds. *Your Private Sky: R. Buckminster Fuller, the Art of Design Science*. Baden, Switzerland: Lars Muller, 1999.

———. *Your Private Sky: R. Buckminster Fuller, Discourse*. Baden, Switzerland: Lars Muller, 2001.

Kubler, George. *The Shape of Time: Remarks on the History of Things*. New Haven, CT: Yale University Press, 1962.

Kuhn, Thomas S. *The Structure of Scientific Revolutions*. 2nd ed. Chicago: University of Chicago Press, 1970.

Kuo, Michelle. "9 Evenings in Reverse." In *9 Evenings Reconsidered*, 31–43. Cambridge, MA: MIT List Visual Arts Center, 2006.

———. "'To Avoid the Waste of a Cultural Revolution': Experiments in Art and Technology (E.A.T.), 1966–1979." PhD diss., Harvard University.

Kurtz, Kevin. "Black Mountain College, Its Aims and Methods." *Black Mountain College Bulletin*, no. 8 (1944): 3 [NC State Archives]. Reprinted from *Haverford Review* 3, no. 1 (Winter 1944).

Lahusen, Susanne. "Oskar Schlemmer: Mechanical Ballets?" *Dance Research* 4, no. 2 (Autumn 1986): 65–77.

Lambert, Carrie. "Moving Still: Mediating Yvonne Rainer's 'Trio A.'" *October* 89 (Summer 1999): 87–112.

Lamberti, Marjorie. *The Politics of Education: Teachers and School Reform in Weimar Germany*. New York: Berghahn Books, 2002.

Lane, Mervin, ed. *Black Mountain College: Sprouted Seeds; An Anthology of Personal Accounts*. Knoxville: University of Tennessee Press, 1990.

Lee, Alan. "A Critical Account of Some of Josef Albers' Concepts of Color." *Leonardo* 14, no. 2 (1981): 99–105.

Leonard, George J. *Into the Light of Things: The Art of the Commonplace from Wordsworth to John Cage*. Chicago: University of Chicago Press. 1994.

Locke, John. "An Essay concerning Human Understanding." In *The Empiricists: Locke, Berkeley, and Hume*, compiled by Jean Austin, 7–133. New York: Anchor Press, 1974.

Lorance, Lorenza. *Becoming Bucky Fuller*. Cambridge, MA: MIT Press, 2009.

Lupton, Ellen. "Herbert Bayer: Designs for 'Universal' Lettering, 1925 and 1927." In *Bauhaus 1919–1933: Workshops for Modernity*, edited by Barry Bergdoll and Leah Dickerman, 200–203. New York: Museum of Modern Art, 2009.

March, Linda Davis. "Asheville Has Become a Cultural Center for Art." *Asheville (NC) Citizen-Times*, September 15, 1997.

Margolin, Victor. *The Struggle for Utopia: Rodchenko, Lissitzky, Moholy-Nagy, 1917–1946*. Chicago: University of Chicago Press, 1997.

Markoff, John. *What the Dormouse Said: How the Sixties Counterculture Shaped the Personal Computer Industry*. New York: Penguin, 2005.

Markoski, Kate. "'Alone Together': On Merce Cunningham and the Question of Black Mountain College's Artistic Legacy." [Typescript provided by author.]

Marks, Robert W. "Man of Science: Bucky Fuller's Dymaxion World." *Science*

Illustrated, November 1948, 30–31. Reprint, New York: McGraw Hill, 4 pp.
Marshall, Steve. "John Cage's *I Ching* Chance Operations: The Visual Art of John Cage." n.d. www.biroco.com/yijing/cage.htm. Accessed Spetember 12, 2013.
Marter, Joan, ed. *Off Limits: Rutgers University and the Avant-Garde, 1957–1963*. New Brunswick, NJ: Rutgers University Press, 1999.
Martin, Reinhold. "Forget Fuller?" *ANY*, no. 17 (1997): 14–15.
———. "Fuller's Futures." In *New Views on R. Buckminster Fuller*, edited by Hsiao-Yun Chu and Roberto G. Trujillo, 176–87. Stanford, CA: Stanford University Press, 2009.
———. *The Organizational Complex: Architecture, Media and Corporate Space*. Cambridge, MA: MIT Press, 2003.
McCall, Debra. "Reconstructing Schlemmer's Bauhaus Dances: A Personal Narrative." In *Oskar Schlemmer*, edited by Arnold Lehman and Brenda Richardson, 150. Baltimore: Baltimore Museum of Art, 1986.
McCormick, Seth. "Fête in Venice." *Art Journal* 70, no. 4 (Winter 2011): 113–16.
Menand, Louis. *The Metaphysical Club: A Story of Ideas in America*. New York: Farrar, Straus and Giroux, 2001.
———, ed. *Pragmatism: A Reader*. New York: Vintage, 1997.
Millar, Jeremy. *Every Day Is a Good Day: The Visual Art of John Cage*. London: Hayward, 2010. Distributed in North America by D.A.P./Distributed Art Publishers.
Miller, Dana. "Thought Patterns: Buckminster Fuller the Artist/Scientist." In Hays and Miller, *Buckminster Fuller*, 21–43.
Miller, Timothy. "The Sixties-Era Communes." In *Imagine Nation: The American Counterculture of the 1960s and '70s*, edited by Peter Braunstein and Michael William Doyle, 327–52. New York: Routledge, 2002.
Moholy-Nagy, László. "The Coming Theater—the Total Theater" [ca. 1927]. From "Theater, Circus, Variety," chap. 3 in *The Stage of the Bauhaus*, vol. 4 of the *Bauhaus Books*. Munich: Albert Langer, n.d. Reprinted in Wingler, *The Bauhaus*, 132.
———. *The New Vision: Fundamentals of Bauhaus Design, Painting, Sculpture, and Architecture* [1938]. Reprint, Mineola, NY: Dover, 2005.
———. "Theater, Circus, Variety." In Schlemmer, Moholy-Nagy, and Molnar, *The Theater of the Bauhaus*, 49–70.
Moholy-Nagy, Sibyl. "The Diaspora." *Journal of the Society of Architectural Historians* 24, no. 1 (March 1965): 24–26.
Molesworth, Helen. "Before Bed." *October* 63 (Winter 1993): 68–82.
Monod, Jacques. *Chance and Necessity*. New York: Alfred A. Knopf, 1971.
Morris, Catherine, ed. *9 Evening Reconsidered: Art, Theatre, and Engineering, 1966*. Cambridge: MIT List Visual Arts Center, 2006.
Morris, Michael, et al. *Ray Johnson: How Sad I am Today*. Vancouver, BC: Morris and Helen Belkin Art Gallery, University of British Columbia, 1999.
Motherwell, Robert. *The Dada Painters and Poets: An Anthology*. 2nd ed. Cambridge, MA: Harvard University Press, 1981.
Mouffe, Chantal, ed. *Deconstruction and Pragmatism*. London: Routledge, 1996.
———. *The Return of the Political*. London: Verso Press, 1993.
Müller, Ulrike. *Bauhaus Women: Art, Handicraft, Design*. Paris: Flammarion, 2009.
Munroe, Alexandra, ed. *The Third Mind: American Artists Contemplate Asia*, 1860–

1989. New York: Guggenheim Museum, 2009. Exhibition catalog.
Nesbit, Molly. "Readymade Originals: The Duchamp Model." *October* 37 (Summer 1986): 53–64.
Nicholls, David, ed. *The Cambridge Companion to Cage*. Cambridge: Cambridge University Press, 2002.
North Carolina Literary Review. "The Black Mountain College Issue." Special issue, *North Carolina Literary Review* 2, no. 2 (1995).
Nyman, Michael. *Experimental Music: Cage and Beyond*. Cambridge: Cambridge University Press, 1999.
Obrist, Hans Ulrich, and Barbara Vanderlinden, eds. *Laboratorium*. Antwerp, Belgium: Provincial Museum of Photography, 1999.
O'Doherty, Brian. "Critically Literate; Provocations: Writings by John Coplans." *Artforum*, February 1998, 11–12.
Oswalt, Philipp, ed. *Bauhaus Conflicts, 1919–2009: Controversies and Counterparts*. Ostfildern, Germany: Hatje Cantz Verlag, 2009.
Pang, Alex Soojung-Kim. "Dome Days: Buckminster Fuller in the Cold War." In *Cultural Babbage: Technology, Time and Invention*, edited by Francis Spufford and Jenny Uglow, 167–92. London: Faber and Faber, 1997.
Passlof, Pat. "1948." *Art Journal* 48, no. 3 (Autumn 1989): 229.
Patterson, David. "Appraising the Catchwords, c. 1942–1959: John Cage's Asian-Derived Rhetoric and the Historical Reference of Black Mountain College." PhD diss., Columbia University, 1996.
———. "Celebrating a Life" [on David Tudor]. *Musicworks*, no. 67 (January 1997): 57–58.
Payant, Felix, ed. "Black Mountain College." Special issue, *Design* 47, no. 8 (April 1946).
Paz, Octavio. "The Ready-Made." In *Marcel Duchamp in Perspective*, edited by Joseph Masheck, 84–89. Englewood Cliffs, NJ: Prentice Hall, 1975.
Pepper, Ian. "From the Aesthetics of Indifference to Negative Aesthetics: John Cage and Germany, 1958–1972." *October* 82 (1997): 30–47.
Perloff, Marjorie, and Charles Junkerman, eds. *John Cage: Composed in America*. Chicago: University of Chicago Press, 1994.
Pezolet, Nicola. "Bauhaus Ideas: Jorn, Max Bill, and Reconstruction Culture." *October* 141 (2012): 86–110.
Picon, Antoine. "Fuller's Promised Land." *ANY*, no. 17 (1997): 28–30.
Pincus-Witten, Robert. "Against Order: Poetical Sources of Chance Art." In *Against Order: Chance and Art*, 5–18 (unpaginated). Philadelphia: Institute of Contemporary Art, University of Pennsylvania, 1970. Exhibition catalog.
Po, Huang. *The Zen Teaching of Huang-Po: On the Transmission of Mind*. With a preface by P'ei Hsiu. New York: Grove Press, 1994.
Popper, Ian, ed. "Reconsidering John Cage, Part Two." Special issue, *October* 82 (Fall 1997).
Potter, Michelle. "'A License to Do Anything': Robert Rauschenberg and the Merce Cunningham Dance Company." *Dance Chronicle* 16, no. 1 (1993): 1–43.
Pritchett, James. *The Music of John Cage*. Cambridge: Cambridge University Press, 1993.
Rabinbach, Anson. *In the Shadow of Catastrophe: German Intellectuals between*

Apocalypse and Enlightenment. Berkeley: University of California Press, 2001.
Rainer, Yvonne. "Looking Myself in the Mouth." *October* 17 (Summer 1981): 65–76.
Rawson, Josie. "Return to Black Mountain: Resurrecting the Spirit of the American Avant-Garde." *Utne Reader*, September–October 1996; www.utne.com/arts/black-mountain-college-american-avant-garde.aspx#axzzzenfoeujl. Accessed September 13, 2013.
Reynolds, Katherine Chaddock. *Visions and Vanities: John Andrew Rice of Black Mountain College*. Baton Rouge: Louisiana State University Press, 1998.
Rice, John Andrew. *I Came out of the Eighteenth Century*. New York: Harper and Brothers, 1942.
Richter, Hans. *Dada: Art and Anti-Art*. London: Thames and Hudson, 1964.
Robinson, Julia. "The Brechtian Event Score: A Structure in Fluxus." *Performance Research* (UK) 7, no. 3 (September 2002): 111–23.
———, ed. *John Cage*. Cambridge, MA: MIT Press, 2011.
Rockett, Will H. *Devouring Whirlwind: Terror and Transcendence in the Cinema of Cruelty*. Westport, CT: Greenwood Press, 1988.
Rodenbeck, Judith F. *Radical Prototypes: Allan Kaprow and the Invention of Happenings*. Cambridge, MA: MIT Press, 2011.
Roland, Rhonda, and Stephen Jay Gould. "Hidden in Plain Sight: Duchamp's 3 Standard Stoppages, More Truly a 'Stoppage' (An Invisible Mending) Than We Ever Realized." *Tout-fait*, no. 1 (April 1999), http://www.toutfait.com/issues/issue_1/News/stoppages.html.
Rose, Barbara. *Rauschenberg*. New York: Random House, 1987.
Rosenberg, Karen. "Primary Season at the Modern." *New York Times*, March 4, 2008.
Ross, Alex. *The Rest Is Noise: Listening to the Twentieth Century*. New York: Farrar, Straus and Giroux, 2007.
Roth, Moira. "The Aesthetic of Indifference." *Artforum* 16, no. 3 (1977): 46–53.
Roy, Lindy. "Geometry as a Nervous System." *ANY*, no. 17 (1997): 24–27.
Rumaker, Michael. *Black Mountain Days: A Memoir*. Asheville, NC: Black Mountain Press, 2003.
Sadao, Shoji. *Buckminster Fuller and Isamu Noguchi: Best of Friends*. Milan: 5 Continents Editions, 2008.
Saletnik, Jeffrey. "Josef Albers, Eva Hesse, and the Imperative of Teaching." *Tate Papers*, no. 7 (April 1 2007); www.tate.org.uk/download/file/fid/7298. Accessed September 12, 2013.
Saletnik, Jeffrey, and Robin Schuldenfrei, eds. *Bauhaus Construct: Fashioning Identity; Discourse and Modernism*. London: Routledge, 2009.
Sandford, Mariellen R., ed. *Happenings and Other Acts*. New York: Routledge, 1995.
Sandler, Irving. *Abstract Expressionism and the American Experience: A Re-Evaluation*. New York: Hudson Hills Press, 2009.
———. "The School of Art at Yale, 1950–1970: The Collective Reminiscences of Twenty Distinguished Alumni," *Art Journal* 42, no. 1 (Spring 1982): 14–21.
Santner, Eric. *My Own Private Germany*. Princeton, NJ: Princeton University Press, 1997.
Satie, Erik. *A Mammal's Notebook: Collected Writings of Erik Satie*. Edited by Ornella Volta. London: Atlas Press, 1996.
Schapiro, Meyer. "Looking Forward to Looking Backward: A Dossier of Writings on

Architecture from the 1930s." Edited by Felicity Scott. Compiled in *Grey Room* 6 (Winter 2002): 67–109.
Schawinsky, Xanti. "From the Bauhaus to Black Mountain." *Drama Review: TDR* 15, no. 3 (Summer 1971): 30–44.
———. "My 2 Years at Black Mountain College, N.C.," 1973 [BMC Research Project, NC State Archives].
———. "Spectodrama: Contemporary Studies." *Leonardo* 2, no. 3 (July 1969): 283–86.
Schimmel, Paul. "The Faked Gesture: Pop Art and the New York School." In *Hand-Painted Pop: American Art in Transition, 1955–62*, edited by Russell Ferguson, 19–65. Los Angeles: Museum of Contemporary Art; New York: Rizzoli, 1993.
———, ed. *Out of Actions: Between Performance and the Object, 1949–1979*. Los Angeles: Museum of Contemporary Art; New York: Thames and Hudson, 1998.
Schlemmer, Oskar. "Abstraction in Dance and Costume" [1928]. Reprinted in Wingler, *The Bauhaus*, 472.
———. "Man and Art Figure." In Schlemmer, Moholy-Nagy, and Molnar, *The Theater of the Bauhaus*, 17–46.
———. "Stage" [1927]. Lecture delivered March 16, 1927, Dessau, Germany. Published in *Bauhaus Journal*, no. 3 (1927). Reprinted in Wingler, *The Bauhaus*, 474.
———. "The Stage and the Bauhaus" (1926). Reprinted in Wingler, *The Bauhaus*, 117.
———. "Theater." In Schlemmer, Moholy-Nagy, and Molnar, *Theater of the Bauhaus*, 81–101.
Schlemmer, Oskar, László Moholy-Nagy, and Farkas Molnar. *The Theater of the Bauhaus*. Middletown, CT: Wesleyan University Press, 1961.
Schmitt, Natalie Crohn. "John Cage, Nature, and Theater." In *A John Cage Reader in Celebration of His 70th Birthday*, edited by Peter Gena and Jonathan Brent, 18–37. New York: C. F. Peters, 1992.
Schnapp, Jeffrey. "Border Crossings: Italian/German Peregrinations of the Theater of Totality." *Critical Inquiry* 21, no. 1 (August 1994): 80–123.
Schrijver, Lara. *Radical Games: Popping the Bubble of 1960's Architecture*. Rotterdam: NAi, 2009.
Scott, Felicity. "Acid Visions." *Grey Room* 23 (Spring 2006): 22–39.
———, ed. *Ant Farm: Living Archive 7*. Barcelona: Actar; New York: GSAPP, 2008.
———. *Architecture or Techno-utopia: Politics after Modernism*. Cambridge, MA: MIT Press, 2007.
———. "Fluid Geographies: Politics and the Revolution by Design." In *New Views on R. Buckminster Fuller*, edited by Hsiao-Yun Chu and Roberto G. Trujillo, 160–75. Stanford, CA: Stanford University Press, 2009.
———. "On Architecture under Capitalism." *Grey Room* 6 (Winter 2002): 45–65.
Shaw-Miller, Simon. "'Concerts of Everyday Living': Cage, Fluxus and Barthes, Interdisciplinarity and Inter-media Events." *Art History* 19, no. 1 (March 1996): 1–25.
Shklovsky, Viktor. "Art as Technique." In *Art in Theory 1900–2000: An Anthology of Changing Ideas*, edited by Charles Harrison and Paul Wood, 279–80. Oxford: Blackwell, 2003.
Shultis, Christopher. *Silencing the Sounded Self: John Cage and the American*

Experimental Tradition. Boston: Northeastern University Press, 1998.

———. "Silencing the Sounded Self: John Cage and the Intentionality of Non-Intention." *Music Quarterly* 79, no. 2 (Summer 1995): 312–50.

Singerman, Howard. *Art Subjects: Making Artists in the American University*. Berkeley: University of California Press, 1999.

———. "A History of the Whitney Independent Study Program—In Theory and Practice," *Artforum* 42, no. 6 (February 2004): 112–17, 170–71.

Smith, Matthew Wilson. *The Total Work of Art: From Bayreuth to Cyberspace*. New York: Routledge, 2007.

Smithson, Robert. "Entropy Made Visible"; interview with Alison Sky. In *Robert Smithson: The Collected Writings*, edited by Jack Flam, 301–9. Berkeley: University of California Press, 1996.

Snelson, Kenneth. FAQs site, http://www.kennethsnelson.net/faqs/faq.htm. Accessed September 12, 2013.

Solomon, Larry J. "The Sounds of Silence: John Cage's *4′33″*" (1998). http://solomonsmusic.net/4min33se.htm.

Sontag, Susan. "Happenings: An Art of Radical Juxtaposition" [1962]. Reprinted in *Against Interpretation and Other Essays*, 263–74. New York: Octagon Books, 1982.

Steinberg, Leo. *Other Criteria: Confrontations with Twentieth-Century Art*. New York: Oxford University Press, 1972.

Sternfeld, Joel. *Sweet Earth: Experimental Utopias in America*. Gottingen: Steidl, 2006.

Stiles, Kristine, and Peter Selz. *Theories and Documents of Contemporary Art: A Sourcebook of Artists' Writings*. Berkeley: University of California Press, 1996.

Tampa Museum of Art. *The Black Mountain Connection: John Cage, Merce Cunningham, Irwin Kremen, M. C. Richards*; the Tampa Museum of Art, September 13–November 22, 1992. Tampa, FL: Tampa Museum of Art, 1992.

Thompson, Nato, and Greg Scholette, eds. *The Interventionists: Users Manual for the Creative Disruption of Everyday Life*. North Adams, MA: MASS MoCA, 2004; Cambridge: MIT Press, 2005.

"Thoughts of Buckminster Fuller." *Whole Earth Catalog*, Winter 1968, 3–4.

Tomkins, Calvin. *The Bride and the Bachelors: Five Masters of the Avant-Garde*. New York: Viking Press, 1965.

Troy, Nancy. "The Art of Reconciliation: Oskar Schlemmer's Work for the Theater." In *Oskar Schlemmer*, edited by Arnold Lehman and Brenda Richardson, 27–147. Baltimore: Baltimore Museum of Art, 1986.

Turner, Fred. *From Counterculture to Cyberculture: Stewart Brand, the Whole Earth Network, and the Rise of Digital Utopianism*. Chicago: University of Chicago Press, 2006.

Tytell, John. *The Living Theatre: Art, Exile, and Outrage*. New York: Grove Press, 1995.

Vaughan, David. *Merce Cunningham: Fifty Years*. New York: Aperture, 1997.

Vidler, Anthony. "Cities of Tomorrow." *Artforum* 51, no. 1 (September 2012): 484–91.

Walch, John. "When the Bamboo Is Gone, Black Mountain's Spirit Lives On." *Austin (TX)-American Statesman*, December 31, 1998.

Wark, McKenzie. *The Beach Beneath the Streets*. London: Verso, 2011.

Watts, Harriet Ann. *Chance: A Perspective on Dada*. Ann Arbor, MI: UMI Research Press, 1980.

Weber, Nicholas Fox, et al. *Josef Albers: A Retrospective*. New York: Solomon R. Guggenheim Foundation, 1988.

———. *Josef Albers: Glass, Color, and Light*. New York: Guggenheim Museum, 1994.

Weber, Nicholas Fox, and Martin Filler. *Josef + Anni Albers: Designs for Living*. New York: Cooper-Hewitt National Design Museum; London: Merrell, 2004.

Weinstein, Jeff. "Anni Albers, the Jewish Museum, New York." *Artforum* 39, no. 2 (October 2000): 140.

"What Became of the Fuller House." *Fortune* 37 (May 1948): 168.

White, Leigh. "Buck Fuller and the Dymaxion World." *Saturday Evening Post*, October 14, 1944. Reprinted in Krausse and Lichtenstein, *Your Private Sky*, 132.

Whitford, Frank, ed. *The Bauhaus: Masters and Students by Themselves*. Woodstock, NY: Overlook Press, 1993.

Wick, Rainer. *Teaching at the Bauhaus*. Stuttgart: Hatje Cantz Verlag, 2000.

Wiener, M. Norton. *The Human Use of Human Beings: Cybernetics and Society*. 2nd ed. New York: Doubleday, 1950.

Wigley, Mark. "Network Fever." *Grey Room* 4 (Summer 2001): 82–122.

———. "Planetary Homeboy." *ANY*, no. 17, 1997: 16–23.

———. "Whatever Happened to 'Total Design?'" *Harvard Design Magazine*, no. 5 (Summer 1998): 1–8.

Williams, Bob. "Black Mountain College Revisited." *Black Mountain (NC) News*, August 26, 1999.

Williams, Raymond. "Base and Superstructure in Marxist Cultural Theory." In *Problems in Materialism and Culture*, 3–16. London: Verso Press, 1974.

———. *Keywords: A Vocabulary of Culture and Society*. New York: Oxford University Press, 1976.

Wilson, William. *Black Mountain College Dossiers: Ray Johnson*. Black Mountain, NC: Black Mountain College Museum and Arts Center, 1997.

Wingler, Hans. *The Bauhaus: Weimar, Dessau, Berlin, Chicago*. Cambridge, MA: MIT Press, 1969.

Wise, M. Norton. "Making Visible." *Isis* 97 (2006): 75–82.

Young, R. V. "The Lesson of Black Mountain: Liberal Education's Short-Lived Utopia." *Weekly Standard*, August 31, 1998, 31–34.

Zelov, Chris, and Phil Cousineau, eds. *Design Outlaws on the Ecological Frontier*. Philadelphia: Knossus, 1997.

index

Note: Page numbers in boldface indicate illustrations.